9TH EDITION
MAUI REVEALED
THE ULTIMATE GUIDEBOOK

ANDREW DOUGHTY
DIRECTOR OF PHOTOGRAPHY LEONA BOYD

WIZARD
PUBLICATIONS
INC

Honolua Bay, right side, taken from the cliffs above.

MAUI REVEALED
The Ultimate Guidebook 9th Edition

Published by Wizard Publications, Inc.
Post Office Box 991
Lihu'e, Hawai'i 96766–0991

ISBN: 978-1-949678-04-8   2129
Library of Congress Control Number 2019940453
Printed in China

Cataloging–in–Publication Data

Doughty, Andrew
    Maui revealed : the ultimate guidebook / Andrew Doughty – 9th ed.
Lihue, HI : Wizard Publications, Inc., 2020.
    324 p. : col. illus., col. photos, col. maps ; 21 cm.
    Includes index.
    Summary : A complete traveler's reference to the Hawaiian island of Maui, with full-color illustrations, maps, directions and candid advice by an author who resides in Hawaii.
    ISBN 978-1-949678-04-8
    LCCN 2019940453

1. Maui (Hawaii) – Guidebooks. 2. Maui (Hawaii) – Description and travel. I. Title.

DU 628   919.6921__dc21

Cover imagery courtesy of Earthstar Geographics (www.earth-imagery.com).
Cartography by Andrew Doughty.
All artwork and illustrations by Andrew Doughty and Lisa Pollak.

We welcome any comments, questions, criticisms or contributions you may have, and have incorporated some of your suggestions into this edition. Please send to the address above or e-mail us at **aloha@hawaiirevealed.com.**

Check out our website at **www.hawaiirevealed.com** for up-to-the-minute changes. Find us on **Facebook, YouTube, Twitter** and **Instagram.**

Dedicated to Leo Doughty,
whose love of flight and adventure has left its mark,
and who has always paid his dues in silence.

(Continued...)

CONTENTS

CONTENTS

ACTIVITIES
178

ADVENTURES
257

ISLAND DINING
270

Maui is the undisputed playground of Hawai'i. No other island has the range of activities and scenery available to you here. There's almost nothing you can't do on Maui: hike in pristine rain forests, snorkel in an extinct crater, coast a bicycle 10,000 feet down a volcano, walk along miles of beaches, frolic under a waterfall, dive into a natural freshwater pool, lie on a black or even red sand beach, or sip a drink as the sun sets over nearby islands. Whatever fantasy you have, Maui is bound to deliver.

Most travel publishers send a writer or writers to a given location for a few weeks to become "experts" and to compile information for guidebooks. To our knowledge, we at Wizard Publications are the only ones who actually *live* our books.

We hike the trails, ride the boats, eat in the restaurants, explore the reefs and do the things we write about. It takes us two *years*, full time, to do a first edition book, and we visit places *anonymously*. We marvel at writers who can do it all in a couple of weeks staying in a hotel. Wow, they must be *really* fast. Our method, though it takes much longer, gives us the ability to tell it like it is in a way no one else can. We put in many long hours, and doing all these activities is a burdensome grind. But we do it all for you—only for you. (Feel free to gag at this point.)

We have found many special places that people born and raised here didn't even know about because that's *all we do*—explore the island. Visitors will find the book as valuable as having a friend living on the island.

In this day of easy-to-access online reviews from countless sources, you can get "ratings" for nearly every company out there. What you get from our reviews is a single source, *beholden to none*, with a comprehensive exposure to all of the companies. There are two critical shortcomings to online reviews. One is that you don't know the source or agenda of the reviewer. Nearly every company that offers a service to the public *thinks* they are doing a good job. (But as you know, not everyone does.) So who can blame a company for trying to rig the system by seeding good reviews of their company at every opportunity or having friends write good reviews? Many also encourage *satisfied* customers to write favorable online reviews (obviously *not* encouraging *unhappy* customers to do so). But maybe their enemies or competitors retaliate with bad reviews. The point is, you never *really know* where those reviews come from, and it's almost impossible to reconcile terrible reviews right next to glowing ones for the same company. Which do you believe?

The other problem is a lack of a frame of reference. A visitor to Hawai'i goes on a snorkel boat and has a great time. (Hey, he snorkeled in Hawai'i, swam with a turtle—*cool!*) When he goes back home, he posts good reviews all around. That's great. But the problem is, he only went on *one* snorkel boat. We do 'em all. If only he'd known that another company *he didn't even know about* did a much better job, had way better food, and a much nicer boat for the same price.

We are also blessed with hundreds of thousands of readers—from our books as well as our smartphone apps—who alert us to issues with companies and places. *Every single message* from our readers is received, placed in a special database that we constantly have available while we're out and about, and we personally follow up on every observation made by our readers. So when we walk into a business or restaurant, we check to see what our readers say and tips they send us, and we use them to our advantage. (Thanks for the head's up about that incredible coconut cake at such-and-such restaurant—I know what *I'll* be ordering for dessert today.) With such a resource, and after two decades reviewing companies in Hawai'i full-time, there ain't much that's gonna get past us.

A quick look at this book will reveal features never before used in other guidebooks. Let's start with the maps. They are more detailed than any other maps you'll find, and yet they omit extraneous information that can sometimes make map reading a chore. We know that people in unfamiliar territory sometimes have a hard time determining where they are on a map, so we include landmarks. Most notable among these are mile markers. At every mile on main roads, the government has erected numbered markers to tell you where you are. We are the first to put these markers on a map so you can use them as reference points. Where needed, we've drawn legal public beach access in yellow, so you'll *know* when you're legally entitled to cross someone's land. Most guidebooks have the infuriating habit of mentioning a particular place or sight but then fail to mention how to get there! You won't find that in our book. We tell you exactly how to find the hidden gems and use our own special maps to guide you.

As you read this book, you will also notice that we are very candid in assessing businesses. Unlike some other guidebooks that send out questionnaires asking a business if they are any good (gee, they *all* say they're good), we've had personal contact with the businesses listed in this book. One of the dirty little secrets about guidebook writers is that they sometimes make cozy little deals for good reviews. Well, you won't find that here. We accept no payment for our reviews, we make no deals with businesses for saying nice things, and there are no advertisements in our book. What we've seen and experienced is what you get. If we gush over a certain company, it comes from personal experience. If we

rail against a business, it is for the same reason. All businesses mentioned in this book are here by *our* choosing. None has had any input into what we say, and we have not received *a single cent* from any of them for their inclusion. (In fact, there are some who would probably pay to be left out, given our comments.) We always review businesses as anonymous visitors and only later as guidebook writers if we need more information. This ensures that we are treated the same as you. (Amazingly, most travel writers *announce* themselves.) What you get is our opinion on how they operate. Nothing more, nothing less.

Sometimes our candor gets us into trouble. More than once we've had our books pulled from shelves because our comments hit a little too close to home. And powerful local businesses that don't like our reviews and their friends in the media have stirred up lots of trouble for us on Maui. That's ok, because we don't work for the people who *sell* the book; we work for the people who *read* the book. It's also true that a handful of local residents have become upset because we've told readers about places that they'd rather keep for themselves. Ironically, it's usually not people born and raised here who have this selfish attitude, but rather the newcomers who have read about these places *in our book* (of all things), then adopted the *I'm here now—close the door* mentality.

Maui Revealed is intended to bring you independence in exploring Maui. We don't want to waste any of your precious time by giving you bad advice or bad directions. We want you to experience the best that the island has to offer. Our objective in writing this book is to give you the tools and information necessary to have the greatest Hawaiian experience possible.

We hope we succeeded.

Andrew Doughty

From the bottom of the ocean to their summits above the clouds, the Hawaiian Islands owe their existence to enormous volcanic and seismic pressures.

HOW IT BEGAN

Sometime around 70 million years ago a cataclysmic rupture occurred in the Earth's mantle, deep below the crust. A hot column of liquid rock blasted through the Pacific plate like a giant cutting torch, forcing liquid rock to the surface off the coast of Russia, forming the Emperor Seamounts. As the tectonic plate moved slowly over the hot spot, this torch cut a long scar along the plate, piling up mountains of rock, producing island after island. The oldest of these to have survived is Kure. Once a massive island with its own unique ecosystem, only its ghost remains in the form of a fringing coral reef, called an atoll.

As soon as the islands were born, a conspiracy of elements proceeded to dismantle them. Ocean waves unmercifully battered the fragile and fractured rock. Abundant rain, especially on the northeastern sides of the mountains, easily carved up the rock surface, seeking faults in the rock and forming rivers and streams. In forming these channels, the water carried away the rock and soil, robbing the islands of their very essence. Additionally, the weight of the islands ensured their doom. Lava flows on top of other lava, and the union of these flows is always weak. This lava also contains countless air pockets and is crisscrossed with hollow lava tubes, making it inherently unstable. As these massive amounts of rock accumulated, their bases were crushed under the weight of subsequent lava flows, causing their summits to sink back into the sea.

What we call the Hawaiian Islands are simply the latest creation from this island-making machine. Someday they

Life forms found nothing but stark rock to greet them, so algae became Maui's first inhabitant.

will disappear, existing as nothing more than footnotes in the Earth's turbulent geologic history. Kaua'i and Ni'ihau are the oldest of the eight major islands. Lush and deeply eroded, the last of Kaua'i's fires died with its volcano a million years ago. O'ahu, Moloka'i, Lana'i, Kaho'olawe—their growing days are over as well. Maui is in its twilight days as a growing island. After growing vigorously, Hawaiian volcanoes usually go to sleep for a million years or so before sputtering back to life for one last fling. Maui's youngest volcano, Haleakala, is in its final eruptive stage. It *probably* last erupted around 1790 (see page 143) and will continue to sporadically erupt for a (geologically) short time before drifting off into eternal sleep.

The latest and newest star in this island chain is the Big Island of Hawai'i. Born less than a million years ago, this youngster is still growing. Though none of its five volcanic mountains is considered truly dead, these days Mauna Loa and Kilauea are doing most of the work of making the Big Island bigger. Mauna Loa, the most massive mountain on Earth, consists of 10,000 *cubic miles* of rock. The quieter of the two active volcanoes, it last erupted in 1984. Kilauea is the most boisterous of the volcanoes and is the most active volcano on the planet. Kilauea's most recent eruption went almost continuously from 1983 until 2018. Up and coming onto the world stage is Lo'ihi. This new volcano is still 3,200 feet below the ocean's surface, 20 miles off the southeastern coast of the island. Yet in a geologic heartbeat, the Hawaiian Islands will be richer with its ascension, sometime in the next 100,000 years.

These virgin islands were barren at birth. Consisting only of volcanic rock, the first life forms to appreciate these new islands were marine organisms—algae and microscopic animals. Then fish and mammals discovered this new underwater haven and made homes for themselves. Coral polyps attached themselves to the lava rock, and succeeding generations built upon these, creating what would become coral reefs. A plant called coralline algae also created (and still creates) vast reefs.

Meanwhile, seeds carried by water, wind and birds were struggling to colonize the rocky land, eking out a living and breaking down the lava rock. Storms brought the occasional bird, hopelessly blown off course. The lucky ones found the islands. The even luckier ones arrived with mates or were carrying eggs. Other animals, stranded on a piece of floating debris, washed ashore against all odds and went on to colonize the islands. These introductions of new species were rare events. It took an extraordinary set of circumstances for a new species to actually make it to the islands. Single specimens were destined to live out their lives in lonely solitude. On average, a new species was successfully deposited here only once every 20,000 years.

As with people, volcanic islands have a lifecycle. When a volcanic island is old, it is a sandy sliver, devoid of mountains. When it's middle-aged, it can be a lush wonderland, a haven for anything green, like Kaua'i. And when it's young, it is dynamic and unpredictable, like the Big Island of Hawai'i, but lacking the scars of experience from its short battle with the elements. Maui is unique among the Hawaiian islands because it's in its prime—young enough to show the dynamism of its volcanic

heritage, yet old enough for the elements to have carved lovely lines of character onto its face. The first people to occupy these islands were blessed with riches beyond their wildest dreams.

FIRST SETTLERS

Sometime around the fourth or fifth century A.D., a large, double-hulled voyaging canoe, held together with flexible

Water and plants take turns converting lava into paradise.

The ancient Hawaiians went to great effort to create temples (heiau) for their gods. The massive Pi'ilanihale Heiau near Hana, reclaimed from the jungle, is a particularly grand example.

sennit lashings and propelled by sails made of woven pandanus, slid onto the sand on the Big Island of Hawai'i. These first intrepid adventures, only a few dozen or so, encountered an island chain of unimaginable beauty.

They had left their home in the Marquesas Islands, 2,500 miles away. Though some say it was because of war, overpopulation or drought, it was more likely part of a purposeful exploration from a culture that had mastered the art of making their way through the featureless seas using celestial navigation and reading subtle signs in the ocean. Their navigational abilities far exceeded all the other "advanced" societies of the time. Whatever their reasons, these initial settlers took a big chance and surely must have been highly motivated. They could not have known that there were islands in these waters since Hawai'i is the most isolated island chain on Earth. (Though some speculate that they were led here by the golden plover—see facing page.)

Those settlers who did arrive brought with them food staples from home: taro, breadfruit, pigs, dogs and several types of fowl. This was a pivotal decision. These first settlers found a land that contained almost no edible plants. With no land mammals other than the Hawaiian hoary bat, the first settlers subsisted on fish until their crops matured. From then on, they lived on fish, taro, sweet potatoes and other vegetables. Although many associate throw-net fishing with Hawai'i, this practice was introduced by Japanese immigrants much later. The ancient Hawaiians used fishhooks and spears, for the most part, or drove fish into a net already placed in the water. They also had domesticated animals, which were used as ritual foods or reserved for chiefs.

Little is known about the initial culture. Archeologists think that a second wave of colonists, probably from Tahiti, may have subdued these initial inhabitants around 1000 A.D. Some may have resisted and fled into the forest, creating the legend of the Menehune.

Today Menehune are always thought of as being small in stature. The legend initially referred to their social stature, but it evolved to mean that they were physically short and lived in the jungle away from the Hawaiians. (The ancient Hawaiians avoided living in the jungle, fearing that it held evil spirits, and instead stayed on the coastal plains.) The Menehune were purported to build fabulous structures, always in one night. Their numbers were said to be vast, as many as 500,000. It is interesting to note that in a census taken of Kaua'i around 1800, some 65 people from a remote valley identified themselves as Menehune.

The second wave of settlers probably swept over the islands from the south, pushing the first inhabitants ever north. On a tiny island northwest of Kaua'i archeologists have found carvings, clearly not Hawaiian, that closely resemble Marquesan carvings, probably left by the doomed exiles.

This second culture was far more aggressive and developed into a highly class-conscious civilization. The society was governed by chiefs, called ali'i, who established a long list of taboos called kapu. These kapu were designed to keep order, and the penalty for breaking one was usually death by strangulation, club or fire. If the violation was serious enough, the guilty party's family might also be killed. It was kapu, for instance, for your shadow to fall across the shadow of the ali'i. It was kapu to interrupt the chief if he was speaking. It was kapu to prepare men's food in the same container used for women's food. It was kapu for women to eat pork or bananas. It was kapu for men and women to eat together. It was kapu not to observe the days designated for the gods. Certain areas were kapu for fishing if they became depleted, allowing the area to replenish itself.

While harsh by our standards today, this system kept the order. Most ali'i were

Hawai'i's First Tour Guide?

Given the remoteness of the Hawaiian Islands relative to the rest of Polynesia (or anywhere else for that matter), you'll be forgiven for wondering how the first settlers

found these islands in the first place. Many scientists think it might have been this little guy here. Called the kolea, or

Before they leave for Alaska.

golden plover, this tiny bird flies over 2,500 miles nonstop to Alaska every year for the summer, returning to Hawai'i after mating. Some of these birds continue past Hawai'i and fly another 2,500 miles to Samoa and other South Pacific islands. The early Polynesians surely must have noticed this commute and concluded that there must be

land in the direction that the bird was heading. They never would have dreamed that the birds leaving the South Pacific

When they return.

were heading to a land 5,000 miles away, and that Hawai'i was merely a stop in between, where the lazier birds wintered.

INTRODUCTION

Kalolopahu—Olowalu's Day of Infamy

In the first 20 years of Western contact, there were numerous incidents of Hawaiians killing westerners for weapons and westerners killing Hawaiians for revenge or to demonstrate superiority. But no skirmish between Hawaiians and westerners compares to the massacre of Kalolopahu.

A dozen years after Captain Cook was killed on the Big Island, a trading ship run by a vicious, contemptible captain named Simon Metcalfe stopped at the Big Island to trade goods. His ship was followed by a small, six-man sloop carrying the captain's son. A chief tried to climb on board Metcalfe's ship, and a crewman smacked him with a rope to prevent it. The chief was humiliated and vowed to take revenge on the next foreign vessel that came by. It was a vow that would change the destiny of the islands.

Metcalfe then went to Maui and began trading. One night, north of Lahaina, a Hawaiian sneaked over to the ship, cut loose the ship's cutter, killed the guard in the boat, then dragged the small boat to shore to break it up. (The Hawaiians didn't care about the boat; they wanted the iron.) When Metcalfe found out what happened, he fired his cannons into the nearest village in rage, then kidnapped some Hawaiians who told him that people from Olowalu did it (which was true). Metcalfe then moved his ship to Olowalu.

At this time, a high chieftess had declared the bay around Olowalu off limits. She was celebrating a family function, and the penalty for a commoner going into the water was to be burned alive. (Naturally, no one violated the kapu.) When she finally lifted the order three days later, commoners rushed in their canoes to begin trading with the foreign ship (Metcalfe's). Metcalfe told all the Hawaiians to line their canoes up on one side of the ship. When they were crowded around, Metcalfe unleashed his revenge. He opened fire with all his cannons (loaded with small shot) and muskets. More than 100 innocent Hawaiians were slaughtered (but not the one who had stolen the boat; he wasn't even there). The screaming and wailing went on for hours, and the natives named the place Kalolopahu, meaning the place of spilt brains.

But remember the man who Metcalfe's crew had smacked with a rope? He got his revenge, too, beyond his wildest dreams. He didn't know about the Olowalu massacre, but as fate would have it, that first foreign vessel he found was the one carrying Metcalfe's son. The chief and some warriors went on board on the pretense of trade, seized the sloop, killed young Metcalfe and all but one of his crew, then stripped the boat of its weapons, including a cannon. The one person from the sloop he let live, along with a man from the senior Metcalfe's ship whom King Kamehameha had captured earlier, soon became Kamehameha's trusted advisers. They helped Kamehameha defeat his island neighbors using the stolen cannon and guns, starting with the battle at 'Iao Valley described on page 71. Kamehameha eventually became king of all the islands.

As for Simon Metcalfe, he was unable to find his son and eventually went back to the U.S. mainland. He had no idea that his presence had forever changed the politics of the islands.

sensitive to the disturbance their presence caused and often ventured outside only at night, or a scout was sent ahead to warn people that an ali'i was on his way. All commoners were required to pay tribute to the ali'i in the form of food and other items. Human sacrifices were common and war among rival chiefs the norm.

By the 1700s, the Hawaiians had lost all contact with Tahiti, and the Tahitians had lost all memory of Hawai'i. Hawaiian canoes had evolved into fishing and interisland canoes and were no longer capable of long ocean voyages. The Hawaiians had forgotten how to explore the world.

OUTSIDE WORLD DISCOVERS HAWAI'I

In January 1778 an event occurred that would forever change Hawai'i. Captain James Cook, who usually had a genius for predicting where to find islands, stumbled upon Hawai'i. He had not expected the islands to be here. He was on his way to Alaska on his third great voyage of discovery, this time to search for the Northwest Passage linking the Atlantic and Pacific oceans. Cook approached the shores of Waimea, Kaua'i at night on January 19, 1778.

The next morning Kaua'i's inhabitants awoke to a wondrous sight and thought they were being visited by gods. Rushing aboard to greet their visitors, the Kauaians were fascinated by what they saw: pointy-headed beings (the British wore tri-cornered hats) breathing fire (smoking pipes) and possessing a death-dealing instrument identified as a water squirter (guns). The amount of iron on the ship was incredible. (They had seen iron before in the form of nails on driftwood but never knew where it originated.)

Cook left Kaua'i and briefly explored Ni'ihau before heading north for his mission on February 2, 1778. When Cook returned to the islands in November after failing to find the Northwest Passage, he visited the Big Island of Hawai'i.

The Hawaiians had probably seen white men before. Local legend indicates that strange white people washed ashore on the Big Island sometime around the 1520s and integrated into society. This coincides with Spanish records of two ships lost in this part of the world in 1528. But a few weird-looking stragglers couldn't compare to the arrival of Cook's great ships and instruments.

Despite some recent rewriting of history, all evidence indicates that Cook, unlike some other exploring sea captains of his era, was a thoroughly decent man. Individuals need to be evaluated in the context of their time. Cook knew that his mere presence would have a profound impact on the cultures he encountered, but he also knew that change for these cultures was inevitable, with or without him. He tried, unsuccessfully, to keep the men known to be infected with venereal diseases from mixing with local women, and he frequently flogged infected men who tried to sneak ashore at night. He was greatly distressed when a party he sent to Ni'ihau was forced to stay overnight due to high surf, knowing that his men might transmit diseases to the women (which they did).

Cook arrived on the Big Island at a time of much upheaval. The mo'i, or king, of the Big Island had been militarily spanked during an earlier attempt to invade Maui and was now looting and raising hell throughout the islands as retribution. Cook's arrival and his physical appearance (at 6-foot-4 he couldn't even stand up straight in his own quarters) almost guaranteed that the Hawaiians would think he was the god Lono, who was responsible for land fertility. Every year the ruling chiefs and their war god Ku went into abeyance, removing their power so that Lono could return to the land and make it fertile again, bringing back the spring rains. During this time all public works stopped, and the land was left alone. At the end of this *makahiki* season, people would again seize the land from Lono so they could grow crops and otherwise make a living upon it. Cook arrived at the beginning of the makahiki, and the Hawaiians naturally thought *he* was the god Lono coming to make the land fertile. Cook even sailed into Kealakekua Bay, *exactly* where the legend predicted Lono would arrive.

The Hawaiians went to great lengths to please their "god." All manner of supplies were made available. Eventually they became suspicious of the visitors. If they were gods, why did they accept the Hawaiian women? And if they were gods, why did one of them die?

Cook left at the right time. The British had used up the Hawaiians' hospitality (not to mention their supplies). But shortly after leaving the Big Island, the ship broke a mast, making it necessary to return to Kealakekua Bay for repairs. As they sailed back into the bay, the Hawaiians were nowhere to be seen. A chief had declared the area kapu to help replenish it. When Cook finally found the Hawaiians, they were polite but wary. *Why are you back? Didn't we please you enough already? What do you want now?*

As repair of the mast went along, things began to get tense. Eventually the Hawaiians stole a British rowboat (for the nails), and the normally calm Cook blew his cork. On the morning of February 14, 1779, he went ashore to trick the chief into coming aboard his ship, where he planned to hold the chief hostage until the rowboat was returned. As Cook and the chief were heading to the water, the chief's wife begged the chief not to go.

By now thousands of Hawaiians were crowding around Cook, and he ordered a retreat. A shot was heard from the other side of the bay, and someone shouted that the Englishmen had killed an important chief. A shielded warrior with a dagger came at Cook, who fired his pistol (loaded with small shot). The shield stopped the small shot, and the Hawaiians were emboldened. Other shots were fired. Standing in knee-deep water, Cook turned to call for a ceasefire and was struck in the head from behind with a club, then stabbed. Dozens of other Hawaiians pounced on him, stabbing his body repeatedly. The greatest explorer the world had ever known was dead at age 50 in a petty skirmish over a stolen rowboat.

KAMEHAMEHA THE GREAT

The most powerful and influential king in Hawaiian history lived during the time of Captain Cook and was born on the Big Island around 1758. Until his rule, the Hawaiian chain had never been ruled by a single person. He was the first to "unite" (i.e., conquer) all the islands.

Kamehameha was an extraordinary man by any standard. He possessed herculean strength, a brilliant mind and boundless ambition. He was marked for death before he was even born. When Kamehameha's mother was pregnant with him, she developed a strange and overpowering craving—she wanted to *eat* the eyeball of a chief. The king of the Big Island, mindful of the rumor that the unborn child's real father was his bitter enemy, the king of Maui, asked his advisers to interpret. Their conclusion was unanimous: The child would grow to be a rebel, a killer of chiefs. The king decided that

the child must die as soon as he was born, but the baby was instead whisked away to a remote valley to be raised.

In Hawaiian society, your role in life was governed by what class you were born into. The Hawaiians believed that breeding among family members produced superior offspring (except for the genetic misfortunes who were killed at birth), and the highest chiefs came from brother/sister combinations. Kamehameha was not of the highest class (his parents were merely cousins), so his future as a chief would not come easily.

As a young man Kamehameha was impressed by his experience with Captain Cook. He was among the small group that stayed overnight on Cook's ship during Cook's first pass by Maui. (Kamehameha was on Maui valiantly fighting a battle in which his side was getting badly whupped.) Kamehameha recognized that his world had forever changed, and he shrewdly used the knowledge and technology of westerners to his advantage.

Kamehameha participated in numerous battles. His side lost many of the early ones, but he learned from his mistakes and developed into a cunning tactician.

What rice is to Asians, taro is to Hawaiians—their most important food.

When he finally consolidated his rule over the Big Island (by luring his enemy to be the inaugural sacrifice of a new temple), he fixed his sights on the entire island chain. In the 1790s his large company of troops, armed with some western armaments and advisers, swept across Maui, Moloka'i, Lana'i and O'ahu. After some delays in taking Kaua'i, the last of the holdouts, its king finally acquiesced to the inevitable and Kamehameha became the first ruler of all the islands. He spent his final years governing the islands peacefully from his Big Island capital and died in 1819.

MODERN HAWAI'I

During the 19th century, Hawai'i's character changed dramatically. Businessmen from all over the world came here to exploit Hawai'i's sandalwood, whales, land and people. Hawai'i's leaders, for their part, actively participated in these ventures and took a piece of much of the action for themselves. Workers were brought from many parts of the world, changing the racial makeup of the islands. Government corruption became the order of the day, and everyone seemed to be profiting, except the Hawaiian commoner. By the time Queen Liliʻuokalani lost her throne to a group of American businessmen in 1893, Hawaiʻi had become directionless. It barely resembled the Hawaiʻi Captain Cook had encountered in the previous century. The kapu system had been abolished by the Hawaiians shortly after the death of Kamehameha the Great. The "Great Mahele," begun in 1848, had changed the relationship Hawaiians had with the land. Large tracts of land were sold by the Hawaiian government to royalty, government officials, commoners and foreigners, effectively stripping many Hawaiians of land they had lived on for generations.

The United States recognized the Republic of Hawaiʻi in 1894 with Sanford Dole as its president. It was annexed in 1898 and became an official territory in 1900. During the 19th and 20th centuries, sugar established itself as king. Pineapple was also a major crop in the islands, with the island of Lanaʻi purchased in its entirety for the purpose of growing pineapple.

As the 20th century rolled on, Hawaiian sugar and pineapple workers found themselves in a lofty position—they became the highest paid workers for these crops in the world. As land prices rose and competition from other parts of the world increased, sugar and pineapple became less and less profitable. Today, these crops no longer hold the position they once had. The "pineapple island" of Lanaʻi has shifted away from pineapple growing and is focused on tourism. And the sugar era officially ended in Hawaiʻi with the demise of the last plantation on Maui at the end of 2016.

The story of Hawaiʻi is not a story of good versus evil. Nearly everyone shares in the blame for what happened to the Hawaiian people and their culture. Westerners certainly saw Hawaiʻi as a potential bonanza and easily exploitable. They knew what buttons to push and pushed them well. But the Hawaiians, for their part, were in a state of flux. The mere presence of westerners seemed to bring to the surface a discontent, or at least a weakness, with their system that had been lingering just below the surface.

In fact, in 1794, a mere 16 years after first encountering westerners and under no military duress from the West, Kamehameha the Great *volunteered* to cede his island over to Great Britain. He was hungry for western arms so he could defeat his neighbor island opponents. He even declared that as of that day, they were no longer people of Hawaiʻi, but rather people of Britain. (Britain declined the offer.) And in 1819, immediately after the death of the strong-willed Kamehameha, the Hawaiians, of their own accord, overthrew their own religion, dumped the kapu system and denied their gods. This was *before* any western missionaries ever came to Hawaiʻi.

Nonetheless, Hawaiʻi today is once again seeking guidance from its heritage. The echoes of the past seem to be getting louder with time, rather than diminishing. Interest in the Hawaiian language and culture is at a level not seen in many decades. All of us who live here are very aware of the issues and the complexities involved, but there is little agreement about where it will lead. As a result, you will be exposed to a more "Hawaiian" Hawaiʻi than those who might have visited the state a generation or two ago. This is an interesting time in Hawaiʻi. Enjoy it as observers, and savor the flavor of the islands.

If you fly directly into West Maui, you'll miss the spectacular shoreline highway.

GETTING HERE

In order to get to the islands, you've got to fly here. While this may sound painfully obvious, many people contemplate cruises to the islands. But remember—there isn't a single spec of land between the west coast and Hawai'i. And 2,500 miles of open water is a pretty monotonous stretch to cover.

When planning your trip a travel agent can be helpful, though that method is becoming less and less common. The Internet has many options, including our website, where you can book flights, hotels and rental cars with packaged discounts. If you don't want to or can't go through these sources, there are large wholesalers that can get you airfare, hotel and a rental car, often cheaper than you can get airfare on your own. **Pleasant Holidays** (800-742-9244) provides complete package tours.

Another option is our smartphone app, *Hawaii Revealed* which has reviews of every resort as well as powerful filters that let you find the resort that has all the features that are important to you. You can get it from the iTunes store or Google Play and the **Where to Stay** section is free. The prices listed in **Where to Stay** reflect the rack rates, meaning the published rates before any discounts. Rates can be significantly lower if you go through a travel company or book online.

When you pick your travel source, be sure to shop around—the differences can be dramatic. A diligent effort can make the difference between affording a *one-week* vacation and a *two-week* vacation.

Maui Flights & Airports

Though most visitors fly into Honolulu before arriving, there are plenty of direct flights to Kahului. Not having to cool your heels while changing planes on O'ahu is a *big* plus since interisland flights aren't quite as convenient—or cheap—as they used to be. If you fly to Maui from Honolulu, the best views are *usually* on the left side (seats with an "A") coming in, and also the left side departing (for most routes). When flying to Honolulu from the mainland, sit on the left side coming in, the right going home. Interisland flights are done by **Southwest** (800-435-9792), **Hawaiian** (800-367-5320) and **Mokulele Airlines** (866-260-7070). (We like Southwest's two free checked bag policy.) Flight attendants zip up and down the aisle hurling juice at you on most of the short interisland flights.

If you're staying in West Maui, it's tempting to look at a map and decide to fly into **Kapalua West Maui Airport** for the sake of convenience. Though it is nearby, we still recommend flying into Kahului. That's because the drive around the coastline into Lahaina during the day is dramatic and worth the extra time. It's during your drive along the coastline to either west or south Maui that you realize that this island, more than any other Hawaiian island, has an extremely intimate relationship with the water. No other Hawaiian island has highways that embrace the ocean so much.

If you're staying in Hana and don't have time for the beautiful drive there, **Mokulele** and **Makani Kai** (808-834-1111) have daily flights and usually at reasonable prices.

WHAT TO BRING

This list may assist you in planning what to bring. Obviously you won't need everything on the list, but it might make you think of a few things you may otherwise overlook:

- Water-resistant, reef-safe sunscreen (SPF 30 or higher, with the ingredients zinc oxide and/or titanium dioxide)
- Hiking sticks (carbide-tipped ones are good for boulder-hopping hikes)
- Shoes—flip-flops, trashable sneakers, water shoes, hiking shoes
- Hat or cap for sun protection
- Mask, snorkel and fins
- Camera with lots of memory
- Warm clothes (for Haleakala trips) and junk clothes for hikes, etc.
- Light rain jacket
- Small flashlight for Haleakala sunrise
- Cheap, simple backpack—you don't need to go backpacking to use one; a 10-minute trek to a secluded waterfall is much easier if you bring a pack
- Shorts and other cool cotton clothing
- Mosquito repellent for some hikes (Lotions with at least 10 percent DEET seem to work best)

GETTING AROUND
Rental Cars

Rental car prices in Hawai'i *can be* (but aren't always) cheaper than almost anywhere else in the country, and the competition is ferocious. Nearly every visitor to Maui gets around in a rental car, and for good reason. Many of the island's best sights can only be reached if you have independent transportation. Maui prices fluctuate more than the other islands. Cheap at times, crazy high at others. Expect to pay an extra $10 or so per day in fees to pay for the new rental car facility and other goodies the government wants to charge you for. This seems like a good place to mention **Uber** and **Lyft** both have a presence on the island.

It's a good idea to reserve your car in advance since companies can run out of cars during peak times. Cars are also available at the Kapalua and *maybe* Hana airports.

Many hotels, condos and rental agents offer excellent room/car packages. Find out from your hotel or travel agent if one is available.

Here's a list of rental car companies. Some have desks at various hotels. Also check the rates from **Discount Hawaii Car Rental** (800-292-1930), which can get good deals from the most of the national rental car agencies mentioned below.

The Big Guys

Below are the main national rental car agencies:

Alamo	**(877) 222-9075**
	Kahului: (808) 871-6235
	Kapalua: (808) 661-7181
Avis	**(800) 321-3712**
	Kahului: (808) 871-7575
	Kihei: (808) 874-4077
	Ka'anapali: (808) 661-4588
Budget	**(800) 527-0700**
	Locally: (808) 871-8811
Dollar	**(800) 800-4000**
	Locally: (866) 434-2226
Enterprise	**(800) 261-7331**
	Kahului: (808) 871-1511
	Ka'anapali: (808) 661-8804
Hertz	**(800) 654-3131**
	Kahului: (808) 893-5207
	Lahaina: (808) 661-7735
National	**(877) 222-9058**
	Locally: (808) 871-8851
Sixt	**(888) 749-8227**
Thrifty	**(800) 367-5238**

The Little Guys

Below are the local car rental agencies:

AllSave (808) 875-9200
(Rents to 18–25 year olds)

Aloha (877) 452-5642
Kahului: (808) 877-4477

Bio-Beetle (808) 873-6121
(Eco car rentals)

Kihei (800) 251-5288
Locally: (808) 879-7257

Kimo's Rent a Car (808) 280-6327

Maui Car Rentals (800) 567-4659
Local: (808) 877-3300
(aka **No Ka Oi Motors**)

Maui Cruisers (877) 749-7889
Wailuku: (808) 249-2319

4-Wheel Drive

On Kaua'i and especially the Big Island we've strongly recommended getting a 4WD vehicle, but it isn't as important on Maui. The drive past Hana doesn't require one, despite what you may read elsewhere. A few places in remote parts of West Maui will allow 4WDs to get *slightly* closer, but it's hard to justify the increased price here. Skip the 4WD.

The only exception is the road to Polipoli Spring State Recreation Area. If you're intent on hiking there, you need 4WD. Otherwise, if you want to splurge, spring for a convertible instead. They can be fun, especially on the Hana drive.

On the Hana Highway, a roadside shrine, ensconced in a natural lava cave, utilizes flowers from nearby.

In East Maui, even the plants have plants.

Motorcycles & Scooters

If you think riding a hog is something you do at a lu'au, you may want to skip this section. There's something about Harleys. Maybe it's the sound, or maybe the looks. But riding a Harley-Davidson around Maui is a blast. If you want to rent one to experience things on your own (freedom, after all, is what hogs are all about), you can get them from you can get them from **Maui Motorcycle Co.** (808-877-1859) in Kahului, **Lahaina Harley-Davidson** (808-667-2800) in Lahaina, or **Eaglerider** (808-667-7000) in Kihei and Ka'anapali. Expect to pay (gulp!) $140–$230 for 24 hours.

If you want to rent a scooter, try **Aloha Motorsports** (808-667-7000) in Ka'anapali and **Hawaiian Cruisers** (808-446-1111) in Kihei at the far back side of Azeka Makai Shopping Center. Scooter rentals start at around $45–$70, and you need a driver's license. Also in Kihei, **Maui Scooter Shack** (808-891-0837) has a Pitbull Moped that has a tougher, motorcycle look than a regular moped.

Classic & Exotic Cars

Maui has a few opportunities to rent a flashy ride. If you want a fast car, **Hertz** (808-893-5207) in Kahului has Mustang convertibles and Camaros for $100–$300 per day. If you're looking for more of a classic car look, **Maui Roadsters** (808-339-6204) has reproductions of 1957 Porsche 356 Speedsters for around $329 for 12 hours. **Aloha Motorsports** (808-667-7000) has Polaris Slingshots for $200–$350 a day. Another way to find a wide range of vehicles is on the car-sharing website **Turo**, where prices can range $35–$400 a day. Bear in mind that there are no opportunities to bust loose with an exotic car—we have no wide open highway straightaways—but if you just want to experience the thrill of driving a fast car and you have a wad burning a hole in your pocket, give it a shot.

A Few Driving Tips

Seat belt and **child restraint** use is required by law, and local police will pull you over for this alone. Open roads and frequently changing speed limits make it easy to accidentally speed here. Sobriety checkpoints are not an uncommon police tactic on Maui. And it's a $300 ticket for even *holding* a **cell phone** while driving.

It's best not to leave anything valuable in your car. There are teenagers here who pass the time by breaking into cars. It's not a huge problem, but it does happen. Thieving scum will work an area until the heat gets too hot, then move on to another area. When we park at a beach, waterfall or any other place frequented by visitors, we take all valuables with us, leave the windows up, and leave the doors unlocked. (Just in case someone is curious enough about the inside to smash a window.) There are plenty of stories about people walking 100 feet to a waterfall, coming back to their car and finding that something expensive-looking has walked away. And don't be gullible enough to think that trunks are safe. Someone who sees you put something in your trunk can probably get at it faster than you can with your key.

If you are between the ages of 21 and 25, **Maui Cruisers** (808-249-2319) and **Bio-Beetle** (808-873-6121) don't charge extra for the crime of being young and reckless. Most other rental companies tack on a premium of $25 or more per day. **AllSave** (808-875-9200) will rent you a vehicle *regardless of age* (18+) as long as you have a valid driver's license (including international licenses) and a major credit card, but you will pay an extra $15 per day. If you're between 18 and 21, you can also rent a scooter or take the bus.

If renting from one of the smaller, local companies, be aware that many of their vehicles are older models and have seen some miles. While you may blend in better when parking at the beaches (lack of a tan aside), we have had readers complain through the years about the quality of some vehicles.

Buses

Maui doesn't have a typical public bus system. Our version is called the **Maui Bus** (808-871-4838), mainly used for shopping. Fare is $2; call for schedules and routes, or go to their website.

A Word About Driving Tours

A word on driving tours before you get started: Maui is split into geographic regions. We are well aware that for some regions, our chapter names such as *South Maui Sights*, aren't geographically accurate. Hey, don't blame us; we didn't invent these names. Other regions, like the "North Shore" are also strangely worded, since it's not where you'd think. It refers to the Hana Highway coastline, not the real north shore of the island. But this is how people here refer to the areas, so who are we to argue?

Most main roads have **mile markers** erected every mile. Since Hawai'i is mostly devoid of other identification signs, these little green signs can be a big help in knowing where you are at a given time. Therefore, we have placed them on the maps represented as a number inside a small box. We will often describe a certain feature or unmarked road as being "0.4 miles past mile marker 22." We hope this helps. Note that some roads have half-mile markers, with a ".5" at the bottom. We don't show them on the map and don't confuse them with the whole mile markers.

For directions, locals usually describe things as being on the *mauka* (mow-ka) side of the road—toward the mountains— or *makai* (ma-kigh)—toward the ocean.

Beaches, activities and adventures are mentioned briefly but are described in detail in their own chapters. Note that the direction of the driving tours won't necessarily match the order we use in the *Beaches* chapter. Driving tours reflect the way we think you'll drive (or recommend that you drive).

GETTING MARRIED ON MAUI

Maui is a wildly popular place to get married. Every romantic setting from a beach at sunset, a tropical garden or a waterfall is here for you to use as a background on your important day. Note that the state charges a small shakedown fee if you get married on a beach.

Finding a good person or company to help you isn't easy, and in this section we can't review the companies the way we normally would. (After all, it's not exactly practical to get married 25 times and rate the performance of a company.)

Here's a list of some full-service wedding coordinators you can contact for information about their wedding packages. Discuss your arrangements in detail with the coordinator to avoid misunderstandings over what your ceremony will be like and what it will cost.

A Dream Wedding Maui Style
(800) 743-2777 or (808) 661-1777
Romantic Maui Weddings
(800) 808-4144 or (808) 280-1214
A Paradise Dream Wedding
(808) 298-7448

Almost all the large resorts on Maui have wedding coordinators to help you arrange your wedding at their hotels. Be aware that site fees can be pretty high. Some of the popular resorts for weddings are the **Four Seasons**, the **Grand Wailea**, the **Hyatt**, **Fairmont Kea Lani**, the **Westin**, the **Travaasa Hana**, and the **Ritz-Carlton**.

Obtaining a Marriage License

Contact the **State Department of Health** (808-984-8210) on Maui (or visit their website) to obtain an application or to get the names of license agents on Maui. Both parties must be at least 18. No residency or blood tests are required. The fee is $60 *in cash*, and the license is good for 30 days. Both parties must be present with photo IDs at the time of the appointment with the marriage license agent.

WEATHER

How's the weather on Maui? A picture speaks a thousand words. The photo (on the facing page) is very typical of the cloud and rain coverage on Maui and, to a practiced eye, tells you exactly what to expect around the island.

As ceremony locations go, this beats a chapel in Vegas any day of the week.

You can see how the windward areas (meaning areas exposed to the trade winds out of the northeast) get most of the clouds and how Hana is dry, but farther uphill it's cloudy, feeding the waterfalls. Kihei and Lahaina (called *leeward* areas) are warmer, drier and sunnier than the rest of the island because they are shielded from the northeast trade winds.

Notice how the clouds don't go all the way to the top of Haleakala, except where they are squeezed into the Ko'olau Gap; it's because of a temperature inversion at the 6,000 foot level. (The air actually gets warmer above that for a few thousand feet, causing the temperature-sensitive clouds to dissipate.) The top of West Maui Mountain is cloudy, as usual. The northeast trade winds build up along the bottom of Haleakala, heading southwest along the flank, and are directed off into the sea near La Pérouse Bay, leaving Kihei and Wailea calmer. This is quintessential Maui trade wind weather until about 1 p.m. Then more clouds will build as the island heats up, causing the air to rise, cool and condense into clouds. The summit of Haleakala may cloud up. Winds will increase all around the island as ocean air rushes in to replace the rising air.

To get current **weather forecasts**, call (808) 944-3756. Call (808) 572-7873 for a **surf forecast** or check our website.

The Different Weather Regions

What does all this mean? It means the weather is radically different around the island. Many times we've been at the airport in Kahului and seen people coming off the plane looking gloomy and worried. "It's so windy and rainy here," they often say. Sometimes we wish the county would erect a sign at the airport saying, *"No worry, da weatha stay mo betta in Kihei and Lahaina."*

In the leeward area of **South Maui**, **Kihei** and **Wailea** will be warmer and drier. Winds that have just been squished between the two mountains will travel south along the Kihei coast, veering slightly offshore, so winds will be lighter the farther you go down the Kihei coast until you get to La Pérouse Bay. There the fierce wind from the bottom of the island meets calm air, creating a distinct wind line over the span of about 100 feet. That means mornings are usually calm from Makena to South Kihei. In the afternoon, however, onshore breezes will form to fill the void from the heated rising air, and the trade winds that have been absent along the coast at Makena and Wailea will start wrapping around the island parallel to the coast here. This means strong afternoon winds. Winters are less windy. The sunnier and hotter it is, the stronger the afternoon winds will be. If there's heavy cloud cover over much of Haleakala, the afternoon winds will diminish. (We're trying to avoid sounding like weather geeks, but if you understand the weather processes here, it helps you plan your day.)

High temperatures will average 80 °F in the winter, 86 °F in the summer. South Maui nights can be cooler than in Lahaina because the air that has built up atop Haleakala during the day will tumble down to the bottom. If your condo has a

Rainfall Map

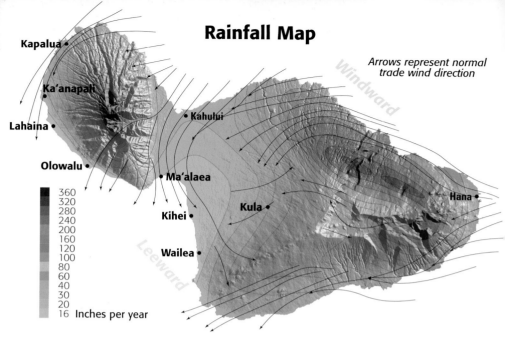

Arrows represent normal trade wind direction

Kapalua

Ka'anapali

Lahaina

Olowalu

Kahului

Ma'alaea

Kihei

Kula

Wailea

Hana

Windward

Leeward

360
320
280
240
200
160
120
100
80
60
40
30
20
16 Inches per year

skylight, you may notice puffs of cool air coming down from it at night.

Rainfall in leeward areas is light and variable. For instance, one year there were only seven days with rain in Kihei. It was going to total 4.75 inches for the year until New Year's Eve brought *another* 4.75 inches, doubling the year's rainfall tally. Other years have seen 20 or more inches of rain.

In **Lahaina**, **Ka'anapali** and **Kapalua**, the exact direction of the trade winds is crucial. Lahaina is usually protected from the trades. There are fewer afternoon breezes in Lahaina than Kihei, making it warmer. High temperatures are 82 °F in January and 88 °F in August and September. As you head toward Ka'anapali, at some point the trade winds that you've been protected from in Lahaina will complete their wrap-around from the other side, making wind a semi-constant companion. That's good if you like cool breezes, bad if you are trying to get a golf ball from Point A to Point B. It also means that the ocean is more susceptible to whitecaps and poor visibility north of Lahaina. **Kapalua**, farther north, is even

windier, more drizzly and has the worst weather of any of the resort areas.

Just south of Lahaina, **Olowalu** would normally be protected from the trade winds, except for one slight detail. Its large, rain-cut valley leading to the center of West Maui Mountain connects with rain-cut 'Iao Valley on the windward side, cracking the mountain in two and making a natural diversion ditch for the wind to rip through, leaving Olowalu windy.

Kahului gets a concentration of winds deflected along the northern part of Haleakala that slither around the island here and are squeezed between the two mountains. So it's *almost always* windy in Kahului. This has made Kahului one of the greatest places on the planet for windsurfing and kiteboarding. Big-time riders from all over the world make pilgrimages here.

Ma'alaea at the south end of the valley gets a concentration of wind and dust that has been squeezed between the mountains, making it one of the windiest places on the island.

Hana is sunnier than most people think since the clouds usually form farther uphill, but it is more vulnerable to whatever the trade winds bring to the island. Most of the time Hana has beautiful weather, but sometimes systems can bring rain that can last for days, especially in the winter. The temperature is incredibly equitable. Average high in February is 78 °F, and the average high in September is only 84 °F. How's *that* for a change of season?

The summit of **Haleakala** has an average high of around 50 °F and low of 32 °F in February and reaches a scorching 58 °F and a low of 38 °F in August. It's *usually* not as windy *after sunrise*, but any wind on a cold morning can cut right through you.

Upcountry areas, such as **Kula** and **Pukalani**, are cooler due to their elevation and less windy.

Average humidity around the island ranges from 65–75 percent.

In general, windward areas like Hana and Kahului get most of their rain at night and in the early morning. Leeward areas like Kihei and Lahaina get their more sporadic rain in the late afternoon and early evening.

Ocean temperatures average 75 °F in February, 80 °F in September.

GEOGRAPHY

The island of Maui is made up of two large volcanoes called… well, that's a little confusing. The largest mountain, on the east side, is commonly referred to as **Haleakala**, meaning *house of the sun*. To the ancient Hawaiians, Haleakala referred only to a portion of the summit of the mountain, not the whole mountain. In fact, as far as we know, they had no name for either of the two large mountains that make up Maui. But the word Haleakala has been used so often in recent years to describe the entire mountain that it's now generally accepted.

The other great mountain is topped by a small peak called Pu'u Kukui, or *hill of the candlenut tree*. A bit duller, huh? That name has never been used to describe the entire mountain, so it's commonly referred to by its less-than-exotic name, West Maui Mountain. Even scholarly geology books refer to them as Haleakala and West Maui Mountain. Annoyed at the western name, visitor bureaucrats are now pushing to refer to West Maui Mountain as Mauna Kahalawai, but that name was never accepted by Hawaiian linguists. We've also heard tour guides, such as boat captains, refer to West Maui as Halemahina, or *house of the moon*. Sounds so symmetrical next to the *house of the sun*, but it's bogus.

West Maui is the older of the two mountains. Streams have cut deeply into its slopes, and the results are lovely. Though you'd expect more erosion on the wet side, an accident of geology capped the wet side with more erosion-resistant lava, so big valleys aren't as prevalent as they normally would be.

Haleakala is the younger, still-active mountain. It's just over 10,000 feet high, but it wasn't always so. At one time it rose to 15,000 feet, making it the tallest mountain in the world at over 32,000 feet high (when measured from its base at the bottom of the ocean). But Haleakala is crushing itself under its own weight. Someday it will sink back into the sea. (But probably not before your trip here.) Its smoother slopes and 10,000-foot height hide an enormous volume of rock. The Hana side is a lush wonderland whose beauty is legendary. Kihei is in the dry rain shadow of the mountain, so there are few streams or eroded areas. The summit features the awesome

Haleakala Crater. (Actually it's an erosion crater; see page 129 for more.)

At one time, all the islands surrounding Maui formed one big island, which geologists called Maui Nui. (Meaning *Big Maui*—darned clever, those geologists.) In fact, if you'd visited here just

Maui is the only place we've ever seen where you can get waterfall fatigue. There are so many beautiful ones, like Wailua Falls here, that you start to take them for granted.

18,000 years ago, during a mini ice age that drastically lowered the sea level, you could have driven from Maui to Lana'i and on to Moloka'i. (Of course, finding a rental car might have been an issue.) As the volcanoes sank and the seas rose, the mountains separated, forming today's configuration. They continue to sink, and in about 15,000 years Maui will be two separate islands. We live in an era when Maui is perfectly arranged to easily explore the two sides. Enjoy our fortunate timing.

WHERE SHOULD I STAY?

Most Maui visitors stay on the leeward side of the island—Lahaina to the Kapalua area in the west, or Kihei–Wailea in the south. Fifty years ago all the major towns were on the windward side, where rain was abundant and crops grew vigorously. Few lived on the leeward side because it was harder to grow things there. (Lahaina has been around longer than most Hawaiian leeward towns because it was a good whaling port in the 1800s.)

But the rain that makes everything so beautiful and lush on the windward side also makes short-time visitors leery. So with the advent of jets and mass travel, the heretofore sparsely populated leeward sides of the islands became developed and a magnet for travelers. Sure, the rain on the windward side makes things green, but it also means the ocean will have more runoff, the surf will be higher, and clouds will obscure the sun. On the leeward side you don't have the tropical lushness you may associate with Hawai'i, but you usually have clear weather, calm oceans, sparkling water and lots of sunshine. (And, after all, you can always *drive* to the lush areas.)

It's hard to decide *which* leeward side of the island to stay on: West or South. West Maui has more activities because it has a working harbor, and it doesn't get as windy off Lahaina in the afternoon as it does off South Maui, though they get plenty of wind north of Lahaina. Activities such as submarine rides, Jet Skis and dinner cruises are common there, but helicopter flights are more convenient from South Maui. West Maui is more remote, making drives to Hana, Haleakala or Kahului much longer. Parking in Lahaina is a mess. Also, it's hotter in Lahaina than in Kihei or Wailea, though northwest Maui (i.e., Ka'anapali and Kapalua) gets lots of cooling winds. South Maui has better access to Molokini, and South Maui reefs are better. West Maui has easier access to Lana'i and Moloka'i. Beaches are less crowded in South Maui, and its beach accesses don't fill up as often.

Shopping is better in West Maui, and its backdrop is more scenic, but it is also more densely developed. Food is better and more varied in West Maui, but South Maui has some of the most kickin' resorts. Golf is better in South Maui, and so is the diving and snorkeling. If you're traveling with kids, West Maui is more popular with families, though South Maui has two parks that are very kid-friendly. West Maui has more cheap condos, but gas and grocery prices seem higher in West Maui. Both sides are hugely popular, but West Maui has a busier and more crowded feel.

So which is better? After living here and spending countless hours exploring and experiencing both sides, in our professional opinion, we have to say... we don't know. Each area has advantages and disadvantages that sway us back and forth. Consider the pros and cons listed above, and the answer may become obvious to you.

Detailed Resort & Condo Reviews

Maui has it all, accommodations-wise, and as you consider where you want to stay—hotel or condo, by the beach or with a mountain view—you might find it intimidating to wade through the vast number of choices.

So here's what we did. We have *personally reviewed* every resort on Maui. We have *exhaustively* cataloged all the amenities, formed opinions on what different properties have to offer and created comprehensive reviews. Sure, you can go online and look at reviews by people who have been to one or maybe two resorts. But none of those sources can compare one to the other.

Because this information is so exhaustive, there isn't enough room in our book to include it all. So we have put all of our reviews in our smartphone app, *Hawaii Revealed*, and made that portion available *for free*. There you can sort and sift through the resorts in a matter of minutes using our special filters. We also include our own aerial photos, so you'll know if oceanfront *really* means oceanfront.

For instance, you might say, *I want a hotel in West Maui, on a beach, that's good for families, has an outdoor lanai, a children's pool, and takes service animals. Oh, and a swim-up bar would be nice.* With the filters in our app, you can cut through the 135 or so resorts and get to exactly what you want by reading our in-depth, brutally honest review. How's that for cutting through the noise?

IS MAUI TOO EXPENSIVE?

Maui has a reputation of being pricey. That's because... well, it *is* pricey. The truth is that eating out costs more here than on the other islands. So do groceries and almost everything we can think of. Anyone who says otherwise hasn't lived on the different islands. Also, many of the activities available involve giving a company money to show you something, such as boat trips, SCUBA, aerial tours, lu'au and more. So spending time on Maui is synonymous with spending money. Some activities, like helicopters, cost more here than on other Hawaiian islands while others, like SCUBA diving, cost less.

This doesn't mean that Maui has to put you in hock for the next decade. There are *lots* of things to do that don't involve spending a fortune, and there are some tremendous values in restau-

Notice anything missing on this sunny day? Shadows! Hawai'i is the only place in the U.S. where the sun can ever be directly overhead, near the summer solstice. We call it Lahaina Noon. And you should call it a real good reason to wear sunscreen, because it'll burn you faster than you think.

rants—if you know where to look. Some of our favorite restaurants are some of the cheapest, and we point them out in Restaurants. The *Activities* and *Adventures* chapters have some delightful things to do that won't cost you a cent. Also, if you have a Costco membership or want to sign up for one, the Costco in Kahului near the airport is where most of us here buy lots of our groceries and other items. If you're here for a week or more, a Costco run can save you a bundle. Also consider shopping at Walmart or Target in Kahului, which can be found on the map on page 70.

That said, count on spending some dollars on this trip. Some of the paid activities are definitely worth the splurge. Others are a rip-off, and we'll try to point them out. You're coming to an island where milk is so expensive, you'll wonder if the cows are housed at the Ritz.

HAZARDS

Just because you're in a tropical paradise doesn't mean there's nothing here that can threaten you. The sun, sea and island critters can all ruin your day. Knowing what to look for is what this section is all about.

The Sun

The hazard that by far affects the most people (excluding the accommodations tax) is the sun. Maui, at 20 degrees latitude, receives sunlight more directly than anywhere on the mainland. (The more overhead the sunlight, the less atmosphere it filters through.)

If you want to enjoy your *entire* vacation, make sure that you wear a strong sunscreen. We recommend a water-resistant sunscreen with an SPF of at least 30. Apply 30 minutes before exposure for the most effectiveness. *Physical* sunblocks (those containing zinc or titanium oxide) are said to be more reef-safe than *chemical* sunblocks, which are more common.

Many visitors who get burned do so while snorkeling. You won't feel it coming because you're in the water. We *strongly* suggest that you wear a T-shirt while snorkeling, or you may get a nasty surprise.

Try to avoid direct exposure between 11 a.m. and 2 p.m. when the sun is particularly strong. If you are fair-skinned or unaccustomed to the sun and want to soak up some rays, 15–20 minutes per side is all you should consider the first day. You can increase it a bit each day. *Beware of the fact that our breezes will hide the symptoms of a burn until it's too late.* You might find that trying to get your tan as golden as possible isn't worth it. Tropical suntans are notoriously short-lived, whereas you are sure to remember a bad burn far longer.

If, after all our warnings, you *still* get burned, aloe vera gel works well to relieve the pain. (Some gels also come with lidocaine in them.) Ask your hotel front desk if they have any aloe plants on the grounds. Peel the skin off a section and make several crisscross cuts in the meat, then rub the plant on your skin. *Oooo,* it'll feel so good!

Water Hazards

The most serious water hazard is the surf. Though more calm in the summer and on the leeward side, high surf can be found anywhere on the island at any time of the year. The sad fact is that more people drown in Hawai'i each year than anywhere else in the country. This isn't said to keep you from enjoying the ocean, but rather to instill in you a healthy respect for Hawaiian waters. See *Beach Safety* on page 154 for more on this.

Ocean Critters

Hawaiian **marine life**, for the most part, is quite friendly. There are, however, a few notable exceptions. Below is a list of some critters that you should be aware of. This is not mentioned to frighten you out of the water. The odds are overwhelming that you won't have any trouble with any of the beasties listed below. But should you encounter one, this information should be of some help.

Hawai'i does have **sharks**. Most are the essentially harmless white-tipped reef sharks, plus the occasional hammerhead or tiger shark. Contrary to what most people think, sharks live in every ocean and don't pose the level of danger people attribute to them. Shark attacks are rare on Maui, averaging less than one per year over the decades, and fatalities are extremely uncommon. Considering the number of people who swam in our waters during that time, you are statistically more likely to get mauled by a hungry timeshare salesman than be bitten by a shark.

If, in the rare instance that you happen to come upon a shark, however, swim away slowly. This kind of movement doesn't interest them. *Don't* splash about rapidly. Doing so makes you look like a fish in distress, which is appealing to sharks.

The one kind of water you want to avoid is murky water, such as that found in river mouths. Most shark attacks occur in murky water at dawn or dusk since sharks are basically cowards who like to sneak up on their prey.

In general, don't worry about sharks. *Any* animal can be threatening. (Even Jessica Alba was once rudely accosted by an overly affectionate male dolphin.) **Portuguese Man-of-War** are related to jellyfish but are unable to swim. They

are instead propelled by a small sail and are at the mercy of the wind. Though small, they are capable of inflicting a painful sting. This occurs when the long, trailing tentacles are touched, triggering hundreds of thousands of spring-loaded stingers, called nematocysts, which inject venom. The resulting burning sensation is usually very unpleasant but not fatal.

Fortunately, the Portuguese Man-of-War is not a common visitor to Maui. When they *do* come ashore, however, they usually do so in great numbers, jostled by a strong storm offshore, and usually land on north-facing beaches. If you see them on the beach, don't go in the water.

If you do get stung, immediately remove the tentacles with a gloved hand, stick or whatever is handy. Rinse thoroughly with salt or sea water to remove any adhering nematocysts. Then apply ice for pain control. If the condition worsens, see a doctor. The old treatments of vinegar or baking soda are no longer recommended. The folk cure is urine, but you might look pretty silly applying it.

Sea Urchins are like living pin cushions. If you step on one or accidentally grab one, remove as much of the spine as possible with tweezers. *After* they are out, soak the wound in warm vinegar. See a physician if necessary.

Coral skeletons are very sharp and, since the skeleton is overlaid by millions of living coral polyps, a scrape can leave proteinaceous matter in the wound, causing infection. This is why coral cuts are frustratingly slow to heal. Immediate cleaning and disinfecting of coral cuts should speed up healing time. We don't have fire coral around Maui.

Related to the jellyfish, **sea anemones** also have stingers and are usually found attached to rocks or coral. It's best not to touch them with your bare hands. Treatment for a sting is similar to that of a Portuguese Man-of-War.

Bugs

The worst are **centipedes**. They can get to be six or more inches long and are aggressive predators. They shouldn't be messed with. You'll probably never see one, but if you get stung, even by a baby, the pain can range from a bad bee sting to a moderate gunshot blast. Some local doctors say the only cure is to stay drunk for three days. Others say to use meat tenderizer or a mushy ripe papaya.

Cane spiders are big, dark and fast, and they look horrifying, but their bite isn't a danger to humans. (But they seem to think they are. I've had them chase me across the room when I had the broom in my hand.) We don't have no-see-ums, those irritating sand fleas common in the South Pacific and Caribbean.

Mosquitoes were unknown in the islands until the first stowaways arrived on Maui on the *Wellington* in 1826. Since then they have thrived. A good mosquito repellent containing at least 10 percent DEET will come in handy, especially if you plan to go hiking. Forget the guidebooks that tell you to take vitamin B12 to keep mosquitoes away; it just gives the little critters a healthier diet. If you find one dive-bombing you at night in your room, turn on your overhead fan to help keep them away.

Bees and **wasps** are more common on the drier leeward sides of the island and in Haleakala Crater. Usually, the only way you'll get stung is if you run into one. If you rent a scooter, beware; I received my first bee sting while singing *Come Sail Away* on a motorcycle. A bee sting in the mouth can definitely ruin one of your precious vacation days.

Regarding cockroaches, there's good news and bad news. The bad news is that here, some are bigger than your thumb and can fly. The good news is that you probably won't see one. One of their predators is the gecko. This small, lizard-like creature makes a surprisingly loud chirp at night. Geckos are cute and considered good luck in the Islands (probably 'cause they eat mosquitoes and roaches).

Snakes

There are no snakes in Hawai'i (other than some reporters). There is concern that the brown tree snake *might* have made its way onto the islands from Guam. Although mostly harmless to humans, these snakes can spell extinction for native birds. Government officials aren't allowed to tell you this, but we will: If you ever see one anywhere in Hawai'i, please *kill it* and contact the Pest Hotline at (808) 643-7378 or on their website. At the very least, call them immediately. The entire bird population of Hawai'i will be grateful.

Rat Lungworm Disease

Almost sounds like a bad heavy metal band's name. You can get it from accidentally eating a slug. Slugs love to munch on our produce and if your fruit or veggies aren't washed and rinsed really well, it's possible a small slug can end up in your salad. Symptoms usually show up 1–3 weeks after exposure, and be anywhere from non-existent to including fever, tingling of the extremities, vomiting and can even cause a rare

form of meningitis. If you're cooking at your rental or love picking up local produce from farmers markets or roadside stands, be sure to inspect your stuff and *always* wash it in clean water (leafy greens especially).

Swimming in Streams

Maui offers lots of opportunities to swim in streams and under waterfalls. It's the fulfillment of a fantasy for many people. But there are several hazards you need to know about.

Leptospirosis is an infectious disease caused by bacteria found in some of Hawai'i's fresh water. It is transmitted from animal urine and can enter the body through open cuts, eyes and by drinking. Around 100 people a year in Hawai'i are diagnosed with the bacteria, which is treated with antibiotics if caught relatively early. You should avoid swimming in streams if you have open cuts, and treat all water found in nature with treatment pills before drinking. (Many filters are ineffective for lepto.)

While swimming in freshwater streams, try to use your arms as much as possible. Kicking an unseen rock is easier than you think. Also, consider wearing water shoes or, better yet, tabis, while in streams. (Tabis are sort of fuzzy mittens for your feet that grab slippery rocks quite effectively. You can get them at Walmart in Kahului or any Longs Drugs.)

Though rare, flash floods can occur in any freshwater stream anywhere in the world, and they can happen when it's sunny where you are but raining up the mountain. They happen quickly, and staying alert for them is crucial. Flowing water will speed up, water will become muddy, and the water level will rise. If this happens, look for the highest ground and get there fast. Don't attempt to cross any flooding streams—wait it out until the water levels go back down.

Lastly, remember while lingering under waterfalls that not everything that comes over the top will be as soft as water. Rocks coming down from above could definitely shatter the moment—among other things.

Dehydration

Bring and drink lots of water when you are out and about, especially when you are hiking. **Dehydration** sneaks up on people. By the time you are thirsty, you're already dehydrated. It's a good idea to keep lots of water in your car. Our weather is almost certainly different than what you left behind, and you will probably find yourself thirstier than usual. Every time you think about it, *suck 'em up* (as we say here).

Pigs

We're not referring to your dining companion. We mean the wild ones you may encounter on a hiking trail. Generally, pigs will avoid you before you ever see them. If you happen to come upon any piglets and accidentally get between them and their mother, immediately bark like a big dog. Wild pigs are conditioned to run from local dogs (and their hunter masters), and Momma will leave her kids faster than you can say, "Pass the bacon."

Frogs

There are some irritating visitors that first arrived on Maui in the late '90s and won't leave. (Well, besides the in-laws.) They're small coqui tree frogs that emit a whistle all night long. Cute at first, like a bird. But they're incessant and ultimately irritating. Most of the resorts do their best to deal with them, but there's a chance that some errant froggies may occasionally give you a long night. West

Maui seems to be slightly froggier (I *swear* that's a real word) than South Maui.

Traffic

Traffic can be a problem here. West Maui traffic between Lahaina and Kapalua is notoriously bad, especially at pau hana (quittin' time). Allow extra time during that part of the day. Traffic into Lahaina from central Maui along Hwy 30 can be bad any time after noon. Road work also slows things down a great deal, and on Maui, road projects seem to be measured in decades rather than months or years. In South Maui, both South Kihei Road and Hwy 31 can be terrible during commute hours (and other times as well).

Grocery Stores

A decided hazard. Restaurants are expensive, but don't think you'll get off cheap in grocery stores. Though you'll certainly save money cooking your own food, a trip to the store here can be startling. Questions such as, *They charge how much for milk?* echo throughout the stores. Even items grown a mile from the store may cost more here than you would pay for them on the mainland. Go figure. If you're stocking up, consider buying groceries at Kahului stores and at the **Costco, Island Grocery Depot,** or **Target.** If you hate shopping, **Maui Grocery Service** (808-280-7526) will shop and deliver for a fee.

Nudity

Not sure if nudity is a hazard or not. Depends on your outlook (and if you're traveling with kids). A number of reader emails have pointed out unexpected fully nude beach users, and most were none too happy about it. This is a naked violation of state laws (and there are stiff penalties), but don't be surprised if you encounter it. Topless sunbathing isn't technically against the law, but it is tolerated at some beaches more than others.

TRAVELING WITH CHILDREN (KEIKI)

Should we have put this under *Hazards*? It's been our observation that visitors with kids are far more numerous in West Maui than South Maui, perhaps because most of the Ka'anapali resorts have such good keiki programs and services. If you want to stay in the south, the **Grand Wailea** seems the most keiki-friendly.

Baby's Away (208-669-1175) has the usual assortment of keiki paraphernalia for rent, such as car seats, strollers, cribs, bathtubs, etc. **Akamai Mother's Rentals** (808-298-1336) has similar services, often for better prices. **Maui on the Fly** (888-497-1113) has indoor and outdoor gear for keiki and some great package deals.

Each large town on Maui has at least one playground. One of the largest that is also close to dining options is **Kalama Park** in Kihei between Welakahao and Auhana on South Kihei Road. It has lots of lawn, a playground, a skateboard park, an inline skating park and a ball field. The largest and best playground can be found above Ha'iku along Kokomo Road at **4th Marine Division Memorial Park**. If you're already exploring the upcountry area with your keiki, it makes for a welcome spot to stretch your legs.

Maui Golf & Sports Park (808-242-7818) has mini golf, bumper boats, a climbing wall and a trampoline. A bit cramped (they pack a lot of stuff into a small area) but a viable keiki diversion. In Ma'alaea next to **Maui Ocean Center** on Hwy 330 near Hwy 310.

Rainy days bring a new set of challenges for those looking to keep kids entertained. Our local aquarium, **Maui Ocean Center**, is a great diversion when the weather doesn't cooperate. The **Ultimate Air Trampoline Park** (808-214-5867), off Hwy 380 and Maui Lani Pkwy, is another good option with rates starting at $22/hour. Free, educational options can be found around Kihei at the visitors centers of the **Hawaiian Islands Humpback Whale National Marine Sanctuary** on South Kihei Road and **Kealia Pond National Wildlife Refuge** on Hwy 311.

There are also farms, ranches and animal sanctuaries that offer outdoor, hands-on fun for kids and adults. **Surfing Goat Dairy**

Maui Ocean Center's aquarium in Ma'alaea is a hit with kids—and us not-so-kids.

Make time for Hawaiian time.

(808-878-2870) on Omaopio Road in Kula is a goat dairy farm where your kids will be able to milk other kids (the four-legged kind) for $15–$39, depending on tour type. **Leilani Farm Sanctuary** (808-298-8544) is a refuge for a variety of rescued animals that offers tours Mondays, Wednesdays and Saturdays for $30 per person (reservations required). The director, Laurelee, has a passion for the animals that is contagious, and it's cute to see how happy all the animals look in their lush, Haʻiku home. **Maui Animal Farm** (808-280-2597) near Launiupoko in west Maui also offers petting zoo tours for $25 per person ($20 for children) and must be booked in advance. **Ohana Ranch of Maui** (808-298-5864) in Kula has a little more action. They offer riding lessons for keiki as young as 2 on their ridiculously cute, miniature horses.

The accommodation reviews describe the resorts with good keiki programs. By the way, if your objective was to get *away* from the kids, then maybe these resorts won't be at the top of *your* list.

Kids who want to try something more involved than snorkeling may want to try SNUBA. (See page 247 for more.)

Lastly, you should know that it's a big fine plus a mandatory safety class if your keiki isn't buckled up in a car. And booster seats are required for kids under 8.

SOME TERMS

A person of Hawaiian blood is **Hawaiian**. Only people of this race are called by this term. They are also called **Kanaka Maoli**, but only another Hawaiian can use this term. Anybody who was born here, regardless of race (except whites), is called a **local**. If you were born elsewhere but have lived here a while, you are called a **kamaʻaina**. If you are white, you are a **haole**. It doesn't matter if you have been here a day or your family has been here for over a century—you will always be a haole. The term comes from the time when westerners first encountered these islands. Its precise meaning has been lost, but it is thought to refer to people with no background (since westerners could not chant kanaenae—praise—of their ancestors).

The continental United States is called the **Mainland**. If you are here and are returning, you are not "going back to the states" (we *are* a state). When somebody leaves the island, they are **off-island**. Similarly, if you're here, you're **on-island**.

HAWAIIAN TIME

One aspect of Hawaiian culture you may have heard of is Hawaiian Time. The stereotype is that everyone in Hawai'i moves just a little bit more slowly than on the mainland. Supposedly, we are more laid-back and don't let things get to us as easily as people on the mainland. This is the stereotype... OK, it's *not* a stereotype. It's real.

Hopefully, during your visit, you will notice that this feeling infects you as well. You may find yourself letting another driver cut in front of you in circumstances that would incur your wrath back home. You may find yourself willing to wait at a red light without feeling like you're going to explode. The whole reason for coming to Hawai'i is to experience beauty and a sense of peace, so let it happen. If someone else is moving a bit more slowly than you want, just go with it.

SHAKA

One gesture you will see often and should not be offended by is the *shaka* sign. This is done by extending the pinkie and thumb while curling down the three middle fingers. Sometimes visitors think it is some kind of local gesture indicating *up yours* or some similarly unfriendly message. Actually it is a friendly act used as a sign of greeting, thanks or just to say, *Hey*.

Its origin is thought to date back to the 1930s. A guard at the Kahuku Sugar Plantation on O'ahu used to patrol the plantation railroad to keep local kids from stealing cane from the slow-moving trains. This guard had lost his middle fingers in an accident, and his manner of waving off the youths became well known. Kids began to warn other kids

that he was around by waving their hands in a way that looked like the guard's, and the custom took off.

THE HAWAIIAN LANGUAGE

The Hawaiian language is a beautiful, gentle and melodious language that flows smoothly off the tongue. Just the sounds of the words conjure up trees gently swaying in the breeze and the sound of the surf. Most Polynesian languages share the same roots and many have common words. Today, Hawaiian is spoken *as an everyday language* only on the privately owned island of Ni'ihau, 17 miles off the coast of Kaua'i (see *Introduction*). Visitors are often intimidated by Hawaiian. With a few ground rules you'll come to realize that pronunciation is not as tough as you might think.

When missionaries discovered that the Hawaiians had no written language, they sat down and created an alphabet. This Hawaiian alphabet has only twelve letters. Five vowels; **a, e, i, o** and **u**, as well as seven consonants; **h, k, l, m, n, p** and **w**. The consonants are pronounced just as they are in English with the exception of W. It is often pronounced as a V if it is in the middle of a word and comes after an E or I. Vowels are pronounced as follows:

A—pronounced as in *Ah* if stressed, or *above* if not stressed.

E—pronounced as in *say* if stressed, or *dent* if not stressed.

I—pronounced as in *bee*.

O—pronounced as in *no*.

U—pronounced as in *boo*.

One thing you will notice in this book are glottal stops. These are represented by an upside-down apostrophe ' and are meant to convey a hard stop in the pronunciation. So if we are talking about the type of lava called 'a'a, it is pronounced as two separate As (AH-AH).

Another feature you will encounter are **diphthongs**, where two letters glide together. They are ae, ai, ao, au, ei, eu, oi, and ou. Unlike many English diphthongs, the second vowel is always pronounced. One word you will read in this book, referring to Hawaiian temples, is *heiau* (HEY-YOW). The e and i flow together as a single sound, then the a and u flow together as a single sound. The Y sound binds the two sounds, making the whole word flow together.

If you examine long Hawaiian words, you will see that most have repeating syllables, making it easier to remember and pronounce.

Let's take a word that might seem impossible to pronounce. When you see how easy this word is, the rest will seem like a snap. The Hawai'i state fish is the **humuhumunukunukuapua'a**. At first glance it seems like a nightmare. But if you read the word slowly, it is pronounced just like it looks and isn't nearly as horrifying as it appears. Try it. **Humu** (hoo-moo) is pronounced twice. **Nuku** (noo-koo) is pronounced twice. A (ah) is pronounced once. **Pu** (poo) is pronounced once. A'a (ah-ah) is the ah sound pronounced twice, the glottal stop indicating a hard stop between sounds. Now, you can try to pronounce it again. **Humuhumunukunukuapua'a**. Now, wasn't that easy? OK, so it's not easy, but it's not impossible either.

Below are some words that you might hear during your visit:

'Aina (EYE-na)—Land.
Akamai (AH-ka-MY)—Wise or shrewd.
Ali'i (ah-LEE-ee)—A Hawaiian chief; a member of the chiefly class.
Aloha (ah-LO-ha)—Hello, goodbye, or a feeling or the spirit of love, affection or kindness.
Hala (HA-la)—Pandanus tree.
Hale (HA-leh)—House or building.

Hana (HA-na)—Work.
Hana hou (HA-na-HO)—To do again.
Haole (HOW-leh)—Originally foreigner, now means Caucasian.
Heiau (HEY-YOW)—Hawaiian temple.
Hula (HOO-la)—The storytelling dance of Hawai'i.
Imu (EE-moo)—An underground oven.
'Iniki (ee-NEE-key)—Sharp and piercing wind (as in Hurricane 'Iniki).
Kahuna (ka-HOO-na)—A priest or minister; someone who is an expert in a profession.
Kai (kigh)—The sea.
Kalua (KA-LOO-ah)—Cooking food underground.
Kama'aina (KA-ma-EYE-na)—Long-time Hawai'i resident.
Kane (KA-neh)—Boy or man.
Kapu (KA-poo)—Forbidden, taboo; keep out.
Keiki (KAY-key)—Child or children.
Kokua (KO-KOO-ah)—Help.
Kona (KO-na)—Leeward side of the island; wind blowing from the south, southwest direction.
Kuleana (KOO-leh-AH-na)—Concern, responsibility or jurisdiction.
Lanai (LA-NIGH)—Porch, veranda, patio.
Lani (LA-nee)—Sky or heaven.
Lei (lay)—Necklace of flowers, shells or feathers.
Liliko'i (LEE-lee-KO-ee)—Passion fruit.
Limu (LEE-moo)—Edible seaweed.
Lomi (LOW-me)—To rub or massage; lomi salmon is raw salmon rubbed with salt and spices.
Lu'au (LOO-OW)—Hawaiian feast; literally means taro leaves.
Mahalo (ma-HA-low)—Thank you.
Makai (ma-KIGH)—Toward the sea.
Malihini (MA-lee-HEE-nee)—A newcomer, visitor or guest.
Mauka (MOW-ka)—Toward the mountain.

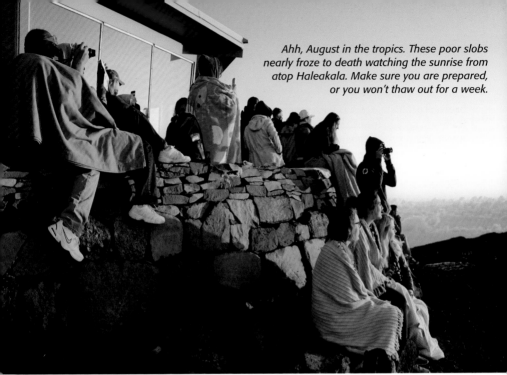

Ahh, August in the tropics. These poor slobs nearly froze to death watching the sunrise from atop Haleakala. Make sure you are prepared, or you won't thaw out for a week.

Moana (mo-AH-na)—Ocean.
Moʻo (MO-oh)—Lizard.
Nani (NA-nee)—Beautiful, pretty.
Nui (NEW-ee)—Big, important, great.
ʻOhana (oh-HA-na)—Family.
ʻOkole (OH-KO-leh)—Derrière.
ʻOno (OH-no)—Delicious, the best.
Pakalolo (pa-ka-LO-LO)—Marijuana.
Pali (PA-lee)—A cliff.
Paniolo (PA-nee-OH-lo)—Hawaiian cowboy.
Pau (pow)—Finish, end; pau hana means quitting time from work.
Poi (poy)—Pounded kalo (taro) root that forms a paste.
Pono (PO-no)—Goodness, excellence, correct, proper.
Pua (POO-ah)—Flower.
Puka (POO-ka)—Hole.
Pupu (POO-POO)—Appetizer, snacks or finger food.
Wahine (vah-HEE-neh)—Woman.
Wai (why)—Fresh water.
Wikiwiki (WEE-kee-WEE-kee)—To hurry up, very quick.

Quick Pidgin Lesson

Hawaiian pidgin is fun to listen to. It's like ear candy. It is colorful, rhythmic and sways in the wind. Below is a list of some of the words and phrases you might hear on your visit. It's tempting to read some of these and try to use them. If you do, the odds are you will simply look foolish. These words and phrases are used in certain ways and with certain inflections. People who have spent years living in the islands still feel uncomfortable using them. Thick pidgin can be incomprehensible to the untrained ear (that's the idea). If you are someplace and hear two people engaged in a discussion in pidgin, stop and eavesdrop for a bit. You won't forget it.

Pidgin Words & Phrases

Ainokea—I no care/I don't care. Try saying it slowly to hear it.
All bus—Drunk.
An' den—And then? So?
Any kine—Anything; any kind.

Ass right—That's right.
Ass why—That's why.
Beef—A problem one has with another.
Brah—Bruddah; friend; brother.
Broke da mout—Delicious.
Buggah—That's the one; it is difficult.
Bus laugh—To laugh out loud.
Chicken skin kine—Something that gives you goosebumps.
Choke—Plenty; a lot.
Cockaroach—Steal; rip off.
Da kine—A noun or verb used in place of whatever the speaker wishes. Heard constantly.
Das how—That's right.
Fo days—plenty; "He get hair fo days."
Geevum—Go for it! Give 'em hell!
Grind—To eat.
Grinds—Food.
Hold ass—A close call when driving your new car.
How you figga?—How do you figure that? It makes no sense.
Howzit?—How is it going? How are you? Also, Howzit o wot?
I owe you money or wat?—What to say when someone is staring at you.

On a clear day—and most days on Maui are clear days—West Maui looks like it's a separate island from South Maui.

Lolo—Crazy, stupid.
Lose money—What you say when something bad happens, like if you drop your shave ice.
Mek ass—Make a fool of yourself.
Mek house—Make yourself at home.
Mo' bettah—This is better.
Moke—A large, tough local male. (Don't say it unless you *like scrap*.)
No can—Cannot; I cannot do it.
No mek lidat—Stop doing that.
No, yeah?—No, or is "no" correct?
'Okole squeezer—Something that suddenly frightens you ('okole meaning derrière).
Pau hana—Quit work. (A time of daily, intense celebration in the islands.) Also another name for Happy Hour.
Poi dog—A mutt.
Shahkbait—Shark bait, meaning pale, untanned people or a beach newbie.
Shaka—Great! All right!
Shoots, den—Affirmative/Okay, then. As in "We're meeting for lunch at noon." *Shoots, den.*
Shredding—Riding a gnarly wave.
Slippahs—Flip-flops, thongs, zoris.
Stink eye—Dirty looks; facial expression denoting displeasure.
Suck rocks—Buzz off, or pound sand.
Talk stink—Speak bad about somebody.

Talk story—Shooting the breeze; to rap.

Tanks ah?—Thank you.

Tita—A female moke. Same *scrap* results.

Training brah—A haole trying (unsuccessfully) to speak pidgin.

Yeah?—Used at the end of sentences.

MUSIC

Hawaiian music is far more diverse than most people think. Many people picture Hawaiian music as someone twanging away on an 'ukulele with their voice slipping and sliding all over the place like they have an ice cube down their back. In reality, music here can be outstanding.

There is the melodic sound of the more traditional music. There are young local bands putting out modern music with a Hawaiian beat. There is even Hawaiian reggae. Hawaiian Style Band, the late Israel Kamakawiwoʻole (known locally as Bruddah Iz) and Willie K are excellent examples of the local sound. Even if you don't always agree with the all the messages in the songs, there's no denying the talent of these entertainers.

Major-name entertainers perform regularly around Maui, including legendary guitarists Willie K and George Kahumoku, as well as younger, equally talented artists. Consult local listings for specifics.

Local radio station, **KPOA 93.5 FM** is a great way to hear Hawaiian music done Maui-style. If you get a chance, stop by **Barnes & Noble** (808-214-6807) in the Maui Marketplace in Kahului. They have a good selection of Hawaiian music. **Request** (808-244-9315) in Wailuku on Market Street is a local music store with *pleny kine* music, new and used.

THE HULA

The hula evolved as a means of worship, later becoming a forum for telling a story with chants (called mele), hands and body movement. It can be fascinating to watch.

When most people think of the hula, they picture a woman in a grass skirt swinging her hips to the beat of an 'ukulele. But in reality there are two types of hula. The modern hula, or hula 'auana, uses musical instruments and vocals to augment the dancer. It came about after westerners first encountered the Islands. Missionaries found the hula distasteful, and the old style was driven underground. The modern type of hula came about as a form of entertainment and was practiced in places where missionaries had no influence. Ancient Hawaiians didn't even use grass skirts. They were brought later by Gilbert Islanders.

The old style of hula is called hula 'olapa or hula kahiko. It consists of chants, is accompanied only by percussion and takes years of training. It can be exciting to watch as performers work together in a synchronous harmony at major hula events like the annual Merrie Monarch Festival on the Big Island. Both men and women dance, with women's hula a bit softer and more graceful (though no less disciplined) and men's hula more active. This type of hula is physically demanding, requiring strong concentration. Keiki (children's) hula can be charming to watch as well.

See local listings for hula performances and festivals around the island, or take in authentic hula at a lu'au. Your resort may offer introductory hula lessons, too.

FARMERS MARKETS

Maui's market choices seem to keep increasing each edition. You can find amazing produce not seen in most places on the mainland, but be sure to shop around. Organic and non-GMO markets (and farms) have also increased in popu-

A dreamy Haleakala sunrise worth getting up early for.

larity. Most of these farmers markets occur at the same time, year round. Check our website for any changes before trekking too far.

West Maui—In the Farmers Market parking lot across from Honokowai Beach Park Mon., Wed. and Fri. 7–11 a.m. Also, there is Napili Farmers Market Wed. and Sat. 8 a.m.–noon, across from Napili Plaza.

Central Maui—Inside the Queen Ka'ahumanu Center on Tues., Wed. and Fri. 8 a.m.–4 p.m.

Upcountry—In Kula at 17 Omaopio Road Wed. 8 a.m.–1 p.m. Also, next to the Pukalani Longs Drugs every Sat. 7–noon.

South Maui—Every Sat. 8:30–10:30 a.m. at 95 Lipoa St. in Kihei. Also next to the ABC parking lot at the corner of Uwapo and South Kihei Road Mon.–Fri. 8 a.m.–4 p.m.

East Maui—At Hasegawa General Store in Hana every Mon. and Thurs. (all day). Also at Hana Medical Center Mon.–Fri. 10 a.m.–2 p.m.

BOOKS

There is an astonishing variety of books available about Hawai'i and Maui—everything from history, legends, geology, children's stories and just plain ol' novels. **Barnes & Noble** (808-214-6807) in the Maui Marketplace on Dairy Road in Kahului has a dazzling selection. Also **Maui Friends of the Library** (808-877-2509) at the Queen Ka'ahumanu Center in Kahului has an even more extensive selection of new books on all aspects of Hawai'i and Maui. Walk in and lose yourself in Hawai'i's richness.

THE INTERNET

Recent changes, links to cool sites, the latest satellite weather shots, calendar of events and more can be found on **our website** (www.hawaiirevealed.com). It also has links to every company listed that has a site—both those we like and those we don't recommend. For the record there are *no advertisements* on the site. (Well... except for our own books and apps, of course.)

If you brought your own computer, you'll find that hot spots are numerous and fairly easy to find.

A NOTE ABOUT ACCESS

If lawful landowners post a *No Trespassing* sign on their land, you need to respect their wishes. That seems simple enough. But here's where it gets tricky.

It's common in Hawai'i for someone who doesn't own or control land to erect their own *No Trespassing, Keep Out* and *Road Closed* signs. Picture a shoreline fisherman who doesn't want anyone else near his cherished spot, putting up a store-bought sign to protect his solitude. Or a neighbor on a dirt road who hates the dust from cars driving by, so he puts up a sign that he knows that locals will ignore but might dissuade unwary visitors.

In the past we did our best to try to ferret out when *No Trespassing* signs were valid and when they were not, and we took *a lot* of heat from residents who thought we were encouraging trespassing when we weren't. But the current environment doesn't permit us to do that anymore. So if you're heading to one of the places we describe, and you encounter a *No Trespassing* sign, even if you think it's not authorized by the landowner (and even if it's on *public* land), we have to advise you to turn around and heed the sign. All descriptions in our book come with the explicit assumption that you have obtained the permission of the legal landowner, and unfortunately, it'll usually be up to you to determine who that is and how to get it. But please, under no circumstances are we suggesting that you trespass.

Plain and clear: Don't trespass... ever... for any reason... period.

A NOTE ABOUT PERSONAL RESPONSIBILITY

In the past we've had the sad task of removing places that you can no longer visit. The reason, universally cited, is *liability*. Although Hawai'i has a statute indemnifying landowners, the mere threat of legal action is often enough to get something closed. Because we, more than any other publication, have exposed heretofore unknown attractions, we feel the need to pass this along.

You need to assess what kind of traveler you are. We've been accused of leaning a bit toward the adventurous side, so you should take that into account when deciding if something's right for you. To paraphrase from the movie *Top Gun*, "Don't let your ego write checks your body can't cash."

Please remember that this isn't Disneyland—it's nature. Mother Nature is hard, slippery, sharp and unpredictable. If you go exploring and get into trouble, whether it's your ego that's bruised or something more tangible, please remember that neither the state, the private land owner nor this publication *told* you to go. You *chose* to explore, which is what life, and this book, are all about. And if you complain to or threaten someone controlling land, they'll rarely fix the problem you identified. They'll simply close it... and it will be gone for good.

Sometimes even good intentions can lead to disaster. At one adventure site, a trailhead led hikers to the base of a wonderful waterfall. There was only *one* trail, to the left at the parking lot, that a person could take. Neither we, other guides nor websites ever said, "Stay on the trail to the left" because at the time there was only one trail to take.

The state (in their zeal to protect themselves from liability at an unmaintained trail) came along and put up a *Danger—Keep Out* sign at the trailhead. Travelers encountering the sign assumed they were on the wrong trail and started to beat a path to the right instead. But that direction started sloping downward and ended abruptly at a 150-foot-high cliff. Hikers retreated and in a short time a previously non-existent trail to the right became as prominent as the correct (and heretofore *only*) path to the left. Not long after the state's well-intentioned sign went up, an unwitting pair of hikers took the new, incorrect trail to the right and fell to their deaths. They probably died because they had been dissuaded from taking the correct trail by a state sign theoretically erected to keep people safe.

Our point is that nothing is static, and nothing can take the place of your own observations and good judgment. If you're doing one of the activities you read about in our book, app or someplace else and your instinct tells you something is wrong, *trust your judgment* and go do another activity. There are lots of wonderful things to do on the island, and we want to keep you safe and happy.

And also remember to always leave the island the same way you found it.

MISCELLANEOUS INFORMATION

Plastic bags are banned on the island, and rather than spring for paper bags, many stores will simply hand you your purchases, no matter how numerous. Consider bringing your own reusable bags whenever you are shopping. You can often buy island-themed reusable bags at grocery stores here and, once back home, get jealous looks from people when you flaunt your Hawaiian bags at your local stores.

It is customary here for *everyone* to remove their shoes upon entering someone's house (sometimes their office).

The **area code** for the entire state of Hawai'i is (808).

All prices listed are before sales or other taxes unless otherwise noted.

If you are going to spend any time at the beach, woven bamboo beach mats can be found all over the island for about $4. Some roll up; some can be folded. The sand comes off these more easily than it comes off towels.

If you're looking for a church to attend, the Saturday *Maui News* has complete listings and times.

Around the island you'll see signs saying *Visitor Information* or something similar. Allow us to translate. That's usually code for *We Want to Sell You Something*.

If you want to arrange a lei greeting for you or your honey when you disembark at Kahului Airport, **LeiGreeting.com** (800) 665-7959 can make the arrangements for around $25. Nice way to kick off a romantic trip, huh?

If your checkout time and departure flight are hours apart and you don't want to haul your luggage around, **Paradise Self Storage** (808-877-7783) in Kahului offers daily storage lockers.

The local hospital, **Maui Memorial Medical Center**, (808-244-9056) is at 221 Mahalani St. in Wailuku. See map on page 70.

SMARTPHONE APP

We love books, which are naturally and instinctively approachable. They convey information in a way that is timeless. But at the same time, new technology allows us to do things with smartphones that can't occur in books. Our app, *Hawaii Revealed*, is unlike *any* travel app you've ever seen. All the information from the books is there, but the app costs a little extra because we have also harnessed *and invented* features that will blow you away.

For instance, you want to go to Honolua Bay to snorkel today? You can flip to the page in the book and read all about it. But with our app, you tap to the entry and you can read all about it *and* find out that today isn't a good day to get into the water due to high surf. Want to do a hike off the Hana Highway? Well, the author woke up this morning, saw that the weather was going to be bad on the windward side, circled a part of the map that he thought might be affected and for how long, and every entry in that area that is weathersensitive will be updated to reflect the bad weather.

Want to find a restaurant that matches perfectly to your vision? *I want to dine at a place in Wailea, that has a romantic atmosphere, an ocean view, is vegetarianfriendly, full bar, easy parking, outdoor seating, not part of a national chain... oh, and has gluten-free options?* With the filters in our app you can cut through all of the restaurants and get to *exactly* what you want, read our in-depth and brutally honest review and get directions. How's *that* for cutting through the noise?

There's more—*a lot* more. Visit the iTunes or Google Play store and check out our app, including a free preview.

With no natural enemies, the endemic nene evolved to be pretty friendly birds.

Playtime in West Maui.

West Maui—playground of the rich and famous? Those are the words that could have described this area hundreds of years ago, when Hawaiian royalty spent considerable time frolicking in West Maui waters and sampling its delights. Today, West Maui serves as a playground for the rest of us. Calm waters, some great beaches, limitless activities and an exciting, dynamic town: West Maui delivers on its legacy of fun.

Whether you're staying in West Maui or just passing through, there's only one road in and out—Hwy 30, which changes its name to Hwy 340 once you get past the populated areas. We'll describe it as most see it, coming from Central or South Maui going clockwise.

MA'ALAEA TO LAHAINA

Before we get started, you need to know that traffic getting into and out of West Maui can be pretty bad. Despite the addition of a four lane bypass above Lahaina, the two lane road south of Lahaina feeding this part of the island is grossly inadequate, and you can expect slowdowns—sometimes even gridlock—in either direction any time of day. The state is aware of the crisis and has responded by increasing Maui's hotel tax to build a 20-mile-long, $10 billion light rail—on O'ahu, spending a you-gotta-be-kidding $100,000 *per foot*. For a train... But they want you to know they are studying West Maui's miseries *real* hard.

Between mile markers 7 and 8 you'll see a road on the left leading to **McGregor Point and Lighthouse** (actually a beacon). This is a good place to watch a sunset or look at whales during the season (mid-December through mid-May).

Past mile marker 8 is the more popular **scenic lookout**. In addition to a beautiful

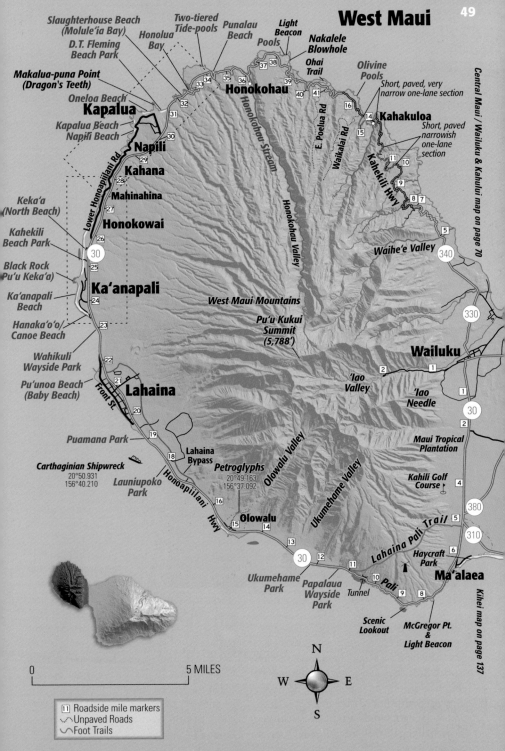

Slaughterhouse Beach
(Moluleʻia Bay)

Two-tiered
Tide-pools

Punalau
Beach

Light
Beacon

D.T. Fleming
Beach Park

Honolua
Bay

Pools

Nakalele
Blowhole

Makalua-puna Point
(Dragon's Teeth)

Ohai
Trail

Olivine
Pools

Short, paved, very
narrow one-lane section

Oneloa Beach

Honokohau

Kapalua

33 34

35

36

37 38

39

40 41

16

14

Kahakuloa

Kapalua Beach
Napili Beach

31

32

15

Short, paved
narrowish
one-lane
section

30

Napili

11

10

Kahana

Honokohau Stream

9

29

Lower Honoapiilani Rd.

Mahinahina

28

8 7

Keka'a
(North Beach)

27

Kahekili Hwy

E. Poelua Rd

Waikalai Rd

Honokowai

26

Kahekili
Beach Park

Honokohau Valley

Waiheʻe Valley

340

30

Black Rock
Pu'u Keka'a)

25

Ka'anapali
Beach

24

Ka'anapali

West Maui Mountains

330

Hanaka'o'o/
Canoe Beach

23

Pu'u Kukui
Summit
(5,788')

Wailuku

Wahikuli
Wayside Park

22

2

1

Pu'unoa Beach
(Baby Beach)

21

'Iao
Valley

'Iao
Needle

1

Front St.

Lahaina

20

30

Puamana Park

19

2

Carthaginian Shipwreck
20°50.931
156°40.210

18

Lahaina
Bypass

Maui Tropical
Plantation

Launiupoko
Park

Petroglyphs
20°49.163
156°37.092

Olowalu Valley

Kahili Golf
Course

4

16

Honoapiilani Hwy

15 14

Olowalu

Ukumehame Valley

380

5

310

13

Lahaina Pali Trail

6

Ukumehame
Park

30 12

11

Haycraft
Park

Ma'alaea

Papalaua
Wayside Park

10

Pali

9

Tunnel

Scenic
Lookout

McGregor Pt.
&
Light Beacon

Central Maui / Wailuku & Kahului map on page 70

Kihei map on page 137

N
W   E
S

0 ———————— 5 MILES

11 Roadside mile markers
··· Unpaved Roads
⌒ Foot Trails

From the shoreline highway, it's easy to pull off the road and lose yourself in an idyllic setting.

Less known is the good snorkeling and diving below the lookout. See *Beaches* on page 166 for more.

Highway 30 is a modern, two-lane highway. In the old days (which anthropologists define as any time before TVs had remote controls) there was a narrow, winding road along West Maui. Parts are still visible in places, such as near the tunnel. It's possible to awkwardly scramble up to the old road and walk along it (if you're so inclined). You get an idea of how something as "permanent" as a road can be quickly consumed by nature, even on this dry side of the island. This part of West Maui is called the **Pali** (cliffs) and soon gives way to a shoreline highway.

In ancient times there was a legendary female robber named Kaiaupe. She would lure men to get friendly with her at the edge of the pali, then kick them over the cliff and rifle their body for valuables (a practice that was named Ka-ai-a-Kaiaupe in her honor). So if you see a woman hitchhiker with a big *K* embroidered on her clothes... you might want to pass.

Descending to sea level, you'll find yourself constantly stealing glances toward the water. Views up the mountain are also scrumptious, and you'll probably want to pull over around mile marker 13 and take them in.

view of South Maui, it's a well-known whale-spotting place. In fact, there must be an underwater sign for the whales, because they seem to approach this area a lot. Maybe it's a scenic lookout for them, too, where they can come and observe us humans in our natural habitat. Morning and early afternoon bring more spottings, since the light winds produce less choppy seas, making the behemoths easier to spot.

At **Mile Marker 14** you'll see lots of cars. This area is listed in virtually all visitor information as having some of the best snorkeling on the island. Don't waste your time. That's *way* out of date. Runoff (perhaps from the old sugar operations) has created cloudy water with terrible visibility. Farther offshore it's good, but the shoreline snorkeling usually stinks. See page 165 for more.

At mile marker 15 is the pea-sized town of Olowalu, the site of the massacre of **Kalolopahu** (see page 16) and the only place on Maui where you can see all three offshore islands. It's also here that you'll find Maui's best **petroglyphs**. (See map on page 49.) In an era before pen and paper, the best way to record your thoughts was to scratch them on lava rock. At this site, pre- and post-contact Hawaiians left their artistic impressions in the smooth lava. (These had been augmented by mindless mutts leaving behind their more modern thoughts, but a group of volunteers now keeps the area graffiti-free.) To get there, turn at Luawai Street (past mile marker 14, before Olowalu), continue about 0.5 miles until the the road bears hard right and dirt roads branch to the left of a large hill. Take the dirt road to the other side of the hill. You'll know you're in the right spot when you see **Olowalu Cultural Reserve** sign. You can't get close up to the petroglyphs, you'll view them from the road at the interpretive sign.

Beware of wasps nesting in the area. And don't drive much past the petroglyphs, or you'll become familiar with what a genuine Hawaiian pig farm smells like.

Back on the highway, more ribbons of beach come and go. Past mile marker 16, the road veers away from the shoreline to become the Lahaina Bypass (Hwy 3000) where the mile markers reset to 0. Feeder

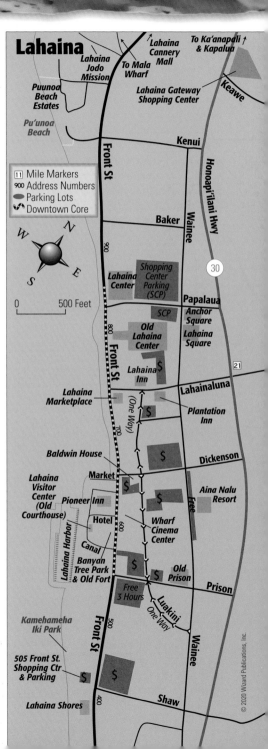

Lahaina

- 11 Mile Markers
- 900 Address Numbers
- ⬤ Parking Lots
- ✈ Downtown Core

0   500 Feet

© 2020 Wizard Publications, Inc.

roads extend to the shore and the original highway, Honoapiilani (aka Hwy 30), where parks such as Launiupoko dot the shoreline. As you ascend the bypass road, you'll get views over Lahaina and the offshore islands. Though the valleys up mauka are beautiful, there are no roads to the center of West Maui, and only a few private subdivision roads that penetrate a short distance. To get into Lahaina town, three main roads descend from the bypass: Hokiokio Place, Lahainaluna Road and Keawe Street (the latter is what the bypass becomes after mile marker 4.5). Lahainaluna is the only road that goes all the way down to Front Street, right into the middle of the action. If you want to drive Front Street from start to finish, Hokiokio will bring you to the south end of town where you jump on Honoapiilani Highway for 0.2 miles, then turn left onto Front Street. The intersection of Front and Shaw streets is where the shops and restaurants of Front Street begin.

LAHAINA TOWN

Lahaina is the only town in all of leeward Maui with a *real* downtown. If someone told you to meet them in downtown Kihei, you wouldn't have any idea where they meant. Same goes for Wailea, Kapalua, Ka'anapali or Napili. Though it's only 1.5 miles long, downtown Lahaina is well-defined and bursting with things to see and do.

The biggest problem with Lahaina is that it's crowded. And even when it's not crowded... *it's crowded.* A secluded stroll along Front Street is about as likely as a snowy day in Miami. But Front Street has an electricity that defies explanation. No matter how much you curse its popularity, you can't deny Lahaina's charm. It's busy, tacky, weird and wonderful. It's full of old world character and new world annoyances. It manages to energize and relax at the same time. If you visit West Maui without strolling along Front Street (abiding by that old Yogi Berra axiom, "*Nobody* goes there anymore; it's too crowded"), then you missed out on more than you think. Because for all its faults, Lahaina works.

Lahaina should be viewed as an event, not a place. You *do* Lahaina. You go there to eat, shop, walk and gawk. Lots of activities, especially boating-related, are centered around Lahaina. (This was, after all, an old whaling port.)

Ironically, as a place to stay, Lahaina lacks many of the things that make West Maui special. Namely good, clean beaches, cool breezes and a slow pace. Plus, there are relatively few places to stay in town. (Nearly all West Maui accommodations are north of Lahaina, in Ka'anapali, Honokowai, Kahana, Napili and Kapalua.) Of course, what it lacks in some areas, it makes up for by having a better nightlife, tons of restaurants and a more happenin' feel.

Lahaina means *cruel sun*. According to one legend, there was a chief named Hua

NOT TO BE MISSED!

many generations ago who, in a huff, killed all his priests. Drought soon followed, and villagers referred to the area as the land of the cruel sun. Today, that ever-present sun is the very thing that attracts people from all over the world, though it can get pretty hot in the summer.

Parking in Lahaina is a *buggah!* If anything can bring on that old-fashioned mainland road rage, this is it. Lahaina is woefully under-equipped in the parking department (though fully staffed in the *enforcement* department). The state makes a tidy sum from unsuspecting visitor naïveté, and parking fees have created a cash bonanza for the ever-hungry state coffers. Even at night, big brother is watching. An example: There's a three-hour lot near the harbor, but if you park there at 5 p.m. for a sunset cruise and return at 8:10, you may find that the ever-efficient parking paratroopers have targeted you for a fee. Be very careful, or you'll end up paying for some new carpet at City Hall. Here are a few tips.

Parking is free on Front Street for three hours if you can get a stall, and yes, they *do* keep an eye on your car. If you're having a hard time finding *any* spots in Lahaina, the pay lot on Dickenson near Wainee seems to fill up later than other lots. Don't forget to try the free lots (see map on page 51). They're usually full, but you may get lucky. (We don't mean it *that* way.) If you're doing an early morning boat trip, there is free parking on Wainee Street (south of Dickenson) where you can park for longer than three hours.

Your best parking opportunities are in the morning. Arrive in Lahaina between 9 and 10 a.m., and you stand a reasonable chance of getting a street-side stall. You'll also find the shops and streets much less crowded.

There is a huge, four-hour lot at Lahaina Center. The first hour is free. After that you can get validated if you purchase something from a merchant who's happy with the transaction.

While strolling around town, your personal tastes will dictate which shops and attractions work for you. Additional Attractions (all labeled on the map on page 51) include the **old courthouse** (where they have a detailed brochure describing all historic sites in town),

Believe it or not, this is a single tree. Banyan Tree Park in Lahaina seems to go on forever. But you gotta wake up pretty early in the morning to find—and photograph—it this empty.

Banyan Tree Park (an incredible must-see tree that encompasses an entire park), Baldwin House (as the oldest house on the island, you get an idea how the missionaries lived) and the old prison (called Hale Pa'ahao, or "stuck in irons house"). It's kind of interesting to visit this last site, made with coral walls, to get an idea of the kind of crimes that people were imprisoned for in the 1850s. They include "profanity, furious riding, adultery and fornication (the second most common offense), refusing to work on the road, giving birth to bastard children, lewd conversation, and affray." (We had to look up that last one; it basically means disturbing the peace.)

While on Front Street, you'll notice that activity salesmen are unusually aggressive. Lines like, *You folks have any questions? Ya need some coupons?* or *Interested in any activities?* are sales speak for, *I want to sell you something* or *Want to see a timeshare presentation?* See page 178 for more on activity brokers.

And the best show we've ever seen in Hawai'i, Warren & Annabelle's (see page 315), is on Front Street near Papalaua.

As you leave Lahaina town going north along Front Street, you'll find a beautiful Buddhist temple at the end of Ala Moana Street near the Mala Boat Ramp. The Lahaina Jodo Mission has a giant Buddha statue that was erected in 1968 to commemorate the centennial of Japanese immigrants arrival to Hawai'i. And there's a towering red pagoda that makes for some great photos, especially at sunset. Next to it is an old cemetery being swallowed by a sand dune.

KA'ANAPALI TO KAPALUA

Ka'anapali was part of a large sugar plantation when the sugar company's board met in 1956 and hatched a plan that would soon be repeated around the globe—the master planned destination resort, the first in Hawai'i. The large landowners had their pick of where to put the resort, and they chose the fantastic Ka'anapali Beach as their showcase to the world. (If *you'd* owned the entire island back then, you, too, probably would have chosen this beach.) It opened in 1962 and has been admired ever since.

The sunset torch lighting ceremony at Black Rock is followed by a plunge into the ocean.

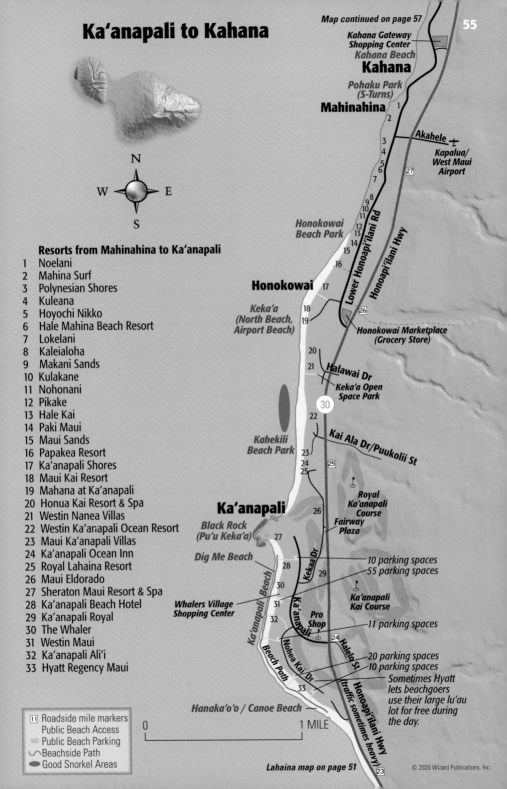

Ka'anapali to Kahana

Map continued on page 57

Kahana Gateway
Shopping Center
Kahana Beach
Kahana
Pohaku Park
(S-Turns)
Mahinahina

Akahele

Kapalua/
West Maui
Airport

Honokowai
Beach Park

Lower Honoapi'ilani Rd

Honoapi'ilani Hwy

Honokowai

Keka'a
(North Beach,
Airport Beach)

Honokowai Marketplace
(Grocery Store)

Halawai Dr

Keka'a Open
Space Park

Kai Ala Dr/Puukolii St

Kahekili
Beach Park

Royal
Ka'anapali
Course
Fairway
Plaza

Ka'anapali

Black Rock
(Pu'u Keka'a)

Dig Me Beach

10 parking spaces
55 parking spaces

Ka'anapali
Kai Course

Whalers Village
Shopping Center

Pro
Shop

11 parking spaces

20 parking spaces
10 parking spaces

Sometimes Hyatt
lets beachgoers
use their large lu'au
lot for free during
the day.

Kekaa Dr

Ka'anapali Dr

Nohea Kai Dr

Halelo St

Beach Path

Honoapi'ilani Hwy
(traffic sometimes heavy)

Ka'anapali Beach

Hanaka'o'o / Canoe Beach

Resorts from Mahinahina to Ka'anapali

1. Noelani
2. Mahina Surf
3. Polynesian Shores
4. Kuleana
5. Hoyochi Nikko
6. Hale Mahina Beach Resort
7. Lokelani
8. Kaleialoha
9. Makani Sands
10. Kulakane
11. Nohonani
12. Pikake
13. Hale Kai
14. Paki Maui
15. Maui Sands
16. Papakea Resort
17. Ka'anapali Shores
18. Maui Kai Resort
19. Mahana at Ka'anapali
20. Honua Kai Resort & Spa
21. Westin Nanea Villas
22. Westin Ka'anapali Ocean Resort
23. Maui Ka'anapali Villas
24. Ka'anapali Ocean Inn
25. Royal Lahaina Resort
26. Maui Eldorado
27. Sheraton Maui Resort & Spa
28. Ka'anapali Beach Hotel
29. Ka'anapali Royal
30. The Whaler
31. Westin Maui
32. Ka'anapali Ali'i
33. Hyatt Regency Maui

Roadside mile markers
Public Beach Access
Public Beach Parking
Beachside Path
Good Snorkel Areas

0   1 MILE

Lahaina map on page 51

Half a dozen fancy resorts line the beach. There's a wonderful paved **beachside path** that runs along all the resorts. It's an excellent place to stroll at sunset and can take an hour or more. Beach accesses are shown on the map on page 55. You can also park at the **Whalers Village Shopping Center**. Any shop will validate if you spend around $20. (Heck, you can practically knock that out with a scoop from Häagen-Dazs.)

Separating the two halves of the great beach is **Black Rock**. As mentioned earlier, Hawaiian volcanoes fall asleep for up to a million years before awakening for a last series of eruptions. West Maui had only four small eruptions during its final days. Black Rock was one. (Another is the rock where the Olowalu Petroglyphs are located.)

The ancient Hawaiians believed Black Rock, which they called Puʻu Kekaʻa, was the jumping off point for their spirits or souls, called ʻuhane, leaving this world. Each island had such a point. When Hawaiians died, it was here that their souls would leave this life and join their ancestors forever. If there were no ʻaumakua, or family spirits, to receive them, they would wander around the area, attaching themselves to rocks and generally causing mischief. That's why it's considered unwise to take any rocks from this area. You may bring back a spirit itching to get back home.

The **snorkeling** around Black Rock is excellent. Check out page 163 for more.

Kahekili was the last king of Maui. He was utterly fearsome looking, with tattoos almost blackening one side of his body from head to foot, but completely clean on the other. He loved the sport of lele kawa (cliff diving), and legend states that he once jumped from as high as 350 feet. Though terrifying to look at (even Captain Cook made reference to his scary appearance in his logs), Kahekili had a tiny, weak voice (sort of an ancient version of boxer Mike Tyson). This is the man who Kamehameha fought so hard to defeat when he conquered all the islands. It was only years later that Kamehameha learned that Kahekili was actually his father. **Kahekili Beach Park**, a great beach north

A REAL GEM

Some say that West Maui beaches are getting a bit crowded. This couple at Kahekili Beach Park knows better.

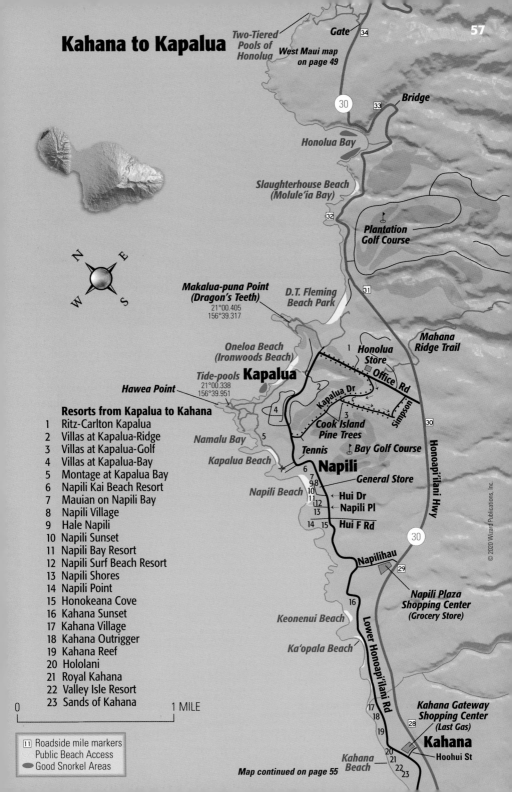

Kahana to Kapalua

Two-Tiered
Pools of
Honolua

Gate 34

West Maui map
on page 49

Bridge

30   33

Honolua Bay

Slaughterhouse Beach
(Molule'ia Bay)

32

Plantation
Golf Course

Makalua-puna Point
(Dragon's Teeth)
21°00.405
156°39.317

D.T. Fleming
Beach Park

31

Mahana
Ridge Trail

Oneloa Beach
(Ironwoods Beach)

1 Honolua
Store

Office Rd

Tide-pools **Kapalua**
21°00.338
156°39.951

Hawea Point

2

Kapalua Dr

Simpson

30

Resorts from Kapalua to Kahana

1   Ritz-Carlton Kapalua
2   Villas at Kapalua-Ridge
3   Villas at Kapalua-Golf
4   Villas at Kapalua-Bay
5   Montage at Kapalua Bay
6   Napili Kai Beach Resort
7   Mauian on Napili Bay
8   Napili Village
9   Hale Napili
10 Napili Sunset
11 Napili Bay Resort
12 Napili Surf Beach Resort
13 Napili Shores
14 Napili Point
15 Honokeana Cove
16 Kahana Sunset
17 Kahana Village
18 Kahana Outrigger
19 Kahana Reef
20 Hololani
21 Royal Kahana
22 Valley Isle Resort
23 Sands of Kahana

Namalu Bay

4

5

3

Cook Island
Pine Trees

Tennis

Bay Golf Course

Honoapi'ilani Hwy

© 2020 Wizard Publications, Inc.

Kapalua Beach

6   **Napili**

7
8
9   General Store
10
11   ← Hui Dr
12   ← Napili Pl
13

Napili Beach

14 15   Hui F Rd

Napilihau

30

29

Napili Plaza
Shopping Center
(Grocery Store)

16

Keonenui Beach

Ka'opala Beach

Lower Honoapi'ilani Rd

Kahana Gateway
Shopping Center
(Last Gas)

17
18

28

19

Kahana

20   Hoohui St
21
22
23

Kahana
Beach

0   1 MILE

11 Roadside mile markers
    Public Beach Access
●   Good Snorkel Areas

Map continued on page 55

Dragon's Teeth at Kapalua is a bizarre lava formation that owes its existence to the wind and sea. But the nearby labyrinth owes its existence to someone with way too much time on their hands.

of mile marker 25, is one way islanders remember him.

We should alert you that **Grocery Stores** are renowned for their *hurt me* prices. Prepare for the stomping of your life the first time you go in for some milk here.

Also, allow for **traffic** when driving to Lahaina in the afternoon from Kaʻanapali or Kapalua. Pau hana (end of work) traffic can be a problem, at its worst between Kaʻanapali and Lahaina.

There are dozens of condos north of Kaʻanapali. This is where the more reasonably priced West Maui accommodations are found. Unfortunately, a few of the beaches north of Kaʻanapali can be cloudy for the same reasons listed on page 166 for north Kihei. The first great beach after Kahekili Beach is **Napili Beach**, see page 160. (Ah, and what a wonderful beach it is...)

Sugar has been the symbol of West Maui since before the American Civil War. All who grew up here lived their lives in its shadow. A single company dominated all commerce here. Surprisingly, it was a German company that ran the sugar operations until WWI, when an irritated U.S. government seized the company and sold it to Americans. (In an *eat this* gesture to the Germans, they named it American Factors, and their retail stores were named Liberty House.)

The waning days of the 20th century brought an end to sugar in West Maui. Even after nearly two decades, nobody still really knows how the previously sugar-laced slopes will look in the years to come. Longtime sugar workers have moved on to other industries. The large mill off the highway is idle. Ironically, pineapple contributed to the demise of sugar here. Sugar is an intensely thirsty crop, and the sugar company was never able to get as much water as they needed, in sharp contrast to HC&S's water bounty in Central Maui. Their single best source of water dried up when their water supplier decided to start growing Pineapple Industry and cut them off from their source.

Farther north, Kapalua is an incredibly manicured oasis of green in this wind-swept part of the island. The gardening bill must be immense because no dead leaf goes unpunished. *Expensive* is the operative word at these resorts. Some of the beaches, such as Kapalua Beach, are excellent. The wind tends to be strong here, and it's also more prone to drizzle than any other leeward resort area.

Where Lower Honoapiilani Road becomes Office Road, there's a little road turnout with a parking lot. Walk toward the shoreline along the golf course next to the short hedge to a long point of lava that separates two large beaches. Called Makalua-puna Point, it's worth the 5-minute stroll. The trachyte lava here is different than most Hawaiian lavas. Light-colored, dense and fine grained, bleached white in some areas, it flowed during the dying days of the West Maui volcano half a million years ago. Salt spray on the upwind side has etched the lava into thrusting shapes known as Dragon's Teeth. Other areas on the point have other types of lava objects embedded in them. In some places the ocean has eroded holes completely through the lava rocks. Walk over to the left (west) side and look at Oneloa Beach, often calm and protected on the nearest side. You'll also spot a strange labyrinth on the ground. Readers have pointed out signs that seem to deter you from getting to Makalua-puna Point. The signs are there to prevent you from walking onto the golf course to the left (our old friend liability again) and to keep you from walking onto the ancient burial ground to the right. Stay just to the right of the golf course signs, and you'll find a worn path just downhill.

The Green Flash

Ever heard of the green flash? No, it's not a superhero. We'd heard of the green flash for years before we moved to Hawai'i. We assumed that it was an island myth, or perhaps something seen through the bottom of a beer bottle. But now we know it to be a real phenomenon, complete with a scientific explanation. You may hear other ways to experience the green flash—but this is the only true way.

On days when the horizon is crisp and clear with no clouds in the way of the sun as it sets, you stand a reasonable chance of seeing the green flash. Avoid looking directly at the sun until the very last part of the disk is about to slip below the horizon. Looking at it beforehand will burn a greenish image onto your retina, creating a "fool's flash" (and possibly wrecking your eyes). The instant before the last part of the sun's disk disappears, a vivid flash of green is often seen. This is because the sun's rays are passing through the thickest part of the atmosphere, and the light is bent and split into its different components the way it is in a rainbow. The light that is bent the most is the green and blue light, but the blue is less vivid and is overwhelmed by the flash of green, which lingers for the briefest of moments as the very last of the sun sets.

For a variety of reasons, including our latitude, Hawai'i is one of the best places in the world to observe the green flash. But if you aren't successful in seeing the real green flash, try the beer bottle method—at least it's better than nothing.

The huge lawn in front of Dragon's Teeth has a tumultuous history. The Ritz-Carlton Kapalua inland was supposed to be an oceanfront hotel. The lawn was to be its location. The only things standing in their way were approximately 2,000 ancient Hawaiians buried in the area. The developers began digging up the graves, and when the Hawaiian community learned of it, they began a series of emotional protests. Nearly 900 remains were dug up before common sense prevailed, and the hotel decided to relocate the buildings and reinter the bones in 1990. A state law was enacted after this to prevent such a thing from ever happening again.

PAST KAPALUA; OVER THE TOP

Like the highway past Hana along the bottom of Haleakala, the drive along the top of West Maui suffers from a long out-of-date reputation. Chances are you'll read that the road is not passable in a rental car or the ridiculous statement that you need 4WD. Years ago the road was nearly impossible to drive. Poor pavement gave way to no pavement, and the narrow spots would make a stunt driver sweat. But today the road is much better—the whole thing is paved. The real caveats are the two sections where it is one lane. About 1.5 miles of the highway are a *very* narrow paved one-lane road, and another 2.5 miles are a narrow*ish* one lane. There are some turnouts on these stretches, and timid drivers may want to evaluate if this is for them. (If two cars meet where there's no turnout, etiquette dictates that the driver heading *downhill* needs to back up because that's easier to maintain control.) Just drive the one-lane portions very slowly.

For what it's worth, we think this is one of the least appreciated drives on the island. It's like the Hana Highway without the traffic. Though nowhere nearly as lush as the Hana drive (nor as long), the windswept charm of this almost forgotten piece of Maui makes it worth the drive—if you can stand the curviness and the narrow sections. Along the way are some unforgettable sights, including one we discovered that amazed us with its perfection.

Our description assumes you will be driving this section from west to east, in a clockwise direction. We strongly suggest you do it this way for several reasons: The sights are better from that direction. Also, drivers rarely discover the road from the Wailuku side, so most traffic, sparse when compared to Hana traffic, will be flowing *with* you. Blind corners seem more blind when driving from Wailuku. Lastly, when on a narrow road, it's more comforting to be on the *inside* lane. Passengers can get uncomfortable when you're on the outside lane as you would if you came from Wailuku.

Beaches Past Kapalua

There are still some popular attractions past Kapalua. There's the *lovely sounding* Slaughterhouse Beach, after mile marker 32, with its concrete steps down to the shoreline and, before mile marker 33, Honolua Bay with its outrageous snorkeling in the summer, monstrous waves in the winter and its beautiful walking trail any time of year. Both are worth stopping for if your destination is the water. Both are described further in the *Beaches* chapter.

A dirt road along the sea cliffs after you've climbed above Honolua Bay past mile marker 33 offers a tremendous view of Honolua. Try to ignore the voluminous black plastic embedded in the ground there. It's one of the less glamorous legacies of growing pineapple. It was used to reduce the amount of water and pesticides needed. Pretty ironic, isn't it? That plastic litter is all over the place to protect the environment. (Gee—thanks, guys.)

At times you'll see a yellow/orange stripe in the lava cut by the road or erosion. These are deposits of ash from the island's youth. At that time huge volcanic explosions covered much of the mountain in ash that was then covered with lava flows. Though quiet now, West Maui was very violent in its younger days.

Still one last beach remains along this stretch, though you'd have a hard time finding many visitors or even locals who know about it. Called Punalau Beach, the access is 0.7 miles past mile marker 34. It's always uncrowded during the week. Past here you won't find any sand beaches until you reach the other side of West Maui Mountain at Wailuku. There's a nice view of Punalau and the coastline in general from the top of the turnout just past mile marker 34.

The road begins its sinuous 25-mile trek to central Maui from here. Dynamite coastal views are common. Now, 25 miles might not *seem* very far, but you're likely to drive slowly and stop often, so don't assume you'll be there in an hour. There are countless places to pull over and gawk at the untamed shoreline—sometimes from cliffs above, sometimes from along the shore. And don't count on cell phone coverage here; it's sparse.

HONOKOHAU TOWN

Past mile marker 36 is the village of Honokohau. There's a road that leads to the back of the valley, but expect plenty of stink eye if you try to go. They don't seem too neighborly there.

Like a jet engine firing into the sky, Nakalele Blowhole rocks when the ocean rolls.

Drive around the corner after mile marker 38.5 to the second of two parking lots across the street from a wood post fence. About 1,200 feet from the road (and 205 feet below you) is one of the more spectacular sights in West Maui. Called the Nakalele Blowhole, the ocean here has undercut the shoreline, pounding underneath the lava shelf, where it spits through a man-sized hole in the lava.

A REAL GEM

The blowhole varies *tremendously* with the tide and size of the surf. We were here once when the blowhole wasn't blowing a thing. Zero water was issuing from the hole. Four hours later we returned and found the blowhole shooting 70 feet into the air every few seconds with such vicious, explosive force that it made the ground tremble, and we were convinced the earth was going to split beneath our feet. It was like a jet engine rocketing seawater into the air with amazing fury. High tide is your best bet, and high surf adds to the fury.

Remember, this is wilderness. There's no guardrail to stop you from shrinking the gene pool should you use bad judgment and fall into the hole. If the blowhole is pumping (which is quite common in the winter), get only as close as common sense dictates. It's hard to predict which waves will make it scream. Huge waves sometimes produce nothing, while wimpy-looking waves sometimes surprise you. Never stand between the hole and the ocean. The area to the left (west) of the blowhole is some of the most amazing-looking landscape you'll ever see. It looks like an alien war zone where combatants fought with acid. Over countless eons, billions of tons of sea spray have shot through the blowhole and been blown on the wind. The spray attacks the fracturous rocks on contact, literally eating the land, and the results are never to be forgotten. Rock hounds will enjoy seeing how the elements have tortured the rocks into various bizarre and jagged formations. And off to the right of the blowhole, if you look around, you'll find a heart-shaped hole in one of the rocks that has become a sensation on Instagram.

If the blowhole isn't overly angry while you're there, you'll notice a whole community of life living off this phenomenon. Crabs tempt the ocean by lining the steamy hole during pauses, eating algae growing on the sides, in constant danger of being swept away from a wave. Primitive-looking blennies (also called rockskippers since they can leap from pool to pool) live their whole lives in the 3 inches of water that remain from the splashes that shoot out of the hole. There's a natural lava viewing ledge above the blowhole, but you are still in the potential wet zone there.

The trail starts at the turnout mentioned above and goes down toward the ocean slightly to the left. (It's not the more obvious-looking road cut slightly

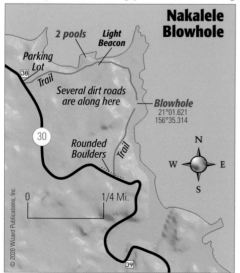

Nakalele Blowhole

2 pools
Light Beacon
Parking Lot
38
Trail
Several dirt roads are along here
Blowhole
21°01.621
156°35.314
30
Rounded Boulders
Trail
N
W — E
S
0   1/4 Mi.
39

© 2020 Wizard Publications, Inc.

Kahakuloa Head is a prominent landmark when you're cruising around the top of West Maui.

to the right, see map on page 62). You don't have to be a billy goat to get down the slippery trail with a few large step downs (but it doesn't hurt—flip-flops aren't a good footwear option for the trek). While on the trail, take note of the huge amount of olivine encrusted in much of the lava rock. We've found dime-sized specimens of this semiprecious gem in the area. If you're interested in a longer, more beautiful hike to the blow-hole, see page 215.

This is probably a good time to warn you of the mindless cows and horses that often wander onto the road. Cows aren't known for their smarts, but they seem especially clueless along this route, so be on the lookout for them. We've also seen a couple of donkeys on the road—and they're very friendly—so watch for them.

At 0.3 miles past mile marker 40 is a small turnout on the ocean side. It presents a truly kickin' view along the coast. If the blowhole is pumping, you'll see the results from here. The ocean is directly beneath you, and you don't need to go more than 10 feet from your car.

Just past mile marker 40.5 is a parking area. There's a concrete path leading to an unimpressive lookout. Even better is a 20 plus-minute hike called the **Ohai Trail**. We called it "remarkably dull" in a previous edition. We were right... yet we got it dead wrong. We discovered it's important to do this trail counterclockwise. See page 216.

At 0.9 miles past mile marker 40 the road opens up around a corner, exposing the peak of majestic 636-foot high **Kahakuloa Head** off in the distance. More on that later.

If you notice a strange feeling in your lungs about now, there's a technical reason for it. It's called *perfectly clean air*. The air here has drifted over the landless Pacific for many weeks. Skies are often crystal clear along this part of the island. So when you're at a sea cliff, suck in a deep breath; this is as clean as air can get.

Shortly after the sign reads "End of State Road," you'll find a turnout and trails leading toward the shoreline. One leads to a **mushroom-shaped rock**. From

Unwanted hitchhikers on the West Maui Highway.

mountain side. Odds are, however, you'll simply look like some fool mindlessly whacking a rock.

Right after the Bellstone is a dirt road on the ocean side. (It's almost kitty-corner to a dirt road on the mauka side with a gate leading inland.) Various signs have popped up over the years to dissuade you. Note that this is *public* land, unattributed signs notwithstanding. If you walk the short distance toward the ocean (veering to the right at the second intersection), you'll come to some nicely placed rock platforms 150 feet above the shoreline. (See map on page 66.) People occasionally go there and then turn around because some maps erroneously label the area as containing the Nakalele Blowhole. Until we revealed this site, however, few, if any, realized what they were missing below.

When you write guidebooks for a living and actually *do* and experience the things you write about, you get used to discovering exciting new things. But we were unprepared for the grand perfection of this totally unexpected oasis, which had never appeared in print. Judging by its pristine appearance when we found it, we'd say that not more than a handful of people on the island even knew about it, even though it's on public land.

We called it the **Olivine Pools** because of its gem-like quality, the color of the

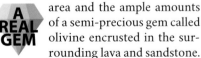

area and the ample amounts of a semi-precious gem called olivine encrusted in the surrounding lava and sandstone. They are numerous natural lava swimming pools ensconced in an ancient lava shelf,

there, you'll find one of the best places in West Maui from which to observe the beautiful ferocity of the ocean during high seas. The unchecked pounding violence has tortured and scarred the helpless lava into a fantastic array of grotesque and wonderful shapes and textures. It's mesmerizing from this secluded spot to watch the creation and destruction happening at the shoreline. Be careful on the trail down; it's slippery when wet. The ocean is 175 feet below you. 4WDs can go much of the way.

This area has some very nice hiking, though it is less structured and often trail-less. Just stop at any particularly inviting piece of shoreline and dig in. One very nice hike from here is described on page 216.

Now that you're on a county road the mile markers will start at 16. At 0.5 miles past the "End of State Road" but *before* mile marker 16, on the mauka side of the road, is the **Bellstone**. This large, round boulder *can* make a mildly metallic clank if you hit it at the right spot on the offering an outrageous and usually safe place to swim with the restless ocean pounding at you on three sides. (Large surf, especially in the wintertime, can turn the pools into a washing machine). It's reminiscent of the Queen's Bath on Kaua'i but far more grand and with more pools. The setting is as idyllic as any we can imagine. One of the pools is extremely deep and cool with a natural step to enter and exit. From this pool, your vantage point to the ocean cauldron beyond makes you feel snug and smug. Another pool is just deep enough to sit in, which makes it shallow enough for the afternoon sun to occasionally heat it to about 90 °F in the summer. Another pool has only one way in and out. Water shoes are fine, but we've walked around barefoot and not had a problem since the lava is pretty smooth, and there are no nasty sea urchins to kill your feet. It can be slippery, however. Perched above the pools is an amazingly flat platform, a perfect place to stretch out your towel to sun yourself. Natural lava steps lead to the pools themselves.

As the tide rises, splashes from the ocean may trickle into some of the pools and flow from one to another, sometimes forming small waterfalls. As far as we've observed, only high surf or prolonged heavy rain seems to ruin the area. (Big waves make it—and any part of the shoreline—dangerous.) Big rains *occasionally* cause the pools to form one large silty pond that you'd never recognize from our above description. When spoiled like this, nature usually cleans it up within a week. *Rarely*, long periods of south winds and low surf may cause it to get a bit stagnant. Observe for yourself to see if conditions are good. Very high surf, above 10 feet, could spoil it during *all* tides. And don't get too close to the unpredictable ocean, which could always send a large wave to pick you off. People standing at the water's edge instead of in the pools can *and have* been killed by large waves. And we've even heard of people getting scraped up *in the pools* when large waves came crashing ashore. Bottom line: Use

Some deep, some shallow, the Olivine Pools can be a calm playground in a restless sea.

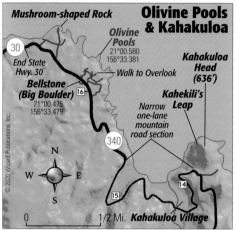

Olivine Pools & Kahakuloa

Mushroom-shaped Rock

Olivine Pools
21°00.580
156°33.381

Kahakuloa Head (636')

30
End State Hwy. 30

Walk to Overlook

Bellstone (Big Boulder)
21°00.475
156°33.479

16

Kahekili's Leap

Narrow one-lane mountain road section

340

N
W   E
S

15   14

0   1/2 Mi.   Kahakuloa Village

© 2020 Wizard Publications, Inc.

common sense and stay out if the ocean appears threatening.

There's a small blowhole off to the side that rarely does much, and next to it is the hole where most of the water drains to return to the ocean. (Be careful around the hole; falling into it would be a *big* problem!) This area tends to be windy, though it's partially blocked by some lava. Sometimes, especially during the summer, it can get so windy that you'll want to blow off this attraction (so to speak).

Since we revealed the Olivine Pools in our first edition, we no longer find it empty all the time like we used to. *Great!* You can't imagine how good it makes us feel to share this discovery with people. It seems tailor-made for recreation *if* the ocean's cooperating.

From the pools, take a look at the unusually intriguing lava formations around you. Some look like lava chessmen sentries. Above the pool is one formation that looks like a lava admiral's chair facing the ocean.

To get to the Olivine Pools from the rock platform overlook, look down the cliff and to your left for a lava bench below you. You should see a heart-shaped pool on the lava bench. There is faint trail leading down to the bench. Footing can

be awkward, rocky and a bit slippery. Flip-flops are not advised for the trail. Please be certain to bring everything out that you bring in. Also, it's easy to sunburn in the placid pools, but we're worried that too much sunscreen may harm the pools. Try to refrain if you can while in the water. Though it's tempting to bring back rock souvenirs, you should know that Hawaiians strongly believe that any rocks that leave the islands bring bad luck due to a curse from the volcano goddess Pele. True or not, we can tell you that readers often mail rocks to us after they've returned home and experienced a string of bad luck. So it's up to you, but we advise you to leave everything where you find it.

Soon the highway gets narrow—*very* narrow—as it descends along the side of the mountain. Skittish passengers may *hate* this 1.5 mile part. (We've seen some who had expressions as if they had just unexpectedly bungee-jumped into hell.) Soon their nightmare is over as they descend into **Kahakuloa Village**.

Kahakuloa is a tight-knit community isolated from the rest of the island, though some locals commute to work out in the "real world." In the village on the left side is **Panini Pua Kea Fruit Stand**. They have an unusual handmade coconut candy that's pretty addictive. As you are leaving Kahakuloa and the road is just beginning to ascend, **Julia's** is a stand on the left next to a wet-looking taro patch that makes the best **banana bread** on the planet (cash only). Makes my mouth hurt just writing about it. (Hmm, raising the bar pretty high, aren't we?) When they're closed, Panini Pua Kea (above) often becomes their outlet.

As you're leaving Kahakuloa town, you ascend the valley walls on the narrow road. At the top of the road is a turnout, if your nerves are shot and you want a nice view of the village and bay. After this the road widens, and you'll see a fence and gate with a path through a cattlestop leading down between the 636-foot high **Kahakuloa Head** (which means *the tall lord*) and a 547-foot high hill to the right called **Pu'u Kahuli'anapa**. The short trail between the hills offers some good views of the back side of Kahakuloa Head towering above you.

If you're feeling adventurous, from near the cattlestop you could make your way to the top of the hill to the right. It's fairly steep, and you won't pick up the cattle trails until toward the top. We've hiked to the top, and the views are second to... well, one, actually. You see, the much steeper Kahakuloa Head to your left has a summit that can only be reached by a death-defying, 'okole-squeezing, nail-biting scaling of the crumbly rock wall. Thanks, but no thanks. But while exploring this area from the air in an ultralight, I discovered something quite impressive. At the peak of the mountain were *two folding lawn chairs*. Someone apparently loved nothing better than to climb this beast in order to relax at the top while enjoying the views. Whoever you are, *bruddah*, you've earned it!

Part of Kahakuloa Head used to be called **Kahekili's Leap**. Why? Because the 18th-century Maui King Kahekili used to sometimes reside up here, according to legend. At a place part of the way down (but more than 200 feet above the ocean) he would regularly dive into the water, then climb back up the cliff face for his breakfast.

After Kahakuloa Head you'll pass **Karen Lei's Gallery & Gift Shop**. They have a nice selection of Maui-made jewelry, art and furniture (plus a restroom if you are truly a shopper). Prices are expensive.

After mile marker 11 is the sharpest **hairpin turn** we've ever seen. Look as you're approaching it, and you'll see that the upper road is almost literally on top of the lower road. (We've tried photographing it but couldn't capture it until we used a drone.)

Just after mile marker 10 is the **Turnbull Studios and Sculpture Garden**, an apt description. Open weekdays only, the area is replete with wood and bronze sculptures, and it's worth a stop.

Around mile marker 8 is something you probably haven't seen on this side of the island—a waterfall below the road. **Lower Makamaka'ole Falls** is visible from just past the turnout at pole telephone #174–viewed slightly farther ahead through buffalo grass. Attention Maui County—this would be an *awesome* place for a scenic lookout. It is a multi-tiered falls and is refreshing after all the dryness you've seen. Its name means without friends. (How sad.)

One last thing. For some odd reason, as you're pulling into Wailuku after the

Now that's a hairpin turn.

long drive, the last 0.1 miles of this road is one way—the wrong way—at the Vineyard intersection. We've seen some terribly close calls here as tired drivers plunge into oncoming traffic. Go left on Vineyard, then right on Central.

WEST MAUI BEST BETS

Best Hike—Acid War Zone to the Blowhole (0.5–0.75 Miles One Way)

Best Place to Find Old Whaling Industry Artifacts—Old Courthouse

Best Beach to Learn to Snorkel—Pu'unoa Beach

Best Sunset Stroll with Your Shoes On—Ka'anapali Beachside Path

Best Sunset Stroll with Your Shoes Off—Ka'anapali Beach

Best Beach to Start Your Day—Kahekili Beach Park

Best Place to Watch a Guy Jump Off a Rock—Black Rock from Sheraton at Sunset

Best Place to See the Ocean Explode—Nakalele Blowhole

Best Beach to Frolic—Napili Beach

Best Banana Bread (on the Planet)—Last Stand in Kahakuloa

Best Place to Find Golf Balls While Snorkeling—Oneloa Beach

Best Place to Kiss Off Snorkeling—Mile Marker 14 Beach

Best Protected Beach—Kapalua Beach

Best Place to See Just How Narrow a Road Can Be—Hwy 340 Segment Going Toward Kahakuloa

Best Snorkeling—Right Side of Honolua Bay When Calm, or Black Rock Snorkeling from Sheraton Side

Best Way to Recapture Mainland Road Rage—Trying to Park in Lahaina

Best Place to Sandblast Your Da Kines—D.T. Fleming Beach Park in Wind

Best Swimming Pool—Hyatt Regency Maui

Best Place to Lose Your Voice—Yelling at the Person Next to You at the Waterfall Grotto Bar at the Hyatt Regency Maui

Best Tree—Banyan Tree Park on Front Street

Best Evening Show—Warren & Annabelle's

Makamaka'ole is just one of the pretty gulches along this stretch of the island.

Although the islands have bid aloha to sugar grown commercially, you'll still see lots of it in this area while the landowner switches to other crops.

Central Maui is your introduction to the island. You'll land here. You'll shop here. You'll also come through here when you head to Hana, up to the top of Haleakala or after circling West Maui. But with all that exposure, few people come to Central Maui just to see Central Maui. It's like the Denver Airport of Maui. Everyone passes through, yet few look around. But don't blow it off completely. Central Maui does have some reasons to stop and stay a while.

Since there's no logical way to organize this area, we're going to describe it in a scattershot manner.

WAILUKU

The county seat, center of power and, most importantly, home to a few good restaurant bargains. (How's *that* for a reason to come here?)

Think of it as a once-grand hub of island activity that's now in the shadow of Kahului, often forgotten and showing its age. There is a certain charm to Wailuku, but not enough to lure many visitors. Too bad. In its day, Wailuku was quite a place: where sugar barons wined and dined, island leaders made important proclamations, and people came from all over to be entertained. One part of town is known as **Happy Valley**, even to this day. The origin is uncertain, but the age-old rumor says it's related to the fact that the area was known for its collection of brothels. (Hard to imagine in sleepy little Wailuku.)

Most people simply drive through Wailuku on their way to ʻIao Valley and the ʻIao Needle. This was a sacred burying place for chiefs and the location of Maui's last giant battle for supremacy.

Central Maui / Wailuku & Kahului

Kitesurfing prohibited

Spreckelsville Beach

Hana map on page 82

Hana Hwy

Haleakala Hwy

37

3

Pa'ia 4 miles

Kalo

Heliport

Tower

Haleakala Hwy

Kahului Airport

Terminal

Kanaha Beach

Ka'a Point

Kitesurfing

Amala

Kanaha Pond

Overflow Parking

Aalele

Marriott

Keolani

Costco

Haleakala Hwy

Hana Hwy

2

36

Pulehu

Hookele

Hansen Rd

Sugar Mill

Maui Marketplace

Walmart

Home Depot

Target

1

333 Dairy

Dairy Rd

Hukilike

Maui Veterans

311

Haleakala & Upcountry map on page 121

Alamaha

Wakea

Puunene Ave

Hana Hwy

36A

32A

Amala

Maui Mall

0

Kahului Mall

3500

Lono

Kihei map on page 137

To Kihei

0

Kuihelani Hwy

To Lahaina

2

380

Kahului Beach Rd

(Hotels along here)

Kane

Ka'ahumanu Center

2

Kamehameha

Kahului Harbor

Wailuku Beach Rd

Kanaloa

Wahinepio

Maui Arts & Cultural Center

Skateboard Park

Wakea

Kahului

Papa

Dunes At Maui Lani Golf Course

1

Waiehu Beach Park

Waiehu Beach Rd

Lower Waiehu

Lower Main

'Iao Stream/Wailuku River

War Memorial

Lower Main

Mill

Mahalani

Maui Memorial Medical Center

Maui Lani

West Maui map on page 49

3400

2

Kuihe

Haleki'i & Pihana Heiau

Banana Bungalow

Happy Valley

Central

Main

Kaahumanu

1

Wailuku

Wai'ale Rd

340

2

330

1

Market St.

33

Church

Koahu

High

30

Old Wailuku Inn

Kehalani Pkwy / Honoapi'ilani Hwy

1

320

To 'Iao Valley & Needle

Bailey House Museum

Waihe'e Ridge & Valley Trails map on page 218

Waiehu Stream

1 MILE

0

N E W S

© 2020 Wizard Publications, Inc.

The king of the Big Island was Kamehameha the Great. In 1790 he decided that the time was right to invade Maui (again). After he had personally killed the leading chief of Maui, his forces swept into Kahului and Wailuku. The two sides were fairly equal except for one thing: the cannon Kamehameha had nabbed from the seized sloop belonging to Metcalfe's son. (See page 16 for more on that.) With this cannon, which the natives affectionately nicknamed Lopaka (Robert), and some captured (though now happily compliant) westerners as advisers, Kamehameha was able to utterly annihilate the Maui forces.

They steadily rolled Lopaka along the rocky trails into 'Iao Valley, backing the troops into a corner, and proceeded to slaughter almost everyone. Many of the women and children had been moved higher up the cliffs and saw their loved ones die as Robert, loaded with shells and sometimes rocks, blasted away. The carnage was so great that the bodies clogged up the stream. Even by Hawaiian standards of the time, the killing was appalling. The natives called the battle Ka'uwa'u-pali (clawed off the cliff) and Kepaniwai (damming of the waters).

Today 'Iao (pronounced as if someone just burned your arm—eee-ow) is a peaceful, beautiful valley. It seems impossible to imagine the death that once permeated the area. The valley stream is lovely, and there are short trails looping around the bottom. (Parking is $5.) The 'Iao Needle is a prominent point sticking up from the valley.

NOT TO BE MISSED!

Looking at it straight on, it's easy to understand why Hawaiians viewed it as a fertility symbol. But it's actually the end of a long, winding knife-edge ridge called an erosional remnant. (If you saw it from

the side, you'd probably call it the 'Iao Plate.) It's 134 baby steps to get to the upper lookout. This valley is what remains of the central caldera (crater) of the West Maui volcano. See map on page 70.

You'll likely see people playing in small clear pools below the bridge (especially popular during hot summer days—parking can be non-existent). There's a sign that warns "Swimming in 'Iao Stream is not recommended. The rocks are very slippery and the water is flowing fast." That's not the same as prohibited, so use good judgement and enjoy. The walking paths are mostly paved (the dirt trails next to the stream are occasionally closed after heavy rain and flooding), feature Hawaiian-style gardens and plants, and should only take around 20 minutes to explore.

Kepaniwai Heritage Gardens, which you passed on your way into the 'Iao Valley, is a small park filled with elaborate displays honoring various ethnic groups that settled on Maui. It has seen better days, but there is plenty to take in and learn wandering the scenic grounds, so it's worth a quick stop. Plus, it's free. In the section honoring Chinese immigrants, there is a statue of Sun Yat-sen. In case you're not up on your Chinese history, he was a revolutionary who was instrumental in the 1912 overthrow of the Qing dynasty, ending more than 2,000 years of imperial rule. He then served as the first president of modern-day China. So... that explains why there'd be lots of statues of him over there. But why here? Well, he lived on both O'ahu and Maui with his older brother, a successful businessman, for many years at several different points in his life. (While on O'ahu he attended the elite Punahou School in Honolulu. That same school was attended by Sanford Dole, who went on to become the first president of the Republic of Hawai'i, and later Barack

Obama, who became president of the United States. Three presidents of three different countries from one Hawaiian school. Pretty impressive.) His experience in Hawai'i helped convince him China must modernize, or be conquered.

On Main Street on your way to 'Iao Valley the cerebral-oriented should consider the **Bailey House Museum** (808-244-3326), the former mid-19th century home of missionary Edward Bailey. Now a museum, it's is a good place to check out artifacts from the past—such as a century-old redwood surfboard that belonged to Duke Kahanamoku, Hawaiian stone tools, spinning wheel, a Hawaiian Bible, quilts, dresses almost two centuries old, and even more surprising items, such as an opium scale and pipe. Bailey was also a painter, and his renditions of Maui in the 1800s provide literal looks back in time. Some of his landscapes look surprisingly current. Entry fee is $7 for adults, $2 for kids. Closed Sunday.

In Wailuku are the remains of the **Haleki'i** and **Pihana heiau**. These are former luakini temples (places of human sacrifice). The view from this strategic hill is impressive. You can see all of Wailuku and Kahului. As you gaze from the top of the heiau, your views of the mountains are mixed with views of the surrounding houses, creeping close to the heiau. Instead of houses, what would the ancient priests have seen when they looked out from here? Houses... and taro. This area was called Na Wai Eha, or Four Waters, and was one of the largest taro-growing areas in the state. The streams around here provided abundant water, so it would have looked similar to rice fields but with broad-leafed taro instead of rice. Thousands of Hawaiians lived here. Instead of shingles, their houses had thatched roofs. Instead of a two-car garage, they had a two-canoe shed. But this area has always been home to lots of people.

The heiau park is not well maintained by the state, which is surprising, given how few ancient relics there are on Maui. (Well, except in the state government.)

The 'Iao Needle and stream make a splendid diversion in Central Maui.

To get there, take Waiehu Beach Road to Kuhio to Hea. (See map on page 70.) You'll have to park at the bottom of the parking lot access road and walk up "due to land dispute issues," we were told.

KAHULUI

People who live on Maui find themselves coming to Kahului all the time. What do they come for? Malls, movies, restaurants and—most important on an island where things cost a lot—*Costco.*

Kahului is where people come to take care of business. The biggest mall, **Queen Ka'ahumanu Center** on Hwy 32, hosts lots of events (like a farmer's market every Tuesday, Wednesday and Friday), as well as the nicest branch of **Maui Friends of the Library** bookstore where you can find new copies of many Hawaiian books. And **Maui Marketplace** on Dairy Road is where you'll find the island's **Barnes and Noble** bookstore. **Maui Mall** has the island's giant **Whole Foods Market** and largest movie theater.

Visitors will most likely pass *through* Kahului on their way somewhere else. There's just not much otherwise that's meant to attract visitors. Hotels tend to be less expensive here (though not as cheap as you'd hope) and only a handful of dining options really stand out (like **Tin Roof**). If you have some time on either end of your trip that requires you be close to the airport, it's a good place for food and last minute gifts. That's about it.

Kahului is nearly always windy. And on those few occasions that it's not windy—it's *real breezy.* If you rent a large vehicle, like a minivan, it'll often feel like someone's outside rocking your car.

THE VALLEY

This is the reason Maui is called the Valley Isle—the large flatland separating East and West Maui. And up until 2017 it was dominated by only one crop—*sugar.* A single company—Alexander & Baldwin's subsidiary, HC&S (Hawaiian Commercial & Sugar Company)—owned all 37,000 acres of the farmland you see. Before people came to these islands, a thin, dry-land forest existed here. The Hawaiians quickly cut down the trees when they discovered the island, and the area became a barren desert, after which the Hawaiians had little to do with it. When western man arrived, he saw an opportunity to grow sugar in this unused region and began building ditches to bring water to this thirsty land. But it's hard to make money in sugar in such a remote place as Hawai'i, and now the crop that literally *defined* agriculture in the state since 1835 is no more. (Without the constant irrigation of these fields, the arid nature of the area quickly takes over and the scars of brush fires now char many areas in the valley.) In 2018, Alexander & Baldwin sold 41,000 acres of Central Maui land to a farming company, Mahi Pono (a Hawaiian phrase that means "to farm or cultivate morally and properly). *Diversified agriculture and cattle* is the mantra of the new landowner, and only time will tell how this valley evolves.

At one time, all of the islands surrounding Maui formed a single large island. Then the ocean rose and the land sank to isolate each of the volcanoes into different islands. The valley separating East and West Maui is the last land bridge remaining, and its days are numbered, too. Given the present sinking rate, East and West Maui will be separate islands in about 15,000 years when this land-bridge disappears. (Gives the realtors something to worry about, huh?)

On Honoapi'ilani Hwy (30) heading toward the west side, you'll find **Maui**

Tropical Plantation (808-244-7643) between mile markers 2 and 3—60 acres of assorted tropical fruits and plants. It's a classic tourist trap, and it'll cost you $24 to ride the tram to see the gardens. You can, however, stroll the grounds at no charge, and their repurposed sugar mill equipment gives a new look to the history of the area. The place seems more geared to tour buses. The tour can be marginally interesting, and it's *definitely* well cared for and pretty, but it's definitely *not* a must-see. Its best asset is the awesome **Mill House Restaurant**. Also, the best **zipline** on the island cuts across the land above this part of the West Maui Mountains—not to be confused with the Plantation's own zipline more geared toward kids. See *Ziplines* on page 254.

If you drive along Hwy 311 on your way toward South Maui, you'll pass Maui's ugliest sight (except for the line at the rental car counter when you're late for your flight home). A sugar mill looking like it belongs more in the 19th century (which is when it was built) has been permanently closed with the demise of sugar on the island. At press time the company was looking to sell it and have it hauled away. At the corner of Hwy 311 and Hansen Road you'll find the **Sugar Museum** (808-871-8058). It has everything you ever wanted to know but were afraid to ask about sugar harvesting and refining. It's $7 for admission, and the place is loaded with relics and artifacts. You'll feel hot and stuffy just *looking* at the outfits that field workers had to wear in the hot sun.

PA'IA

If you're heading in the direction of Hana, the last town you'll visit is Pa'ia. This town has accomplished something few Hawai'i towns can claim: It has become an attraction without any attractions other than itself. No great views, no waterfalls, no scenery, no big institutions like an aquarium. Pa'ia's sights lie in its character—and characters. The odd and bizarre add color to Pa'ia like no other Maui town. An example—one morning we saw the following: a guy with a feather stuck in the top of his head (not his hat), a 90-year-old couple on a Harley (she was driving), a woman whose entire body was covered with tattoos, one gentleman with more dirt in his dreadlocks than a medium-sized canefield, a guy having a serious argument with himself (and losing), and a man in a hard hat carrying a full-sized cross. (Unfortunately, we *just missed* the naked woman painted green doing her Christmas shopping at the various shops.) Welcome to Pa'ia, where it's *still* the Age of Aquarius, and shoes are always optional in the streets. It's not a quiet town (even the name means *noisy* in Hawaiian), but it's unique.

Residents along these windward towns are so used to the frequent, short, passing showers that they don't even seem to notice when it starts to rain. They often just go about doing exactly what they were doing, oblivious to the falling drops.

In addition to people-watching, Pa'ia is a great place to do some **shopping**. Though not as large as Lahaina, the selection is varied, though pricey. Stores like **Alice in Hulaland** and **Lele by Adelina a Mare** are situated near surf shops and lots of places to grab a beer. Every shop has its own style. Even men, who normally don't like shopping, may like wandering around Pa'ia. And there are some surprisingly good restaurants.

If you're looking to stock up on foods and want to visit the best independent health food store we've seen, stop by **Mana Foods** just up Baldwin Avenue. It's a strange experience: It looks tiny and

dumpy from the outside. Then you walk in, and you'll be blown away by the size and selection. (Good prices, too.)

Go another block up Baldwin to find a unique cultural experience—a **Buddhist Prayer Wheel**. It's a short diversion and fits right into the Pa'ia atmosphere.

Up Baldwin Avenue, **Holy Rosary Church**, across from Pa'ia School, is a beautiful birch and glass building. They also have a nice memorial to **Father Damien** of Moloka'i, the priest (and now saint) who worked with Hansen's Disease patients at the leprosy settlement described on page 151.

While in Pa'ia, wave bye-bye to that last stoplight. If you're heading toward Hana, you won't see another light until you've almost completely circumnavigated Haleakala to Kula, 100 miles around.

Leaving Pa'ia, the **Ho'okipa Lookout** just before mile marker 9 is a perfect place to watch the surf. When it's pounding, there's no better place to be than along this shoreline. Breakers can pound with such ferocity in the winter that it

I'll bet you never realized that those sweet pineapples you enjoy are guarded by nature's version of razor wire and land mines.

makes the ground tremble. Much of the year, expert **windsurfers** (see page 253) ride the waves after 11 a.m., often streaking faster than the wind, and it's quite a sight to see. Wind is so predictable here—and it runs almost parallel to the shore—that it's considered the single best beach in the United States to windsurf.

CENTRAL MAUI BEST BETS

Best Restaurant View—Mama's Fish House

Best Place to Watch Windsurfers Race the Wind—Ho'okipa Beach Park

Best Place to Find Weird People Doing Odd Things in a Strange Way—Pa'ia

Best Place to Pick Up Healthy Food—Mana Foods in Pa'ia

Best Pizza—Flatbread Company

Best Signs to Ignore—Any Sign That Says "Last Food Before Hana"

If heaven had a highway…

The road to Hana is without question the most famous and desired drive in all Hawai'i, the crown jewel of driving. It's been compared to driving through the garden of Eden: a slow, winding road through a lush paradise that you always knew existed—somewhere.

If you're in a hurry to get to Hana, you're missing the point. Unless you're staying the night in Hana, you probably won't spend much time there. You're heading somewhere else. (Those who spend the night in Hana will have more time to sample its delights.) At the risk of sounding like a Chinese fortune cookie, fulfillment lies in the journey, not the destination. The whole reason to drive this route is to see the Hawai'i of your dreams, the tropical fantasy that becomes reality along the way. This is a drive through wonderland, and the only thing at the end—is the end

of your discovery. As you drive, don't feel the need to hurry up to get "there," because you may find that there is no there there.

If you're going to be staying in Hana for a couple of days (which we *highly* recommend), then you'll have a chance to see and do much of what the following two chapters present. But if you'll be seeing this part of the island on a one-day tour (as most do), then you won't have a chance to experience even a third of the things we've discovered on the road around Haleakala. If you're a one-dayer, we suggest you read through the following two chapters before you leave so you can prioritize the things that interest you most. Maybe you want to do some bodysurfing at the best beach on the island for it. Then Hamoa Beach on page 102 is what you want. If you want to see a drop-dead gorgeous view of the coast, make sure you take Nahiku Road on page 93. If you want to dig your toes in a genuine volcanic black sand beach, then Waiʻanapanapa on page 97 is a must-see. Want to see crazy fools make daring leaps into the water? Gotta check out page 88. Want to take a powered hang gliding flight along the coast? You need to see Armin on page 184. This is just a small portion of what's available. The point is, you can't do it all, so decide which adventure is most important to you.

The road to Hana is two lanes with lots of one-lane bridges. Tourist literature says there are 600 turns, though I don't know exactly how they classify a turn since the road is never straight. (Your steering wheel *certainly* changes direction more than that.) Whether you find the Hana Highway wild or tame depends on your experience. We've noticed that people who have lived most of their lives in flat areas—where a straight line *really is* the closest distance between two points and you can always see what's a mile in front of you—find the constant winding road and blind turns unnerving. Those of us who grew up with crooked roads find it a joy. We once met some visitors from the midwest who were highly adventurous. They skydived, flew ultralights and thought nothing about jumping off the 60-foot bridge over ʻOheʻo Gulch into the water. But they refused to drive the Hana Highway again because it "made us nervous." Ironically, they were traveling with timid couch potatoes who grew up in Northern California and loved the "relaxing feel" of the highway. So I guess it depends on what you're used to.

BEFORE YOU START DRIVING THE HIGHWAY

There are many myths associated with the Hana Highway. Let's dispense with the biggest and most entrenched.

Myth—You can't drive a regular car all the way around Haleakala; you need a 4-Wheel Drive and high clearance past Hana, and even if you could, it would violate your rental car agreement.

Fact—The road past Hana is nearly always perfectly driveable and *may* not violate your rental car agreement. You *don't* need high clearance or 4WD. Years ago, the road to Hana was a tortuous drive. The sadistic pavement was full of potholes and ill-conceived pothole fills beating up you and your car along the way. But today, the road to Hana is smooth, though a winding and narrow two lanes much of the way. *Yeah, but what about the part past Hana?* Well, 14 miles past Hana, after mile marker 39 (the number sequence changes at Hana), the road goes from pavement to gravel that is regularly graded. After a few miles of bumpy gravel (its bumpiness depends on when you catch it during the maintenance cycle), it becomes blacktop again, though it is roughly textured from countless poor patch jobs. After 6 miles of bumpy blacktop the smooth highway returns. *Very* rarely, extremely heavy rains may close the road at one point where a normally dry stream crosses the road, but it is usually reopened as soon as they can get a crew out there.

Most rental car contracts we've seen restrict you from using the car on "unpaved" or sometimes "unimproved" roads and don't specifically mention the road to Hana. In the past that language certainly covered the latter part of the road. But now those terms don't sound as if they apply. After all, the paved portion would seem to be legitimate, and the gravel portion is certainly "improved" constantly. Besides, if it's so bad, how come large tour buses are able to drive all the way around daily? The fact is, the second half of the road has a very out-of-date reputation, and all the free magazines and maps that tell you otherwise need to have their people drive it for themselves. Even if you are violating your rental car agreement, what does that mean? According to the rental car companies we contacted, it means the extra insurance you took out *may* not cover you there (and you may not want to pay for that anyway because your own car insurance may cover you), and it means they won't come get you if you get into trouble. And the first thing a tow truck driver will ask this far out is, *Do you own your own home?*

Driving all the way to Hana and then turning around—which the vast majority of visitors do—is like shave ice without the ice cream on the bottom. (I'm a shameless shave ice lover—sorry.) It means missing the windswept backside of Haleakala in the late afternoon. The way the light casts deep shadows in the water-scoured gulches, the incredibly expansive views of the coastline, the impossibly blue sky against the brown and red upper slopes of the volcano, the angry, wind-ravaged seas, and the utter lack of civilized development—these are the things that make a drive along the bottom part of the island worthwhile. It won't look like the jungle-y Hana drive; you just *saw* that. But it will pass from Eden-like lushness to the land of sun and wind. It's hard to believe that the backside is part of the same mountain.

DRIVING THE ROAD

The usual way of driving to Hana is to travel a clockwise direction so you can take advantage of the sun. The Hana side is sunny in the morning, shady in the afternoon, and its waterfalls are best before 11 a.m. However, if you travel *counterclockwise*, you will probably feel like you have the road to yourself, and you'll be able to enjoy the views instead of worrying about the guy braking in front of you. The downsides to this direction are that the lighting on the Hana Highway will be bad (you'll want to hope for cloudiness to make the sights better), and you will have close encounters with all the traffic coming at you on the narrow roads—and you'll be on the outside lane. We have found that passengers, staring down the hill on their side during tight squeezes, don't like the route that does Southeast Maui first and Hana Highway second. That's why we suggest traveling clockwise from Pa'ia.

It's best to start the road to Hana *early,* so you'll have time to see and experience as much as possible. Unfortunately, we're not the only ones who give this advice, so everyone else seems to be leaving early, too. On average, between 1,500 and 2,000 cars per day drive the road to Hana. Most leave Kahului between 8:30 and 10 a.m. *We* know, we know. You're supposed to be here on vacation, and we *really* hate to suggest something as regimented as a timetable, but let us make one recommendation. If you're not going to be staying in Hana overnight, we strongly suggest you leave early enough to be passing Kahului by 8 a.m. This lets you avoid the crowds, see the sights in good light and allows you to take your time. If you're staying in Hana, leave after 10:30 a.m. when the road's more empty.

Both of these scenarios help you avoid being stuck in a procession of cars. This can take away *much* for the driver. *We can't emphasize this enough.* Whether they realize it or not, drivers focus almost constantly on the car ahead. You can't help it; it's instinctive. But when no one's ahead of you, your eyes tend to sweep and record the road ahead and then fall onto the delicious scenery. That's why we're more than happy to pull over repeatedly to allow cars to get far enough ahead so that we can drive to Hana and enjoy ourselves. We've done informal surveys and found that people who drove behind another car didn't think the drive was *nearly* as nice as those who drove it with no one in front of them. And if you notice a long line behind you, (and we can't emphasize this enough) *pull over* to allow the faster ones to get by. There's virtually no place for them to pass on this highway. Some Hana locals do, but they know the road—though some drivers are aggressive to the point of recklessness. As we say on Maui, *If someone is on your 'okole, let da buggah pass.*

WATERFALLS

Everybody loves waterfalls. They seem to universally affect people with a peaceful, soothing feeling. On this drive, waterfalls near the road are easy to find. This part of Maui was tailor-made for waterfall production because it has the two necessary ingredients—constant elevation changes **WATERFALL** and lots of rain up the mountain. But many of the lovelier ones are off the road, often accessible from trails. We have identified many with this graphic.

ALERT!

We tried to photograph most of the waterfalls flowing about halfway between abnormally pumping and abnormally light. You'll find them sometimes higher (usually winter), sometimes lower (usually summer).

One thing you need to understand is the extremely variable nature of waterfalls. At different times, the same falls can be an unimpressive trickle, a world-class wa-

There are a lot of waterfalls. Some, like this one after mile marker 6, you'll never even see as you zigzag your way along the Hana Highway.

Admit it. You've always wanted to do this...

terfall in a lovely setting, or a brown, swollen mass of water and mud after a heavy rain. We have found most of these falls in all three states at different times. During some wet winter months, you may find more waterfalls than we mention. Sometimes, during dry months, some of our favorites may shrivel to a pathetic dribble, but you'll never see fewer than six falls between Kahului and Hana, if you know when and where to look.

A FEW BASICS

East Maui Irrigation Company (EMI) has ditches that run most of the way to Hana. At times, you may find dry falls as EMI diverts the water to feed their fields in Central Maui and for some residential use. Be aware that some of these falls may be on land controlled by EMI. Much of the land here is *state-owned* forest reserve, not private. EMI merely leases the water rights on a revocable month-to-month basis. Here and under *Hiking* we describe several awesome hikes in this area. It's mandatory that you contact EMI in advance to get a waiver to hike to some of the falls. Don't expect to be able to get permission while at the falls themselves

because you'll rarely find any EMI personnel at the falls to ask. You'll need to go to their office in Pa'ia. EMI has been stingy with hiking permits in the past, but with the demise of sugar, local farmers fighting them for water rights, and considering EMI's reported short-term grasp on the leased land, who's to know if, by the time you read this, they have a lease on the land or not? You'll need a waiver, or you'll have to join one of the commercial hiking groups granted access by EMI. Our descriptions are not meant to encourage you to trespass. (See page 44 for more on that.) They are merely so you'll know which hikes you want to request from EMI or one of their authorized groups.

Car break-ins can occur at scenic spots, such as waterfalls. Though not exactly common along the Hana road, all it takes is one or two scumbags smashing windows to create a problem. So avoid leaving valuables in the car, especially visible on the seat.

The car of choice for the Hana Highway is the convertible. There are many times that you'll see striking greenery above you that others will miss. Start the trip with a full tank of gas.

Bring a good pair of sunglasses—the road weaves in and out of shaded jungle and sunlit coastline, making for blinding light contrasts.

Many of the businesses along this road are closed on Sundays. Bring cash as most businesses do not accept credit cards.

The **weather** on the Hana Highway is notoriously difficult to predict. Parts of it get a *lot* of rain; that's why it's so beautiful and the waterfalls so plentiful. You can call (808) 944-3756 for a weather update or go to our website. One thing that Hana road veterans know is that as you start the drive, if you observe bad weather, it usually (but not always) gets better past Nahiku, so don't turn around assuming it will be raining the whole drive. More times than we can count, we've hit heavy rain much of the way only to have it disappear just before the Hana Airport.

This stretch of road, more than any other in the state, suffers from **the lemming effect**. (Lemmings are rodents known for going over cliffs *en masse* because the ones in front of them are doing it.) The drive is so special that everyone's afraid of missing something, so when you pull over, you'll likely see others pulling up behind you to see what they might be missing. We are well aware that many of the sights that we've discovered—some of them never mentioned anywhere else—attract others who pull in behind our readers. But at least *you* know what to look for, and *they* are the lemmings. And just because you see others on the side of the road, don't think they know something you don't. Odds are they don't.

We noticed (and voluminous reader e-mail confirms) that a conspicuous few East Maui residents have forgotten what **aloha** means, permeating their area with unfriendly signs and rude behavior. We promise you, most Maui residents *aren't* like that and would be embarrassed by it. If you do run into any unfriendly people or attitudes, we strongly request that you simply smile and wave at them. Maybe, in some way, you'll help them get their aloha back. And please make sure you leave the areas you visit just as you found them. You might even take it a step further and pick up any litter you see at the waterfalls.

PA'IA TO HIGHWAY 360

The first part of the drive starts on Hwy 36 after you've passed Pa'ia. (That town is described in *Central Maui Sights*.) The map on page 121 covers this first part. As you pass mile marker 10, you'll cross **Maliko Gulch**. An older bridge and train trestle were erected 0.5 miles up mauka (toward the mountain) in 1913. The sugar company that built it had lots of trouble getting people to work on the foundations. It required swinging into the 300-foot gulch on ropes, and nervous workers kept refusing to go. Finally the boss/owner of the sugar company grabbed the rope and swung into the ravine. None of the other workers ever refused again. You see, the boss, Henry Baldwin, did it while recovering from a recent accident— in which he had *lost an arm*. Baldwin swung into the gulch armed with only... well, you know. After that, no worker had the nerve to refuse to do something with two arms that the boss man had done with one. The bridge was eventually torn down to prevent indestructible teenagers from repeating the feat.

ON HIGHWAY 360

Soon the highway changes its name to 360 (now it's a county road), and the mile markers start again at 0. The *Hana Highway Map* starts on page 82. You

Hana Highway

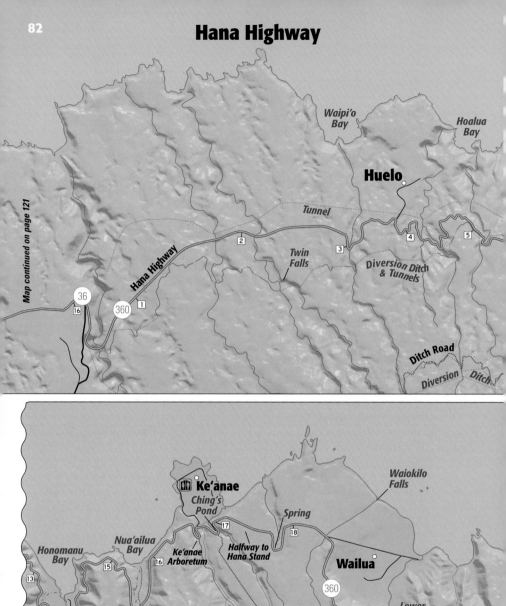

Map continued on page 121

Waipi'o Bay

Hoalua Bay

Huelo

Tunnel

36

360

1

Hana Highway

16

2

3

4

5

Twin Falls

Diversion Ditch & Tunnels

Ditch Road

Diversion Ditch

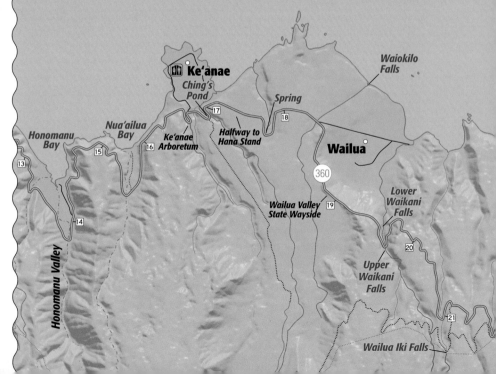

Waiokilo Falls

Ke'anae

Ching's Pond

Spring

Honomanu Bay

Nua'ailua Bay

Ke'anae Arboretum

Halfway to Hana Stand

Wailua

13

15

16

17

18

360

14

Wailua Valley State Wayside

19

Lower Waikani Falls

20

Honomanu Valley

Upper Waikani Falls

21

Wailua Iki Falls

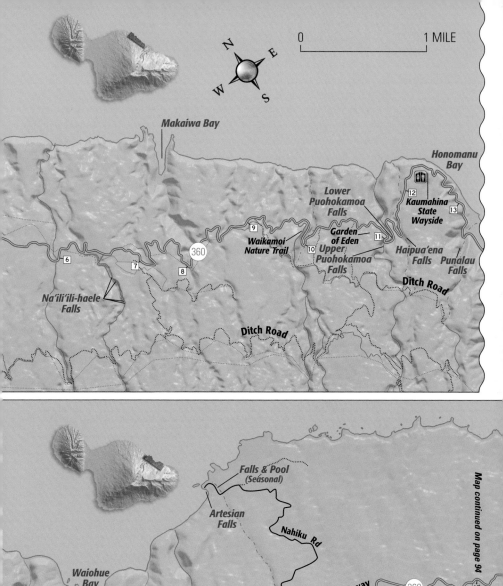

Makaiwa Bay

Honomanu
Bay

Lower
Puohokamoa
Falls

Kaumahina
State
Wayside

12

13

Garden
of Eden

11

Haipua'ena
Falls

Punalau
Falls

9

Waikamoi
Nature Trail

10

Upper
Puohokamoa
Falls

Ditch Road

360

6

7

8

Na'ili'ili-haele
Falls

Ditch Road

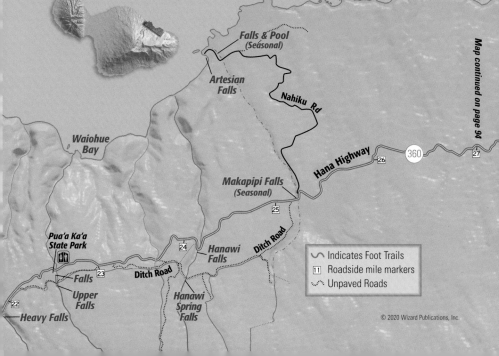

Falls & Pool
(Seasonal)

Artesian
Falls

Nahiku Rd

Map continued on page 94

Waiohue
Bay

Makapipi Falls
(Seasonal)

Hana Highway

360

26

27

25

Pua'a Ka'a
State Park

24

Hanawi
Falls

Ditch Road

Falls

23

Ditch Road

Upper
Falls

22

Hanawi
Spring
Falls

Heavy Falls

Indicates Foot Trails

11 Roadside mile markers

Unpaved Roads

© 2020 Wizard Publications, Inc.

should reset your odometer so you'll always have a general idea where you are, but bear in mind that the mile markers aren't always precisely placed a mile apart as they should be. We refer to their *actual* location, not where they're *supposed* to be. So if we say something is 0.3 past mile marker 8, you can reset your odometer back to 0 at mile marker 8 so you'll know when you're 0.3 miles past it. Also, we've noticed that some of the markers are buried in buffalo grass and hard to spot.

The first half of the drive is more tightly enclosed by vegetation, so you won't get too many expansive views. There's a fruit stand and lots of people just past mile marker 2. A series of roads and trails leads to **Twin Falls**, actually six or seven waterfalls, none very spectacular compared to what's ahead. People tend to spend too much time here because it's the first available falls—though a longer walk than they might want—and then rush by better opportunities. You might wait for the nicer, less-mobbed waterfalls

Kamehameha Fights to the Death

Just before Holokai Road between mile markers 15 and 16 (on Hwy 36) there is a hill visible a mile up mauka. This hill became famous during the time of Kamehameha, the only king to conquer all the islands. While he was here battling for Maui in the late 1700s, the Maui king's top warrior was sent with troops to repel Kamehameha. One night Kamehameha camped at that hill and paraded an image of his war god Ku around the camp to see how the feathers on the head of the god would look. It was believed that the more erect the top feathers bristled, the better the battle would go. The feathers cooperated. The next day a fierce battle was fought beyond the hill at a place called Kokomo. Though most battles were fought by lower-ranking soldiers, here Kamehameha himself fought in a battle to the death with Maui's top warrior. Kamehameha had practiced making war since he was a child, even going so far as to have some of his top men surprise him from time to time by throwing spears at him when he wasn't looking, just to keep him sharp. (He prided himself on being able to dodge or catch as many as five spears thrown at once.) The battle began the way most Hawaiian battles did—with both leaders on opposite sides of the battlefield hurling insults back and forth to stir each other up. When the Maui warrior landed a particularly cruel blow (accusing Kamehameha of having no royal blood, but rather descending from slaves—yes, the Hawaiians did keep slaves), Kamehameha roared. Both leaders shot sling stones at each other. Then they charged each other with spears. In hand-to-hand combat, Kamehameha landed a vicious blow with his leiomanu, a club studded with shark's teeth, opening the Maui warrior's chest. The Maui warrior stabbed Kamehameha with a wooden dagger, but Hawai'i's future king finished off his opponent with his club. Maui's top warrior was slaughtered on the field of battle in front of the Maui troops, who were so demoralized that the taking of their island became inevitable.

Upper Puohokamoa Falls is a classic example of a beautiful waterfall that is now closed due to liability concerns. The landowner told us he'd open it if he could get insurance to cover it. So, hey. If you're in the insurance biz and can help this guy out, we'll celebrate with a cool swim below the falls.

later. But the fruit stand itself is pretty good with lots of fresh fruits, decent banana bread and great juices.

Little more than a half mile past mile marker 3 is a road on the left that leads to **Kaulanapueo Church**. Built in 1853, it's still in use and is an excellent example of a 19th-century church, though it will probably be locked when you visit.

At 0.6 miles past mile marker 6 is a turnout. A trail that begins there leads to *four waterfalls*. Many of the waterfall trails along the Hana Highway are in this section, but this one's harder to get to and is in *Adventures* on page 258. A couple tenths of a mile past that trailhead you'll see some **rainbow eucalyptus** trees on the left side and a place to park farther ahead (don't hop the fence to get closer). These trees have a beautiful bark that looks especially good when wet. There's another stand not long after mile marker 7 that you can get right next to—the trees are on the left and a pullout can be found on the right side just past them.

Between mile markers 9 and 10 on the mauka side of the Hana Highway is the **Waikamoi Nature Trail**. Two nature loops—one about 10 minutes, the other about 30—make it a pleasant place to stretch your legs a bit, but it's not a hugely compelling hike. It's good for families, and you gain, at most, 200 feet. If you venture past the main trail, a pretty waterfall awaits. See *Hiking* on page 224 for more. No restrooms here.

Waikamoi Stream just before mile marker 10 is usually dry, but after a heavy rain it can become a giant cauldron with a large waterfall up the mountain and a slippery trail to a smaller one. You'll know whether to bother by the amount of water flowing under the bridge.

Soon you come to the **Garden of Eden** (808-572-9899). Pretty tough name to live up to; it's an arboretum and botanical garden. The $15 per person entrance fee seems a little high at first, but you soon realize that this is a meticulously maintained and very beautiful garden. Everything is scrupulously labeled. You can either drive it or walk a separate path. They have a picnic area with good views down the coast, a food truck serving items such as tacos, smoothies and coffee, and there's a restroom.

At 0.8 miles past mile marker 10 on the ocean side of the road is a turnout with a telephone pole. This is a well-known path to **Lower Puohokamoa Falls**, which is now fenced off by the landowner. Too bad, as it is an impressive waterfall. To be fair, the trail past the waterfall is treacherous.

Just past mile marker 11 is a path to **Upper Puohokamoa Falls**. The landowner has erected a large fence and won't allow people to access it from the near side. The *far* side of the stream has a trail to the falls and is on state land. You'll have to find a place to park after you pass the stream up the road a ways. But that far side trail was also fenced off at press time and the community was up in arms because it was on state land, but reportedly erected by the landowner on the near side without authorization. If you can't go to it, don't worry. We got more falls for you further up the road. And if that fence causes you to rethink patronizing the **Garden of Eden**, you have that right.

Half a mile past mile marker 11 there's a small turnout on the far side of the bridge and a trail that leads 30 seconds or so to a pool and small waterfall called **Haipua'ena Falls**. It's worth a stop. There's another, larger falls just upstream, but the trail to the second falls, even on a dry day, has a short stretch where it's easy to fall. (An ugly fall at that.) Not worth it; stay at the first waterfall.

Past mile marker 12 you come across the **Kaumahina State Wayside Park** with its restrooms. The **restrooms** at Ke'anae 5 miles ahead are usually less crowded (and usually not quite as nasty), even though there are fewer of them. The wayside also has a series of short nature loops heading uphill from the ocean overlook.

There's a place on the right side past the **Kaumahina State Wayside** where the road opens up, exposing the very scenic **Ke'anae Peninsula**, but there's no place to pull over. You'll get a chance to pull over at mile marker 13. What a view! As you cruise along, consider that cars couldn't make it to Hana from central Maui until an unpaved road was cut in 1926. Before that, Hana was isolated and quiet. Even with the new road, driving was only for the brave and the well insured. It remained unpaved until 1962. The paving job was awful, and the paved Hana Highway deteriorated until it was almost worse than the old unpaved road it replaced. The state finally did it right in the 1980s, creating the smooth (though still narrow) ride you enjoy today.

If you've been itching for your very own private waterfall, you *may* be in luck. One quarter mile past mile marker 13 there's a *tiny* turnout on the far side of the bridge and another one kitty-corner up the road. Even when it looks dry, there *may* (or may not) be more water flowing unseen under the rocks near the highway, so it's hard to gauge the flow here. About 800 or so feet upstream is a pretty and lacy unnamed falls on the Punalau stream. We'll call it **Punalau Falls**. This is one of the few falls along the way that you can visit with a reasonable chance of having it to yourself for three reasons: You can't see it from the road, it's never been written about, as far as we know, and you'll have to walk on the (usually) dry stream boulders nearly the whole way. (When the boulders are wet, they're pretty slippery.) It'll take between 10 and 25 minutes to get there (depending on your rock-hopping aptitude). A pair of walking sticks is invaluable for stream walking; you'll go from being

WATERFALL

ALERT!

WATERFALL

ALERT!

The ocean along the raw, younger Ke'anae coastline is often bathed in beautiful, violent chaos.

a two-legged animal to a four-legged one. Even if the falls are a trickle (EMI has a ditch upstream), the area around the falls is an impossibly narrow, vertical-walled chasm bursting with ferns and moss and a cool pool for swimming.

On the highway just past mile marker 14 there's a paved-then-dirt road that leads to **Honomanu Bay**. The road hardly gets any maintenance and is often closed to vehicles—4WD (or hiking down) is necessary. The beach here is gravelly and the swimming poor, but in the early morning or late afternoon, the sun creates a magnificent golden green on the gouged-out valley walls, reminding you why you came to Hawai'i.

The present government road to Hana is by no means the first. Back in the 1500s a king named **Kihapi'ilani** decided that trips around the island were too perilous. Many of the gulches you have passed along the way were well known places for robberies, since the thieves could easily get away. So the king had trails cut and paved with smooth stream stones all around Haleakala—quite a feat at the time.

It took years (though probably less time than the current county government seems to take these days when they repave it). It was said that the king didn't want to be forgotten when he died. His public works project succeeded, because five centuries later he is still remembered fondly, and another public works project, Pi'ilani Highway, bears his name and the name of a 17th-century governor. His 500-year-old stone road was still visible in places until the jungle consumed the last of it in the early 1900s.

After mile marker 14 there are several pullouts, but the county has let vegetation block most of them. Just over 0.5 miles past mile marker 14 there's a long pullout on the right and a small puka on the left where you can still see a tranquil view of Honomanu Bay and Valley and of the zig-zagging Hana Highway working its way up the cliffs. If vegetation blocks the view too much, the YMCA camp just ahead has some great views for those willing to make the 5-minute walk along the grounds. Take your time here and savor the smashing scene. The upper part of the valley you're looking at is full of burial sites. The old Hawaiians refused to walk there at night, believing that the spirits of chiefs buried there roamed the valley.

Off the highway just before the road into Keʻanae Peninsula is the **Keʻanae Arboretum**. Neglected for years, the state puts a tad more effort into maintaining it, but overall this is an expendable diversion. The paved and unpaved path is a 25–30 minute stroll and good for those with limited mobility. Bring mosquito repellent unless you're a practiced bloodletter.

KEʻANAE TO NAHIKU

Next comes the road into **Keʻanae Peninsula** and village. (The YMCA camp you just passed has cabins for rent see page 209) The dead end road hugs the coastline for a time, and at one place there's an excellent photo op with the ocean tearing through some jagged lava boulders. Very striking, especially at high tide. The impossibly blue water against the rich lushness of the Hana coast is a feast for the eyes.

DIVERSION

ALERT!

Farther ahead are some restrooms near a park. (Before the park, a stand called **Aunty Sandy's** on the right sells **banana bread** and snacks—avoid the burgers in favor of the giant hot dogs.) The coastline across from the restrooms is a good place to watch the waves beat up the shoreline. The land here is younger than the rest of the island, and it shows.

There's an extraordinary legend about the origin of the taro fields at Keʻanae that can't be confirmed but ties in nicely with what we know about the geology of the land. The legend states that in ancient times there was a chief who was constantly at war with the neighboring village of Wailua. At that time Keʻanae was mostly a barren lava field. The chief decided that he needed more taro-growing land and

more people living in the area. So he decreed that every man, woman and child would go to the upper valley, gather soil in baskets and fill the peninsula with enough soil to grow taro. In time, the peninsula became a prime taro-growing area. True story? Who knows? It's a legend. But what a task it would have been. Imagine hiking miles up the valley, hauling a basket of heavy dirt back, dumping it on the lava rock and heading back uphill. The definition of a thankless, Dilbert-like job!

Keʻanae was nearly wiped out by the tsunami (tidal wave) of 1946. Nearly every building was destroyed, leaving only the immovable stone church.

Back on the highway, just before mile marker 17, is a pullout on the right and a bridge. (It's a popular stop and there's usually a number of cars parked here.) **WATERFALL** The path about 75 feet to the left leads down to a marvelous pool, known locally as **Ching's Pond**. The swimming is particularly good, and most drivers never even see this pond. Above the narrow stream portion (just before it opens up to the pool) there's a concrete platform on the right side. We've seen daring young locals *diving* out and away from the cliff into the tiny part they claim is deep enough so you don't hit rocks. We're talking about a 25 foot or so drop with *zero* margin for error. *That's* what we call an 'okole squeezer. (We'll let you guess what an 'okole is.) Obviously you shouldn't do this unless you name us as beneficiaries on your life insurance.

ALERT!

About 0.3 miles past mile marker 17 is a stand generally known as **Halfway to Hana**. (Actually, you're two-thirds of the way from Kahului.) We review theirs and Aunty Sandy's banana bread every time we travel the road. (Just to be thorough, you understand. We do it for you, only for you.) Currently they are neck and neck (but completely outshined by *Julia's* in Kahakuloa, West Maui). Halfway to Hana also has fruits, beverages, some sandwiches and so-so burgers, and other snacks. If you're getting hungry, there are more dining options a dozen miles ahead. By the way, take a peek at the house behind the stand to see if they still have all those pigs' heads hanging on the wall.

About 0.7 miles past mile marker 17, pull over and walk to the white concrete bridge. Look down on the ocean side of the bridge, and you'll see water gushing out of the mountain, surrounded by flowers and some huge elephant ears (called 'ape) in a garden setting tailor-made for a postcard (though they sometimes let the jungle overgrow the area). This is a **spring-fed gusher**, originating here. Any pipes you see under the flowers are tapping the water, not feeding it. When they keep it welltended, it's a lovely sight, but it sometimes gets overgrown.

You may see **Uncle Harry's** stand on the left side. Snacks, pork tacos, burgers and banana bread; food can be hit or miss, just like his hours.

The tiny settlement of **Wailua** sits off the road not far past mile marker 18. This community is mostly built around growing taro, the plant Hawaiians use to make poi, the purple, less-than-tasty paste you may try—*once*—at a lu'au. Wailua Road is deadon straight. (Bowlers may get sweaty palms imagining the possibilities. It's strange to be driving on straight pavement again; your hands are searching for something to do.) Keep an eye on your right for a glimpse of the enormous, multi-tiered Waikani Falls, which drop 1,000 feet in several stages just under the highway. (You can't see the large lower falls from the highway.) For what it's worth, we (and readers) seem to get more stink eye here than just about any other place on the island.

Just before mile marker 19, most people blow by without even noticing the **Wailua Valley State Wayside** on the mauka (mountain) side. Take the stairs to the right to the top, and on the ocean side you'll see the village of Wailua with its fields of taro beneath you. Turn around and look up mauka. You'll see (clouds permitting) the

A cliff diver at Ching's Pond leaps into the only space deep enough.

Koʻolau Gap at the top of the mountain. Notice how steep the valley walls are, yet the floor is so broad and flat. This valley used to be thousands of feet deep, cutting into the very core of the volcano. It was filled in at the same time as the Kaupo Gap on the other side of the volcano. (See page 117 for the full story.) The relatively new lands of Wailua and the Keʻanae Peninsula were formed by the same flows that filled the gaps.

Just a bit up the road from here are some concrete picnic tables if you need a break.

Many of the one-lane bridges along here are close to 100 years old. The county wants to replace them, but there's a hitch. In order to get federal (meaning your) dollars, the bridges usually need to be two-lane. (The feds don't like paying for one-lane bridges.) The problem is that Hana residents don't *want* two-lane bridges. Since the county is perpetually short of funds, it's a safe bet that some two-lane bridges are on their way. In fact, in Kaupo on the bottom of the island before mile marker 27 you'll notice two nice, expensive concrete two-lane bridges—connecting two halves of a one-lane road. We Maui residents thank you for your support.

Between mile markers 19 and 20 there's a very popular waterfall to photograph **WATERFALL** called **Upper Waikani Falls**, sometimes called **Three Bears Falls** (the upper cousin to the huge falls partially visible from **ALERT!** Wailua village).

These falls vary dramatically, depending on flow. In case you're wondering, yes, you *can* get to the falls themselves. At the

Most people seem to think that the heavier the water flow, the prettier the waterfall. These two shots of Upper Waikani Falls (AKA the Three Bears) are an example of how sometimes less is more.

far side of the bridge (on the mauka side) is a fairly easy, short path—it's just the first step that's pretty ugly. Standing near the falls, you'll realize that they're a lot bigger than you thought. At press time there were "No Parking" signs at the falls, and police were ticketing those who ignored them. So "for your safety" you are forced to drive about 800 feet past the falls to an inadequate parking area and walk the narrow road back. Thanks for looking out for our safety, Maui county.

Remember, the secret to shooting waterfalls is a long exposure. If your camera has adjustable shutter speeds, the longer the exposure (say around one-tenth of a second), the better the shot looks—if you can hold the camera still enough. If you flunked out of surgeon school because your hands shake, use a tripod or prop the camera on a rock. Also, see page 35 for precautions on swimming in streams. This is probably a good time to tell you that while swimming in natural pools, use your hands as much as possible to avoid kicking unseen rocks. (Voice of experience with the stubbed toes to prove it.)

The stream just before mile marker 21 is sometimes almost dry. That's because most of the water is diverted less than 0.5 miles upstream. But 0.2 **WATERFALL** miles past mile marker 21 is a hunters' road called **Wailua Iki**. The "Private Property" sign **ALERT!** there seems to be off the mark because this land is part of a giant *state land* parcel, not private.

A 10-minute walk from there (at the top of the dirt road turn right) leads to a very nice waterfall and pool, as well as a *gorgeous* valley. (See page 80 for hiking in this EMI area.) There are two more falls farther upstream, but they're harder to reach. By the way, *if* there's water flowing at the highway, the real view is from about 250 feet up the highway (there's a one-car turnout just up the hill), where the water that flows under the highway plunges off the cliff in a very dramatic fashion.

At 0.9 miles past mile marker 21 is one of the heavier-flowing falls along the coast called **Kopiliula**. (It's heavy because there's no ditch upstream robbing its water.) Unfortunately, it's just barely out of sight (except maybe the top of the two falls as you're driving up) 500 feet inland. This whole area is part of the Koʻolau Forest Reserve, but **EMI**, which has the water rights, has infrastructure there that dissuades you from visiting the falls. Assuming they give you their blessing to hike to it, you'll find a trail on the right side of the stream leading most of the way to the falls. If you're willing to get your feet wet and the stream flow isn't too high, you can also access the trail from the far side of the bridge and cross the stream in front of the ditch.

Between mile markers 22 and 23 is **Puaʻa Kaʻa State Park**. (*That's* a hard one **WATERFALL** to say.) Two easily visited small waterfalls make good photo ops, and there are (sometimes **ALERT!** crowded) **restrooms**. The falls are often fairly light, but it's not for lack of water. If you're adventurous, we have a surprise for you. There's an awkward trail on the right side of the upper falls. (We've seen "Trail Closed" signs *sometimes*, but they disappear the next time we visit and the trail is always well-worn, so we aren't sure if it's closed intermittently or simply ignored by other hikers.) It first leads to a short path to the top of the falls, but if you go past it for 5–10 squishy minutes (it's usually muddy), there's a much heavier untapped falls and pool just above the diversion ditch that's taking much of the lower falls' water. When the trail gets to the elevated waterway (viaduct), you have to walk along it, then turn right and cross it at the end of the handrail *before* the second viaduct. Only 100 more feet upstream is your prize. The falls make an ideal photo op—you know, the *me under a waterfall* shot, if the flow's not too heavy—and it's a pretty dependable waterfall, even during the driest times. (But it's pretty cold, indicating the presence of spring water.) The trail goes around a hill and narrows as it goes down to the pool.

It's a fine line at Makapipi between viewing the falls—and becoming part of them. So don't lean too far forward.

By the way, there are boreholes in the Pua'a Ka'a highway bridge to answer that question that's troubled you all your life—how thick are these bridges anyway? And if you look straight down from the downstream side of the bridge, you realize you're missing a *beautiful* waterfall and pool. We've tried to find a safe way down to the base but have been unsuccessful, so consider this one a tease.

Two turnouts after mile marker 23 (left side) you see a cave on the mauka side of the road. If you have a flashlight (and are willing to do some stooping), the cave loops to the right and emerges in an ethereal green scene guarded by banyan tree roots next to a babbling stream. It's short, but sweet. To be precise, it's 140 feet long—we measured it. (*Yeah*, we can be a bit too detail-oriented at times.) Climb out of the cave there, or retreat back to your car. These caves are **lava tubes**, created when lava from volcanic vents forms a river that crusts over on top. These tubes can transport the lava for more than 20 miles, losing a mere 20°F along the way. Lava tubes tend to collapse over time, so young islands like the Big Island are loaded with them, whereas older islands like Kaua'i have relatively few.

After mile marker 24, yet another pretty waterfall called **Hanawi Falls** awaits. It's particularly attractive. If you take a photo from the bridge, be careful. The guardrail is shorter than it looks. There have been people who have sat on the rail for a photo, only to careen backward onto the rocks. When the flow is heavy, this becomes one of the nicest waterfalls on the whole coast. It splits around the rocks,

WATERFALL

ALERT!

Nahiku Road is heaven for anything green.

and the portion on the left adds to the portion on the right, making it a dream.

OK, OK. I know you've probably seen a number of nice waterfalls by now. Been there, done that. But *when it's flowing,* this next one is different. Pull over on the far side of the bridge shortly past mile marker 25. If you walk out onto the bridge (there's no walkway for you) to the middle of the ocean side, look straight down. (Be *really* careful not to topple over—somebody fell to **WATERFALL** his death here in 2012.) You'll see something you don't normally get to see. You are *directly* **ALERT!** above the spot where **Makapipi Falls** plunges unfettered into a large pool.

Enjoy the excellent vantage point as you follow the stream with your eyes as it burrows through the vegetation on its way to the ocean. Makapipi is more seasonal than most falls and is dry about half the time.

NAHIKU

Next to the falls, **Nahiku Road** leads 2.5 miles down through the luxuriant community of Nahiku. If you **DIVERSION** think the road to Hana looked lush and beautiful, wait till you see Nahiku. When plants **ALERT!**

go to heaven, Nahiku must be their destination. Everything green seems so happy and healthy, you can almost hear all of them giggling. Life bursts from every corner at the bottom half of the road. Nahiku was formed in 1905 as a rubber tree plantation, but the effort went flat a decade later.

Drive slowly; children play in the streets. Several honor system fruit stands are often present.

Before the road ends, you'll find that the bridge that leads to the bottom of Nahiku Road has been closed to vehicles since 2015. The bridge is in poor condition (there are a few holes), but you can still walk across to access the end of the road. (The "Local Traffic Only" sign is a holdover from when they allowed cars.) One caveat is parking, which can be tricky. Nahiku is a small community that deserves the respect of anyone who comes to marvel at its beauty. Please don't park in front of the mailboxes or in the school bus turnaround here. There is limited space in *front* of Nahiku Church (but please don't park during service hours) as well as some space along the adjacent dead end road near the banyan tree. From the church it is about 700 yards down to the shoreline, or a 10-minute walk.

Once at the bottom of Nahiku Road, you're in for a treat—a jaw-dropping view of the shoreline all the way back to Keʻanae. There's a little path on the left that leads to a variable but charming little artesian waterfall and pool, right next to the ocean. What a spot! As you stand there in your own private heaven, you can't help but wonder if there's a more beautiful place in the world. Perhaps you can't see forever, but you can see all the way to paradise. This is one of our favorite spots to sit and gaze along the Hana coast. You'll take in miles of coastline as the sounds of the surf and the small falls perfectly accent your surroundings. A grassy area near the ocean makes a good place to have lunch.

As you depart and the road leaves the shoreline, you may think that Nahiku has delivered everything it can. But during rainy times there's one surprise left. About 150 feet uphill from the shoreline guardrail, the stream to your left forms a big pool with a small wa- terfall. (It can dry up in the summertime.) The whole setting is ensconced in an idyllic area packed with more shades of green than you ever knew existed. It's a flawlessly sculpted natural setting. Only the mosquitoes remind you that it's still the real world. There's a short path down to the pool.

DINING OUTSIDE OF HANA

Before mile marker 27 you'll start to see pre-Hana dining opportunities. Hours are squirrelly, some may be temporary businesses and many are cash only. Standouts include the small but light banana bread at **Nahiku Roadside**, coffee and smoothies (plus Wi-Fi) at **Hana Harvest** and the ridiculously good, dairy-free ice cream (made from coconut milk) at **Coconut Glen's** past mile marker 27.

At **Nahiku Marketplace** (before mile marker 29) they have a half-dozen eating stands. Fish and chips plus tasty shrimp dishes at **Island Chef** and good tropical

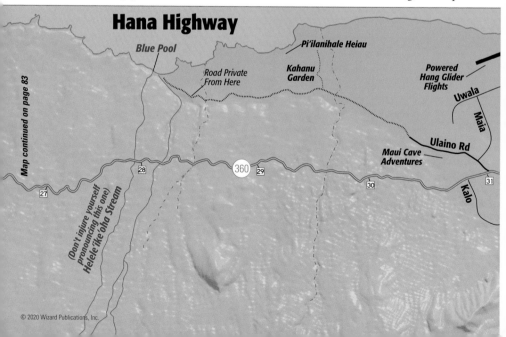

Hana Highway

Blue Pool

Piʻilanihale Heiau

Road Private From Here

Kahanu Garden

Powered Hang Glider Flights

Uwala

Maia

Ulaino Rd

Maui Cave Adventures

Map continued on page 83

28

360

29

30

31

Kalo

27

(Don't injure yourself pronouncing this one)
Heleleʻikeʻoha Stream

© 2020 Wizard Publications, Inc.

coconut cake (when they have it) at the **Nahiku Café**. We also like **My Thai** (which has no mai tais).

More dining options pop up on the approach to Hana. **Hana Farms** is a convenient stop with to-go sandwiches, salads and road snacks, plus nice restrooms. A quarter mile before mile marker 34, **Hana Fresh** often has incredible cherry tomatoes and unusual smoothies. (They

An idyllic Nahiku pond that looks so perfect it can't possibly be real.

are right in front of the health department, which is comforting.)

In Hana town, just before Hasegawa General Store, are a handful of food trucks with reliably good food such as **Surfing Burro** and **Ae's Thai Kitchen**.

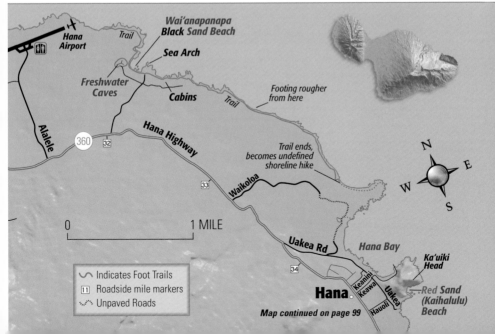

Map continued on page 99

NAHIKU TO HANA

Back on the highway, you'll notice that the terrain is changing. It's less eroded because the land is relatively new here.

Near mile marker 31 is 'Ula'ino Road, and a couple unique attractions. Drive 0.4 miles and the first you come to is **Hana Lava Tube** (808-248-7308). Their land has access to Ka'eleku Cave, a lava tube from Hana's past. The cave has some nice formations. This isn't like mainland mineral caves. Lava tubes aren't as colorful, but it's a cool journey through a volcanic pipeline. They have $12 self-guided tours with signs discussing various -*ologies*, and they've marked formations with signs explaining what you're seeing. You'll have access to .25 miles of the 2-mile cave. (State law says that lava tubes belong to whoever owns the land above, so once you get to the property line underground, you'd be trespassing.)

By the way, if you ever wanted to see what utter blackness looks like, the kind where you can't tell whether your eyes are open or closed, have everyone turn off their lights. That's darkness like you've never seen.

Drive a couple miles farther down 'Ula'ino and you come to an even grander attraction—**Kahanu Garden** (808-248-8912), part of the National Tropical Botanical Garden. They have self-guided tours (which take around 30 minutes) from 9

Wai'anapanapa State Park has the only volcanic black sand beach (created from a lava flow) on Maui. Good facilities, freshwater caves; the only thing difficult about this park is pronouncing it.

a.m. to 4 p.m. Mon.–Fri. and Sat. 9 a.m. to 2 p.m. for $10. The garden is set among spacious grounds, and the emphasis is on native and Polynesian-introduced plants, not ornamental flowers. The love and care is evident, and the plants are well labeled. The most extraordinary feature is not a plant at all, but rather the **Pi'ilanihale Heiau** (shown on page 14). This massive temple, the largest in the state, was largely forgotten and buried under vegetation until the garden restored it in the late 1990s. The first time we saw it, we were unprepared for its immensity. When you first spot it, it looks enormous. But after you get close and go around a corner, you realize how utterly colossal it really is. It covers almost *three acres* and took an estimated 128,000 man-days to build, starting in the late 1200s A.D. The second phase was completed around 1570. You won't be allowed to walk on it, and your vantage point isn't as good as our aerial photo, but you'll get a feel for its sheer size.

Past here the road eventually becomes private, ending at a stream crossing. You may read about a lovely waterfall past the crossing called **Blue Pool**. It's a fantastic site with a tall, delicious waterfall on one side of the pool and the ocean on the other. Unfortunately, access has become a tangled mess. It's on a single large parcel with dozens of owners. Some of the owners of this single parcel are inviting you onto their land, evidenced by their signs near the end of the road saying you can park for $2. At least one of their fellow owners apparently *doesn't* want you there, evidenced by a purportedly grumpy greeting at the end of the road and sometimes even threats, according to numerous e-mails we've gotten from readers. We're very concerned about someone getting hurt and can't recommend going to Blue Pool any longer.

Back on the highway, you'll pass the tiny **Hana Airport. Mokulele Airlines** has daily flights from Kahului. If you want a thrilling adventure, consider a **powered hang glider** flight in a seated ultralight along the Hana coast. The views along the coast are unreal. See page 184 for more.

WAI'ANAPANAPA BLACK SAND BEACH

Just past mile marker 32 is the road to **Wai'anapanapa Park**. (Gee, that really rolls off the tongue, huh? Blew a gasket in the old spell-checker on *that* one. It sounds like why-a-nah-pah nah-pah.) The park is clean and well maintained. They even have cabins for rent. Other facilities include restrooms, showers, picnic tables and camping. Its main draw? It has a volcanic black sand beach.

If you've heard of **volcanic black sand beaches**, you may have thought they were all on the Big Island. *Au contraire.* **Pa'iloa Beach** here at Wai'anapanapa Park is 100 or so feet wide and attests to the newness of the land here. The beach was formed when lava flowed and fountained into the sea near here, shattering on contact with the ocean. Fragments smashed against each other and formed the sand you see. (Don't believe books that tell you that the beach was formed by cliff erosion.) Maybe Rome wasn't built in a day, but this beach may have been, because these types of beaches are often formed in days or weeks. We've watched black sand beaches being created on the Big Island, and it's an awesome sight. They usually have a short life span since the source of the sand stops as soon as the lava stops flowing. Usually within a few hundred to a thousand years they vanish as the ocean gradually sweeps away the precious sand. (White sand beaches have organic sources like coral and shells, which are renewed.) Occasionally the sand is deposited in a perfectly shaped bay like this one, which allows it to stay a little longer. Some lava flows nearby are only 500 years old, according to a dated sample taken a mile south of here. There's a pretty coastal hike that leads to the source of all this sand. It's described on page 223.

Older islands like Kaua'i and O'ahu have no volcanic black sand beaches. (They can sometimes have the other type of black sand beach, like the one at Hana Bay, created when water chips off flecks of lava from stream beds and piles them up onshore.) Since the sand supply here is finite, please try to refrain from taking samples back home with you, except the stowaways lodged in your bathing suit.

Don't swim during high surf because currents can form in the bay.

If you read somewhere about the spring-fed freshwater caves here, forget about it. In 2017 a visitor decided to do some underwater cave exploring, using a cellphone in a plastic bag as his light source. Tragically, he drowned, and the state responded not only by closing the caves off to swimming, but also by erecting barriers so you can't even *look* at the caves. They also posted a "Falling Rocks" sign to imply that it's dangerous to even approach the caves.

HANA

Hana doesn't hit you, it seeps into you. Living on Maui, we had driven through Hana many times and thought we knew it well. But it wasn't until the first time we spent a week in Hana that we truly connected with it. The peace that Hana exudes can only penetrate when you're here at leisure, not on a mission. Today, Hana is

Serious jungle action, brah!

one of our favorite places to go to get away from the hellacious rigors of guidebook writing. (You have no idea how hard it was to write that last sentence with a straight face.) If you're on Maui for a week or more, we strongly suggest you consider spending the last couple of days in Hana.

Hana has the reputation of being a rainy place. In fact, they get just over 80 inches of rain per year at the Hana Airport, though it varies quite a bit. That may sound like a lot (actually it *is* a lot), but hidden in that number are two things you need to know. First, it's *way* less rain than what falls farther up the mountain (which is what feeds the waterfalls), and it's less than what they get to the northwest, around Nahiku. This is because Hana is relatively flat and the orographic rain engine that waters most of Hawai'i misses Hana more than most people think. (The photo on page 27 is typical. Notice how Hana itself is sunny, with the clouds starting farther uphill?) Second, most of the rain falls at night and early mornings due to the same effect. During the day, heavy five-minute showers also contribute to those rain stats. Don't get us wrong: You can still come for a week and have it rain every day. They occasionally get monstrous rains, especially in the winter. It can happen anywhere in Hawai'i. But it's much less likely in Hana than you may guess by simply looking at raw stats.

Things move slowly in Hana, and if you try to rush, you'll only end up frustrated. Businesses may close for any reason. The only bank is open 1.5 hours a day—3 on Fridays. (How's *that* for bankers' hours?)

Here are some of the things you'll want to check in, and just south of, Hana.

HANA BAY

Hana Bay has a large, black sand beach. The sand source is lava eroded from a

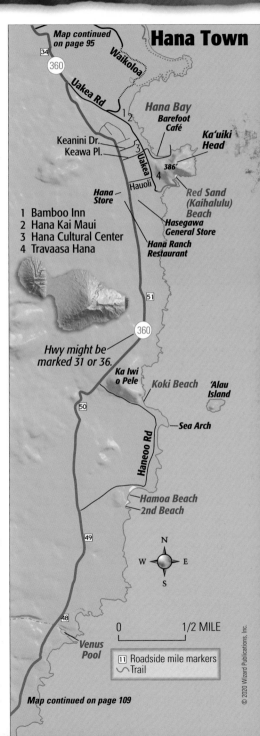

Hana Town

Map continued on page 95

34
360
Waikoloa
Uakea Rd

Hana Bay
Barefoot Café
Ka'uiki Head

Keanini Dr.
Keawa Pl.
1 2
3
Uakea
386'
4
Hauoli

Hana Store

1 Bamboo Inn
2 Hana Kai Maui
3 Hana Cultural Center
4 Travaasa Hana

Red Sand (Kaihalulu) Beach
Hasegawa General Store
Hana Ranch Restaurant

51
360

Hwy might be marked 31 or 36.

Ka Iwi o Pele
Koki Beach
'Alau Island

50
Sea Arch

Haneoo Rd

Hamoa Beach
2nd Beach

49

N
W E
S

48

Venus Pool

11 Roadside mile markers
Trail

0   1/2 MILE

Map continued on page 109

Little gems, like this tiny red sand pocket beach near Hana Bay (not the larger, more famous Red Sand Beach), are here to be discovered for those not in a hurry to get to the "Seven Sacred Pools."

nearby stream. This is usually the safest place to swim along the coast. It's also good place to picnic with a meal from the food trucks in town. On the north (left) side of the bay you may spot an area where the waves come in and seem to die at a certain place. Called **Ke'anini,** Hawaiian legend says there was once a visiting Tahitian chief who wanted to go surfing there. He asked the gods to give him waves, and this they did. As he was surfing, two beautiful local girls saw the handsome chief from shore and fell in love with him. Competing with each other for his attention, they both removed their pa'us—skirts—the only things they wore. The chief saw them and was so startled by the sight that he stopped right there in the water, and the wave went no farther. That is why the waves always stop at that surf site today.

On the right side of the bay is the **Hana Pier.** Nearby, there is a trail that leads 200 or so yards along **Ka'uiki Head.** There's a plaque at the end of the trail marking the spot near a cave where Ka'ahumanu (King Kamehameha the Great's "favorite" wife) was born. The real reasons to take the trail are to visit a small but unknown **red sand pocket beach** that varies seasonally (not *the* Red Sand Beach mentioned on page 101) and to get up close and personal with the geology of this part of the island a little farther along. This hill was formed in geologically recent times when a volcanic vent sprayed lava high into the air. The hill came into being as airborne, gas-frothed lava was caught by the trade winds and piled up here. Near the plaque area you see places where globs of lava plopped and piled up. The deep burgundy color (especially at the small beach) is from iron in the lava. It's literally rusting before your eyes. There's an isthmus connecting the end of the trail to a small islet that houses a light beacon. During *real* calm seas you can cross it. The cove below the end of the trail is an excellent snorkeling spot, and it's common to see kayakers there.

If you ever decide that you need to make a stand somewhere, this hill is the place to do it. For generations invaders from the Big Island would capture this hill and were nearly impossible to dislodge due to the hill's easy defense. From up top they could harass area residents and plan general mischief.

RED SAND BEACH

Though we usually describe all beaches in the *Beaches* chapter, Hana is so far that you'd never come here simply for a day at the beach. So we're deviating from our usual format and describing Hana's beaches here. The far side of Ka'uiki Hill hides one the area's more exotic looking beaches, **Red Sand Beach** (Hawaiian name is **Kaihalulu**). There's a photo on page 176. It's made from the same crumbling red and black cinders that make up the hill. The swimming is often poor except during calm seas. There's a strip of jagged lava that forms a semi-pool at the head of the beach, but it sometimes has the perverse effect during high seas and high tide of making the water more chaotic and disorienting, like swimming in a washing machine. The snorkeling opportunities are usually marginal. To make matters worse, the trail is on the side of the hill, with loose cinders making the footing treacherous in several spots. (And you wouldn't want to slip and fall down the side of the hill—regular shoes are preferred over flip-flops). And one part of the trail is along the shoreline, exposing you to rogue waves.

In the past the landowner, Hana Ranch, had "No Trespassing" signs to dissuade you. We're *thrilled* that they finally saw the light and now allow access under a Hawai'i law that clears them of liability.

(So don't complain to them if you get hurt; *you* are legally responsible for your own safety.) So we often have marginal swimming much of the time, marginal snorkeling and an awkward, potentially injurious five-minute walk. Is it worth going to? To us, it sure is! This is a striking beach, at least worth a look. The rainbow of colors in the lava cinders along the way, the electric blue waters outside the cove, the menacing-looking lava rock inside the bay, the ironwood trees, the layered cinder walls and the untouched beauty make this a memorable place to visit. It's popular and sometimes used by nudists, though nudity is particularly resented by the Hana community, and locals sometimes make their displeasure known in a big way, so you might want to take your bare *da kines* elsewhere.

To get there, park on Uakea near Hauoli. (See map on page 99.) Even though it's a dead-end street, make sure you park facing the correct direction. Furiously *underworked* Hana cops will give tickets for this heinous crime. Just after the Hana Community Center and before the Sea Ranch Cottages there's a large lawn area owned by the county. Look to the right for the obvious trails leading downhill. Continue straight down, taking a left just near the shore. The trail has seen better days, and parts can be downright treacherous without proper footwear. After your initial descent from the lawn, the trail splits. Do not take the uphill path; instead go along the shoreline but only if there are no waves washing over it. You then climb back up to the hillside path, which is not as steep, but loose gravel can make it slippery. The smaller your steps going downhill, the better control you'll have. Don't hike if the trail is muddy, and be careful on the slippery cinders. People have broken bones and badly injured themselves on this trail. All told, it's about a 10-minute walk.

KOKI BEACH

This beach is a mixture of black sand (from the nearby crumbling hill) along with white sand from pulverized coral. It's a good place to sit and observe the ocean under the nearby trees with a dramatic view of the red hill behind you, a sea arch off to the left and the coconut tree-topped 'Alau Island off to the right. Swimming is unprotected and can be hazardous, except when calm. Boogie boarding can be good here. The shape and direction the beach faces make it a good place for beachcombing. Fishing nets, Japanese net glass floats and other flotsam often wash ashore. Local residents have made strong efforts to keep down the litter that once plagued Koki. Be careful not to leave anything valuable in your car here or at Hamoa as we've seen the beach cased many times by young thieves looking for an opportunity.

The large hill next to the beach is called **Ka Iwi o Pele**, said to contain the bones of the volcano goddess Pele, left behind after she had a battle with her sister. The hill and adjacent land is currently owned by Oprah Winfrey. There's a second Koki Beach around the corner (to the left), but unless you're a friend of Oprah's, you gotta do a sketchy swim to get to it.

HAMOA BEACH

A great beach! Tons and tons of fine salt and pepper sand, some shade, showers, clear water and the best **body-surfing** on the island make this one of the island's primo beaches. The thickness of the sand toward the middle is so great that you don't have to worry as much about stubbing

A REAL GEM

Hamoa Beach, in the early morning, is where you'll find the best bodysurfing on the island.

Hana's offshore 'Alau Island.

your toe on rocks as at most north- or east-facing Hawai'i beaches (though it's always possible). Toward the center of the beach the sand drops abruptly a little way offshore, meaning that the waves tend to break at the same spot each time—exactly what you want for bodysurfing. If you've never done this before, be really careful and only do it on small waves. The ocean is unprotected here—no reef to break things up—so the waves have more power here and can drill you into the sand if you're not cautious.

To bodysurf, you simply stand in place, wait for a wave to break right about where you are, and jump forward with your arms extended, turning yourself into a surfboard. I use a mask and snorkel while doing it to keep the salt out of my eyes since I wear contacts. (The mask sometimes gets torn off, so to keep from losing it, I bite down harder on the snorkel when I feel the wave coming.) Many an hour I've spent bodysurfing this beach. Don't try it during high surf; it's too dangerous. Snorkeling is marginal, and there are currents at the two ends of the beach; best to stay in the middle. Located at the south end of

Haneo'o Road, there's a paved path leading down. There is a small dirt parking lot mauka of the bus stop here, but it's often full. There's limited parking along road, but make *sure* you park facing the right way. There are other facilities here designated only for guests of **Travaasa Hana**, but the showers and restroom are used by all.

Around the rocks to the right (south) is another beach, which is usually deserted. Best to swim to it, conditions permitting, as the rock scrambling may be difficult.

DINING IN HANA

We normally put dining reviews in *Island Dining*, but we're putting them here for the same reason we put beaches here. Hana is so far out, *nobody* drives here just for the food.

Braddah Hutt's BBQ Grill
(808) 264-5582

ono This place is an institution in Hana. Braddah Hutt's was essentially the only game in town for years (besides the resort). They outlasted everyone else by offering delicious food, reasonable prices, big portions and lots of aloha. We're happy to say that they still do. (If it ain't broke…) Grilled pork and chicken are the specialty, but the pasta (which comes with chicken or shrimp) is large enough for two to share and is always a hit. Add to that killer fresh fish tacos, and you've got a little something for everyone. Only ding is that waits can be long when they serve tour buses—if you see more than two in the lot, consider another food truck in town. $11–$18. Closed weekends. Just past Hana town on the ocean side of the highway.

Hana Ranch Restaurant
(808) 270-5280

When this was nearly the only game in town, it was our poster child for an awful, arrogant restaurant. (OK, perhaps we were a bit over the top when we begged *don't eat here, don't eat here, don't eat here* at the beginning of the review.) You have more choices in Hana these days, and this place is not as bad. But it sure ain't good, and you pay a lot for mediocrity here. The menu is mostly half-pound burgers, some sandwiches and salads, with some local-style items. The burgers aren't great, but hey... they're just burgers, and venturing to other items might bring heartache (especially if you choose the fish). Stick with burgers or salads, or take a pass. The setting at the outdoor tables is quite nice. $20–$35 for lunch or dinner. Open 11 a.m.–9 p.m. daily. No bathing suits allowed. The mai tai has a kick, which eases the pain.

The Preserve Kitchen & Bar
(808) 248-8211

ono This is Hana's version of fine dining, and it's the best food in Hana. They get an an *ono*—with a qualifier. The menu is steak and seafood with more selection these days than we've seen from them in the past. Flavors are

School's out…forever. (Hopefully you know the song.)

great, and the ingredients are high quality. Most are locally produced, but when it comes to steak, they import it because Maui cattle are grass-fed, which means there's not enough marbling for tenderloins and ribeyes. Preparation is usually—though not always—spot on. Their bartending skills are unexpectedly solid for such a remote location. Consider the candied ginger gimlet or tasty mai tai. And the lanai tables have tranquil views of the distant ocean. But the price of quality is breathtakingly high here. Expect double what you're used to at home. Appetizers are around $20 and entrées are $40–$60. If you can accept that, then you'll probably be happy. Reservations are required (even when things are slow).

As an alternative, if you're staying in Hana, you can always pick up something cookable at Hasegawa's Store and fix it back at your accommodations.

ALSO IN HANA

The **Hana Cultural Center** (808-248-8622) is a tiny museum on Ke'anini Street with a small display of Hawaiian stone tools, quilts, shells, Chinese and Japanese bottles as well as re-creations of thatched huts and a canoe shed. (Dugout canoes required serious labor, and the ancients always built a garage for them.) The museum is somewhat interesting and asks for only a $3 suggested donation, but the place is expendable if your time is precious. Open only when a volunteer is available. Closed weekends. Check out the courthouse next door. It's only used one day a month, when they fly in a judge to hear all of Hana's court cases. He's usually finished by lunch.

Hana-Maui Kayak & Snorkel Reef Watch (808-248-7711) has short, fun kayak/snorkel trips at Hana Bay. For $99 you take a 2-hour tour of Hana Bay and/or some nearby areas. Depending on seas, you may get some nice snorkeling, and owner Kevin is a good guide. Extras include Rx masks, rash guards, digital photos of you, and for $50 extra you can try their underwater scooter.

Hasegawa General Store (808-248-8231) has the most widely diverse assortment of... stuff we've ever seen. That's the only word that describes it. Stuff. Where would you find men's dress socks? Next to the shower curtain rings, of course. And the aloha shirts? To the right of the epoxy. How about fishing spears? Across from the movie rentals. Really need some muffler tape? Turn right when you see the red cabbage; it's between the dried cuttlefish and the lawn mowers. By the way, they also have tabis, great for walking on wet rocks. (They're next to the galvanized pipe.) Some items are a decent deal. Milk was actually cheaper here than at the confiscatory Safeway in Kahului. Other items can be breathtakingly expensive. (I remember going in for a few items once. When I checked out, the total came to $68. I was convinced that this must be a running total from the last few customers... *it wasn't*.)

HANA HIGHWAY BEST BETS

Best View of Coastline—From YMCA Camp near Ke'anae

Best Bodysurfing—Hamoa Beach

Best Exotic Beach—Red Sand Beach

Best Place to See Every Shade of Green—Nahiku

Best Place to See a Cliff Diver—Ching's Pond

Best Attraction to Skip—Twin Falls

Best Place to Get Swept Off A Rock—Ke'anae if You Venture Too Far Out

Best Breakfast on the Way—Baked On Maui in Ha'iku

What a difference from the wet, windward side. The dry mountaintop above Kaupo is 9,000 feet high.

After the inspiring Hana Highway, what else can there be? *Plenty!* Past Hana the road goes through beautiful Kipahulu, past the ʻOheʻo Gulch (formerly called the Seven Sacred Pools) and along the bottom of the island, where jungly forest is replaced with wide open expansiveness. The road to the pools is good. Past that you have a decision to make. To go around the bottom...or not to go? The answer is on page 77.

KIPAHULU

If you've driven the entire Hana Highway today, it's easy to fall into a sort of beauty fatigue by now. In fact, it wasn't until we stayed in Hana the first time and drove this part of the road in the morning that we realized how utterly gorgeous it was. Only when we were fresh and had allowed Hana to melt our bones did Kipahulu seep in. The mountains are so stunning and the waterfalls unspoiled; it's hard to believe that the highway can still deliver after all these miles. Those making the all-day drive are now getting tired. It's after noon, and they are looking for the payoff at ʻOheʻo Gulch, AKA Seven Sacred Pools. But if you're lucky enough to be in Kipahulu in the morning, when the light is best, you have the highway pretty much to yourself, and any waterfalls you find are yours and yours alone.

Back on the highway, the mile markers have changed and are now counting down. (Until 16, then they jump back to 20 and start going down again—*go figga*.) You'll notice a looong lava rock wall starting near the 51 mile marker. Visitors would be stunned to find out how expensive lava rock walls are to build. This one goes on forever and must have cost in the mid six-figures. We won't mention the name of the private landowner who can spend that kind of cash. Let's just say her name rhymes with *okra*.

Leaving Hana, there is a surprise waiting for you if you have time to venture to it. It's one of the largest and nicest freshwater pools on the island. Called **Waioka** by the Hawaiians, its physical appearance has spawned a new age name that seems to have stuck—**Venus Pool**. It looks like a painting that you would normally dismiss as being too contrived, too perfect, yet here it is. It's located next to the ocean with a hala tree-capped ball of lava symmetrically dividing the sea view. There you'll find numerous places that people jump from, deep water in several spots, the pounding ocean just on the other side of the gravel and some perfect areas on the mountain side from which to sit and cogitate. The aura is unforgettable. If you go in the morning or late afternoon, you'll sometimes have it to yourself. The water is slightly brackish (salty) from the ocean but usually very clean since it is partially spring-fed and not dependent on the seasonal stream it resides in. During whale season we've seen the leviathans breaching close to shore. All told, it's a fifteen-minute hike from your car. If you're looking for a unique place to swim or ponder, this will definitely ring your wow meter.

To get there, you'll first need to assess the parking situation. There is space for four to five cars on the ocean side of the highway just before the bridge. (You must face the legal direction and have all tires off the road or risk getting a $45 ticket.) If these spots are taken, across the bridge is the souvenir and shave ice shop, **Hana Treasures**. For $7 you can park facing the legal direction in their lot all day long, but they usually aren't open weekends. Near the Hana side of the bridge is a short trail running parallel to the road that turns toward the ocean (left) at the gulch. The trail comes to a pass-through at the fence (it keeps livestock in while letting people through) and continues straight toward the ocean. Hana Ranch has allowed access along this trail in recent years, even erecting a sign reminding you that a state law protects them if you hurt yourself on

Watch your step when entering Venus Pool.

their land while recreating. (Which is true; *you* are responsible for your own safety in this case, so please don't harass them if you stub your toe or something more serious.) It was a gracious move on Hana Ranch's part, which we applauded. Just before the path hits a weird, large, round concrete... thing (it's actually an old Portuguese bread oven), veer to the right toward the stream. Be careful of slippery rocks, and don't jump unless you've checked out what's below. (Look around to find the best place to get in and out of the water.) Avoid if the flow is too heavy from the stream. Occasionally, very long dry spells make the water a bit stagnant. One other caveat—it's not the best place to take small children. Exiting the water requires pulling yourself up on rocks and can be awkward even for adults and teenagers.

Weather permitting, look for the Big Island peeking above the clouds. Its massive mountains, over 13,000 feet tall, are impressive to see.

There may be a small waterfall at mile marker 46. Then, before mile marker 45, you'll notice a cross erected in memory

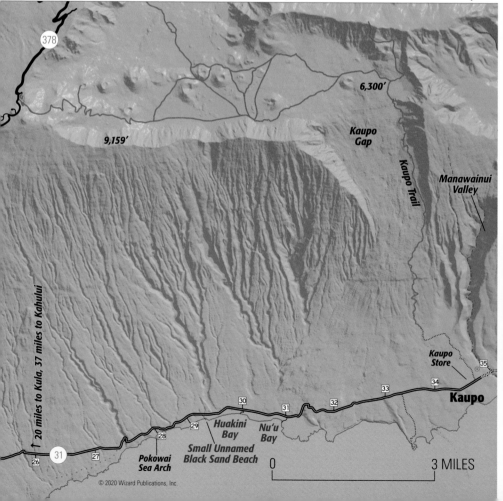

378

6,300'

Kaupo
Gap

Kaupo Trail

Manawainui
Valley

9,159'

Kaupo
Store   35

34

Kaupo

33

32

30

31

Huakini
Bay

Nu'u
Bay

29

28

20 miles to Kula, 37 miles to Kahului

31

27

26

Pokowai
Sea Arch

Small Unnamed
Black Sand Beach

0   3 MILES

© 2020 Wizard Publications, Inc.

of Helio Koaeloa, one of the earliest Hawaiian Catholic priests. The narrow trail leading to the bottom takes about 10 minutes but tends to be overgrown, and it could take another 10 minutes to pick your way to the shore. You are rewarded at the end with a rounded boulder beach that makes a cool rumbling sound when waves break over it. There's sometimes a pretty little waterfall near the sign called **Paihi Falls**.

After you cross the Wailua Stream (where we have an adventure hike on page 263), yet another *(sigh)* sweet waterfall called **Wailua Falls** on the next stream awaits. (*Why isn't Wailua Falls on the nearby Wailua Stream?* Not sure, but hey, don't be judgmental. Remember, the London Bridge ain't in London, it's in *Arizona*. Just sayin'…)

WATERFALL ALERT!

Wailua is best in the morning when the sun shines on it. The flow varies *a lot*. (See photo on page 30.) Its water pattern can be exceptionally idyllic—even for Maui—or a light, pathetic trickle. Later in the day vendors sometimes congregate there, selling handmade souvenirs.

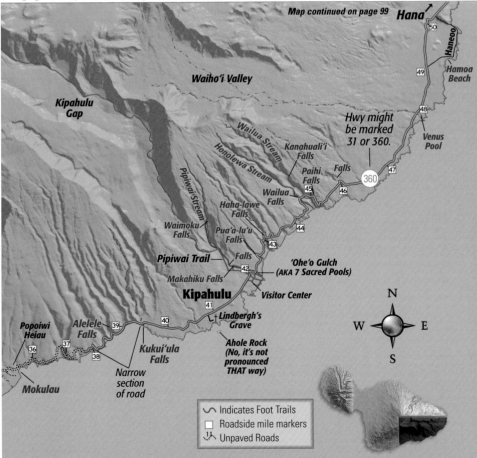

Map continued on page 99

Hana

Haneoo

Hamoa Beach

Venus Pool

Waiho'i Valley

Kipahulu Gap

Hwy might be marked 31 or 360.

Wailua Stream

Honolewa Stream

Pipiwai Stream

Kanahuali'i Falls

Paihi Falls

Falls

Wailua Falls

Haha-lawe Falls

Waimoku Falls

Pua'a-lu'u Falls

Pipiwai Trail

Falls

Makahiku Falls

'Ohe'o Gulch (AKA 7 Sacred Pools)

Kipahulu

Visitor Center

Lindbergh's Grave

Popoiwi Heiau

Alelele Falls

Kukui'ula Falls

Narrow section of road

Mokulau

Ahole Rock (No, it's not pronounced THAT way)

N
W E
S

⌒ Indicates Foot Trails
☐ Roadside mile markers
Unpaved Roads

Southeast Maui/Kipahulu & Kaupo

Are we at the Seven Sacred Pools yet? No, sorry. You'll have to endure **WATERFALL** yet another falls called Pua'a-lu'u Falls just past here. We apologize for the inconvenience. The falls are to the left of the bridge and also fall under it. Driving past these falls, look for a Blessed Mother Shrine in a remnant from an old lava tube. It's lovingly maintained by a retired woman in the area. A priest chose this location because Pua'a-lu'u Falls always flows, so there's always water available nearby for blessings and for cleaning the statue.

Those 'Ohe'o Gulch—aka Seven Sacred Pools are just ahead.

'OHE'O GULCH–AKA SEVEN SACRED POOLS

OK, enough of these single waterfall scenes; now comes the big daddy. This series of waterfalls and pools at the shoreline is the most popular attraction in all of east Maui. Why? Because the old name, Seven Sacred Pools, sounds so appealing you just gotta check 'em out.

Also because the swimming is usually so good and the setting so beautiful. What's not to love? Back when nobody had ever heard of Hana, the owner of the Hotel Hana Maui (now called Travaasa Hana) wanted desperately to attract people here. He had a choice: Tell people they could visit the fabulous "Ohe'o Gulch or the wondrous *Seven Sacred Pools* (which he made up). Which do *you* think looked better on a brochure? (For the record, there are not seven of them, and they never were sacred.)

When a retired airline executive from the mainland named Sam Pryor planned to build a house right near the pools back in 1960, articles began to appear in local papers warning that access to the pools would become a thing of the past. Pryor realized that the pools were so beloved by residents that he contacted the people who sold him the land and insisted that they trade it for land elsewhere, saying the pools should belong to everyone. He later contacted his old friend Laurance Rockefeller and convinced him and others to buy 52 acres around the pools and eventually donate it to Haleakala National Park. So today, the pools are protected forever.

The park became one of the best places in the world to jump off waterfalls because they were so user-friendly, and for decades people came from all over the world to do just that. Falls, pool, falls, pool, falls, pool. It's an ideal playground where visitors jumped for joy into deep pools to their hearts' content. But an accident, lawsuit and subsequent giant settlement in 2009 changed all that. Park officials responded by banning people from jumping off anything, plastered the area with warning signs, and now rangers vigorously patrol the pools. You will be fined and perhaps even arrested if you jump off anything. Their message is quite clear: *We want to save you from yourself... and we want to save ourselves from your lawyer.*

What about swimming in the pools or just walking around them? We hate to say this, but odds are you *won't* be able to do either of those. You *might*, just don't *count* on it. They'll often close them off to public access at the mere hint of rain up in the mountains (which is common in this area) and for months at a time if they even get a twitch. And when the pools are closed to swimming, they're closed to people who want to just walk around them, too. Only the trail above the gulch is available and they let vegetation cover the view from most of the trail.

When you *can* swim here, it's absolutely great and the views are gorgeous. People *staying* in Hana have it best, because they

ALERT!

A **REAL GEM**

Whether you get to swim in them or not, the pools at 'Ohe'o Gulch are some of the most scenic on the island.

can get here before the crowds do. There is often nobody at the falls in the morning. In the afternoon, expect *a lot* of people to join you in the fun.

Park at the prominent parking lot on the left. The lot sometimes fills up around peak time (2 p.m.). The loop trail from the lot to the pools and back is just over 0.5 miles.

Part of Haleakala National Park, it's $30 per car for entrance here, credit card only. This fee also gets you into the park at Haleakala's summit for three days and vice versa, so save your receipt.

Camping is available; see page 208 for more. There are restrooms at the park and a water fountain. At the visitor center there are opportunities to learn about Hawaiian culture and its people's relationship with the land, sometimes from local Hawaiians. You can also go on guided hikes or visit a taro farming area. Check with park personnel to find out what's available.

The huge valley above the pools, stretching all the way up the mountain to Haleakala Crater, is a wondrous area. Called Kipahulu, it has resisted the intro-duction of most foreign plants brought by man, making it one of the more pristine forests in the state. Endemic birds and plants, found nowhere else in the world, thrive in the waterlogged rain forest above you. It has been designated a biological reserve, and entry past the end of the Pipiwai Trail is closed. Park officials are engaged in a never-ending battle with pigs in this valley. Despite their best efforts, pigs abound here and can wreak havoc on endemic plants.

PIPIWAI TRAIL

Above the pools lies one of the best hikes on the island. You certainly won't have it to yourself, but you get more *wowie* views and settings per mile on this trail than almost any other. All told, it's almost 2 miles each way, and you gain 650 feet (not 800, as the park brochure says) from the highway, though the grade is fairly gentle. (The first part is the steepest, and it's not that steep.) Called the Pipiwai Trail, it's smashing and takes anywhere from 2.5–5 hours, depending on how much of a hurry you're in.

The mystical mountains of Kipahulu will be your last tropical view before you get to drier Kaupo.

Trails are usually described in *Hiking*, but we deviate here to make things simpler because there's no chance you woke up, decided you wanted a good hike and drove way over to these-here parts to do it. The trailhead is down the highway toward the 'Ohe'o Bridge near mile marker 42. (See map on page 109.)

The trail basically follows the stream. You'll want mosquito repellent in places if you deviate from the main path. Early into the hike you see a concrete derrick with a pulley on top. Another is on the far side of the bridge. Back when sugar was king, they were used to haul sugar cane across the gorge on its way to the mill down the road. Around 0.7 miles into the hike you come to the Makahiku Falls overlook. This massive falls drops 200 feet.

Back on the trail, you'll go through a gate, and in a few minutes there's an intersection. Check out the wise-looking banyan tree with its aerial roots along the way. Without a doubt, banyans are the most ancient-looking trees you'll ever see.

A hundred yards after the banyan you can take a side trail to one of the louder waterfalls you'll find. It free falls and smacks onto rocks, then runs into a particularly emerald green pool that has undercut the mountain, forming a cave. You can see more of the falls by following the rock steps to the right.

More diversions await, including a pool at least a football field long. Then a pair of bridges soon enables you to cross the magnificent stream you've been following. (And yes, foolhardy buggahs jump off the first one here, too.) The vantage point from the bridge is tongue-wagging.

What next? Why, a beautiful, thick, vigorous bamboo forest, of course. (Bamboo, which is a grass, makes an excellent walking stick.) After the long, impressive boardwalk—constructed to keep you out of the perpetually muddy areas—you eventually come to the end of the line. (Well, you still have to go back, of course.) Slicing 400 feet down the back of a three-way sheer wall of lava, Waimoku Falls marks the instantaneous beginning of this canyon. What a way to end a trail! You could walk under the falls, but remember that any debris falling from above will feel like getting hit by a meteorite. Did you bring your hard hat? Best to view it from a little distance and comply with the park's sign. During abnormally dry times in the summer the water flow can diminish somewhat, but it's mostly spring-fed, so its flow is not as rain-dependent.

PAST THE PARK

About 0.1 miles past mile marker 41 is an easy-to-miss paved road that leads to **DIVERSION** Palapala Ho'omau Church where the world's greatest aviator, Charles Lindbergh, is buried. **ALERT!** See page 115. Lindbergh's grave is on the ocean side of the church, through the cement post openings, and straight past the older graves on the corner.

Just past the grave is a big lawn that leads to a tiny park. Walk to the far end for a scrumptious view of the jagged coastline, or munch on a snack at the shaded picnic tables. The church was recently restored and if it's open, you can go inside and perhaps make a small donation, if you are so inclined, that goes toward upkeep of the graveyard.

At 0.3 miles past mile marker 41 you'll see the Laulima Fruit Stand. In addition to fruits, they'll make you a salad from their freshly grown greens or pour you a cup of coffee from beans grown on their trees. Take whatever you get to one of two tables ensconced in a thick bamboo stand.

At 0.6 miles past mile marker 40, the road begins to skirt the side of a cliff and you get utterly glorious view of the Kipahulu coastline. The road's about to get narrower for a few miles with many blind turns, so be alert for oncoming cars.

At the bottom of this first valley, pull over past the small bridge (called Kaapahu) onto the short gravel driveway to the ocean. Walking onto the gravelly beach and looking back the way you came, you'll usually see 'Opelu Falls plunging into the ocean. (You can't reach the falls by land, and we have the scars to prove it.) It only occasionally runs dry.

OK, here's your last chance to frolic at a waterfall, and it's a sweet one. The cliffside road looks sketchy here. (Maybe that's because it *is* sketchy.) About 0.3 miles past mile marker 39 is a white bridge with the word "Alelele" on it. There are several trails, all leading 5–10 minutes inland. It's fairly easy (though you'll have to cross the stream at one point, usually keeping your feet dry). Alelele Falls is around 40–50 feet high and has the cleanest, clearest and coldest water you'll find. We believe that it's partially spring-fed, which accounts for its clarity. The lower pool is lined with lots of pebbles, making entry easy on your feet. The pool's about 6 feet deep. Bring your camera; you'll really like this one. It occasionally slows to a trickle, but not often. Listen for bleating goats who live in the steep valley walls.

At 0.25 miles past mile marker 36 at a grassy corner up on the hill in front of you are the barely visible (if at all due to vegetation) remains of the Popoiwi Heiau, a religious structure. They aren't visually interesting. What's unusual about it is that it wasn't made by the Hawaiians. It was made by the people who were here *before* them. You see, when the first people arrived here from the Marquesas Islands around 300 A.D., they lived untouched for about 700 years. Then another group came, this time from Tahiti. They killed and subdued the first inhabitants, driving them ever farther northwest. (The first inhabitants were called Menehune by the second arrivals, a derogatory term denoting small in class and stature. The legend was later distorted by westerners who didn't understand, and Menehunes became the Hawaiian equivalent of elves.) The last remnants the Menehunes left behind are some decidedly unHawaiian carvings on tiny islands northwest of the main Hawaiian Islands.

Alelele Falls is your last chance to frolic in freshwater.

Where Legends Come to Die

Kipahulu will be forever distinguished as the final resting place of aviation great Charles Lindbergh. Most of those from our generation know very little about Lindbergh, and that's a shame. In 1927 the world held its collective breath as this 25-year-old airmail carrier fought weather and fatigue-induced hallucinations for 33.5 hours to become the first man to cross the Atlantic solo in an airplane. One of the greatest feats of his time, it was celebrated as much in its day as the moonshot was decades later. Lindbergh hadn't been able to sleep the night before his flight left New York, so when he landed in Paris, he had been awake for nearly 60 hours. Some 150,000 screaming well-wishers met his plane when it landed in France. (More than 4 million people later turned out for him when he returned to New York.) He had no idea when he landed in Paris that he had the world in the palm of his hand. All he wanted was to take a nap.

After the flight, Charles Lindbergh became the century's first media superstar. His life was followed with more interest than any man alive at the time. He represented the very heart and soul of aviation and was a worldwide hero. When his baby was kidnapped a few years later, the ransom demands went on for two and half months, and the baby was eventually found dead just a few miles from his house. (The infant never even made it out of the house alive; he died when the kidnapper's ladder broke on the way out the window.) The Lindbergh baby kidnapping trial was called the trial of the century (before anybody had ever heard of O.J.).

In later life, when Lindbergh's old friend Sam Pryor told him, "I have found heaven on earth, and it is at Kipahulu, Maui," Lindbergh visited his friend and was immediately smitten with this part of Maui. He built a home here and spent the last six years of his life in East Maui.

In 1972 Lindbergh was diagnosed with lymphosarcoma. Over time he tried various treatments in New York, but the cancer eventually spread to his lungs. His doctors told Lindbergh that his time was very short. He phoned his physician in Hawai'i and said, "I have eight to ten days to live, and I want to come back home to die. I would rather spend two days alive on Maui than two months alive here in New York."

Against his New York doctors' wishes, he was flown on a stretcher in a commercial 747 (the other passengers had no idea who was behind the curtain in first class) back to his beloved Maui. He spent the next week meticulously planning all facets of his funeral, even designing his coffin and picking the lining. Lindbergh wanted the wild plum tree next to his grave removed, but his grave digger convinced him to let it live there with him. Just over a week later, on August 26, 1974, he died. As the small funeral procession passed tourists visiting the "Seven Sacred Pools," none had any idea who it was for. Fewer than 15 people were invited to attend, and Lindbergh had asked that his pallbearers wear their work clothes. A Hawaiian hymn was sung as the casket was lowered into the ground, and one of Lindbergh's sons said the hymn "just soared out and away with the wind and the crashing of the waves below us."

A short distance from Lindbergh are the graves of Sam Pryor (the friend who lured Lindbergh to Maui) and Pryor's wife. Between Pryor's and Lindbergh's graves you'll find six small graves. These were some of Sam's "children," including Keiki, George, Lani, and his favorite, Kippy. They don't have last names because his "children" (as he always referred to them) were actually Asian gibbons. Sam took these apes with him wherever he went. Townsfolk rarely saw him without one of his children.

The inscription on Lindbergh's grave, from the 139th Psalm, reads, "If I take the wings of the morning, and dwell in the uttermost parts of the sea." The rest of that passage, not on the stone, is, "Even there would Thy hand lead me. And Thy right hand would hold me."

In remote and sparsely populated Kaupo, St. Joseph's Church, built in 1862, only holds services if there's a fifth Sunday in a month.

Less than a mile after mile marker 36 (across from two mailboxes) there's a road on your left that angles back toward the ocean and leads to **Huialoha Church** and cemetery. It's a dirt road, but 2WD vehicles are usually OK unless it's been raining. Drive to the end, and you'll see why it's called **Mokulau**, or "many islets." Dozens of lava outcroppings in the water defying the relentless waves make a dramatic photo op as the water pounds and twists to get past them. The area has an unmistakably peaceful feel. Keep an eye out for Hawaiian monk seals that sometimes beach themselves here. The nicely restored and well-maintained church has restrooms.

If you see signs saying the road is private (or a chain blocking access), it's not true. County records show (and the church owner confirms) that the road and the parcel at the end of the road are *state* land. Huialoha Church and Kaupo community put up the signs and unlocked chain to "prevent casual visitors" because some unsavory residents were abusing the area at night. If you go, please pack out anything you bring, and reattach the chain in order to help their efforts.

Kaupo Store past mile marker 35 is your last chance to pick up snacks. Mostly sodas, chips, ice cream and candy mixed

DIVERSION ALERT!

with an interesting collection of antique cameras, clocks and assorted knickknacks. There's also a restroom out back. Check the dates on any food here as freshness this far out can be hard to maintain.

After umpteen years renting this old wooden building, the landlord (we were told by the shopkeeper) ejected them from the building in 2016 out of structural concerns. So they were next to the building upon our last visit and requesting donations to use the restroom. After 20 years of observing the *never*-changing world of Kaupo, this is the most dramatic development we've ever seen. Just *try* to contain your astonishment.

The road is paved again (though poorly), and it's tempting to ask yourself, *Why don't they pave that last section?* The answer is, the county *wants* to. But Kaupo residents like it just the way it is. They want a certain number of people to turn around when they encounter the dirt road in order to "keep Kaupo the way it is." (What they *do* want is to have the bumpy stretch you're about to encounter to Upcountry smoothed out so they can make their trips to Central Maui easier.)

Looking around in this part of the island, it's easy to think that nothing important ever happened along here. Actually, this area was subject to a vicious invasion in 1775 by the king of the Big Island. He occupied the area and treated his captives so badly that they called it the war of Kalaehohoa (meaning, roughly, *the war where they beat our brains out with clubs*). When Maui's king responded, he routed the Big Island king along the shoreline below mile marker 33. One of his Big Island lieutenants in this defeat was Kamehameha, who would later become king of all the islands. Kamehameha barely escaped with his life.

At 0.5 miles past mile marker 32 just before the road zigzags is one of our favorite spots to pull over and enjoy the views of Haleakala and the broad expanse of shoreline in the late afternoon. The deep gorges, formed by sporadic but intense rain, show up well in the afternoon. Look to the top of the mountain and you'll see the **Kaupo Gap**, the large, wide opening at the top of the mountain. At one time the gap, caused by erosion, was at least 5,000 feet deep, perhaps deeper, and cut into the very core of the mountain. (There's a similar gap on the other side of the mountain, meaning the volcano was essentially cut in half.) Later, lava again poured from the summit, filling the great Kaupo canyon to the shallow level you see now. If you look at the left side of the gap, it's not hard to imagine how the lava dammed up against the side of the older mountain and flooded the canyon and the plains below.

Wind is almost always present along here as the trade winds pile up along the flank of the great mountain. We once saw three helicopters struggling to land on a barren, grassy field next to the road. We soon learned that a wedding coordinator had convinced a group of Germans that this would be an ideal place for a wedding reception, so they chartered the expensive helicopters to fly everyone in. We can still picture them standing there, with the wind blowing champagne all over their shirts, as they looked around, asking each other, "Whose stupid idea was this?"

Just before mile marker 31 on the oceanside of the highway, there's an unlocked gate to Nu'u Preserve. This is the public access to **Nu'u Bay**, the only decent ocean swimming area along this entire stretch of coastline. You'll need to park in the grass along the side of the highway just past mile marker 31 and walk back to the unlocked gate and the 0.2 mile-long road. (You would need 4WD and higher clearance than any rental vehicle has to drive the road.) The road terminates at the

An unnamed black sand beach with no footprints? Yup. Welcome to Kaupo. Read on.

spotty remains of an old cement landing—Nu'u Bay is to your right and a small shoreline trail leads down to the rocky beach. The snorkeling is fairly good to the left (away from the shore), but don't venture beyond the protected point where the water is rougher and there's a current. The only thing marring the plentiful coral scenery is an unusually large number of fishing nets. Local fishermen thoughtlessly abandon them when they become entangled on coral heads, which creates a permanent hazard for sea life. We once found a dead reef shark (a normally docile animal) entangled on the bottom here. That's not a sight we'd like to see again.

If the surf is up, the short dirt road just before mile marker 30 leads to a great place to listen to the surf. **Huakini Bay** is lined with small- and medium-sized rounded stones. When large

DIVERSION

ALERT!

waves rake the shoreline, these stones make a deep rumbling, sometimes thunderous sound that you won't soon forget. The bigger the waves, the better. Just don't get too close to the water. The cliffs behind the bay are said to contain ancient Hawaiian petroglyphs, according to a 19th-century archeological report we read, but we must confess we haven't been able to find them. Let us know if you're more successful. Be careful of the wicked kiawe (mesquite) thorns.

Modern man is not the first to traverse the island along this route. The ancient Hawaiians built a highway centuries ago, paved with lava stones and wide enough for two. This was how they went from east to west. Keep an eye out on the right side for remnants of it.

At 0.6 miles past mile marker 30, a dirt road angles back to the shoreline. This is it—the *last* beach on the island. (And we have the kiawe thorns from walking the shoreline in our hiking shoes to prove it.) It's a small, **unnamed black sand beach** about 60 feet wide. Its sand source is a nearby intermittent stream patiently dismantling its lava streambed. Cloudy water and not good for swimming, but the sand has an exotic look, and there's a small cave in the back shore. Sometimes storms remove the sand for months at a time. You'll find it after the road has dipped across a dry gulch and rises up—after a cattle guard. There is a gravel pullout big enough for three or four cars on the mauka side of the road. Walk across the road, down the faint 2-track toward a small clump of trees toward the ocean.Don't get fooled by the large beach of gravel to the west. This black sand beach is smaller with actual sand instead of just gravel.

Continuing west you'll spot the **Pokowai Sea Arch**, but don't pull over until the road descends to the shoreline. From there

Dry and desolate. Nothing in common with Hana, on the other side of the mountain, except the beauty.

you can get out and get a closer look at the arch and shoreline. Though the ocean is almost always whipped and frothed here, we've seen throw-net fishermen braving the water for their catch.

Soon you'll find a brand new two-lane bridge on this one-lane road. (As with all Hana Highway bridges, federal dollars will only pay for two-lane bridges, even if they are on one-lane roads.) The gulch that the bridge spans is beautiful, however, showing the layers of different lava flows.

As the road leaves the sea on its way up to the 3,000-foot level, you may wonder what you are missing with all that land and shoreline below that you won't get to see. The answer is you're missing *nothing!* The land below the highway past here is the most wretched you'll find on Maui. Harsh and unforgiving lava fields, sparse and scrubby brown grass—there is nothing visually pleasing about this area other than some marginally interesting lava rock ruins. (Even paradise has to have an ugly side—this is it.) The shoreline, though rich in fish, is lashed by heavy seas, making it hazardous. Many maps show a trail that goes from South Maui all the way to where the highway started leaving the shoreline. Yeah, the trail's there, but it's sporadic, miserable and ugly and passes almost nothing of interest. (And we have the kiawe thorns from walking the shoreline in our hiking shoes to prove it.)

Surprisingly, this area used to be heavily populated by Hawaiians. Thousands took advantage of the fishing area and the good sweet potato growing conditions in some pockets where there was soil. There was even a forest in those days, before cattle were introduced. Hawaiian ruins are scattered about the rocky fields. Today, native Hawaiians are in the process of trying to repopulate the higher elevation areas. Over 100 families are working as a group to rebuild this part of Maui, called Kahikinui. It won't be easy. Life was always difficult in this land of little rain and ever-present winds. Easier life elsewhere lured their grandfathers away for a reason, and they abandoned the land. Even today the homesteaders live with no power or running water, and only time will tell if they are successful. The biggest event to happen to this area is the Auwahi Wind Farm near mile marker 21, built to capture the raw wind that courses through this area. Aside from that, Kahikinui remains a blank canvas.

Past mile marker 15 you see Maui Wine (formerly Tedeschi Winery, 808-878-6058). They have a nice wine-tasting room and gift shop (albeit with fairly unremarkable wine, some made from pineapple), and it's worth a stop. The grounds are serene. Check out the wood sculptures out front. They are what remains of 150-year-old cypress trees, carved in place after they had to cut down the dying trees for safety reasons.

Across the street is the Ulupalakua Ranch Store (808-878-2561), a no-frills grill. It's worth going inside just to smell the burgers cooking on the grill. Beef, venison, lamb and elk. Open 10-5.

SOUTHEAST MAUI BEST BETS

Best Surreal Sunrise—Venus Pool
Best Hike—Pipiwai Trail
Best Place to Pay Homage to an Aviation Legend—Where Legends Come to Die
Best Isolated Waterfall—Alelele Falls
Best Place to Hear the Ocean—Huakini Bay if the Surf's Up
Best Place to Loosen a Filling—On the Bumpy Road Past 'Ohe'o Gulch
Best Place to Build a Windfarm—On the Scrubby Land Below the Highway Past the Pokowai Sea Arch

Sunrise from Haleakala Crater can be a surreal, ethereal experience.

People come to Maui for the ocean, palm trees and balmy weather. So why on earth would you want to use up one of your precious vacation days in the center of the island where you won't find *any* of that? Simple. This part of the island has green, rolling hills, switchback roads, cool mountain air and a *lump-in-your-throat crater* at Haleakala National Park. It may not be typical Hawai'i, but it's definitely beautiful.

UPCOUNTRY

Upcountry refers to the cluster of towns located 2,000–4,000 feet up the slope of Haleakala. They aren't pointing directly into the trade winds, so rain is less frequent. Drought happens on occasion, sparking water rationing. Since temperatures fall about 3 °F with every thousand feet, it's cooler up here than at the shore. It's popular with people who want to work or play in the tropics but don't want to *live* there.

Don't tell this to people who live upcountry, but in ancient times, Kula residents were considered dim-witted and dense and were the butt of jokes throughout the islands. It stems from the fact that they lived so far from the water that they possessed little sea knowledge and were thought of as stupid and backward. Sort of the ancient equivalent of *How many Kulans does it take to pound poi? Five! One to hold the pounder and four to raise the bowl over and over. Ha, ha, ha...*

To get upcountry, most people head up the Haleakala Highway on 37. (The

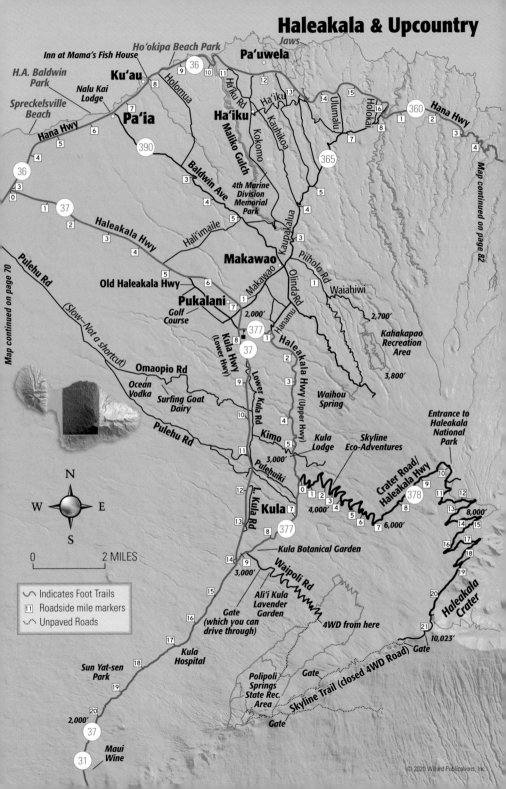

term *Haleakala Highway* and the signs are misleading because it is actually composed of segments from *three different highways,* 37 to 377 to 378. But if you're headed to the national park, the most expeditious route is well-marked and easy to follow.) If it's clear, between mile markers 4 and 5 you get a perspective of just how *big* this mountain really is. It's more than 10,000 feet high, and from here you can tell by the width that this single mountain hides a monstrous amount of rock.

Why are the Days 24 Hours Long? Thank Maui.

The Hawaiians believed that in ancient times there was a demigod named Maui. (A demigod is the offspring of a god and a mortal.) Maui noticed that his mother used to complain that the days were too short for her to dry her tapa cloth. So young Maui set his mind to lasso the sun as it streaked across the sky. He went to Hana to watch the sun rise, then tried to catch it at Haleakala but failed. Later, near Kahului, Maui cut down all the coconuts he could find and made a long fiber rope. He climbed Haleakala and hid at a place across the crater called Hanakauhi. When the sun streaked by, he lassoed many of the sun's rays, weakening it. Maui told the sun, "Now I will kill you for hurrying so fast." The sun answered, "Let me live, and I promise that from now on I'll walk instead of run across the sky." Maui agreed and the sun kept his promise. Today the days are 24 hours long as a result of this agreement. (Weekends were apparently exempt from the deal because they seem much shorter.)

There are areas mentioned in this chapter that you won't pass by coming up Hwy 37, the most notable being Ha'iku and Makawao.

Oh, and if you're looking at the map on page 121 and trying to take a short cut to upcountry via Pulehu Road to Omaopio Road, it's not really a shortcut, but it does pass by two things. One for kids (it's called **Surfing Goat Dairy** (808-878-2870) and it ain't too shabby) and one for adults. The latter is **Hawaii Sea Spirits Organic Farm & Distillery** (808-877-0009). They make vodka and rum here. The Ocean Vodka brand is the most interesting. Usually made out of potatoes or grain, the vodka here is made from sugar cane. Then they add desalinated ocean water that's been sucked from 3,000 feet down off the coast of the Big Island. $15 gets you a 45-minute tour of the process and a small sampling at the end. If you're a sucker for clever packaging, you'll like their bottles.

HA'IKU

Ha'iku is just below the area normally considered upcountry and is probably the least discovered town on Maui. Two pineapple canneries were once the lifeblood of the area. The canneries now house very diverse businesses (from video production to surfboard shaping) and still remain integral to the community. The population is around 8,000, consisting of a mix of old-time locals, hippie farmers and wealthy mainlanders, Maui business owners and computer commuters. Green, wet and quiet is what they come for, and they're not disappointed. Their higher-elevation neighbors sometimes look longingly at Ha'iku's abundance of water. The roads here tend to be narrow. Twenty feet was considered wide enough in the horse and buggy days, and parts of some

DIVERSION

ALERT!

The mystic forest along the upper part of Waipoli Road.

roads have maintained that width. There's usually very little traffic on Ha'iku roads during the week. Look at map on page 121 if you're interested in driving (for no particular reason) some of these pretty places like Ha'iku or Ulumalu roads. The town is worth visiting if you're in a wandering mood or want a treat from the Ha'iku Marketplace (which has some good dining options).

MAKAWAO

Makawao is a major Upcountry hub. It's supposed to be the island's cowboy town. Most visitor informa- **DIVERSION** tion conveys the impression that you'll see old cowpokes riding horses through the **ALERT!** streets. Not likely. If you see anybody on a horse, it'll probably be a teenage girl picking up some brie for her mom's get-together. But it's a pretty cool and interesting place to wander and shop, with some unusual finds. (On weekends, though, hours are pretty spotty.) For instance, the **Rodeo General Store** might sell "island coconut-flavored gourmet kosher Maui-grown coffee." (You know, it's kind of hard to picture a grizzled old Hawaiian cowboy saying, *Hey, Kimo, pass the gourmet kosher coffee, will ya?*) Around

town you'll find a wide range of shops. A few highlights include **Hot Island Glass,** which blows their own glass artworks; the **Makawao History Museum,** a quaint (and free) spot for learning about the area; and **The Dragon's Den,** an herbal remedy shop with everything from alfalfa leaf to *Zhi Gan Cao.* The absolute best is **Komoda Bakery** (808-572-7261) on Baldwin Avenue. Unimpressive on the outside, but unreal baked goods at reasonable prices.

Galleries are also common here and they're friendly. Not like a few years ago when they took themselves pretty seriously saying they were for "peace and the enrichment of humankind with their visions" and they "accept the aloneness in the creative process and celebrate the aloha with their togetherness." Well, damn, that's really good to know. But hey, do you folks sell that painting of the dogs playing poker?

Be aware that mornings can be busy in Makawao since the downhill bicycle tours race through town. You'll want to check your gas tank in Makawao or Pukalani. If you're going up to the park, you've got a lot of climbing ahead, and there's no gas on the way to Haleakala. Also, if you're trying to park and find all those two-hour stalls filled, there is a large, free public parking lot on Makawao Avenue between the library and **Stopwatch Bar & Grill** across from Ai Street.

By the way, no self-respecting Hawaiian cowboy (called a *paniolo*) would ever be caught dead saying, *Get along, little dogie.* Here he would say, *Hele makai* (go to the ocean). Other local cowboy terminology includes:

Hemo kapuka—open the gate
Pipi—cattle
Lio—horse
Oni—let's move out
Kau ka lio—mount your horses
Waha!—yeehaa!

KULA

Think of Kula as everything past **Pukalani** (which itself offers little other than golfing and a few good places to grab local grinds, such as **Pukalani Superette**). Kula is farming country, and there are some downright tasty views of the central valley from up here. The sights in this region are past the turnoff for the national park, so you won't see them on your way up to the summit unless you take a detour.

Though you can see incredible flowers on the drive itself, there are some nice gardens for those who want a closer look. The best is probably the **Kula Botanical Garden** (808-878-1715) on Highway 377 between mile markers 8 and 9. It's well maintained, well marked and there's a nice assortment of tropical plants scattered over 6 acres. They also have two resident nene (native Hawaiian goose) which are the only ones on public display on Maui. Well worth the $10 if you're into gardens.

Just before mile marker 14 is Maui's strawberry farm, **Kula Country Farms** (808-878-8381). It can be a fun stop for families during spring months when you can pick your own strawberries and play their small putt-putt course.

Polipoli Spring State Recreation Area is at the end of that *other* winding road (Waipoli Road) working its way up Haleakala. The road is a wiggly son-of-a-gun that few people ever take, and when it's licked by fog, the disorienting twists and turns can do the same to passenger stomachs. (See map on page 121.) 4WD only the last 4 miles. At the end is an unexpected redwood forest in the middle of this tropical island. The trails are described on page 219. It's cool and misty and would seem to belong more in Northern California than the center of Maui.

Also on Waipoli Road past a gate and cattle guard is **Ali'i Kula Lavender** (808-878-3004). You probably never knew so much could be done with lavender until you come here. They sell lavender chocolates, brownies (yummy), scones (also yummy), coffee, lotions, lemonade (better than the tea), candles, face pillows and more. There's a large variety of plants and flower gardens, which combine nicely with the cool temperature and stellar views. But it's annoying that they charge you $3 for the privilege of going inside and buying stuff from them. We know it's only $3, but just sayin'... Guided 30-minute guided tours are $12, or for $25 you can ride with staff on a golf cart.

Farther up Waipoli Road, just before the tree line, you can find the **Polipoli Disc Golf Course**. Disc golf is a game where you use a specialized Frisbee and try to toss it into baskets in as few throws as possible, a la golf. It's free and open to the public, but it's maintained by volunteers and the 18 holes are not very well marked. We know this is popular on the

Sunrise From Haleakala—Is it *Really* That Good?

Sunrises from atop Haleakala have taken on legendary status. They are said to be comparable to a religious experience, that they will heal your soul, rejuvenate your spirit and perhaps even fix that ingrown toenail you've had lately. In short, they are said to be the best in the world. As a result, sunrises from up here are considered must-dos for visitors. But they ain't free. The park now requires an online reservation—in advance—before they will let you into the park to watch the sun rise. And they charge an extra $1.50 (in addition to the entrance fee) for this "service." If you don't have a reservation from www.recreation.gov, they will turn you around until the sun comes up. (The sunsets are still free, but please don't call this to their attention, or they might start charging for that, too.) You can book a reservation up to two months in advance, and they will open up another 40 tickets at 7 a.m. two days in advance, and you want to be online promptly. There are more requests than tickets available, so some people are gonna be out of luck.

The first time we came to watch the sunrise up here, we thought it was the most overrated, overhyped event we'd seen. Pleasant, yes, but hardly worth the effort. People around us seemed to agree. Also, the first time we were so wretchedly cold that we couldn't have appreciated winning the lottery, much less seeing a sunrise. The second time we did it, however, we were blown away by its majesty. Wouldn't have missed it for the world. What's the difference between pleasant and wow? Multiple trips have cemented a theory. It's simple—clouds. A sea of clouds (especially broken clouds) below you with the sun rising from beneath makes a glorious canvas for the sun to paint. It's like nothing you've seen, and when it's good, it's as good as a sunrise can get. Other times, when it's too clear, it's simply… nice… and cold. And for nice it's hard to justify the hardship. Fortunately, having clouds below you is fairly common, though less common than at sunset.

To get the time of sunrise and a **weather forecast**, call (808) 944-3756, or ask your smartphone. You'll want to get to the summit at least half an hour before sunrise. However, if you don't arrive about an hour before, you run the real risk of not getting a parking spot at the actual summit. You'll have to park at the upper visitor center instead. If you try to park in the dirt, you may get a monstrous ticket. If you park at the visitor center, consider walking the short distance to the Sliding Sands trailhead. (See map on page 126). It's less crowded, and you may find the wind partially blocked by White Hill next to you. Allow just under two hours from Kihei, or a bit over two hours from Ka'anapali. If you don't allow enough time, you'll be one of the poor saps who woke up at 3 a.m. and still missed the good stuff. Bring a small flashlight, if possible; it's easy to fall down in the dark and numbing cold. If you get here while it's still inky dark, you'll probably see more stars than you've ever seen in your life.

No matter how warmly you think you need to dress, dress warmer. Bring every piece of clothing you brought from the mainland, if necessary. If you rented an open-air jeep, here's where you pay the piper. You'll freeze your nuggies off. (In fact, look on the side of the road, and you'll see mounds of formerly frozen nuggies from previous visitors.) If the wind's blowing at that high altitude (which it often is), it'll make a penguin scream. We bring our ski clothes, gloves and a wool cap, and still, we sometimes get cold. The temperature rises quickly when the sun does, but few visitors are properly prepared for the morning cold, even in summer. At the summit there's an enclosed viewing area, but it's usually crowded and noisy in there, and the views are more restricted. If you're properly prepared, consider toughing it outside.

Sunset atop Haleakala is 180 degrees different, literally and figuratively. It's not about the crater; it's about seeing the sun set into clouds below you, and the mountain mainly serves as your elevator to the sky. To observe it from the summit, you have to arrive about 90 minutes before the sun sets if you want to get a parking space. That's when the light will be in the crater. Soon after, a long shadow starts to creep across the crater from the rim you're standing on, consuming all colors as it moves. People gather in the shelter, while the braver (if it's windy) ones walk a short ways to the west edge. You can scurry down the embankment a bit to diminish the screaming east wind, but the cost will be eating the dust of those who scurry down after you, so maybe you want to follow the crowd, not lead it.

mainland, but it seems comparable to playing fetch with yourself. But with views like the ones here, who cares?

Past the park, the last thing between you and the vast lands of Kaupo is **Maui Wine** and **Ulupalakua Ranch**, past mile marker 21 and described on page 119.

HALEAKALA NATIONAL PARK

From Hwy 37 you took 377 then 378, right? (See map on page 121.) You now begin the endless switchbacks necessary to scale the steep slopes of Haleakala. A donut ring of clouds often forms part of the way up, fooling people into thinking that the summit's socked in. Most of the time the clouds clear before the summit. Watch for mindless, wayward cows on this stretch. It's an open ranch, and the witless bovines often wander onto the road. They're occasionally prematurely turned into hamburger by cars traveling too fast in the fog. You will be afforded many outstanding views of West Maui and the valley between the mountains. (Unless you're heading here for the sunrise; then you'll have to see many of the sights mentioned here on your way down.)

A REAL GEM

If you ever want to *see* what **turbulence** looks like, take a look at the cloud formations as you drive up and down Haleakala. As a pilot, this is the only place I know on the island where I can *watch* turbulence (as opposed to feeling it) close up as the clouds roil and boil in all directions. Coming *down* the mountain, after mile marker 8 is often a good place to see it.

After mile marker 10 you'll pay your $30 per car entrance fee and enter the

Haleakala Crater

The crater area is hard to visualize, so it's shown here on an angle. Think of it as a casting of the crater sitting on a table top. The smaller map is how it looks from the other side.

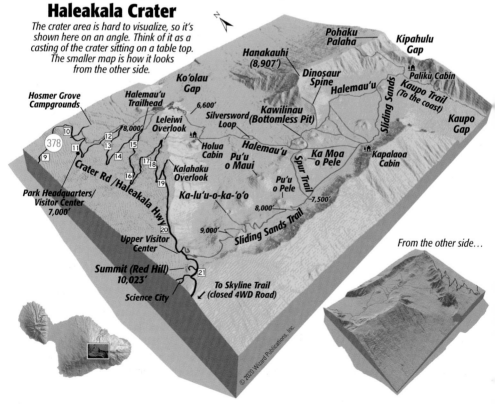

Pohaku Palaha
Kipahulu Gap
Hanakauhi (8,907')
Ko'olau Gap
Dinosaur Spine
Halemau'u
Paliku Cabin
Sliding Sands
Kaupo Trail (To the coast)
Hosmer Grove Campgrounds
Halemau'u Trailhead
6,600'
Kawilinau
Silversword (Bottomless Pit)
Loop
Kaupo Gap
Leleiwi Overlook
8,000'
10
378
9
12
11
13
15
14
17
18
16
19
Holua Cabin
Pu'u o Maui
Halemau'u
Ka Moa o Pele
Kapalaoa Cabin
Spur Trail
Kalahaku Overlook
Ka-lu'u-o-ka-'o'o
Pu'u o Pele
7,500'
8,000'
Park Headquarters/ Visitor Center 7,000'
Crater Rd /Haleakala Hwy
20
9,000'
Sliding Sands Trail
Upper Visitor Center
Summit (Red Hill) 10,023'
21
Science City
To Skyline Trail (closed 4WD Road)

From the other side…

© 2020 Wizard Publications, Inc.

park. For years admittance was often free because (only the government could come up with this kind of logic) they "didn't have the budget for someone to collect money all the time." Can you imagine Disneyland making that policy? Now they do everything by credit card (no cash accepted if unmanned). Anyway, the visitor center and campground are the first things you pass. The visitor center has restrooms and the only phone available. Save your receipt, and you won't have to pay again at Oheo Gulch, aka the Seven Sacred Pools, at Kipahulu within three days.

Walking down Sliding Sands Trail will transport you to another world.

Camping is allowed at several places in the park, including the coveted cabins at the bottom of the crater. See *Camping* on page 208 for more. The campground at **Hosmer Grove** as you entered the park has a 25-minute **nature loop**, which is one of the better trails to catch a glimpse of rare native Hawaiian birds, thanks to its proximity to a restored native forest on Haleakala Ranch lands. This campground is also a good place to see moonbows (rainbows caused by the refraction and reflection of moonlight) when the full moon's rising in the east and it's raining toward the west.

As you've ascended the mountain, note how much the vegetation has changed. You're not in Hawai'i anymore; you're in Alaska. Cold, windy and arid conditions favor plants with needles and very small leaves. One plant that looks like a whisk broom has powder-filled spore casings. Ancient Hawaiians used to come up here and gather the powder to rub into their *da kines* to prevent chafing on long walks.

The visitor center at 7,000 feet has an average high temperature of 59° F and low of 41 °F in February. In August it averages a high of just 66 °F and a low of 47 °F. It's about 10 °F colder at the summit, and every few years they even get a light dusting of snow or ice. Most of the rain at the summit falls in the winter months, but it's still not nearly as rainy as the lower elevations can be with 54 inches at the 7,000 foot level and much drier at the summit. (Our website has a link to current weather readings on Haleakala, including temperature and wind speed.)

HALEAKALA SUMMIT

After mile marker 17 you'll see a parking lot for the **Leleiwi Lookout**. Most people blow right by in their frenzy to get to the summit, assuming that Leleiwi merely gives them another nice view down the mountain to the coast. Too bad, because Leleiwi holds a surprise. Walk five minutes

DIVERSION

ALERT!

The Haleakala Highway is proof that on Maui, the shortest distance between two points is rarely a straight line.

to the end, and the crater itself suddenly explodes into view. What a startling sight! It looks very different than the more traditional view at the top and is well worth the diversion. A small shelter protects you from any wind that may be present. This is a good alternative to the summit for less crowded sunrises.

As you near the summit, keep an eye out for **silverswords** ('ahinahina). You'll know them when you see them. This plant, unique to Hawai'i, first arrived as a California tarweed seed in the feathers of a wayward bird a million years ago and evolved into this striking round silver wonder. They developed their dense covering of silver hairs to live in this difficult environment. It allows them to retain water and ward off the intense sun at this altitude. If you see one blooming with a large stalk of flowers, pay your respects. Silverswords may live up to 50 years, but, like salmon, they only reproduce once (with that large floral stalk), then die. At one time silverswords were endangered when thoughtless people plucked them out of the ground for all sorts of ornamental purposes. Today they are protected, and their numbers have rebounded. Be careful walking around them, however, as the fine for damaging them is more than the cost of your whole vacation. For the ancient Hawaiians, there was nothing silver in

their universe until they met this plant. Their name for it, 'ahinahina, literally means *gray gray*. That's as close as they could get.

There are several trails that are supposed to highlight Silverswords, like the one at the **Kalahaku Overlook** up ahead. But you're more likely to see them from the side of the road nearer the summit. While at Kalahaku, take the time to enjoy the view of the crater, which already looks a bit different than at Leleiwi Lookout.

There aren't many types of birds that can live up here. Flying in thin 30 mph winds, which is common, is not a very efficient means of transportation. So they walk most of the time. The three most successful are the native **nene** and the imported **chukar** and **ring-necked pheasant**. A nene is what results when you take wayward geese from Canada and stick them on an island for a few million years. They've left the water and adapted to high, arid lands, losing much of the webbing on their feet in the process. They were almost extinct at the beginning of this century. Today they are protected, but are often accidentally killed because of their laid-back attitude toward cars. They just don't seem impressed with an auto's size, like frogs at night looking into your headlights as they're squashed. People often accidentally back over them.

As a result, it's more important than usual not to feed them, or they'll get even cozier with cars. They'll likely come up and beg if they see you, and they're hard to resist, but try. They're often visible at the **Halemauʻu Trailhead** between mile markers 14 and 15.

Most visitor information refers to **Haleakala Crater** as the *largest extinct volcanic crater in the world.* Cool! Too bad none of that statement is true. It's not the largest, it's not extinct, and the crater is not volcanic in origin. (In fact, the park now prefers to call this a *basin, valley* or *wilderness area,* but we refer to it as a *crater* because people will look at you funny if you mention *Haleakala Valley.*)

After Haleakala built itself up, it went to sleep for several hundred thousand years as most Hawaiian volcanoes do. During its snooze, two great valleys formed on either side due to erosion. These valleys cut at least 5,000 feet deep, into the very core of the volcano. They worked their way up the mountain until they met at the summit, back to back. Now the mountain was essentially cracked down the middle, separating the east and west sides, with only a thin ridge between the two great canyons. Then Haleakala awoke for one last series of eruptions before falling forever silent and eventually sinking under its weight back into the sea. That's what will happen to all of the Hawaiian Islands. (This last series of eruptions is in its final phase, having last erupted around 1790.)

When it awoke, it did so from the summit, filling the enormous canyons with lava and raising the summit floor you see before you. So, you see, Haleakala Crater is an *erosion* crater that was partially filled with lava and gravel from the crumbling sides, not a volcanic crater like those on the Big Island. When you drive around the bottom of the island, you'll be able to see, from around mile marker 32, where and how the lava flowed through the **Kaupo Gap** and flooded the plains below in an ever-widening flow of molten rock hitting the sea between mile markers 30 and 35.

As you approach the top of the mountain, you may find yourself a bit breathless. You've gone from sea level to almost 2 miles high with no time to acclimate. Take it easy and drink plenty of water. You dehydrate very quickly without noticing at this altitude. If you've been SCUBA diving in the last 24 hours and your blood feels a bit carbonated up here, remember—as far as your body's concerned, you may as well be flying. *You got da bends, brah; go back down.*

The upper visitor center after mile marker 20 has kickin' views but it closes at noon—yeah, noon. Its parking and restrooms stay open. There's also a restroom at Kalahaku Overlook and at the Halemauʻu Trailhead. If you brought a bike for the 38-mile downhill ride, this is the best place to launch. (Commercial tours are banned from the park, and have to start way down at the 6,500-foot level.) See *Biking* on page 187 for more.

The way the clouds race by, clawing at some of the nearby peaks, you could be 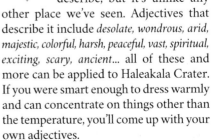 looking at Mt. Everest instead of a Hawaiian peak across the crater. The beauty is hard to describe, but it's unlike any other place we've seen. Adjectives that describe it include *desolate, wondrous, arid, majestic, colorful, harsh, peaceful, vast, spiritual, exciting, scary, ancient...* all of these and more can be applied to Haleakala Crater. If you were smart enough to dress warmly and can concentrate on things other than the temperature, you'll come up with your own adjectives.

Sharp contrasts, impossibly blue skies and a myriad of colors are a feast for your eyes.

If you're here in late afternoon to see the **sunset**, consider staying until past dark for one of the clearest views of the Milky Way you may ever see. You may also be treated to something available in only a few places in the world. It happens as you're standing at the crater's edge with clouds below and in front of you (and relatively close) while the sun is low and directly behind you. (Leleiwi Lookout is a good place to see it since it's close to the Koʻolau Gap's clouds.)

Called **Spectre of the Brocken** or *akaku anuenue* in Hawaiian, it's when you see your own shadow on the clouds with a rainbow surrounding your shadow. It's an *incredible* sight. The Hawaiians felt blessed to experience it because they believed that what they were seeing was their actual soul, and the rainbow was a promise from heaven that their souls would be taken care of. If you're lucky, maybe you'll be blessed, too.

The ancient Hawaiians never lived up here, but they did visit for religious purposes and to hunt birds. Many artifacts have been found in the crater. The Hawaiian historian Kamakau says that commoners used to come up here to toss the

remains of their loved ones into a pit at the bottom they called Kaʻaʻawa, now called **Bottomless Pit** or **Kawilinau.** (Hawaiians were always fearful that others would desecrate the bones of their ancestors, so this bottomless pit was a perfect place to assure that their remains wouldn't be tampered with.) People who lived at the bottom of the mountain in Kaupo believed that their water came from Haleakala Crater, and they used to bitterly complain that the reason their water tasted so insipid was because of this practice. (Hmm, sort of makes you want *bottled* water while driving through Kaupo.)

Hawaiians also came for the rock. Most lava rock is relatively soft. There are several deposits here of harder stone that the Hawaiians used to make adzes (a stone ax) for shaping other tools.

Lastly, Hawaiians came to Haleakala to hide the umbilical cords of their newborns. Hawaiians strongly felt that if rats, notorious thieves, were to steal a baby's umbilical cord, the child would grow up to be a thief. So they hiked to some of the smaller volcanic pits in Haleakala to keep the cords from rats (which aren't native—the Hawaiians brought the Polynesian rat with them from the South Pacific).

At one time imported **goats** were a huge problem in the crater, eating everything in sight and tearing up the ground with their hooves. When they eradicated them, they purposely left a few sterilized males marked with radio transmitters to roam the wilderness. Referred to affectionately as *Judas Goats,* the theory was that lonely males were *far* more effective (and motivated) at locating any unaccounted-for female goats than park personnel could ever hope to be. It worked, and the crater is now goat-free.

Past the upper visitor center parking lot, the road leads to the actual summit itself at 10,023 feet. Winds can be strong up here and can cause windburn if you're exposed to them for an extended period. If it's not windy, as is often the case later in the morning and afternoon, it's tempting to shed your warm clothes. You should know that sunburn happens very quickly up here since the light filters through a thinner atmosphere. (OK, OK, no more nagging.) The peak directly southeast of the summit is called **Magnetic Peak**. Can't find southeast? That's because the iron in Magnetic Peak is messing with your compass.

At mile marker 21, if you avoid the turnoff up to the summit and instead stay to your left, you're heading to **Science City**. The Air Force and the University of Hawai'i have astronomical observatories up here, but they're not open to the public. The Air Force uses their 12-foot diameter scope to optically sweep space, tracking space junk that could collide with existing satellites. The optics alone for this cost $40 million, and it can spot items the size of golf balls in space. (The old space shuttle reportedly lost very few golf balls, but the Air Force

is tracking a wayward glove.) Astronomers also bounce laser beams off retro-reflectors left on the moon by the Apollo astronauts in the '70s. By timing the reflection, they can measure the speed of continental drift. Maui's Pacific plate moves northwest at the same rate that your fingernails grow. (Apparently, their procurement office moves at about the same speed. It wasn't until this millennium that they finally replaced their '70s-era 4mhz computers with newer ones that were only five years out of date. Now *that's* progress!)

We came up here once in the middle of the night to watch a meteor shower, but the shower was mostly a bust. After dozing for a few minutes in the car, we awoke and thought we were hallucinating. *How can this be?* It looked like thousands of shooting stars in line with each other, like a special effect from a *Star Wars* movie. It took a minute to realize it was a pulsating laser shooting all the way to the horizon from one of the university's many science experiments.

On this road to Science City, at the next intersection, there is a locked gate **DIVERSION** and an FAA sign warning that trespassers will be tortured and maimed, or something to that **ALERT!** effect. The sign is apparently incorrect, unauthorized and contradicted by the fact that the state has established a *public access* to Skyline Road. Few people have explored this part of the summit because of the sign. Too bad. We did a little digging and found that the FAA erected the sign to prevent *tour buses* from using the narrow washboard road for (c'mon, everybody, you know the words to this song) *liability reasons.* Then they put up a gate. The FAA does not have a problem with hikers (and bikers) using the road since it's necessary to access **Skyline Road**, a fantastic and lightly used dirt road that meanders down the spine of Haleakala, ending at **Polipoli Spring State Recreation Area**. See page 260.

If you take the 0.6 mile-long federal road, you'll come to a dirt road on your left. That's Skyline, and if you walk on it around the corner for a few minutes, you're treated to a magnificent view of most of Kaho'olawe. Though you're almost 10,000 feet up, the ocean is only 6 miles away. What a sweeping vista! The Big Island—at 4,000 square miles it's almost as big as Connecticut—lives up to its name. It looks positively *huge* from up here.

After all these beautiful sights, it's (literally) all downhill from here. Remember to use a lower gear driving back down; the slope will burn your brakes.

INSIDE THE CRATER

On the other side of the hill next to the upper visitor center is **Sliding Sands Trail**. If you're only going to do one hike at Haleakala, this is the one. The trail descends 2,400 feet fairly evenly over a span of almost 4 miles (it's hard on the knees) to the crater floor, but you don't need to go that far to see some of the gorgeous views from your slow but constant descent. Just go as far as you want, and you'll see how much larger and grander the crater looks from inside. At times it looks big enough to hold another island. The colors inside are amazing. Everything from green, yellow, red, brown, grey and blue are represented.

If you've heard about the amazing horseback ride down into Haleakala Crater, here's the deal. Officials at this national park just *live* to ban things, and after three decades of allowing horseback tours, they have now *banned* commercial companies from taking you there. But they wanted us to tell you that you're perfectly welcome to bring your own horse as long as it's *not* rented locally. Seriously... We'll leave it up to you how you're gonna get 'em on the plane.

The trail leading into the crater is far less windy than up above. The weather is usually sunny, especially in the morning. Clouds will push up from the Ko'olau and Kipahulu gaps as the day progresses. From inside you'll often see the clouds roiling at the head of the Kipahulu Gap at the far end, like a white waterfall, but coming no farther. Quiet prevails inside the crater, and the ever-eroding walls provide endless gravel. In fact, when horses were allowed here, it was necessary to dig up the horse hitch at the bottom of the crater several times. Erosion from the sides of the crater keeps raising the basin floor, creating the illusion that the hitch is sinking.

Inside are numerous hiking trails described under *Hiking*. Though Haleakala's most recent eruption in 1790 was at the coast, the crater is far from dead. Lava flowed in the crater 900 years ago while Hawaiians occupied the island, and perhaps even more recently. And it probably will erupt again.

There are cabins in the crater for the lucky campers. If you get one, enjoy that complimentary firewood. It'll make the most expensive stove fire you've ever had because the park service gets it there by helicopter. Other maintenance is done by rangers on horses and mules.

A NOTE TO THE PARK

I don't want to end this chapter on a negative note, but there's something that's been eating at me, and I just can't keep it inside any longer, because it saddens me. I have been visiting **Haleakala National Park** for two decades and have watched in quiet horror as activity after activity, sight after sight has been taken away

from visitors. I don't know if anyone else is keeping score, but here's what's been lost, all by *park declaration*. Jumping into the pools at **'Ohe'o Gulch**—banned. Visiting the base of **Waimoku Falls**—banned. Visiting the **Infinity Pool**—banned. **Bicycling** down Haleakala roads inside the park with trained guides—banned, unless you go on your own. Watching the sunrise from atop Haleakala—greatly restricted, regulated and now a fee is charged. Numerous trails within the park—closed. Horseback tours inside the crater—banned. Staying in one of the crater's cabins—nearly impossible. All these and more are things you could once do here but can't any longer because bureaucrats have declared it so. Waving the banner of "safety" would undoubtedly be their response, and that's behind *some* of these decisions, but it's impossible to dispute that management here is *ban*-happy, and it's frustrating to see so many of the park's natural assets now off limits. The philosophy seems to be to keep *everyone* from doing *anything* where *someone* just *might* get hurt. We wish they'd look at how other national parks and sites in Hawai'i are run and try to remember that the people who visit the park are not the enemy—they are the owners.

HALEAKALA & UPCOUNTRY BEST BETS

Best Hike—Haleakala Crater Grand Loop as Far as Your Heart Takes You

Best Coup—Getting a Cabin in Haleakala Crater

Best Decadent Treat—Komoda Bakery in Makawao

Best Sign to Ignore—FAA Sign to Skyline Road

Best Place to See Someone Shoot at Klingons—From Science City at Night

Best Way to Freeze Your Da Kines Off—Wear Shorts to Watch the Sunrise

Best Place for Bathroom Break After Sunrise—Maui Lavender and Botanicals on Crater Road

Best Place for Breakfast After Haleakala Sunrise—Grandma's Coffee House in Keokea

Best Campfire—Helicopter-Flown Wood in the Haleakala Crater Cabins

Best Place to Get a Glimpse of Your Soul—Leleiwi Lookout

Best Stargazing on the Island—Haleakala Summit

Calm water, luscious beaches like Mokapu and swanky resorts are why people love South Maui.

Ahh, South Maui. Land of sun and beaches and visions of offshore islands.

Until the mid-1900s, there were few people living in South Maui. Lack of water made it difficult to grow things, and, after all, what else was land good for? Today we know it's good for growing Hawai'i's most important cash crop—*visitors!* South Maui gets so little rain (many years it may only rain three or four times), and its beaches are so extraordinary that it's a mecca for anyone looking for a dreamy, dependable tropical vacation.

If you look at the graphic above, the first thing you notice is that the term *South Maui* is not very geographically correct. *South Central Maui* seems more accurate. But South Maui is what the region has been historically called, so who are we to quibble?

We're going to describe it from Ma'alaea at the top of Hwy 31 heading south as far as you can go.

MA'ALAEA

At the intersection of Hwys 30 and 31, Ma'alaea was feared and despised by early airborne visitors. Because it was here, where the Kealia Pond now exists, that clueless aviation officials chose to place Maui's first airport in 1929. (It looked geographically convenient on a map to early planners.) It didn't last long because this is the windiest spot in Hawai'i. The scouring wind ensured that the inbound flight experience would be as terrifying as possible. There are cows born and raised on the slopes north of Ma'alaea. If the winds stopped, they'd probably fall over.

Maʻalaea is still a transportation hub, only now it's for boats. If you take a snorkel or whale watching trip, odds are very good you'll leave from here.

Maui Ocean Center (808-270-7000) is the other big attraction here and is definitely worth a stop. Opened in 1998, this is a relatively small (compared to some mainland aquariums) but extremely well-done aquarium. The living reef exhibit has a fantastic collection of fish found around the Hawaiian islands, and the sealife seems remarkably well cared for. Turtle Lagoon has lots of honu (the Hawaiian word for *turtle*) roaming around that you can view from above or from a glass wall below the surface. Elsewhere there is a glass tunnel that passes right through a large tank, complete with sharks. Stop in the tunnel's center, and watch the sharks pass right beneath the glass floor. Check out the 3D show, *Humpbacks of Hawaiʻi.* Shown in a 58-ft. diameter sphere (the size of an adult humpback), you end up face-to-face with the behemoths in a way you could never experience out in the ocean. It's only 15 minutes long and it's a cool experience. The gift shop has a surprisingly fine and vast assortment of gift items, many locally made. It's one of the more impressive gift shops we've seen on the island. The aquarium is more crowded when the weather is bad. The $35 entrance fee may seem excessive due to the small size, but the quality shines. (Kids get in for $25.)

Maʻalaea's greatest natural asset is its 3-mile-long Maʻalaea Beach, stretching all the way to north Kihei. If you're looking for a great walking or jogging beach, this is the one. Early mornings and early evenings are best, as winds punish the area during the day. You won't have it to yourself, but you will have an amazingly peaceful stroll. Start at Haycraft Park at the end of Hauoli Street in Maʻalaea, and you won't see another building for 2.5 miles.

While *you* may have come to Maui for the beaches, *birds* visit us for Kealia Pond National Wildlife Refuge. This important wetland is home to several species of native birds. Besides the visitor center off Hwy 311, there's a turnout to an almost half-mile long boardwalk trail (with beach accesses) between mile markers 1 and 2 on Hwy 31. (Also labeled as Hwy 310 on some signs.) This is a good place to bird-watch. After moderate rains, the ponds often fill up and are *beautiful* to see. Ironically, after heavy rains they will only last a short time at their high water mark. (Huh?) That's because there is a sand plug (visible from the boardwalk) that separates the low elevation pond from the ocean. After heavy rains, the pond overflows the plug, eroding it, and the pond drains, leaving the remaining water at the mercy of the tides until the ocean waves replug the hole. During the late summer and fall the ponds dry up.

In the past we were pretty tough on Maʻalaea. The astonishing winds and dust from the sugar operations (which have now ceased) in the past convinced us that staying here was a bad idea. (You'll be forgiven if you think *Maʻalaea* must be Hawaiian for *bad hair day.*) So we spent five months living in Maʻalaea and came away with this conclusion—if you want to experience life in *both* South Maui and West Maui, Maʻalaea can be pretty darned convenient. See the free *Where to Stay* section in our smartphone app.

Until that fence lining the shoreline was installed, hawksbill turtles would occasionally cross the road here in late spring/early summer to lay eggs in the Kealia Pond. Today they lay their eggs on the beach. But that's the only time you're likely to see them. They live and feed in deeper waters, far from shore. The turtles you see while snorkeling are usually green sea turtles, which rarely nest here, preferring French Frigate Shoals, 700 miles away. (Like restless teenagers, sea creatures rarely want to hang around the place they were born.)

KIHEI

As you're entering Kihei, you have a choice of either taking South Kihei Road along the shore or staying on the highway. The latter you'll use when you're simply interested in getting farther south. Though you won't take it every time, we'll describe South Kihei Road from here because that's where all the goodies are.

Kihei is the unplanned outcome of South Maui's explosion of popularity during the 1970s and '80s. It's a linear collection of condos and strip malls. While it certainly lacks the old world charm of Lahaina, Kihei doesn't try to be anything other than what it is—a beach town—where everything is water-related. As for downtown Kihei, there is no such animal. The closest you could come to defining the town center is the Triangle, north of Auhana Street, south of Kihei Town Center. And that's a stretch.

Before it was developed, Kihei looked like what you see up the mountain: dry, scrubby and not overly attractive. Water was scarce. With no water to tap from this dry side of Haleakala, planners drilled wells over in water-rich West Maui and piped it in under the central plain. Most people who live here don't even know this, and when Upcountry experiences its occasional droughts, residents look resentfully down the hill at the green of Kihei and Wailea and wonder where *they* seem to get all their water.

South Kihei Road is quite a sight for first-timers. It's so close to the ocean and beaches, you recognize immediately how important the sea is to this town.

Though it may dry up in the summer, the existence of Kealia Pond, a wetland in perennially dry South Maui, is a surprise to everyone except the birds.

When the Big Island's King Kamehameha invaded Maui for the last (and ultimately successful) time, he came ashore in Kihei at one point. The fighting was fierce with Maui warriors employing a novel weapon—*heated* slingstones. Kamehameha's forces were a bit intimidated by the hot rocks and contemplated retreating. So Kamehameha ordered all of his warriors' canoes destroyed. The message was simple—win or die. With newfound motivation, his troops eventually won (with the help of some western cannons) and went on to conquer all the islands.

Though south Kihei and Wailea have some of the *best* beaches on the island, north Kihei won't get you so excited. In the past the problem was so bad we had to label the whole area as a *don't swim* zone on our map, but it's not nearly as bad these days.

As you pass Cove Park, note the color of the water. Brownish, right? Less than 200 yards south the water will get clean and clear again, and the next beach, Kama'ole Beach, offers fine swimming. From here on, it's nothing but great beach after great beach. All are described in the *Beaches* chapter. Outstanding Keawakapu Beach is the last beach you pass on South Kihei Road. Here the road veers away from the shoreline. You'll take a right

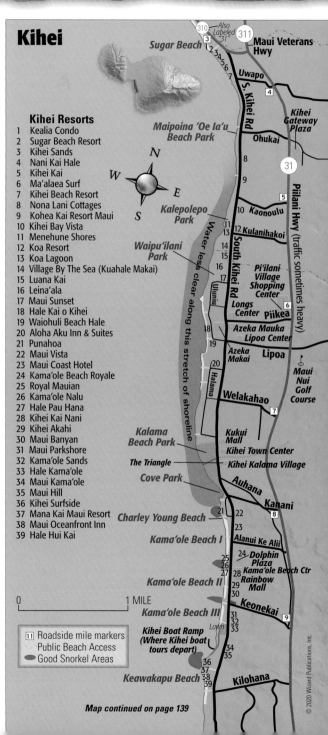

Kihei

Kihei Resorts
1 Kealia Condo
2 Sugar Beach Resort
3 Kihei Sands
4 Nani Kai Hale
5 Kihei Kai
6 Ma'alaea Surf
7 Kihei Beach Resort
8 Nona Lani Cottages
9 Kohea Kai Resort Maui
10 Kihei Bay Vista
11 Menehune Shores
12 Koa Resort
13 Koa Lagoon
14 Village By The Sea (Kuahale Makai)
15 Luana Kai
16 Leina'ala
17 Maui Sunset
18 Hale Kai o Kihei
19 Waiohuli Beach Hale
20 Aloha Aku Inn & Suites
21 Punahoa
22 Maui Vista
23 Maui Coast Hotel
24 Kama'ole Beach Royale
25 Royal Mauian
26 Kama'ole Nalu
27 Hale Pau Hana
28 Kihei Kai Nani
29 Kihei Akahi
30 Maui Banyan
31 Maui Parkshore
32 Kama'ole Sands
33 Hale Kama'ole
34 Maui Kama'ole
35 Maui Hill
36 Kihei Surfside
37 Mana Kai Maui Resort
38 Maui Oceanfront Inn
39 Hale Hui Kai

Also Labeled "31"
310 · 311
Sugar Beach · Maui Veterans Hwy
Uwapo
S. Kihei Rd
Kihei Gateway Plaza
Maipoina 'Oe Ia'u Beach Park · Ohukai
31
Kalepolepo Park · Kaonoulu
Kulanihakoi
Waipu'ilani Park
South Kihei Rd
Pi'ilani Village Shopping Center
Waterless clear along this stretch of shoreline
Uliniu
Longs Center · Piikea
Azeka Mauka Lipoa Center
Azeka Makai · Lipoa
Maui Nui Golf Course
Welakahao
Halama
Pi'ilani Hwy (traffic sometimes heavy)
Kukui Mall
Kalama Beach Park · Kihei Town Center
The Triangle · Kihei Kalama Village
Cove Park · Auhana
Kanani
Charley Young Beach
Kama'ole Beach I · Alanui Ke Ali'i
Dolphin Plaza
Kama'ole Beach Ctr
Rainbow Mall
Kama'ole Beach II
Keonekai
Kama'ole Beach III · Lawn
Kihei Boat Ramp (Where Kihei boat tours depart)
Kilohana
Keawakapu Beach

0 · 1 MILE

11 Roadside mile markers
Public Beach Access
Good Snorkel Areas

© 2020 Wizard Publications, Inc.

Map continued on page 139

on Wailea Alanui Road to continue your southward journey.

Breezes usually stiffen into winds in the afternoon in South Maui. (See *Weather* on page 26.) Most beach activities are best in the morning or late afternoon just before sunset.

If you're watching a sunset from South Maui, and the sky is clear of clouds, take a look behind you as soon as the sun sets. If Haleakala Summit is free of clouds, too, you'll see that the sun still shines there. It's so tall that the sun sets several minutes later on Haleakala, bathing it in sunlight when the sun itself has vanished from your eyes.

WAILEA

This is the premier resort area on the island (Kapalua's and Ka'anapali's claims notwithstanding). Expensive resorts line its heavenly beaches. Some, like the Fairmont Kea Lani, are so posh and exotic, you'll weep when you finally have to go back to the *real* world. While Kihei was an *every man for himself* development, the Wailea area had a single owner with a single vision: grand, green, groomed and golf. With splendid weather (cooler than Kihei and with lighter afternoon winds), phenomenal beaches, clean water and kickin' views of Molokini and Kaho'olawe, Wailea is a grand success.

There are no mile markers here, and some places don't have signs. If you reset your odometer at the corner of Wailea Ike and Wailea Alanui, we've marked distances on the maps or use our geo-aware app map to stay on course.

Many of the best beaches on the island are found right here. In addition to its beaches, Wailea has a glorious beachside path. Though not as long or as well known as Ka'anapali's path, it stretches between

Mokapu and Polo Beaches and is a perfect way for visitors at one Wailea resort to dine at another without messing with cars. It also makes a great place for a sunset stroll or a sunrise jogging path.

Wailea Alanui becomes Makena Alanui past the Fairmont Kea Lani. (That's the goofy-looking, though very luxurious, resort past the Four Seasons—someone was reading *The Arabian Nights* when they designed *that* one.) Segments of the old Makena Road visit less known beaches, such as Palauea and Makena, as well as snorkeling and diving areas like Five Graves. Kayakers often launch at Makena Landing.

One sound that's common in South Maui is the call of the gray francolin. This imported gamebird starts every morning with a surprisingly vigorous call, which sounds something like a car alarm.

MAKENA

Leaving Wailea and heading south, as you round the corner you'll notice a large hill near the ocean. The drama that created that hill was probably witnessed by the ancient Hawaiians.

Haleakala is in its twilight years as an active volcano. Its time is almost up. The typical life cycle for a Hawaiian volcano is to grow slowly beneath the sea through sporadic eruptions. It then begins vigorous, near-constant growth, building an island. Later it falls asleep for 500,000 to 1 million years and then awakens for its last hurrah before dying and eventually sinking beneath the sea under its own weight. O'ahu's Diamond Head is a product of its last gasp 300,000 years ago. Here, on Haleakala's southwestern flank, we see a volcano in its death throes. Its last eruption was around 1790 at the end of the road ahead. It was a "typical" surface flow: Lava squeezed from a vent and flowed downhill.

A REAL GEM

The eruption that created the large hill toward the sea, called Pu'u Ola'i, or Earthquake Hill, was not.

Hawaiian legend states that before the 1790 eruption, this was the last place on the island to erupt. Imagine how it must have looked if there were villagers living here at the time. Lava began quietly pooling beneath the surface in what was supposed to be just another "typical" surface flow. But because it was so close to the shoreline, sea water seeped into the magma pool. This water immediately flashed into steam, building up the pressure in the lava pool. Earthquakes began rumbling as the earth struggled to contain the pressure. Villagers may have begun to notice small amounts of steam coming from the ground. As more lava and seawater combined, something had to give. Suddenly, the ground ripped open with a tremendous explosion as fountains of bright orange and red lava shot into the sky. It must have been spectacularly large, because the entire hill you see before you was created as the gas-frothed lava fell to earth and piled up to form the 360-foot Pu'u Ola'i, perhaps in as little as a week. (Looks taller, doesn't it?)

Hiking up Pu'u Ola'i is more difficult than it looks. The trail to the top marches through the cinders (called *tephra* by geologists, in case you just *had* to know) that make up this mass. So, as you take a step up, the tendency is to fall back a few inches, making the climb more tiring. But the view from the top is magnificent. You can see Big Beach below on one side and much of Wailea on the other. The state closed the trail after an earthquake back in 2006 for "safety evaluation" and forgot to reopen it.

You may see signs in the area warning of deer crossing. These aren't a joke. Nine axis deer from India were brought here

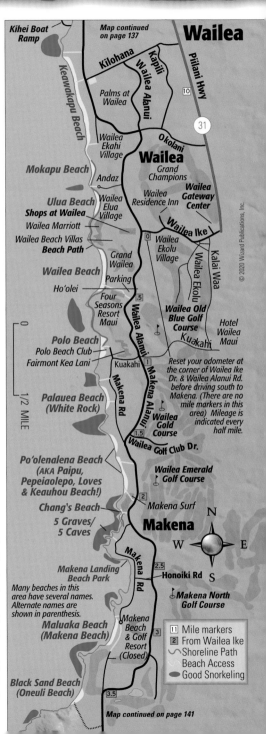

© 2020 Wizard Publications, Inc.

Stand up paddleboarding is all the rage in South Maui, although some people seem to have developed their own unique style.

in 1959. They were supposed to have a low reproductive potential, but Maui's romantic atmosphere apparently affects deer as well, because in the brief time they've been here, they've multiplied to around 8,000 and are considered a nuisance. (There were twice that many before a control program began.) Many of them live in this area and are occasionally whacked by passing cars. Golfers at Wailea's courses may find additional hazards on the greens when the deer come down from the mountains during times of drought Upcountry and leave souvenirs on the greens. They're most plentiful on Pu'u Ola'i.

There might be a few food stands on the side of the road in Makena. Avoid Jawz Tacos.

MOLOKINI

To residents and visitors in the know, the name Molokini conjures up images of crystal clear water and bright, vivid coral. If nature hadn't made this offshore is-

A REAL GEM

land, the Hawai'i Visitors Bureau would have done it. This aquatic wonder was created when an undersea vent, held under pressure by the ocean's weight, busted loose with lava and ash, building up what is called a tuff cone. The northern half has been eroded away by wave action, creating a semi-circular reef far enough offshore to be clear of runoff or sand. So underwater visibility is nearly always 100 feet, sometimes 180.

Visiting Molokini means taking a boat from either Ma'alaea (10 miles away) or Kihei Boat Ramp (6 miles). Though it seems close to Maui, don't try to take a kayak there. Currents and winds between Molokini and Maui are too strong for most kayakers.

The crater is a marine and bird sanctuary. You're not allowed to walk on the island. Once inside the crescent, you'll find the water inviting. See *Boat Tours* on page 189 for more. In the past, the crater was visited often by a lonely monk seal who was famous for swimming right up to divers. Boat captains nicknamed him

Humpy because of his... *unusually* friendly gestures toward swimmers. The seal was apparently unaware of the law prohibiting human contact with monk seals. If any monk seals visit Molokini while you're there, just remember that *they* have to initiate any contact.

The horizontal notch on the back of the crater is caused by wave cuts. If you were to SCUBA dive 250 feet down the back side, you'd find a similar wave cut, evidence that the ocean was *much* lower during a past ice age.

According to lore, the 19th-century King Kalakaua wagered Molokini in a hand of poker with a local rancher. When the king lost the hand, he reneged, proclaiming that he hadn't wagered Molokini, but rather *omole kini,* which is a bottle of gin.

LA PÉROUSE BAY

As you approach the end of the road, look on both sides of you. It appears to be a lumpy, tilled field, just waiting to be planted. That's a field of a'a lava rock, and it looks just the way it did when it erupted two centuries ago. Turn your attention to the split lava mound uphill just before the road's end. This is where the last eruption took place on Maui. Local legend states that there was a family living there at the time. An old woman came one day and asked for a chicken to eat. The family refused, saying that they first had to sacrifice some to the volcano goddess, Pele. The old woman raged, saying that *she* was Pele, and how dare they refuse her? She sent lava flowing their way. The mother and daughter fled toward the mountain, but Pele seized the two and turned them into stone. The hill you see, split in two, is made up of the mother and daughter, forever separated by a vengeful Pele.

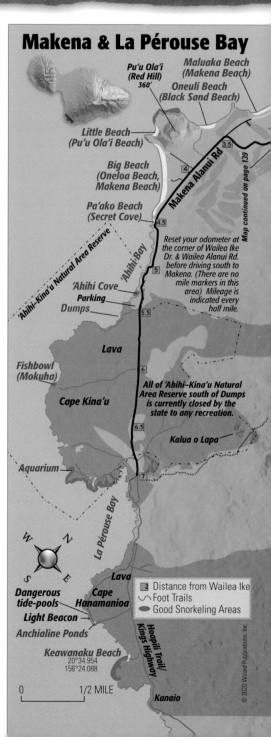

Makena & La Pérouse Bay

Pu'u Ola'i
(Red Hill)
360'

Maluaka Beach
(Makena Beach)

Oneuli Beach
(Black Sand Beach)

Little Beach
(Pu'u Ola'i Beach)

Big Beach
(Oneloa Beach,
Makena Beach)

Pa'ako Beach
(Secret Cove)

Makena Alanui Rd

3.5

4

Map continued on page 139

4.5

'Ahihi–Kina'u Natural Area Reserve

'Ahihi Bay

Reset your odometer at the corner of Wailea Ike Dr. & Wailea Alanui Rd. before driving south to Makena. (There are no mile markers in this area) Mileage is indicated every half mile.

'Ahihi Cove
Parking
Dumps

5

5.5

Lava

Fishbowl
(Mokuha)

Cape Kina'u

6

All of 'Ahihi–Kina'u Natural Area Reserve south of Dumps is currently closed by the state to any recreation.

6.5

Kalua o Lapa

Aquarium

7

La Pérouse Bay

Lava

Dangerous tide-pools

Cape Hanamanioa

Light Beacon

Anchialine Ponds

Keawanaku Beach
20°34.954
156°24.088

Hoapili Trail/
Kings Highway

2 Distance from Wailea Ike
⌃ Foot Trails
● Good Snorkeling Areas

0   1/2 MILE

Kanaio

© 2020 Wizard Publications, Inc.

Perfect days end with a perfect sunset.

La Pérouse Bay is as far as you can go by car in South Maui. It's renowned for two things: dolphins and wind. Dolphins are relatively common early in the morning. A pod patrols the area, and we often see them here around 7 a.m. and at Big Beach by around 10 a.m. But we often go months without seeing them at all. (Maybe dolphins take vacations, too.) Scientists think that, while resting, dolphins are able to turn off much of their brain (including the part that runs their echolocation abilities). They do a sort of snooze-and-cruise at La Pérouse in the early hours, counting on the fact that the shallow water and a light bottom will alert them to predators in the absence of their sonars. This means that, in the morning, dolphins are *literally* operating on half a brain. (Come to think of it, so am I before my coffee.)

It is illegal to chase or harass dolphins or do anything that disrupts their natural behavior. It may be hard to imagine slow, clumsy, human swimmers harassing sleek, fast dolphins, like a lowly crop duster harassing an F-16 fighter. If you're swimming near them, dolphins can distance themselves from you almost instantly with very little effort. But when they're resting, they're not in a very fast mood. They don't *want* to work to distance themselves. So if you swim in the same water near them, don't shoot like a shotgun in their direction. You can slowly meander toward their general vicinity, but you shouldn't try to box them in or head them off at the pass. They may initiate the contact, if they are interested. Many times we've been in the water and had dolphins come over to check us out.

Most of the time, however, they keep themselves at a cautious distance. If they don't stay away, you can only interpret their actions as curiosity. In short, don't harass or chase them or try to grab them if they come close. If people continually bug them, they'll simply stop coming to La Pérouse, and we'll all lose.

Wind is also a La Pérouse trademark. If you look at a *Rainfall Map* on page 28,

When was the Last Eruption on Maui?

Ask most people on Maui, "When was the last time there was an eruption here?" and you'll be told 1790. It's said so often it's considered an unchallenged fact. The truth is, no one knows when it happened. The 1790 date is based on the fact that when George Vancouver visited Maui in 1794, he drew a map showing the lava flow at Cape Kina'u (at the end of the road in South Maui). But when the French explorer La Pérouse visited earlier in 1786, his map didn't show the cape. This, coupled with the fact that the flow looks very young, allowed people to divide the time and conclude that the eruption occurred "around 1790."

The problem is this: As a mapmaker, La Pérouse was terrible. He didn't get anything right. And his map of the shoreline was so crude and inaccurate, you can't use it to determine anything—other than the fact that La Pérouse probably flunked out of cartography school. You'd never recognize these islands from his map. Recent carbon-14 dating puts the eruption closer to 500 years ago, give or take a century. And by analyzing crystals in the lava, they can check the direction of the earth's ever-changing magnetic field. The crystals don't match the flows that have been documented on the Big Island in 1801.

What about historical accounts? There were people living here and, after all, two centuries isn't that long. Didn't they witness it? Sure, they did, but nobody wrote it down. The Hawaiians didn't have a written language until western man invented one in the 1800s. The only known historical accounts of the last lava flow come from two sources. One was from an American missionary who came to Maui in 1841. He said the native Hawaiians had told him their "grandparents witnessed it." Hmm, pretty slim. The only other account is from a Hawaiian cowboy named Charlie Ako. In 1906 he told a reporter that his father-in-law said that his grandfather had seen the flow when he was "old enough to carry two coconuts from the sea to the upper road," which was 4–5 miles. The reporter plugged in various ages and dates, assuming 33 years per generation, and came up with around 1750.

So we have map readers saying 1790, historical accounts saying 1750, and some scientific tests saying around 1490. Since we had to use some date, we mention the 1790 date in this book. But now you know the full story.

So now if someone tells you that the last eruption on Maui took place in 1790, you can look them directly in the eye and tell them with smug certainty... mmmaybe.

you can see that wind coming from the northeast (our usual trade direction) will build up along the bottom of Haleakala and get ejected where the flank ends here at La Pérouse Bay, shooting out toward Kaho'olawe island. The wind-caused chop on the water will usually start at the south end of the bay and work its way north throughout the day. The dividing line between choppy and calm water is often sharp, typically around 100 feet wide.

La Pérouse Bay was well known in ancient times as a place where night marchers could be found. Called Huaka'i po, it refers to spirits who are still trapped on earth and generally cause mischief at night. To this day, there are places Hawaiians avoid at night because of night marchers. On Kaua'i there was a night marcher area that had an unusual string of bad car wrecks, which many believed were due to these spirits. (Police, however, blamed the wrecks on the other type of spirits—the kind in a bottle.)

Past La Pérouse there is a hike to a usually deserted black, white and green sand beach called Keawanaku. The setting is incredible, and the snorkeling can be great there, but the hiking trail has some obnoxious footing. See *Activities* on page 226.

You can see the upper highway less than 3 miles uphill from Wailea. The county has spent 20 years and millions of dollars *studying* a Kahului Bypass to get you upcountry faster. After all that effort, there's still no road, and you should take a look at the graphic to see what route they envision. In 2010, Oprah (yes, *that* Oprah) and her buddies paved their own private highway that goes right up to the upper highway. It's nice to be Oprah. A couple of other parties also have their own private roads. But in the meantime the rest of us will have to drive the 30-mile detour through Kahului to get up the hill.

SOUTH MAUI BEST BETS

Best Place for a Stroll—Shoreline Path from Mokapu Beach to Polo Beach

Best Snorkeling—Between Po'olenalena and Palauea

Best Place to Toast Your Da Kines— Little Beach

Best Time to Wish You Were Oprah's Friend—When You Want to Drive Upcountry From Kihei

Best Example of What Should Be a Misplaced Decimal Point... But Isn't— Up to $1,250 to Use a Cabana for One Day at the Grand Wailea

Best Long Beach Stroll—Ma'alaea Bay

Best Boogie Boarding—Kama'ole III

Best Place to See a Local Music Legend—Mulligan's on the Blue on Wednesdays for the Willie K Dinner Show

Best Nightlife—The Triangle (aka Bar-Muda Triangle) Across from Kalama Beach Park

Kahului

What you gotta do—

County Solution
(Someday in the future)

Where you
want to go

You are
here

Oprah's
Private
Solution
(Now)

Haleakala

Kihei

Wailea

The desolation of uninhabited Kahoʻolawe, its hardpan exposed by unchecked erosion, is a vivid reminder of what both indigenous and modern man can do to the land. West Maui rises in the background.

One of things that adds to the exotic nature of Maui is the abundance of offshore islands. Somehow, seeing multiple islands across the water adds mystery to the scene. Islands are never more intriguing than when they are tantalizingly out of reach. Because of the way they are sprinkled about, no other Hawaiian island has such great views of offshore islands. For instance, when you awaken for your first day at Kaʻanapali, you are confronted by islands dominating your view. Is that Kahoʻolawe? No wait... that's the other part of Maui; the land bridge is below the horizon. Is that Lanaʻi? No, Molokaʻi is where Lanaʻi should be. Here's the general rule. Molokaʻi dominates the view from Kapalua, Lanaʻi is offshore of Lahaina, and Kahoʻolawe is the closest to South Maui.

We haven't attempted to make this a complete guide to other nearby islands, but you may want to know a little about your neighbors. Some can even be visited by boat trips listed on page 189 or by helicopter trips listed on page 179. Since Maui is the gateway to the resorts of Lanaʻi, we're including some information on them here.

KAHOʻOLAWE

If you're staying in Kihei, Kahoʻolawe is the impressive island offshore behind the tiny crescent islet of **Molokini**. Though it looks enticing from afar, Kaho'olawe is an ecological mess.

History revisionists (most of whom have almost certainly never visited Kaho'olawe) attribute Kaho'olawe's ecological woes to either the military or western man in general. The truth can be a little more embarrassing. When the ancient Hawaiians discovered these islands, they found on Kaho'olawe a fragile dryland forest. It was a marginal environment to live in due to its location in the rain shadow of Maui. Dry, thin soil populated by hearty but water-starved trees and shrubs marked the windswept island. In the course of their settlement, the Hawaiians cut down most of the trees on the island to make canoes, for firewood and other purposes. Without roots to hold the soil together, erosion became the thief that stole the essence of Kaho'olawe.

In fact, by the time Captain Cook first encountered the islands in the 1770s, Kaho'olawe was no longer inhabited and was instead used only as a campsite for visiting fishermen. When the king of the Big Island invaded Maui in the 1780s, he made a separate trip over to Kaho'olawe and was furious when he discovered there was nothing to steal or plunder there and only a few fishermen to terrorize. When Maui children of that era asked their parents why nobody lived on the island across the waters, they were told it was because the island was sacred. Perhaps, but it was also used up.

In the mid-1800s the Hawaiian government used Kaho'olawe and Lana'i as penal colonies. Crimes that got you banished to Kaho'olawe included rebellion, theft, divorce, breaking marriage vows and murder. Starvation was rampant there and desperate escape attempts were common.

Later, western man introduced feral animals: goats, pigs and cattle. Their destructive hooves and grazing quickly completed the ecological rampage.

During WWII the military took control of Kaho'olawe and used it for target practice. It was later seized by direct presidential order for exclusive use by the military. But the damage from their target practice was minimal compared to what the island had already experienced and was mostly limited to a smaller area. (Hitting a stationary island of 44.5 square miles is, after all, a pretty poor demonstration of marksmanship. Their goal was to hit a certain *part* of the island.) Often, the military would put an old jeep in an open area and fire at it. Residents of Kihei grew up to the booming sound coming from 7 miles across the water.

After a half-century of live fire, President George H.W. Bush signed an executive order in 1990 halting all target practice on the island. Even after an expensive multi-year "cleanup," a large number of unexploded small ordnance remains scattered about the entire island, enough to make it a dangerous place to wander around.

The result today is an island robbed of topsoil in many places, leaving nothing but an unforgiving hardpan layer. The areas that still harbor plants feature mostly gray shrubs and grasses. There is no permanent source of water other than wells. But despite that, there is a stark beauty to the place. It looks nothing like the rest of Hawai'i.

But don't count on booking your Kaho'olawe vacation anytime soon. The island was transferred to native Hawaiian control in 1994. They are trying to replant native species and increase the amount of soil. It's a hot, tiring job, but it's hoped that future generations will find a

Kahoʻolawe that is much like what long-ago Hawaiians found. An ancient name for the island was *Kohemalamalama-o-Kanaloa*, meaning the shining... birth canal of Kanaloa. It was an important location for wayfinders as they embarked on their voyages to the South Pacific.

Going back in time is a rare event in this world, and islands don't often get a second chance. Maybe the island will benefit from our hindsight and our diligence.

LANAʻI

For most of the 20th century Lanaʻi was known as the pineapple island. Almost 98 percent of the island was owned by Dole Pineapple, and pineapple dominated this 140.5-square-mile island. In the late '80s the owners decided that owning a secluded Hawaiian island was more valuable than owning pineapple fields. So they got out of pineapple and began marketing Lanaʻi as the "private island," complete with two high-end resorts and excellent golfing.

In 2012 the island got a new owner when Larry Ellison acquired his largest trophy property for around $300 million. (He probably bought it with spare change he found in the seats of his private jet. Ellison is one of the richest men in the world, worth over $60 billion.)

Ellison is investing a *ton* of money into the island. The previous billionaire owner was widely perceived to have lost interest, so Ellison's frantic pace of construction has had a profound effect on sleepy Lanaʻi. It has also created tight accommodations because of the need to house so many construction workers. Upgrading both Four Seasons resorts and the smaller Hotel Lanaʻi, as well as a planned resort at the remote site of the former Club Lanaʻi, has drawn workers from all over the state. And until Ellison ramps down his pace, you should consider Lanaʻi a moving target.

In 2017 he announced plans to put another $75 million into the Lodge at Koʻele Four Seasons with the goal of making it a place where people come from afar to improve themselves through meditation, yoga and "serene image immersion." He is also planning to make greenhouses high-tech on the island through the use of computer automation and solar energy. No matter what you think of Ellison, he's certainly putting his money where his mouth is on Lanaʻi, and most residents seem to be pretty glad he's the owner.

Most of the island's 3,200 residents work for the landowner, often paying cheap, subsidized rent. More than once we've seen residents taking the ferry to Lahaina to pick up stacks of pizzas for delivery back to Lanaʻi City. (Lanaʻi is a tad out of Domino's delivery range.)

Lying in the rain shadow of West Maui, Lanaʻi is arid, receiving only 10–20 inches of rain annually in most locations, and it's certainly not the most attractive island you'll visit. Some of its beaches, however, are excellent. Taking the **Expeditions Maui–Lanaʻi Ferry** (808-661-3756) for $30 each way is the most popular way to get there. (Sit on the right/starboard side going over.) There are also flights into the airport on **Hawaiian Airlines** (800-367-5320) and **Mokulele Airlines** (808-495-4188).

Lanaʻi is an amazingly relaxing place to stay. The second day into our first visit, we were tempted to call the front desk and complain that someone had broken into our room and surgically removed our bones. You can actually *feel* motivation and ambition draining from your body. The downside to the relaxing nature is the lack of options available to you here. The island is dominated by a few players who have more control over you than you may realize.

Rental car prices will shock you. In fact, *everything* is expensive on Lana'i. It's easy to let expenses get away from you since nearly every place on the island lets you charge things to your room, including private Jeep rentals. (It's called check-out shock, and it can be fatal for those with weak hearts.) The main rental company outside the resorts is **Lana'i Car Rental** (808-999-0682). Their fleet is limited to 3 vehicle types: Jeep Wrangler Saharas for $195 per day, Ford Transit Minivans for $155 per day, and electric Chevy Volts for $95 per day.

Though resort personnel "aren't supposed to tell you this," there is another company renting Jeeps on the island with better prices. **Lana'i Adventure Club** (808-565-7373) also provides coolers, etc., with the Jeep, has fewer restrictions on where you can drive (*that's important*), and their

mud tires are better than Lana'i Car Rental's. Sure, their Jeeps are a bit more banged up. But that's because they allow *you* to bang 'em. They also have ATV and bicycle rentals and tours.

West of the town you come to the **Garden of the Gods**, a very dramatic collection of weathered boulders eroded over eons in a serene setting best seen in the early morning or late afternoon.

Past here a dirt road leads down to **Polihua Beach**, over a mile long and super wide. Take a tip from us and *don't* drive on the sand at the north end of the beach. Beneath that sand lurks a swampy goo that will snag your vehicle. And you'll spend hours and hours trying in vain to get it free, then someone else will get stuck trying to help and...Sorry, had a flashback.

At the north end of the island you'll find miles of empty beaches and a shipwreck off to the left. (There's another

Epic meals next to an epic beach for epic prices. You'll be forgiven if you start to wonder if Lana'i is the Hawaiian word for, "It costs how much?"

wreck to the west, but it's hard to access.) Driving eastbound along the northern coast you eventually come to the old Club Lana'i and the nearby sugar mill, an abandoned day trip location for sailing trips from Maui.

Before Club Lana'i (an abandoned day retreat) you'll see a wooden church on the mauka side of the road. (Be careful of the numerous wasps often nesting there.) A trail leading inland for 5 minutes takes you to the remains of an old sugar mill from the early 20th century. It only operated three years. This dry, scrubby windswept area was a *profoundly* bad place to grow sugar and may have even been a scam by the land owner at the time to lure unsuspecting investors. But the results of this short-lived sugar attempt were also terrible for the environment. They clear-cut the land, then planted thorny kiawe (mesquite) trees to use as fuel for the mill. The trees now dominate, so watch for the wicked thorns that can go through your shoes. Worse was the runoff that choked the reef. The amount of soil that washed away was so great that it extended the shoreline 300 feet. You can see for yourself by visiting the remains of an old boat across the street from the church. Where the boat currently lies *used* to be the beach. But if you walk past it to the ocean (you won't, unless you brought your Kevlar-lined boots for the thorns), you'll realize just how much soil was washed away.

Back in the center of the island in Lana'i City, to expand your knowledge and appreciation for the island, you'll want to visit the Lana'i Culture and Heritage Center. They showcase an impressive historical collection on all things Lana'i.

The main beach at the hotel is probably among the top 10 beaches in the state. Called Hulopo'e Beach, it has a huge sand deposit and good swimming coupled with unreal snorkeling on the left (southeast) end of the beach. Venture along the rocky shoreline away from the beach, and you're treated to some very dramatic underwater scenery. Not because of the coral (which is sparse) or the fish (which are abundant) or visibility (often a bit cloudy), but because of the canyon-like lattice structure of the lava and dead coral. Chasms, holes, stacks and arches create a miniature Bryce Canyon with exciting possibilities. Avoid during moderate to high surf, however, or it may get *too* exciting due to surginess. Occasionally, large Kona storm runoff causes severe water cloudiness that can last for many months. You can easily walk to the beach from the ferry landing.

Staying on Lana'i

Check out the *Where to Stay* section of our app for reviews of the Four Seasons at Manele Bay, Four Seasons Lodge at Ko'ele and Hotel Lana'i. All resort reviews are in the free section of the app, so it won't cost you a penny. (Which is more than we can say for what your hotel stay will set you back on Lana'i.)

MOLOKA'I

Moloka'i is a long, skinny island of immense beauty and unimaginable sea cliffs. It's 260 square miles, though it was once much larger. The island owes its shape to the type of cataclysmic event that sometimes occurs with Hawaiian volcanoes. Much of the volcano from east Moloka'i broke off and fell into the sea hundreds of thousands of years ago, where *half-mile-sized* chunks of rock rolled to a stop 100 miles away. The landslide created awesome sea cliffs up to 3,000 feet high—the highest in the world—which are continually undercut by the ocean's waves. Think about the mind-boggling forces involved in that event. The entire Pacific rim was affected as tidal waves of skyscraper heights ravaged shorelines thousands of miles away. Moloka'i is not alone in experiencing this kind of apocalyptic event. The Big Island had a slide 120,000 years ago, and the resulting wave swept over Kaho'olawe and tossed chunks of coral up to the 1,000 foot elevation level on Lana'i. Kaho'olawe and probably Lana'i and Ni'ihau also experienced monster landslides.

The population of Moloka'i is around 8,000, and there is not a single traffic light on the whole island. Not all is rosy on Moloka'i, however. The island has a perpetually dismal economy. Most residents are on some kind of government assistance. Though the island's nickname is "the friendly island," you may find just the opposite. Though residents are very friendly with each other (the only repetitive motion injury residents are likely to suffer is from drivers constantly waving at each other), many (though by no means all) tend to be pretty reserved with visitors. The grumpy reputation is, to a certain extent, for effect. Most residents here don't *want* many visitors and don't *want* a friendly reputation, even if they are nice to you on a one-to-one basis. The belief is that community stink eye can help keep the island from being developed and its resources depleted. (It's a favorite island of many visitors because of its undeveloped nature, but many complain of feeling unwelcome.) No trespassing signs are conspicuously few. You either belong somewhere or you don't, and residents don't need signs to tell them that.

Local residents had a nasty little war going on with the island's largest landowner, Moloka'i Ranch, which owns over *a third* of the island (mostly on the drier western half). When the ranch built a pipeline to carry water to another part of the island, vandals destroyed it. While the ranch suffered tens of millions of dollars in losses from their operations, residents stopped them from doing any development. As a last ditch effort to save the business, Moloka'i Ranch threw a Hail Mary. They proposed developing a 500-acre strip of land at La'au Point on the extreme southwestern tip. They agreed to use proceeds from the sale of luxury lots at the otherwise inaccessible land to rebuild the long-closed Sheraton resort and to set aside 50,000 acres (over three-quarters of all their land holdings) for conservation. But residents opposed them. Handmade save la'au signs went up all over the island, and local activists influenced the land use commission to turn down Moloka'i Ranch's plans.

So in 2008 the company essentially quit the island. They closed their two remaining resorts, shut down the gas station and movie complex in Maunaloa and closed off access to their third of the island. After being thwarted in their quest to build windmills on the island and send the electricity to O'ahu in 2014, the war now seems pretty much over… and both sides lost. There is a little activity taking place on their land, but Maunaloa is still a ghost town with only a private general store open next to Moloka'i Ranch's office. Most other buildings have been abandoned and vandalized. The owner put the property on the market in 2017, and it can all be yours for a mere quarter *billion* dollars.

The port town and population center of the island is Kaunakakai. This is where you'll find almost all dining options, grocery stores and Hotel Moloka'i.

Visiting Moloka'i

In the past you could get to Moloka'i by ferry, but today you'll have to fly. **Mokulele Airlines** (866-260-7070), **Makani**

Kai Air (808-834-1111) and Hawaiian (800-367-5320) fly to the main Moloka'i airport from Maui. Package deals that include round trip flights and tours of either the topside or Kalaupapapa's former leprosy settlement are available through Father Damien Tours (808-349-3006). See page 262.

Once on island, your biggest decision is which way to go. Either turn right (east) if the weather's good, or left if it's not. East wanders along the dry, southern part of the island. Private fishponds line almost the entire shoreline. With no one in front and no one in your rearview mirror, Moloka'i feels like it's all yours.

Once 20 miles out of Kaunakakai, the scenery turns dramatic (and the road narrows). The sweet payoff 30 miles from Kaunakakai is the end of the road, and the vista alone is almost worth the trip. Halawa Valley is isolated, quaint and strikingly beautiful. Backed by tall waterfalls, the descent into the valley is marvelous. Once at the bottom, Moloka'i's "friendly" nickname becomes laughable. There's a good dirt road and path leading back to the falls, but makeshift signs tell you not to go, and we strongly suggest, for your own good, that you heed them. (Or pay someone for a guided tour.)

Moloka'i's 3,000 foot sea cliffs are the tallest on the planet, and the offshore scenery they provide is the essence of exotic.

Toward the middle of the island, a 6-mile detour from the highway leads to Moloka'i's biggest must-see, the Kalaupapa Overlook. Moloka'i was notorious in the 1800s as the site of the state's leprosy settlement. Leprosy (now known as Hansen's Disease) may have been brought back to Hawai'i by a chief who had visited abroad in 1840 or by Chinese laborers a bit later. Stricken patients were banished to an isolated peninsula called Kalaupapa when their condition was discovered. They didn't come here to live with the disease; they came to die. It was a hideous and vile place in those days, completely neglected by a Hawaiian government that only wanted to forget it existed.

A 33-year-old priest from Belgium named Father Damien arrived in 1873 and tended to the unfortunates, living closely with them. Giving no thought to his own safety, he eventually contracted the disease and died there in 1889. The method of transmission was baffling to 19th-century doctors. They had no way of knowing that over 95 percent of the human population is naturally immune to the disease, which means that 19 out of 20 priests sent to Kalaupapa could never have contracted it. Damien was genetically unfortunate to be among the 5 percent who could. Though his last 16 years of life were a selfless dedication to the most reviled and abused people among us, Damien was tormented on his deathbed with the fear that he was unworthy of heaven. The Catholic Church felt otherwise, and in 2009 he was officially declared a saint.

Though the disease has a cure now, there are still a handful of elderly, former leprosy patients living at Kalaupapa, which is now a national park. (Some Kalaupapa residents prefer the more modern term, Hansen's Disease; others prefer to leave it as *leprosy*. All hate the term *leper*.) Mule rides down into the area (when available) are the most popular activity on Moloka'i. (See *Adventures* on page 262 for more.)

From the unbelievably beautiful overlook, you realize why 19th-century Hawaiian officials chose this place. After the volcano collapsed and created the sea cliffs, the apparently cold magma chamber came back to life for one last creation. It erupted at the base of the cliff and created land that is adjacent to but utterly apart from the rest of the island. Only a man-made trail, gouged in the side of the cliffs, allows land access.

As you stand at the overlook, with the wind whistling through the trees, the ghosts of misery and pain banished there a century ago can seem all too real. It's ironic that a place once so despised is today a visitor attraction. Perhaps that's the only way to completely clear away the haze of despair that once filled the air.

Most of the workers at Kalaupapa live there, but there are a half dozen workers who hike in every week. *Big deal,* you say! Well, yeah, it is. The hike includes going down and then up a *1,700*-foot-high mountain. They say the biggest haz-

Two miles long and not a soul to be found. Welcome to Moloka'i's west side.

ards are the mules on the trail that don't like to be passed and have a nasty habit of kicking hikers when they try. Now *that's* a commute!

The other attraction near the overlook is Kaule-o-Nanahoa or (Phallic Rock). It's a five-minute uphill walk. To the ancient Hawaiians, the 6-foot-tall stone in the shape of a gigantic... well, *you* know... represents fertility. It's really quite a remarkable... uh, formation. (It may have had some human help.) Even today, some Hawaiians believe that if women sit or sleep on it, they will conceive. Legend states that the rock is what remains of a husband who should have kept his eye on his work.

The west side of Moloka'i is drier and flatter. Vast beaches line much of the shoreline. You'll have the opportunity to create the only footprints in long stretches of sand, though some of the west side beaches are often *very* windy.

Visiting West Moloka'i is both sad and delightful. Sad because so much has been abandoned and vandalized, the result of a feud between the landowners and local residents. Delightful because the enormous beaches on the west side are empty, there is certainly never any traffic, and you will not find a more peaceful place to get away from it all. There is one resort, the old Sheraton, now called Kepuhi Beach Resort (aka Kepuhi Villas), and visiting it is a bizarre experience. The resort fell into disrepair decades ago and half of it closed, along with the restaurant and golf course. But the other half of the units were sold as condos and their owners still live there or rent them out as vacation rentals. You can find them on sites such as Airbnb. They won't be as inexpensive as you might expect, given the remoteness and lack of restaurants within 15 miles, but this is a good choice if you need to de-stress and want peace and quiet as well as access to a beautiful, though often treacherous, beach.

If you're returning your car from either the west or Kalaupapa Overlook, don't bother driving back to Kaunakakai to gas up. Save the 20 minutes and eat the extra few bucks to have the rental car company gas up.

Moloka'i Dining

While in Kaunakakai, there is limited but surprisingly good food options. The best known restaurant also has the best food. Kanemitsu's Bakery, though labeled a coffee shop is so much more. They are open for breakfast and lunch, then shut down until 7:30 for dinner. It is when they open for dinner that the sweet bread comes out fresh, and there is a line pretty much every night. Their sweet bread is an experience unto itself, and all Hawaiians who visit are required (seemingly by law) to bring some back home to their families. Only those in the line up know how good it really is, though. The center is gooey and can be eaten plain, but a variety of toppings can take you to the sweet or savory side. Breakfast and lunch are diner-style with their French toast and fried rice most popular. If you like to spice things up, try the kim chee fried rice. Dinner is made up of changing menu of pasta, steak and seafood.

The local watering hole is Paddler's Inn. Steak, seafood, burgers and a few pupus make up the menu for both lunch and dinner, plus daily specials (which tend to be better than items on the regular menu). Moloka'i Pizza Café (808-553-3288) and Moloka'i Burger (808-553-3533) are both excellent, fast options and as good as any you'd find on Maui. The burger joint is the only drive-through on the island.

We're not saying this is the best beach on Maui. But you can be here eight minutes after picking up your rental car, and you might have it to yourself. Just make sure you walk the correct way at Kanaha Beach.

Of all the Hawaiian islands, Maui probably has the most user-friendly beaches. Nearly all the sand beaches on the island are concentrated in the more protected leeward areas of West and South Maui. If you were designing your own island, that's *exactly* where you'd put them, because the other side of the island is exposed to more surf and runoff. The few beaches in Hana are good, but the remaining windward beaches near Kahului won't ring your chimes.

Because of this topographic blessing, Maui is considered by many to be the *Ocean Island*. In fact, so much of the Maui experience is centered around beaches (to a greater degree than any of the other Hawaiian islands) that we've had to endure countless hours assessing the characteristics of each individual beach. Which ones worked best for snorkeling, boogie boarding, swimming or just plain frolicking? Sometimes this research was as simple as determining if a sunset mai tai worked better at one beach than another. (See, and you thought that writing guidebooks and apps was all fun and games. There's a *serious* work ethic involved.)

Here you can snorkel exceptional reefs, boogie board till you're raw, take a 3-mile beach walk, dig your fingers into genuine volcanic black sand, catch rays on a red sand beach, and sip a cocktail under a palm tree on a golden sand beach. Maui's beaches have earned their legendary status.

BEACH SAFETY

The biggest danger you will face at the beach is the surf. Though most beaches are on the calmer part of the island, that's a relative term. Most mainlanders are unprepared for the strength of Hawai'i's surf. We're out in the middle of the biggest ocean in the world, and the surf has lots of room to build up. We have our calm days when the water is like glass. We often have days where the surf is moderate, calling for respect and diligence on the part of the swimmer. And we have the high surf days, perfect for sitting on the beach, watching the experienced and the audacious tempt the ocean's patience. To get **current weather forecasts**, call (808) 944-3756. For a **surf forecast**, call (808) 572-7873, or go to the **Weather and Surf** link and the **Know Before You Go** section on our website. Don't make the mistake of underestimating the ocean's power here. Hawai'i is the undisputed drowning capital of the United States, and we don't want you to join the statistics.

Other hazards include rip currents, which can form, cease and form again with no warning. Large "rogue waves" can come ashore with no warning. These usually occur when two or more waves fuse at sea, becoming a larger wave. Even calm seas are no guarantee of safety. Many people have been caught unaware by large waves during ostensibly "calm seas." We swam and snorkeled the beaches described in this book on at least two occasions (usually much more than two). But beaches change. The underwater topography changes throughout the year. Storms can take a very safe beach and rearrange the sand, turning it into a dangerous beach. Just because we describe a beach as being in a certain condition does not mean it will be in that same condition when you visit it.

Consequently, you should take the beach descriptions as a snapshot in calm times. If seas aren't calm, you probably shouldn't go in the water. If you observe a rip current, you probably shouldn't go in the water. If you aren't a comfortable swimmer, you should probably never go in the water, except at those beaches that have lifeguards. There is no way we can tell you that a certain beach will be swimmable on a certain day, and we claim no such prescience. For instance, a strong storm and accompanying swells one year swept lots of sand from South Maui beaches and mucked up the water so badly, it took months to recover, making beachgoing a different experience. There is no substitution for your own observations and judgment.

A few standard safety tips: Never turn your back on the ocean. Never swim alone. Never swim in the mouth of a river. Never swim in murky water. Never swim when the seas are not calm. Don't walk too close to the shorebreak; a large wave can come and knock you over and pull you in. Observe ocean conditions carefully. Don't let small children play in the water unsupervised. Fins give you far more power and speed and are a good safety device in addition to being more fun. If you're comfortable in a mask and snorkel, they provide considerable peace of mind in addition to opening up the underwater world. Lastly, don't let Hawai'i's idyllic environment cloud your judgment. Recognize the ocean for what it is—a powerful force that needs to be respected.

This is a good time to repeat that water shoes make entering and exiting beaches that aren't 100 percent sandy *much* easier. Longs Drugs and lots of other stores sell them. Even if you *think* a beach has a completely sandy bottom, toes have well-known magnetic properties and will often attract that lone jagged rock, ruining an otherwise perfect beach day. While snorkeling, we like to use water shoes and fins that fit over them. See the *Snorkeling* on page 245 for more.

Theft can be a problem when visiting beaches. Visitors like to lock their cars at all beaches, but **piles of glass** on the ground usually dissuade island residents from doing that at secluded beaches. We usually remove anything we can't bear to have stolen and leave the car with the windows rolled up but unlocked. That way, we're less likely to get our windows broken by a curious thief. Regardless, don't leave anything of value in your car. (Well... maybe the seats can stay.) You might want to find a place to discreetly stash your keys and other valuables. We don't take a camera (except disposables) to the beach unless we are willing to stay there on the sand and baby-sit it. This way, when we swim, snorkel or just walk, we don't have to constantly watch our things.

Use **sunscreen** early and often. Don't pay any attention to the claims from sunscreen makers that their product is waterproof, rubproof, sandblast proof, powerwash proof, etc. Reapply it every couple of hours and after you get out of the ocean. The ocean water will hide sunburn symptoms until after you're toast. Then you can look forward to agony for the rest of your trip. (And yes, you *can* get burned while in the water; that's where most people here get cooked.)

Water quality around most of Maui can be amazingly clear. (Just look at the photo on page 2.) The Pacific Ocean is kind enough to provide a roughly east-to-west current that constantly replaces our water with clean, clear, open ocean water. There are, however, several spots where geography and human action conspire to mess up the water. They are: **north Kihei**, off **Lahaina** (especially the north part of town), **Kahana** (sometimes),

Kahului Harbor and around **Pa'ia**. Waters in these areas *can be* unpleasant, so avoid them. Runoff from storms inevitably washes lots of nasty stuff into the ocean, especially around any place where fresh water enters the sea. Brown water advisories are the worst of this and you shouldn't go in the water if one is issued.

The Hawai'i Supreme Court ruled in 2006 that all beaches are public to "the upper reaches of the wash of the waves...at high tide during the season of the year in which the highest wash of the waves occurs." This means that you can park yourself on any stretch of shoreline sand you like. The trick, sometimes, can be access. You might have to cross private land to get to a public beach. We've pointed out a legal way to every beach on the island, and some of the maps have access routes in yellow to show you the way.

In general, **surf** is higher and stronger during the winter, calmer in the summer, but there are exceptions during all seasons. Compared to the rest of the island, South Maui waters *tend* to be calmer year round. When we mention that a beach has facilities, it usually includes restrooms, showers, picnic tables and drinking water.

If you encounter any **Hawaiian monk seals** during your beach excursions, be sure to give them plenty of space. They are endangered and beaching is perfectly normal. By not disturbing them, you increase the chances that they will continue to increase their presence on Maui.

Mornings are almost always best. Wind in South Maui and north of Lahaina in West Maui picks up in the late morning and early afternoon.

A few of Maui's beaches have lifeguards at them and are highlighted with this ➊ symbol. They are **D.T. Fleming** and **Hanaka'o'o** in West Maui, the three **Kama'oles** in Kihei, **Big Beach** in Makena, and **H.A.**

Ok, Ok. So the name Slaughterhouse Beach doesn't exactly look good on a postcard. But the beach sure does.

Baldwin, Hoʻokipa and Kanaha near Kahului. Also Hana Bay in the summer.

If you have any other questions about beach safety, refer to *Hazards* on page 32. It gives plenty of insight as to what you may encounter both at the beach and on land.

Lastly, remember that just because *you* may be on vacation doesn't mean that residents are. Consequently, beaches are more crowded on weekends.

We're starting our *Beaches* chapter at the upper left side of the island and working our way down the coast in a counter-clockwise direction.

WEST MAUI BEACHES

West Maui doesn't have *as many* good beaches or good snorkeling areas as South Maui, but the best ones here really shine.

❖ Punalau / Keoneheleleʻi Beach

Also called Keoneheleleʻi Beach and sometimes Windmill Beach, it's 0.3 miles long and backed by abundant shade trees. During high surf (usually in the winter), large, well-formed waves break on a lava bench particularly close to shore, making it a perfect place to watch the surf. During calm seas, the beach is fronted by a bouldery tide-pool and clean water, making the

snorkeling interesting, though shallow. Swimming and snorkeling are only advisable during very calm seas since unusually strong currents can form during higher seas. Access is from a *rough* 4WD dirt road 0.7 miles past (east of) mile marker 34. You're better off walking it a few minutes down to the beach. During the week few visit this beach compared to other beaches in the area. Popular with local kite surfers.

❖ Honolua Bay

A REAL GEM

There's no sand beach—just a rocky shoreline—so you aren't going to come here to relax. And water quality is frustratingly variable due to a stream that tends to muck up visibility in the bay after a heavy rain. But when conditions cooperate, Honolua offers truly *outrageous* snorkeling and SCUBA diving. (See photo on page 2.) Tour companies literally bring paying customers here by the boatload, charging more than $100 per person. But since you were savvy enough to do a little research first, you get to visit for free.

The left side of the bay (from the beach, looking at the ocean) is shallower, and that's where you're more likely to find sea turtles. There are also lots of interesting lava formations with crevasses and gullies to explore. But the better coral formations are to the right side. You'll need to swim a fair way out to get to the good stuff—the bottom near the beach is littered with small boulders covered in silt. Hug the shoreline for about 150 yards, and you'll come to breathtaking underwater scenery.

The middle of the bay has a featureless sand bottom and is used as a boat channel, so it's better to follow the coastline rather than swim directly across to get from one side to the other. If you swim all the way out to the point on the left, you can go around to Slaughterhouse Beach, but be aware of a swirling eddy that usually forms at the point that can churn you around.

Honolua Bay is a reserve, making fishing and spearing illegal, so fish counts *can* be high here. Water is colder due to freshwater springs percolating up from the ground. Unlike most island beaches, mornings aren't *necessarily* best here. Summer is better than winter, which sometimes brings monstrous waves. If you see lots of surfers out around the point to the right, it means waves have stirred things up and snorkeling conditions aren't at their best.

Parking may be a problem. You probably won't see mile marker 32 on Highway 30, but past it are the stairs down to Slaughterhouse Beach. Then 0.5 miles past Slaughterhouse are several small turnouts where you'll find well-worn paths leading a few minutes' walk through vine-covered trees to the water. (The walk is almost as enjoyable as the snorkeling.) Enter the water at an old boat ramp.

If those turnouts are full, you'll have to drive past them and park where you can. Portable toilets on the highway.

Honolua is occasionally canvassed by car break-in maggots, so don't leave anything valuable in your car.

❖ Slaughterhouse Beach

Ooh, doesn't *that* sound inviting? The Hawaiian name is **Mokule'ia Bay** (which itself is often misspelled as **Makuleia**). This beach gets its commonly used name from a long-gone slaughterhouse that used to be above the cliffs. This relatively small pocket beach has lots of sand in the summer, which can almost disappear during winter surf. The snorkeling to the right *can* be good, especially around the point to the right, but the beach is subject to water-clouding runoff from an intermittent stream to the left (southwest). There's some shade in the mornings, but none in the afternoon, and the beach is *partially* protected from afternoon winds. The morning views of Moloka'i are stunning; you won't see more detail from anywhere else on Maui. Slaughterhouse *on a good day* is definitely A Real Gem and can have a very high fish count. Located 0.7 miles north of mile marker 31 on Hwy 30 (you probably won't see the incorrectly placed mile marker 32). Access to the beach, 100 feet below the road, is via a concrete stairway.

➕ D.T. Fleming Beach Park

Swimming is similar to Oneloa Beach: good during calm seas, but vulnerable to rip currents when the surf picks up. In fact, these two beaches used to be one, until the West Maui volcano, in its dying days, sent lava to the coast to form **Dragon's Teeth**, splitting the bay in two. D.T. Fleming is long and wide. There's lots of shade, courtesy of ironwood trees. Picnic tables, BBQs, lifeguards, showers and restrooms all make the beach very popular with locals who come to relax and talk story (shoot the breeze), so weekends can be very crowded. The right side gets occasional runoff, so the ocean isn't as clear as nearby Oneloa. Boogie boarding can be good. Afternoons can bring an irritating wind, so be sure to bring that old BBQ grill you've been meaning to have sandblasted. (Mornings are calmest.)

❖ Oneloa Beach

Not to be confused with the other beach of the same name in South Maui. Despite the huge number of resort dwellings behind this long, luxurious beach, it is surprisingly uncrowded most of the time. It's a deceptive beach. The public access deposits you on the eastern (right) third of the beach, and you quickly conclude that this 0.25-mile long, wide sandy beach has bad swimming and snorkeling because of a lava bench in the near-shore waters seemingly extending the whole length. Visitors often turn around and leave at this point. What they can't see is that the left third of the beach usually has a padded sandy bottom, making the swimming delightful when calm. (Occasionally, the winter surf can temporarily erase some of the sandy bottom.) The snorkeling around the left end can also be very good with lots of fish and some wild rock formations, but don't do it when the surf's up, or a washing machine effect will bounce you around. Plus a rip current forms. Take time to climb up the rocks on the left side to poke around the tide-pools and cove. Boogie boarding on the left side can be good for the intermediate *sponger* (local slang). This beach is susceptible to wind. (The gem designation only applies when the wind and surf are low.) Early mornings are best. The extreme right side is somewhat protected from the wind, but, of course, the swimming and snorkeling aren't very good there. (But we do like hunting for lost golf balls there from the nearby golf course. If you find a club, you know the guy was having an off day.) No shade or facilities except for a shower and powerful faucet and sometimes a hose near the parking lot. From the highway, take Office Road till it dead ends, turn left, then right on Kapalua Place. Parking is in the small lot mauka to the beach trail. If it's too windy for a day here, consider the more protected Napili Bay or perhaps Kapalua Beach.

❖ Kapalua Beach

Well known as one of the best swimming beaches on Maui, the bay is usually very protected, making timid swimmers

The left side of often-forgotten Oneloa Beach in West Maui is usually deserted.

happy. Consistently the best beach for kids due to the protected bay, though it can quickly feel crowded. The water isn't necessarily the clearest, so snorkeling is not that hot unless you swim around point on the right side of the bay. Known as "Cliff House," this cove tends to be much clearer with higher fish counts. Just watch out for the young'uns who use the cliffs to leap into the cove. You'll do well to bring your water shoes so you can walk about in the ocean without fear of stubbing your toe. But Kapalua is a great place to wade into the ocean without worrying about getting beaten up by the surf most of the time, and the palm trees behind the beach are very picturesque (helping to disguise the surprisingly ugly, ultra-expensive condos there). The access is near the Sea House Restaurant at Napili Kai

Grain for grain, Napili Beach seems to invite more fun than any other stretch of sand in the area.

condos. The sign says "Napili Lani," and there's a yellow fire hydrant nearby. Drive down and look for a blue beach access sign. Additional $10 parking is next to the tennis courts across the street accessed from Kapalua Drive.

❖ Napili Beach

An excellent beach that seems to generate more fun per square foot than any other beach in the area. It's very recessed into the shoreline, which blocks much of the afternoon wind along here. The sand is steep, so the waves slap the shoreline then recede quickly, creating an impressive undertow during high surf. The offshore waters are quite sandy. This combination creates the best beach on the island for an activity called Monastery Tag (named after a beach in California where we invented it one day after a SCUBA dive). Now bear with me here, it's going to sound strange, but

we've shown others how to do this, and they *love* it. The three ingredients you need are a steep beach, unchecked (unprotected) waves and a padded, sandy bottom. Basically you lie in the water at the surf's edge and zip up and down the beach up to 40 feet each way on a thin cushion of water, digging feet or hands into the sand to control your ascent and descent. Like a low-to-the-ground sports car, the sensation of speed is greater. Here, you're only inches above the sand, and the trick is to go as far up the shore as possible without getting beached. To people on the beach it looks like you're scraping along the sand, but actually you're unscathed as you orient the shape of your body for maximum efficiency. As with all worthwhile and important endeavors, it takes years of practice and dedication. (You see, and you thought we spent all our time doing only *frivolous* stuff.) A mask and snorkel make it easier. On your back, front, head first or feet first, it's important to master them all. You really feel the power of the ocean this way. Best conditions are usually at the center/right portion of the beach.

The beach can get fairly crowded. Two accesses to the middle and south end are from Hui Drive (cutting through Napili Sunset) and Napili Place (limited parking, and the public access sign is sometimes *conveniently* missing), both off Lower Honoapiilani Road. See map on page 57.

❖ Keonenui Beach

Usually a respectably wide white pocket of sand and fairly attractive. Sometimes natural sand migration strips away much of the beach, making it narrow. Slightly cloudy water, sandy bottom, steep shorebreak. On occasion, seaweed blooms create marginal water quality. Fronting the Kahana Sunset on Lower Honoapiilani Road. Only public access is from the north along the shoreline path.

❖ Ka'opala Beach

Visually inviting piece of shoreline beach, but its water can be affected by a foul creek 0.5 miles south of here. (Current runs north.) In the past it's been downright foul but we've found the waters merely cloudy in most recent visits, especially when the creek's dry. (Interestingly, Ka'opala translates to *trash*.)

❖ Kahana Beach

The sand has eroded significantly in recent years and nearby property owners have responded by shoring up their parcels with sandbags. At least their historical problem with seaweed washing ashore here has dwindled. If you're staying at a resort here you'll probably be beach-going elsewhere.

❖ Pohaku Park

Pretty little park for picnics or sunsets, but the water is often cloudy and sometimes yucky. Also called **S-Turns Park**. Located just north of the Noelani condos.

❖ Honokowai Beach Park

The swimming and snorkeling are poor, but it's a good place to come with your lunch (Honokowai Okazuya Deli is nearby) and eat to the sound of the surf. Playground for the keiki and full facilities plus a *wonderful* strip of protected water (at low to mid tide) for kids. On the southern end of Lower Honoapiilani Road.

❖ Keka'a / North Beach / Airport Beach

This stretch of sand fronts what used to be the old Ka'anapali Airport and runs to Honokowai Beach Park. It's a beautiful beach with full facilities, lots of parking

The south end of Kahekili Beach Park has the sandiest bottom—and the dreamiest water.

and usually not super crowded. So why no Gem? Because the nearshore waters are rocky, so swimming is only marginal. Water shoes will help protect your feet. The (preferred) southern section is accessible from Halawai Drive between mile markers 25 and 26. No facilities there. The northern stretch has a large access with full facilities. If you walk to the right along the beach, avoid the waters in front of the Ka'anapali Beach Club. (See map on page 55.) This is also where there is a reef opening, resulting in a rip current out to sea. Snorkeling is fairly good at the southern section once you get 100 or so feet offshore.

❖ Kahekili Beach Park

Official name **Ali'i Kahekili Nui 'Ahumanu Beach Park** (but everyone calls it simply Kahekili), it's a superb park, glorious beach and excellent facilities, including covered tables, a large parking area, restrooms, showers and lawn area. A windbreak running north of here *partially* protects you from afternoon winds. Kahekili is a popular place for SCUBA diving. Several companies do introductory shore dives here.

Conveniently, the best snorkeling is directly offshore of the pavilion, about 75 feet or so where a nice variety of coral and some fish await. Just plain ol' swimming offshore of the park facilities is not so good, suffering from hidden rocks at the water's edge that you can't see without polarized sunglasses. But if you walk down the concrete path south (left) toward **Black Rock**, you'll find that when the sidewalk ends, so do the hidden rocks in the water (for the most part), and from there all the way to the end of the beach (0.25 miles) is a sandy, frolicker's delight. (Winter surf sometimes temporarily erases some of the sand, exposing rocks not normally present.) A stream near Black Rock brings colder, fresh water onto the surface a few dozen feet from shore but doesn't affect things *near* the shore. There's a rumor that an airplane went into the water between the pavilion and Black Rock. (Ka'anapali Airport used to be to your right.) We've spent many hours looking for it and have been unsuccessful. Let us know if you find it. When surf's up, there's a current that runs from Black Rock along the shore heading north. Bigger surf can make the water cloudy and difficult to enter. If it's not calm and you choose to swim anyway, better to walk down and let the current aid you coming back to the pavilion.

Kahekili is a magnificent place for an early morning swim, or just bring your cup of coffee and set the day's tone here.

Lana'i and Moloka'i are usually bathed in bright light, and the often-tranquil waters create an unusually serene atmosphere.

Access is off Hwy 30 between mile markers 25 and 26. Take Kai Ala Drive. (Puukoli Street is across the street.)

❖ Black Rock

This is the large, black lava rock (called **Pu'u Keka'a**) that separates the two halves of Ka'anapali Beach. (It's also where Hawaiian spirits went to meet their ancestors See page 56 for more.) The snorkeling around the rock is legendary and mostly lives up to the hype. Lots of fish and a decent amount of coral. Start from the Sheraton side and work your way around the rock; it's mostly a wall of coral-encrusted lava. The part nearest the beach is the *least* interesting. Only one area around the corner has a lava shelf. Be careful there of surges. Watch for turtles that come to the area as customers of cleaner wrasse fish stations. When returning back to the Sheraton Maui Resort side, if you notice a current around the corner, swim away from the rock along the beach about 75 feet. The current should end, and you can swim back to the beach. (That current is from the weak longshore current that bumps up against Black Rock and slithers around it.) We're baffled as to why authorities haven't installed rescue buoys to aid swimmers in distress here.

❖ Ka'anapali Beach

This beach has a dozen different, often conflicting names. Pick a handful of free magazines around the island and each may have a different name. Some names were apparently invented out of the blue. Technically, Ka'anapali Beach is everything from Keka'a (North Beach) to Hanaka'o'o (Canoe) Beach, but we'll bow to the more common usage and designate it as the sandy beach from Black Rock south to Canoe Beach, including a section known as **Dig Me Beach**. (See map on page 55.) Ka'anapali is one of the finest beaches you'll find on Maui. This portion fronts most of the Ka'anapali resorts and Whalers Village. There's a **concrete path**

It might not be a hidden, untrampled beach, but Ka'anapali never disappoints.

Lahaina Town only has one beach that's any good—and it tends to be overlooked by most beachgoers.

running the entire length of Ka'anapali Beach, from the Sheraton to the Hyatt. It's a *great* place to be at sunset. This beach turns into a kickin', hoppin', happenin' place as all eyes are cast toward the sunset. Dinner cruises ply the waters, beachside restaurants hum, and couples walk the glorious beachside path holding hands and waiting to greet the night. It's busy but not offensively loud. If you're staying in West Maui, you should strongly consider spending one evening doing a stroll along this path, then dining at one of the restaurants along here. There are five free parking lots along the beach. Since the north end of the beach is best, check for vacancies from north to south. The last one, at the Hyatt, usually has empty spots and, since we often see employees parking there (which they're not *supposed* to do), I'm sure they won't mind if you take one of *their* regular spots. You can also park at the Whalers Village Shopping Center. Any shop will validate if you spend around $20 (which is *easy* to do).

The waters at Ka'anapali are great when calm. Snorkeling at Black Rock on the north end is good. The middle offers a nice sandy bottom and good **bodysurfing** when the waves are right. When the surf's up, waves break on the somewhat steep beach with greater force, bringing strong currents, and swimming is not advised.

The north end of the beach is the best, from Ka'anapali Alii Resort to Black Rock. It's a lovely plain of sand and clean water. The southern end in front of the Hyatt and Marriott has a foot-gouging reef near the shore and the Hyatt has been battling a beach erosion issue in recent years.

✚ Hanaka'o'o / Canoe Beach

A major hub of West Maui activity, you have your choice of jet skiing, boogie boarding, body surfing, watching canoe races and...oh, yeah, swimming. Snorkeling is poor due to bad visibility. There are covered picnic tables and poorly maintained facilities, and the beach is popular with locals, especially on weekends. Access is from the parking lot between mile markers 23 and 24. Wander north from the lot.

❖ Wahikuli Wayside Park

South of Ka'anapali, this long sliver of shoreline is wedged between the highway and the sea. Often nearly empty during the week, there are restrooms and showers, but the restrooms can be pretty scary. (County parks are notorious for their bad restroom maintenance.) The northern end is best, but fairly yucky water and little sand make it a forgettable beach park unless you're just looking for a place to eat your picnic lunch or stroll the paved walking path. Between Lahaina and Ka'anapali. Wahikuli means *noisy place,* an appropriate name given how close the beach is to the highway.

❖ Pu'unoa Beach / Baby Beach & Shark's Pit / Kamehameha Iki Park

Lahaina is good for a lot of things, but beach-going ain't one of 'em. The waters off this busy town are usually murky and not suitable for swimming. **Pu'unoa Beach** at the north end, also known as **Baby Beach**, is your best bet. The beach is protected from waves by a near shore reef that makes it ideal for keiki. Water tends to be shallow, there's some coral and access is easy. Park on the Kenui Road mauka of Front Street and follow the access signs down Kai Pali Place for the short walk. Other Lahaina beaches such as **Shark Pit** and **Kamehameha Iki Park** are less lovable.

❖ Puamana Park

Just south of Lahaina town is tiny Puamana Beach Park. No facilities, it's popular with local families with children.

❖ Launiupoko Beach Park

Farther south at the intersection of the old highway and Kai Hele Ku Street is Launiupoko Park. It's a popular place for beginner surf lessons, though water quality makes it unsuitable for snorkeling. Nearshore waters slope gently, so even small waves last a while. Picnic tables and BBQs make it a good place to bring cookables. A boulder-lined pond is popular with parents with kids, but the water can get stagnant and quality can be questionable, so check it before letting your keiki go in.

❖ Mile Marker 14 Beach

Many dive shops and free magazines steer snorkelers to a spot on Hwy 30 called Mile 14 (referring to the mile marker). To put it bluntly, the snorkeling there usually bites. In fact, we wonder if they have even snorkeled there in the last decade, because its reputation is based on something that doesn't exist anymore: namely, clear water and live coral. Visibility *may* be 20 feet *on a great day*; it's 5 feet on more days than we'd care to admit. And though there is coral, more than 90 percent of it is dead, perhaps choked to death by runoff from a now-defunct sugar company.

From the highway, it *looks* like it will be wonderful. Driving along, you see lots of reef and contrast, giving the *illusion* of good snorkeling, but it's usually cloudy. It varies with the tides and seasons and is sometimes better, but odds are you're likely to be disappointed. However, if you're absolutely terrified of the ocean, this site has two things going for it: It's usually calm and protected, and it's often shallow enough to stand up. You will see some fish up close, but *compared to other island snorkel sites*, it's only suitable for the ultra timid. The best snorkeling is 200 yards out to sea *west* of mile marker 14; snorkel boats take paying passengers here to a place called Coral Gardens. But it's too far away from shore, and the visibility, though improved, can still be topped elsewhere.

❖ Ukumehame & Papalaua Parks

These are stretches of beach lining Hwy 30 between mile markers 11 and 13. Access is easy: Just drive up, open your door and fall out. The only good snorkeling is where the road leaves the shoreline, ascending toward the tunnel heading southeast. The reef and visibility improve markedly. But you'll have to swim from the last stretch of sand at Papalaua, and that can be tiring. Best just to enjoy the beach for what it is—a good place to pull over and revel in the view.

❖ **Scenic Lookout Snorkeling**

Though not a beach, the snorkeling below the scenic lookout between mile markers 8 and 9, 2 miles southwest of Ma'alaea on Hwy 30 is fantastic. Extraordinary fish counts often bless the area. The problem is getting in and especially *out*. The trail from the railings is the easy part. At the bottom, entry and exit from the water are difficult. Intermediate to advanced snorkelers only. Do so only when calm, wear water shoes into the water, and pick your spot carefully. While exiting, remember the difficult-exit rule: Work with the ocean and let it do the work for you. You can use a surge to bring you up onto a rock if you do it right, or you may get badly scraped up. While in the water, snorkeling to the right is best. Be careful of surginess. Divers will find deeper waters fairly quickly.

SOUTH MAUI BEACHES

When it comes to good beaches, South Maui has an embarrassment of riches. This is where the tropical beach dream comes true. Perfect stretches of thickly padded sand usually kissed by gentle surf, clear water and palm trees create an instantly pleasing atmosphere. The surf is usually flat in the winter and very small in the summer. The only downside to South Maui beaches is afternoon wind. Shielded by Haleakala during the morning, winds tend to start slithering around the mountain at north Kihei in the late morning and work their way south throughout the afternoon. At the other end, La Pérouse Bay is where the morning wind starts and works its way northward as the day progresses. This means that *morning* almost always offers the best conditions, both for swimming and snorkeling. The last area to get windy and choppy is usually around Wailea, and

that's also where the best beaches are, so we're in luck.

❖ **Ma'alaea Bay**

If you're looking for a long beach stroll, have we got a beach for you. Stretching from the end of Hauoli Street at Haycraft Park for 2.5 miles down to north Kihei, this beach is a walker's delight with no buildings on the beach. The waters off the Ma'alaea end aren't the friendliest, and winds and *sometimes* seaweed can be irritating, but beach strolls are great here. As you near Kihei, a portion of the shore is known as **Sugar Beach**. Here you can sometimes rent windsurfing boards and other beach paraphernalia. Be careful on the soft sand beyond the tide line as occasional kiawe trees (an odd choice to plant behind a beach) sprinkle painful thorn-filled twigs on the sand. Also—and there's no good way to say this—remote parts of the beach sometimes attract…dirtbags who come out from the trees and harass lone beachgoers.

A great summer surf break starting at the harbor is called *Freight Trains*. When it's going off, it's a long, awesome ride.

❖ **Maipoina 'Oe Ia'u Beach Park to Kalama Beach**

Since we first started writing about Maui we've advised people not to swim along the coastline anywhere from the northern part of Kihei town to Cove Park. We caught *a lot* of flack from politicians, the media and local bigwigs for printing this, but none of them disputed it. Much of the criticism we've received from locals about *Maui Revealed* is really misdirected fury at this disclosure. People in power here simply didn't want us to tell you about it. The water in much of that area *has been* nasty. This problem went on for decades. A discharge ditch running through the center of Kalama Park sometimes drains nasty water into the area. Slow but ever-present northward currents take the nutrient-rich water north until it dissipates. Algae has flourished in this water, making the ocean here a bit smelly, murky, full of seaweed and generally unpleasant. (From Kama'ole Beach I all the way south, the water is *completely* unaffected.) But the situation has gotten much better in recent years. The water is still cloudy, but we haven't seen it nasty in awhile and we can say that swimming here—while certainly not great like it is at beaches farther south—is not something we feel we should warn against.

❖ Cove Park

Surfing lessons are common at Cove Park. Swimming and snorkeling conditions are poor—water clarity is not very good since the cloudy waters from Kalama Park are driven south during the afternoon winds, then partially cleaned out by the currents running north during the less windy evenings. Still, I find it one of the more relaxing places to do stand-up paddleboarding and have spent many a morning here.

➕ Kama'ole Beach

Kama'ole Beach is broken into three parts, cleverly named Kama'ole Beach I, II and III. Kama'ole I is the biggest and best of the three—a long and pretty stretch of fine sand with good swimming much of the time, restrooms, showers and a lifeguard. Access is a snap, and your car is very close to the water. Across the street is a convenience store, in case you get hungry or thirsty, and there's a lawn area at the south end of the park. You'll find very good snorkeling around the rocks bracketing each end, especially the north (right) end. (That end is also called **Charley Young Beach.**) **Kama'ole II** is also a good beach, though not quite as long or as nice as Kama'ole I. Here, too, good snorkeling exists around the rocky points defining the beach. Of the three Kama'oles, **Kama'ole III** is the most popular with locals. There is a small spot here where waves focus, even during calm seas, which makes the boogie boarding as reliable as you're gonna get in South Maui. There's some decent snorkeling at the north end near the rocks, but beware of a particularly bad surge

The three Kama'oles:
Not a Mexican rock group, just a nice trio of beaches.

there if the sea's not calm. There is a *huge* lawn at the south end of Kama'ole III, which makes a great place to fly a kite or toss a Frisbee or football, and there's a limited playground for the keiki. Unfortunately, Kama'ole III is also the messiest of the three beaches due to its usage, and the sand beach area is relatively small. All three Kama'oles are easily identified from South Kihei Road between Alanui Ke Alii and Keonekai roads. All have showers and restrooms. On S. Kihei Road. (See map on page 137.)

❖ Keawakapu Beach

One of the most criminally underrated beaches in South Maui. Very long with gobs of fine sand on and offshore. The only resorts on the beach are at the north end. The rest is lined with *very* expensive houses. The area in front of the main public access has a huge, well-padded sandy bottom, perfect for frolicking with minimal fear of stubbing your toe on a rock. (You've never *really* cursed until you've cursed a beach rock that has attacked your foot.) If you walk to the south (left), the beach widens, and you'll find another large sandy bottom area. This part of the beach is amazingly underused. Farther south is the third Keawakapu entrance. (The first two have parking lots at the intersection of South Kihei Road and Kilohana and near the Mana Kai Resort.) This third entrance (which has a shower) is at the unnoticed end of South Kihei Road, and the water offshore is very well sanded. (This is probably a good time to tell you that sunglasses that are *polarized* are amazing at detecting dark rocks on the sandy bottom.) Mornings are best; afternoons can be windy. One caveat about Keawaka-pu: Some plants on the backshore attract bees, which usually aren't a problem, but it's sometimes possible to step on an errant bee blown onto the sandy shoreline, especially in the windy afternoon. At the south end of S. Kihei Road. (See maps on pages 137 and 139.)

❖ Mokapu & Ulua Beach

These two beaches are usually spoken of in the same sentence since they share the same parking lot north of the Shops at Wailea. When you take the short path down, the beach on your left is Ulua, on the right is Mokapu. The sand at Ulua doesn't extend as far offshore as most of the other beaches in the area. We prefer Mokapu; it's more picturesque, is used a bit less and has slightly clearer water. Ulua is a popular dive spot. Though a tad over-dived, it's nice with a lot of coral, albeit crowded, and the visibility is often poor. Night dives have pretty easy access—a big plus. The 51 parking stalls fill up *early* since most slots are snagged by dive companies taking students here for introductory SCUBA lessons. Access to Mokapu isn't dependent on the parking lot, however. You can park at the southern Keawakapu lot and stroll around the corner along the beach to the left to get to Mokapu. You're at Mokapu when you see a wooden walkway inland.

❖ Wailea Beach

An outstanding beach! Over 0.3 miles long, this classic crescent of sand has been ranked by several beach rankings (yes, there *are* people who do that) as the best beach in America. Terrific clear water, fine-grained sand, picturesque setting, calm waters most of the time, excellent swimming; Wailea should be on your short list of beaches to visit while here. The biggest problems at Wailea are parking and popularity. The resort has provided a parking lot, accessed just past the Grand Wailea, but it may fill up if you don't get there early. (However, the Wailea parking lot usually fills up *after* the **Mokapu/Ulua Beach** parking lot.) Showers and restrooms are provided. As with all South Maui beaches, morning is better than afternoon, though Wailea won't get windy as early as beaches farther north. Snorkeling can be decent at each end when calm. Boogie boarding can be very good for novices at the far south (left) side when there's a little surf. (But remember, small surf is often a South Maui hallmark, so boogie boarding is not always possible.) Waves at Wailea are short, close to shore and easy to catch without fins. Just stand there and jump with them. Stay just far enough away from the rocks at the end of the beach to avoid them. The tiny cove just past the rocks at the south end has a rocky bottom. Good for sunbathing, but not for swimming.

❖ Polo Beach

Easy access and more parking than other Wailea beaches, Polo has restrooms, a shower, picnic tables and BBQ grills on the lawn above the beach. The beach isn't as deep as some other Wailea beaches, and there are a few more hidden rocks in the sand, but it's a fine beach, nonetheless, and the water is usually clear. Parking is ample and rarely fills up. There are beach chairs lining the beach, though they're *presumably* for guests of the Fairmont Kea Lani, which backs the beach. Located 2 miles from the Wailea Ike intersection; see map on page 139.

❖ Palauea Beach

Used primarily by local residents who take the short path through the trees to this lesser-known beach, it's not usually crowded during the week. Also called **White Rock**, the snorkeling around the rocky point on the left is *very* good. It's also good on the right side, though the water isn't as clear as the left side. The gently sloping shoreline is loaded with sand in the middle and provides excellent swimming much of the time. The bay is recessed, so it doesn't get as windy in the afternoon as other beaches. No facilities except *maybe* a Porta-Potty, but

Palauea Beach is one of the lesser-known South Maui beaches.

Po'olenalena Beach is world class. But this lessor known portion, separated by the rocky point at the bottom, is often overlooked by beachgoers.

the easy access and quality of the beach make it a winner. Off Makena Road; see map on page 139.

❖ Po'olenalena Beach

Probably the least known and certainly least used large beach in the Wailua/Makena area. It's also known locally as **Paipu Beach, Pepeiaolepo Beach, Love Beach, Keauhou Beach** and sometimes **Makena Surf Beach.** *(How can something so little known have so many names?)* Nearly 0.5 miles long, there have been times when we've found other Wailea beaches crowded and found this beach nearly empty during the week. (Weekends are busy here, as all beaches can be.) The water offshore is mostly a broad, flat, gentle, sandy bottom with only occasional outcroppings of rock. The beach is gently sloping, making the water especially good for swimming during the normally calm seas. When there's a little surf, the left (south) side can offer good boogie boarding. The beach is interrupted toward the right (north) side by lava. Scramble over the lava rocks or take a shoreline trail, and you may have the northern third of the beach to yourself. (Or you may find nudists baring their *da kines*—sometimes happens.)

The beach is bracketed by lava points on each side, and the snorkeling around them is exceptional and little used compared to other snorkel sites. Tons of fish and a very healthy coral community, especially as you venture away from shore along the points, make it a worthy snorkel destination. Usually *lots* of **turtles** at the left and right sides and even the occasional lobster. (By the way, lobsters are sometimes known locally as *bugs.* When you hear someone say, *Hey, brah, we go catch bugs,* it means he's going lobster diving.) The right end of the beach is rarely snorkeled and is one of our favorite snorkel sites on the island. So let's see... We have great swimming, great snorkeling, easy access, good boogie boarding when there's some surf and a general lack of crowds. *What's not to love?* The two accesses are just past where Makena Alanui meets Makena Road for the first time. The second one is a bit farther south at the Makena Surf and, though limited to nine stalls, is often unused. It's better since it has showers nearby. Go through the unlocked gate and along the walkway. If full, use the first access.

One quick nag: The coral and fish in this area haven't been exposed to lots of people. The coral isn't trampled and broken, and the fish haven't been fed much. Please don't start the tradition. Fish feeding completely messes up the balance, leaving only a few aggressive species while driving away the meeker fish. And while snorkeling, be *real* careful not to bump into the coral with your fins, and don't stand on it or grab it. This will keep the reef here pristine and beautiful. (Ok, end of nag.)

❖ Chang's Beach

Just south of Po'olenalena is a public access (with only six parking stalls) that leads to Chang's Beach. Cut off from Po'olenalena, it's a wonderful little cove with fantastic snorkeling offshore and a sandy beach to lie on (though winter storms sometimes wash the sand away). When there's some surf, the boogie boarding here can be awesome.

❖ Five Graves / Five Caves

A good SCUBA site and fairly good snorkeling. Turtles are common, and there are several caves. Once in the water, divers should head straight out, slightly to the right and look for the caves along the wall. Entry is from a small, semi-protected rocky cove off Makena Road. See map on page 139. You'll walk by a small graveyard

(with *seven* graves that we counted, and probably more in the faint lava rock outlines). Sometimes referred to as 5 Caves, sometimes 5 Graves, but neither seems to be accurate. If you're lucky on a SCUBA dive, you'll find the elusive bubble cave near the shoreline. The air pocket inside is sealed, and the ocean's surge constantly changes the pressure, causing your ears to continuously flux and a cloud of pressure-induced haze to form and dissolve instantly with every surge. *Real* cool.

❖ Makena Landing Beach Park

A marginal place for snorkeling, but it's usually calm with easy entry, making it a popular place to launch kayaks and do intro or night SCUBA dives. The visibility is best on the north side, which also has good coral.

❖ Maluaka Beach / Makena

A REAL GEM

You'll be forgiven if you get confused as to where Makena Beach is. So is everyone else. Ask a local for directions, and you could end up in one of *four* places. Oneloa Beach, also called Big Beach, is often called Makena Beach or sometimes

Why aren't you wet yet? Maluaka Beach in front of the shuttered Makena Golf & Beach Resort has good swimming and great snorkeling.

Big Makena Beach. (It's also called Makena State Park.) Makena Bay, just north of here, which also contains Makena Landing, is sometimes called Makena Beach. Sometimes Poʻolenalena Beach is called Makena Surf Beach. And lastly this beach is sometimes called Makena Beach. It's usually called Maluaka Beach, as the signs often say. Hey, don't blame us—we're just the messengers. For clarification (ha!) we'll call this beach Maluaka Beach.

Fronting the Makena Beach Resort, this wide, pretty beach slopes gently, providing good swimming during calm seas, especially toward the center of the beach where a thick padding of sand awaits. During calm seas keiki (kids) splash about with abandon. There is shade at the south (left) end, as well as restrooms, showers and picnic tables. Parking is past the Makena Beach Resort, where Makena Road backtracks, 3.6 miles south of the Wailea Alanui/Wailea Ike intersection. (See map on page 139.) After parking continue the same direction on the concrete path to the beach. If you want, park a bit closer to the sand, try using Makena Road just south of Honoiki for the north end of the beach.

The snorkeling off to the left (south) is very good with good coral and fish, and usually *lots* of turtles. In fact, this area is one of the famed **turtle towns** that some snorkel boats take people to see. Off to the right also offers good snorkeling.

❖ **Oneuli Beach / Black Sand Beach**

Less known than other beaches in the area since it's not well marked and can't be seen from the road. Those who do know about it usually call it simply *Black Sand Beach*. It's on the north (right) side of that large hill in Makena called **Puʻu Olaʻi**, and you access it from the short, bumpy, but usually passable dirt road shown on the map on page 139. (Keep an eye out for deer on this road.) Though the gate is supposed to be open during daylight hours, the state opens the gate *most* of the time, and you'll have to walk .25 miles if they didn't get around to it on *your* day. Once you're at the salt and pepper beach, it's easy to see how it formed. Puʻu Olaʻi is essentially a large mound of lava cinders created from an enormous lava fountain. Wave action has bitten into the cinder

Oneuli Beach/Black Sand Beach is often lost in the shuffle of world-class South Maui beaches.

cone, causing the loose black cinders to fall into the ocean where they are ground into black sand. Over the years shells have been pulverized into sand and coral has been...well, *processed* by parrotfish, adding salt to the pepper.

The water at Black Sand Beach is usually calm, but the sand gives way to a lava shelf at the water's edge, making the swimming marginal. However, the snorkeling can be great, and turtles are very common on the left side near the hill. Visibility is usually cloudy near the shore, so head out and to the left for lots of coral, turtles and fish. If it's calm, you can snorkel all the way around Pu'u Ola'i, and it gets even better. Beware of any currents by occasionally stopping to see if you are drifting. Kayakers sometimes visit the beach, but it's rarely crowded.

❂ Big Beach / Little Beach / Oneloa / Makena

A REAL GEM

Big Beach is what many people think of when they think of a Hawaiian beach. It is considered by many to be *the* beach on Maui. (Not to be confused with another beach in West Maui also called **Oneloa Beach**.) Almost 0.7 miles long and over 100 feet wide, this beautiful crescent of golden sand is a dream for swimmers, snorkelers, frolickers and sometimes boogie boarders. When seas are calm, the water is very inviting. You won't find it empty; it's one of the more popular beaches. But you *will* find it enchanting.

The sandy bottom can make for excellent swimming, and the snorkeling around the points at both ends of the beach is good during calm seas (which are somewhat rare). During *not calm* seas, the shore break can be very powerful and regularly causes injuries and rip currents. The lifeguards are pretty strict when conditions

are rough, but if you're there after hours you'll have to use your judgement.

During the '60s, hippies from the mainland came to Maui looking to get back to nature, and they found their nirvana at what was then an isolated beach. Unable to remember its Hawaiian name, Oneloa (meaning *long sands*), they referred to it as simply Big Beach, a name that has stuck. (They also called it Makena Beach, which is incorrect. **Makena Beach** is farther north, but that name, too, has stuck.) After several years of hippie occupation, disease outbreaks from a lack of hygiene, lack of proper waste disposal, and contaminated water supplies along with rampant drug use, authorities raided and evicted the illegal "campers" in 1972. Today Big Beach is a state park. Porta-Potties and picnic tables are available.

The large hill on the north (right) end of the beach is called Pu'u Ola'i, or Earthquake Hill. It was the site of the huge eruption described on page 143.

From the right side of the beach, you can take a short trail to a promontory. (Walk up a little, then turn left rather than continuing up the steeper gravel portion.) On the lava promontory, 20 feet above the water, there are several short trails leading shoreward that end at nice places to watch the sunset. The views of Big Beach from up here are delicious. On the other side of the promontory is a smaller beach. Let's see. The big beach is known as Big Beach, so what do you think the hippies called the little beach? Hmm, that's a toughie. How about **Little Beach**? (Darned clever, they were.) This ideal pocket of sand tucked away in a nook of Pu'u Ola'i offers great swimming, snorkeling, boogie boarding and bodysurfing. As it's not visible from the road, it is often used by nudists, which, by the way, is illegal in Hawai'i. (We tell

you this so that if nudity bothers you, you may want to pass on Little Beach. Hmm. I wonder if there's another reason they call it Little Beach...) Another thing you need to know is that Little Beach is occasionally (but not too often) occupied by squatters in makeshift tents, creating an unfriendly atmosphere. Aside from these caveats, you may want to take a peek at Little Beach from the trail on the promontory overlooking the sand to see if it's right for you that day. If it is, head on down and stake a claim to some sand. Weekends at Little Beach can be packed and Sunday afternoons usually bring hippie parties complete with their consumption habits and dress code (or lack thereof). If you swim to Little Beach from Big Beach, the current can make swimming back annoying. Consider walking back if it's a problem that day. Also, Little Beach is becoming well know for its Sunday night parties. Maybe worth gawking, if you are so inclined.

There are two parking lots for Big Beach that you'll see from the road. It's $5 per vehicle to park. Actually, if you're not going to Little Beach, consider driving past the second lot and park on the road at the south (left) end of the beach where there's shade on the beach and less crowds.

You have several food options via road stands nearby. Avoid **Jawz Tacos**.

❖ **Pa'ako Beach / Secret Cove**

This beach is *literally* a hole in the wall, or at least access to it is. That impressive rock wall you see just past (south of) **Big Beach** hides some impressive beachfront homes. But across from telephone pole #E2–3 (the first pole you encounter past Big Beach, in case someone steals the marking) is an opening in the wall, a legal public access. Walk through and you find a beautiful little pocket of sand. This is a popular place to get married, and for good reason. In the morning the views of Kaho'olawe and Molokini from this pocket are outstanding, and the little beach simply looks charming. Since it's small, it doesn't take much to fill it up; mornings are best. Off to the left, in front of a beach house, is a smaller pocket of sand. The beach doesn't really have a name other than Secret Cove. But the point on your right is called Pa'ako, so we'll call it that.

❖ **'Ahihi Cove**

Located just inside the 'Ahihi–Kina'u Natural Area Reserve (where it's illegal to capture or spear fish), the fish life here has been sparse lately. Why? Because it's right next to the road. Aquarium collectors have been stationing a lookout up the road then quickly cast a net, illegally poaching the fish to sell to stores on the mainland. No sand beach, but the cove is usually protected from wind and surf, and access and water entry are fairly easy. Though intimidating signs *imply* you can't snorkel, it's perfectly legal. The state made it hard by taking away every single parking space, but you can park at Dumps and walk 900 feet to the water here. Don't stash your car key here—someone might see you—stash it under a rock on your walk from Dumps. South of Wailea; see map on page 141.

❖ Dumps

Yeah, I went snorkeling on Maui at a place called Dumps. Makes you want to brag to all your buddies back home, huh? Well, the state actually *wants* you to snorkel here, because they closed off access to the shoreline south of here, including the snorkel sites **Fishbowl** and **Aquarium**. Located just past impossible-to-miss 'Ahihi Cove, Dumps (named after a now-vanished rubbish dump) has pretty mature coral and reasonable fish counts. Visibility usually isn't great. The winds can blow you out to sea, and the surge can get rough near the shore. This area is protected (something you may have noted after passing the third warning sign). Basically, the only thing you're allowed to touch is the water. Don't go onshore to the point to the left and avoid standing on anything in the water. Though you'll see lots of life, we suggest this spot only for intermediate snorkelers because entry and exit can be a bit challenging for beginners. After your five-minute walk to the shore (and the only spit of sand near the center of the cove), kick out past the exposed rock, 25 yards out, and go right.

❖ La Pérouse Bay Beach

In South Maui, this is as far as you can go by car. The shoreline is mostly rocky and at first glance it looks like it would be a poor place for any ocean recreation. This is a natural area reserve and it's illegal to do just about anything in the water. But for those with strong legs and the will to use them, snorkeling opportunities do exist. But it's not your typical snorkel experience. See *Adventures* on page 269.

La Pérouse is a common place to see dolphins in the early morning. A large pod seems to cruise this area, heading northward as the morning progresses. We often see them here around 7 a.m., then at Big Beach around 10 a.m. Turtles are also relatively common, though more so just north in 'Ahihi Cove.

❖ Keawanaku Beach

Most locals reading this will say, *where?* That's because this beach really has no name and is virtually unknown. It's past the end of the road in South Maui. You need to hike to it. See *Hiking* on page 226. At times the ocean reclaims the sand here.

THE BOTTOM OF MAUI

Past Keawanaku the shoreline is rocky and windy, and the seas are unusually harsh. Other than one inaccessible pocket at the base of the cliff and a tiny seasonal sand patch, you could explore the entire 30 miles of shoreline (which we've done), and you won't find one sand beach until you get to Hana. The only area frequently accessed (mostly by locals) is **Nu'u Bay**, described on page 117 and the unnamed black sand patch between mile markers 29 and 30.

HANA BEACHES

Hana only has a few beaches. *Ahh*, but what beaches! A red sand beach, a black sand beach and the best body surfing beach on the island. Since there's no way you'd ever drive all the way to Hana just for a day at the beach, we've deviated from our usual format and listed them in *Hana Highway Sights.*

THE NORTH SHORE OF HALEAKALA— FROM HANA TO CENTRAL MAUI

Hana is on the eastern tip of the island, and once you're west of Hana, the shoreline turns rocky. There are a few bays that you can visit (listed in the driving tours), but they don't have sand and are exposed to the higher surf normally present all along the windward coast. Not until the towns of Pa'ia and Kahului will you find beaches, and they are *not* in the same league as South and West Maui's beaches. You may find them best for getting some last minute photos along a beach before returning your rental car, especially Kanaha.

✛ Ho'okipa Beach Park

Near mile marker 9 on Highway 36, this beach is upcurrent of most of the runoff that plagues other area beaches farther west. It's widely recognized as perhaps the best place in the world to windsurf, and boarders from everywhere make their pilgrimage to this spot. If you're not an expert, don't try. If the ocean doesn't get you, the surprisingly territorial windsurfers will. (Novices use Kanaha Beach.) But this is a *great* place to watch the hordes of windsurfers as well as the pounding surf that often racks the shore. (Windsurfing is not allowed until 11 a.m. Surfers own the waves before then.) It's uncommon *not* to have wind here. Car break-ins can be a problem, so don't leave any valuables in your car. And if you try surfing here, make *sure* you talk to somebody about local rules and etiquette. The parking lot is gated and usually gets locked from 7 p.m. to 7 a.m.

Like several areas along the North Shore, the shoreline here is dominated by a rock bench. This blocks much of the waves (in the summer time) and tidepools form between the sand and rock, making for a great place for kids to explore. The area should be avoided in winter time, though.

If you want to get away from the crowd, there's a small beach just to the west (across from Holomua Road) that

Hana doesn't have many beaches, but the few it does have, like Red Sand Beach, are exceptional.

is often deserted. A nearby reef makes swimming difficult but it's a good place to point your face into the stiff wind and smell the salt air.

❖ Lower Pa'ia Park
Just before you get into main Pa'ia town, this beach is a hit with local kids (probably because of the nearby youth center) and has fairly good bodysurfing and boogie boarding. Full facilities and a basketball court.

⊕ H.A. Baldwin Park
At mile marker 6 on Highway 36, it has a huge lawn, a long crescent of sand, good body surfing (though it's easy to get pounded into the sand here), lifeguard, Porta-Potties, pavilion and nice views of West Maui. The downside is cloudy water from nearby runoff and very crowded conditions on the weekend. During the week it's good for a beach stroll. Past the right side of Baldwin (as you're looking at the ocean) after scrambling over boulders is an 800-foot stretch of sand beach that is nicer. Because it's often overlooked, the beach is frequented by nudists which, for the record, is illegal in Hawai'i. Just sayin…

❖ Spreckelsville Beach
Mixed feelings about this one. On the plus side, it's a long, *very* attractive beach with unusually firm sand that's deserted most of the time during the week, with expansive views of the north coast. Several areas have a bench of lithified sand (sandstone) near the water's edge that provides some protection for keiki (kids) and nervous swimmers after you check for safety. On the negative side, current and wind are pretty dependable companions all day long, the water is cloudy, and (the clincher) jets fly over part of the beach as they depart the island, which can really rattle

your jaw. The best part of the beach is farthest from the airport, at mile marker 5 on Highway 36. Take North Onohe to Kealakai. The other part, between mile markers 4 and 5, is avoidable.

⊕ Kanaha Beach
This is where most visitors take their **Windsurfing** and **Kiteboarding** lessons. (See *Activities* for more on these.) As a beach destination it won't make your palms sweaty *unless* you know to walk to your *right* when you get to the sand from the parking area. After scrambling over some rocks you'll find a very pretty little stretch of sand backed by trees that you might have all to yourself. A particularly good place to hang out if you're waiting for someone who's plane is late. (Yup, been there, done that.) In front of Kahului Airport off Amala Street. Park at the second (farthest) parking lot. See map on page 70.

❖ Waiehu Beach
A small but pretty beach in Wailuku with a large lawn next to the sandy shoreline. Though the waters tend to be cloudy and not really suitable for swimming, it's a great place to stop and watch kitesurfers setting up and skimming across the ocean. Worth a stop if you're in the area. Next to Waiehu Municipal Golf Course.

❖ Waihe'e Beach
This beach is the last one on the windward side. Kind of anticlimactic to end it this way after so many great beaches. The beach is mostly used by shoreline fishermen and local residents and doesn't offer much for visitors. The water's a bit murky, the shoreline is rocky, and currents can be a problem. If you're in the area, consider going to the other side of Waiehu Municipal Golf Course where the beach is a bit nicer.

Boat trips are wildly popular on Maui, but we were nervous about publishing this photo. The water is so clean, clear and calm, it makes the photo look like it was retouched. We promise, we don't use tricky photographic filters or computers. This is really how it looks on a good morning.

Pick your fantasy; name your dream. If you had to pick the one thing that keeps people coming back to Maui year after year, this would probably be it. Just about everything you dream of doing in the tropics is available here. This is where it all comes true. But where should you go, and with whom should you go?

Most sources of visitor information, free and not free, tend to steer visitors to the same group of large activity providers, such as boat tours and helicopter companies. Some of these are good companies, but we've found some to be large, arrogant visitor-processing machines that seem to take their status for granted. We've spent countless hours *anonymously* reviewing smaller companies in addition to the larger ones to give you options you won't find elsewhere.

Be *skeptical* when looking at advertisements from different companies. Everyone claims to be the "best." Everyone is "world famous." Everyone claims to have been "voted number one." You could drown in their sea of hype.

Activity providers in Hawai'i are also notorious for using computers to place leaping whales on their ocean tour brochures or showing kayakers paddling up to waterfalls where it's not possible. Or how about the tour company that advertises that with their jungle tour they'll show you "hidden waterfalls" in Hana? Wow, sounds intriguing. Too bad the "hidden waterfall" photo on their brochure is actually the artificial falls in front of the Grand Wailea Hotel in South Maui. There are shameless attempts to capture your business, and you need to be vigilant about picking who you go with.

The activity industry on Maui is *massive*. Be suspicious of recommendations from activity desks and activity booths that often only "recommend" companies that give them the biggest commissions. (Those commissions are *30–50 percent* of the total cost of the activity.) Some are contractually bound to certain companies. Even many hotel concierges work this way. Our reviews reflect our personal observations, opinions and experiences. We actually see and *do* this stuff (always anonymously), and this chapter reflects what we saw. We don't get any money for steering you in a certain direction, a claim that very few can make. While it's true you can *sometimes* get good deals booking though activity companies (or get good deals if you trade some of your precious Maui time for a timeshare presentation), we *strongly* suggest you decide which company you want to go with *before* you see them, and don't let them steer you elsewhere. Also, some companies will give you a *big* discount if you book directly, on the phone or online, cutting out the activity brokers.

July, August and Christmas are busy times on Maui, and it may be difficult getting what you want on short notice. If you have your heart set on a particular activity, consider reserving it from the mainland (by phone or Internet; the latter often has discounts), just to make sure there's room for you.

AIR TOURS

To see Maui from the sky is to explore areas you can't reach by land. Paradise in the tropics is a breathtaking experience from the air. But the kind of experience you have depends on the kind of vehicle you want to take. You can be aloft in a helicopter, airplane (as a passenger or pilot), powered hang glider, motor glider and a paraglider. These are radically different experiences, and we've covered them all.

So you'll know my perspective, I'm a pilot myself and fly traditional fixed-wing planes, seaplanes and microlights. I don't have a helicopter rating, but have flown *in* the choppers (anonymously reviewing them).

HELICOPTER TOURS

We've never been shy about our strong advocacy for helicopter tours of Kaua'i. Kaua'i, aside from being astoundingly beautiful, has three jaw-droppingly compelling reasons to take a helicopter tour: the Na Pali coast, Waimea Canyon and Wai'ale'ale Crater. Maui has… some *very* pretty scenery. But is it worth the big bucks you'll have to shell out for a helicopter flight? It depends.

As a pilot, I can tell you that flying along the Hana coast and through the West Maui Mountains is fantastic, especially when it's been wet. It's incredible, but I don't get the same lump in my throat as when I fly over Kaua'i or the Big Island's Kilauea volcano *when it was flowing*. If a flight over Kaua'i doesn't move you, then you probably can't be moved by anything. But a flight over Maui isn't like that. It's very nice, very pretty, but it's probably not as much of an emotional event. It's simply cool. Maui has much to experience, but helicopters aren't as vital here as they are elsewhere.

Then there's the fact that helicopter flights are more expensive on Maui than on other islands. Even companies with outlets on the Big Island and Kaua'i often charge more for air time on Maui. It might be because of the confiscatory commissions (up to 50 percent) paid to activity booths on Maui, and maybe it's also because that's what the market will bear here.

Choosing a company depends on what you want. They fly similar routes and charge similar prices. **Blue Hawaiian** is probably the tightest operation and flies six-passenger A-Stars and the more-cushy Eco-Stars.

Helicopter Flight Routes

Companies have four main flights, listed with the best ones first.

#1 West Maui/Moloka'i Sea Cliffs

This is the best of the flights to take. After seeing West Maui and the beautiful and inaccessible Honokohau Falls, you fly across the channel and look at the stunning 3,000-foot sea cliffs of Moloka'i— an awesome sight, never to be forgotten. Then slip through the middle of Moloka'i, along the fringing reefs, then back to Maui. After going up Olowalu Valley, into the center of West Maui, you'll come out 'Iao Valley to end the hour-long flight for about $300.

#2 Circle Maui

You won't actually circle the island, and some companies see more of West Maui

than others. For our Air Maui "complete island" flight, the West Maui portion only went into one valley before reversing back to the airport. The benefit over the Moloka'i flight is that you get to see East Maui, which, hopefully, includes a peek into Haleakala Crater (clouds permitting— they aren't allowed to fly *into* it but instead look over the rim) and the Hana coastline. An hour for about $350.

#3 West Maui

You'll see West Maui's 'Iao Valley, another valley with beautiful waterfalls called the Wall of Tears, and the pretty northeast coastline. It's 30 minutes of flight for $170 or more.

#4 East Maui

Similar to the circle island without West Maui. 45 minutes for about $280.

A Few Tips

These prices are list prices. Many companies will give some kind of discount if you ask them. Ask them about coupons, Internet discounts, or tell them you'll book through an activity booth if they don't discount it some. Sometimes they'll deeply discount if you book at the last minute, especially for single passengers. In the late afternoon, call around and ask if they have room the next morning, and you may get a better rate.

If you decide to take a flight, consider doing it early in your trip. It'll help orient you to the island.

Morning is almost always best. Be done by 10:30 a.m. for best viewing conditions.

Company	Phone	Tours	Aircraft Type	2-Way*
Air Maui	(808) 877-7005	1, 2, 3 & 4	6-Pass. A-Star	No
Blue Hawaiian	(808) 871-8844	1, 2, 3 & 4	A-Star & Eco-Star	Yes
Maverick	(808) 893-7999	1, 2 & 4	Eco-Star	Yes
Pacific Helicopter	(808) 866-8165	1, 2, 3 & 4	R-44 & A-Star	Yes
Royal Pacific Air	(808) 824-4369	Big Island Kilauea	Airplane	No
Sunshine	(808) 871-0722	1, 2 & 4	A-Star & Eco-Star	No

* Indicates whether craft contains a microphone for you to talk to the pilot.

Tasty views like this can only be seen with an aerial tour. And you may even catch a glimpse of the Big Island's volcanoes.

Wind and clouds increase as the morning and afternoon progress, and conditions get bumpier.

If approaching a live chopper with blades-a-whirring give you the creeps, only Maverick turns the engine off for loading.

For photos, use a fast shutter speed. Don't let the camera touch the vibrating window. Glare from the window can be a problem while filming. A circular polarizer can cut through almost all of it. Few point-and-shoot cameras will accommodate polarizers, but all SLR cameras will. Dark clothing also reduces glare.

Only **Blue Hawaiian, Pacific Helicopter Adventure Tours** and **Maverick** have a microphone so you can talk to the pilot. This is very nice because often you'll have a question about something you see. Others may say they don't have mics for safety reasons, but that's laughable. For instance, one company has you hand notes to the pilot if you have questions. Which do *you* think is safer—the pilot *hearing* your questions, or *reading* your note while flying? Others probably don't have mics for money reasons or because they don't want to be "annoyed" by your questions.

For some reason, helicopter pilots are notoriously bad with their facts during narrations. Our **Air Maui** and **Sunshine** Helicopters flights had such bad "facts" that we bought the movies of the flights to see how much conveyed was correct. The results were pretty poor, especially Air Maui's.

The state charges extra to park at the Kahului heliport, and the lot often fills up.

Don't wear earrings; they interfere with the headsets.

Here's the deal on seating: The best seats are up front—period. They may tell you otherwise in order to console you with your backseat position, but the front seat offers better visibility and allows the island to rush at you. Seating is *supposed* to be dictated by weight, and lighter people usually go up front. (Though some companies, like Sunshine, will sell you the front seat for extra, somehow getting around the whole weight and balance thing.) Also, single riders often get placed up there since companies don't like to break up couples.

If you are sitting in the back, you want to be on the side where all the action is. On the West Maui/Moloka'i trip, the

Taking a lesson in a powered hang glider surrounded by the waterfalls of Hana—what could be cooler?

left seats are the best because of the route. On the Circle, East or West Maui trips, it depends on the direction they go. If they visit the south part of Haleakala and the crater first, then head up and then along the Hana coast, the left side is best. If they head straight for the Hana coastline, the right side is best. Talk to them on the phone and ask which route they're taking, then request a seat where the main action will be on *your* side. They may not *guarantee* seats, but make sure they know that you'll consider them weasels if you don't get the seat you're looking for. Most of the time you'll be accommodated, even while they claim that "the computer assigns seats" or "the weather dictates our route." If they don't sound accommodating, go elsewhere.

Many companies now take video of the trip and will sell you the DVD afterward. That's kind of cool, and you can hear your pilot on the movie, but the quality of these recordings won't match what you can buy from a pre-recorded DVD, where sights were captured in their best light. It's your call as to which, if any, you want.

Most companies use six-passenger A-Stars. **Blue Hawaiian** and **Sunshine** have some flights on their cushy and roomy Eco-Stars (or Whisper-Stars). All of **Maverick's** flights are on Eco-Stars, and the price reflects the more luxurious aircraft. They're larger inside and the windows are bigger, but it costs 20 to 30 percent more than riding in an A-Star. Think of it as the difference between business class and first class. If you've got the extra cash, it's a heck of a ride.

AIRPLANE TOURS

Without as many narrow valleys as Kaua'i or the Big Island's Hamakua Coast, hovering isn't as important here, so airplane tours are a good alternative to more expensive helicopter flights.

Royal Pacific Air (808-824-4369) advertises tours of the volcano on the Big Island from both Kapalua and Kahului, but when we try to book they say that "the FAA requires them to stay 5,000 feet above the park" so they don't do that any more. Odd. As a pilot I can't find that limitation and neither could the FAA when we called them. They bill themselves as a private charter company, and the charters feature a VIP-style experience with full concierge service, "executive" lounge and a state-of-the-art, $1.6 million hangar. Popular with big name celebrities. Their fleet includes a Cessna Grand Caravan 208B and Piper Navajo. Tours of the volcano vary in price, depending on your place of departure: $449 from Kapalua, $425 from Kahului and $545 from Honolulu. (They still show images of glowing lava on their web site which hasn't occurred for quite some time. You *won't* see that.) They are very difficult to reach, so consider yourself lucky if they answer the phone or return your call.

If you are a pilot (or want a lesson and the chance to fly to another island), **Maui Flight Academy** (808-298-5188) gives lessons in a four-passenger 2007 Cirrus SR22 out of Kahului Airport. You pay for the plane, so if you have three people, you can split the $700 for the hour-long flight that lands at the Kalaupapa peninsula on Moloka'i. They also have a longer flight to the Big Island, which includes landing and lunch for $1,800. This isn't a sightseeing tour. You will actually be *flying* the Cirrus and probably landing it, and in the process you'll learn about the unique challenges of flying around mountainous tropical islands. And if you're a pilot who needs a BFR, you'd be hard pressed to find a better place to do it.

Pilots looking for the cheapest airplane rentals on the island should know that **Maui Aviators** (808-871-6990) has several 172s for $250 per hour wet.

POWERED HANG GLIDERS

First, I need to get something out of the way. Flying a powered hang glider (known as a trike) is different than any other type of aircraft. When I was growing up, I used to have a recurring dream that I could flap my arms and fly like a bird. My father flew little Cessnas, which, though fun, felt more to me like a car in the air than flying like a bird.

I had forgotten my flying dreams until I reviewed a company that gave lessons in this odd little craft called a trike. As soon as my instructor and I took off, I realized that a person *really could* fly like a bird. *This* was what the flying bug felt like! I was so smitten with the craft that I eventually hired the instructor on another island to teach me, and flew trikes myself. So although I have no personal interest in any company teaching trikes in Hawai'i, my perspective isn't as remote as it is for most activities. After all, it's not possible to anonymously review companies like Hang Gliding Maui because I know the pilot. (We're both members of the small lightsport community.)

With that explanation, powered hang gliding is the activity I recommend. Trikes take off and land on regular runways (in this case Hana Airport), have a ballistic parachute recovery system for the whole plane, and the ease and grace of the craft is glorious. (Stream the movie *Fly Away Home* if you want to see what they're like.) It's as close to flying like a bird as any form of flight I know. Trikes are what I have come to love so much and, in my opinion, are the safest form of lightsport flight available. (I'm not a daredevil and wouldn't fly them myself if I felt unsafe in them, though any time you're in the air, you're potentially at risk, even on the airlines.) I grin like a fool every time I fly and have never reviewed an activity that generates more enthusiastic responses from other participants. It seems that whenever I see people coming off a trike (since I use the same airports that the trike companies do), passengers are frothing at the mouth with excitement, proclaiming that it's the best thing they've ever done on vacation.

The local company is **Hang Gliding Maui** (808-264-3287). Located out in lovely Hana the pilot, Armin Engert, is a Certified Flight Instructor and is well known and respected in the light sport and hang gliding communities with a stellar safety record. I can't review him anonymously, but I can tell you that his skill as a pilot is something I aspire to. He has *16,000 hours* of trike flight time—perhaps the most of any one in the world. Armin has a camera mounted on the wing to take photos of you during your lesson for $40—just in case no one back home believes you. (It's $80 for video.) There is a 240-pound weight limit. The cost of a half-hour, in-air lesson is $210, 45-minutes is $280 and $350 for an hour. Reserve in advance. Expensive? Perhaps. But it's so unspeakably cool that the memories will stay with you for a lifetime. No credit cards.

PARAGLIDERS

Paragliding is, in my opinion, a much less safe method of flying. It's is essentially a gliding parachute. You are very susceptible to gusts of wind and to landing where you *don't* want to land. The chutes are prone to collapsing (unlike rigid or flex-wing flyers), and I know too many longtime pilots who've only received injuries while flying this particular type of wing.

Having said that, **Proflyght** (808-874-5433) impresses us with their attention to safety and their record. (We've seen others in this field we can't say that about.) The owner, Dexter, has been flying for years and does a great job of getting you prepared for your flight.

Your first flight is an introductory class. You're not gonna be soaring all the way down to the beach. You'll launch from upcountry Haleakala, and you'll also be landing there. You need to weigh less than 230 lbs. and be able to run—straight down a steep launch area and into thin air. The initial takeoff is the most squirrelly part, but once you're away from the ground, you sit back and basically lounge in an airborne chair and take in the view of almost the whole central valley. No sound—only the wind and your own hoots.

If you have your own camera (a GoPro is perfect here), the instructors are very good at capturing your experience while you steer. They have two launch points: the preferred one with 3,000 feet of descent over 12–15 minutes for $265, or a 1,000-foot descent in 3–5 minutes for $145 (which isn't long enough to get comfortable). Meeting point is on Waipoli Road, next to Ali'i Kula Lavender.

GLIDERS

Gliders are engine-less aircraft that are towed into the sky by another airplane, cut loose, then soar using either thermal updrafts or mechanical updrafts (caused when wind is deflected upward by mountains). Unfortunately, East Maui doesn't have either of those conditions, making soaring nearly impossible. Despite their name, **Skyview Soaring** (808-344-9663) in Hana gets around this by using a motorglider. During the one-hour flight you spend half the time slowly motoring your way up to the top of Haleakala (clouds permitting). Then they cut the motor, and the second half is spent gliding your way back to Hana. It's quiet and peaceful in the hot, cramped, two-person cockpit, and the pilot is good about letting you fly the airplane as much as you want on the way down. (Or you can take photos out the tiny window.) If you want a genuine glider experi-

ence, complete with updrafts, you gotta go to O'ahu. If you want the freedom that an engine brings to see the sights, try Hang Gliding Maui in Hana or one of the helicopter companies. But if you want a relaxed and quiet ride down the slopes of Haleakala, these are the guys to go with. $300 for the one-hour ride, $160 for 30 minutes. 245-pound max. At the Hana Airport. Cash or check only.

ATVS

These are those four-wheeled things that look like Tonka Toys on steroids with knobby tires. They are often used by ranchers these days to chase cows. And they're a lot of fun to ride.

The current leaders in the equipment category are **Maui Off-Road Adventures** (808-495-0950). Their four-seater, Polaris RZRs have a lot of power and are a hoot to drive. Once you've passed their safety talk and assessment, the fun begins. You're able to open up the vehicles and really feel the power a couple of times during the tour. Two or three stops will allow

Paragliding off Haleakala.

One company uses single rider ATVs, the other uses these four-seaters.

you to switch drivers (for those who want to), and you'll climb to around 2,000 feet, making for great vistas and some dirt-smeared selfies. Their tours are set in old pineapple fields above Kapalua, with nice views of Moloka'i and Lana'i. Guides are friendly and tend to be more engaged than other companies. Only dings are a lack of refreshments and next to no facilities offered to clean up at the end of the tour. (Bring some trashable clothes, closed-toe shoes and some wipes). Otherwise, it's one of the better ATV experiences. Prices are steep. $189 per person for groups of 2–4 ($150 for kids 7–17), $99 if you don't drive and just ride with the guide, and $350 if you're a solo driver. Turns out that one isn't just the loneliest number, it's also the most expensive. (Google *Three Dog Night* if you don't get that reference.)

Maui Mountain Activities (808-242-5558) takes you on forested ranch land and trails that skirt Waihe'e Valley. You'll go up just over 1,000 feet for a nice over-look of the valley, then head down to the coastline. There's shade and more of a tropical feel here thanks to being on the windward side of the island. (Don't worry—you'll still have plenty of opportunity to get dusty and dirty.) They use single rider ATVs and offer a morning ride and afternoon ride. Waters, juices and sodas are provided. Tours last 1.5–2 hours, $180 per person. On the pricey side, but the guides are friendly and knowledgeable, plus it's a part of the island you'd otherwise only get to see on horseback.

BIKING

The biking scene on Maui is certainly more varied than on the other Hawaiian islands. In addition to simply pedaling around the neighborhood, there's the famous Haleakala downhill ride, the less-famous Skyline downhill mountain bike ride, cycling for the road and a range of mountain biking opportunities.

FROM HALEAKALA DOWNHILL

You've probably heard about this one since at its peak more than 100,000 people per year were cycling down Haleakala. You need to know how dramatically this has changed since what are affectionately known as "the old days." Back then you started near the summit of 10,000-foot-high Haleakala and cruised downhill virtually the whole way to the ocean. If you opted for the sunrise tour, you'd get to see sunrise from the mountain the Hawaiians called *house of the sun,* which can be glorious—unless you don't dress warmly enough.

Well, in 2007 the park service banned commercial bike riding within the park boundaries, citing "safety concerns." (Oddly, those safety concerns don't extend to bicyclists doing the downhill ride on their own, which it's still legal to do—only with bike companies.) Today, those companies are forced to start their tours from the 6,500-foot level. You'll still see the sunrise if you opt to do so, and park entrance fees are included with tour prices, but afterward you'll drive down a third of the mountain's elevation to start your bike tour.

The companies have improved in recent years and are more upfront about the tours. In the past, photos would depict tour groups biking down from the summit, even after the ban. You'll still see plenty of photos of a Haleakala sunrise on their websites, but all now point out that the actual bike tour starts just outside the park boundaries.

Nowadays most people are picked up at their hotels or condos between 2 and 3 a.m. A quiet or surly stupor fills the van during the two-hour or so drive up the mountain, as thoughts such as, "Whose stupid idea was this?" or "There better not be any darned sing-alongs on the van" dominate the morning.

Once at the top, most people soon learn that they are seriously underdressed. Temperatures from the low 30s to the upper 40s, coupled with 30 mph winds at times, can turn the rarefied air to a symphony of groans and brrrs. See page 125 for more information on the sunrise and how to prepare for it. When you get cold, you can sit in the van and drink coffee to keep warm.

There are two large companies that do this tour and a few small ones. **Mountain Riders** (800-706-7700), which rides 26 miles to the ocean and **Maui Mountain Cruisers** (808-871-6014), which rides almost to the ocean. They take 10–13 people per trip, with a guide in front setting the pace and a van (called a sag wagon) pulling up the rear. Anyone who gets uncomfortable can climb in the van at any time. Both companies use comparable bikes whose wide seats are appreciated if you haven't been on a bike in a while. It's $180–$250 for the sunrise trip, cheaper if you want to sleep in a few hours later. **Cruiser Phil** (808-575-9575) is smaller and a bit more personalized—tours are $220 (less if booked directly). **Maui Easy Riders** (808-344-9489) is another good, small outfit with a great price of $135 for one of the longer, guided rides. **Bike It Maui** (808-878-3364) is $130 and a shorter ride of around 20 miles. **Skyline Eco-Adventures** (808-518-2860) has the shortest guided tour, but you also do their zipline course for $250.

A Word of Warning

Because so many people do this, it's tempting to think that the danger must be minimal. It's not. From road rash to broken bones to deaths, this activity has taken its toll on visitors.

The first time we did it, we invited visiting relatives to go. Back then you went from the summit, and we brought our 15-year-old niece. With only 2 miles left on the ride, a bee landed on her (not an uncommon occurrence) and, distracted, she failed to negotiate a turn and took a vicious tumble end-over-end right in front of us, landing on boulders 15 to 20 feet from the road. Even wearing a motorcycle helmet, she had head injuries (a deep gash all the way to the skull) and was hospitalized. It literally took over a year before her head injury symptoms abated.

Part of the problem is that riders in groups are strongly prodded to ride at least 20 mph, or the tour companies claim they'll be ticketed. And 20 mph (often faster) is pretty fast on some stretches, especially when you're still stiff from the cold or haven't ridden a bike in several years. Though the age limit is 12 years old, we don't recommend it to anyone under 16. (Incidentally, those generous souls at Mountain Riders refused to refund her parents' money, even though they spent much of the day at the hospital. Also, in case they're reading this, our niece is still waiting for her promised complimentary *I Survived the Haleakala Downhill Ride* T-shirt, which seemed particularly appropriate considering how it ended.)

A Few Thoughts

A small flashlight can be handy at the nearly lightless pre-sunrise summit; many people hurt themselves stumbling around. Sunglasses are recommended on the ride because most helmets don't have eye protection. Contact lens wearers should bring drops. The colder you allow yourself to get before the ride, the stiffer you'll be during the ride. Lastly, if you're going to do the sunrise trip, do it early in your trip, when your body clock is still on mainland time.

An alternative to the massive downhill companies is to bike it on your own. Companies will take you to the edge of the park (at the 6,500-foot level) and let you ride down on your own after perhaps first visiting the summit for a sunrise. And if you can arrange your own transportation (commercial companies can't do this), you're allowed to ride all the way from the summit in the park, if you like, just like the good old days. The increased risk of not having a guide in front of you blocking tackle is balanced by the fact that you get to go *at your own*

The view of clouds, ocean and Central Maui below are tempting, but don't take your eyes off the road.

pace. Also, you can choose a different route if you want. For instance, **Bike Maui** (808-575-9575) is located in Ha'iku. Instead of stopping at the 2,000-foot level or having to take Baldwin Avenue at the end, you can take the more scenic Kokomo Road (first stop sign outside of Makawao) into Ha'iku with just a little uphill riding past Makawao. It's $110 for the drop-off at the park boundary; add a sunrise at the summit for $210. A pretty decent outfit, and they have some of the better bikes on the summit, complete with disc brakes and front suspension.

MOUNTAIN BIKE HALEAKALA'S SPINE

One of the most interesting bike rides in Hawai'i is down the lesser-known spiny side of Haleakala. See page 260 for more.

OTHER BIKING OPPORTUNITIES

Of all the Hawaiian islands, Maui has the best biking opportunities.

Maui Cyclery (808-579-9009) is the unofficial cycling headquarters for Maui. This shop is all about the cycling experience and caters to those who have a passion for road bikes and spandex. (They suggest you bring your own cycling shoes, pedals are included.) Offering not just bike rentals, Maui Cyclery also has personalized tours of the best biking routes around the island for single or multiple days, starting at $150. Though they welcome all skill levels, this isn't a downhill cruise. These tours are about *climbing* the mountain, and you should be prepared for a serious workout with lots of elevation gain. These guys are as legit as you get on Maui for cycling.

If **mountain biking** is your thing, the **Kahakapao Recreation Area** above Makawao offers the only mountain bike-specific trails on the island. There are several trails exclusive to bikers, as well as skill tracks with different gravity-oriented features. Most notably, the Pauma (or Pump) Track has berms, tabletop jumps and rhythm sections. Novice and experienced riders will like the Pineapple Express trail. Take the Fong Ridge trail uphill to find it. The Pineapple Express takes you 1.6 miles downhill through the entire Kahakapao trail system and brings you out next to the skill tracks. Helmets are required here. Entrance is free. (See map on page 121 for Piiholo Road.) At 0.5 miles past mile marker 1, left onto Waiahiwi Road. After coming out of the narrow gulch, turn right onto Kahakapao Road and follow it to the top. Two parking lots are available, but use the upper.

RENTING A BIKE

If you want to rent a bike, in West Maui try **West Maui Cycles** (808-661-9005). They have a range of styles for $35–$100 per day.

If you're looking to go biking in South Maui, call **South Maui Bicycles** (808-874-0068). They have a good range of bikes, including Treks for $22 a day.

Most of the mountain biking trails found on Maui are Upcountry, and **Krank Cycles** (808-572-2299) in Makawao has a great selection of top-of-the-line bikes running from $39–$130 a day. They can set you up with the best rig for your skill level and point you to the best trails for that day.

In West Maui, **Ride Smart Maui** (808-633-8553) has pedal-assisted electric bikes for $70–$100 per day. They are in the AAAAA Rent-A-Space Mall in Honokowai.

This is probably the single biggest activity that people pay to do on Maui, and for good reason. The calm, clear waters make it a boater's heaven. Maui's boating conditions are superb due to the shape of its coastline, and it has close island neighbors to visit.

In some ways, this is one of the most difficult sections to write about. The section's length is a testament to your varied options. *So* many choices and fleeting characteristics make it dizzying. We may take a boat tour and rave about it, but the day after we go to press, the boating company may sell their 50-foot sailing yacht and begin taking passengers out on an inflatable raft from Walmart. It's hard to keep up.

Most of the boats leave from Lahaina or Ma'alaea (close to Kihei). A few boats leave from the Kihei Boat Ramp and Ka'anapali Beach.

Boating trips can generally be broken down into four types:

Snorkel Trips
Pure Sailing Trips
Whale Watching mid-Dec.–mid-May
Dinner Cruises

Many of the snorkel trips *claim* they also whale watch, but that usually means they'll simply make a beeline to their snorkeling spot, hoping to spot one of the buggers. It's like calling them fishing boats because they drag a lure behind them on their way to Molokini.

We need to clarify something up front. Taking a boat trip on Maui is like making a dessert with chocolate, ice cream and peanut butter. No matter how you combine the ingredients, you're gonna end up with something sweet and tasty. (See, *that's* what I get for writing while hungry.) The boater's ingredients are the boat, sun, water and fish. Unless the weather is horrible, even if you're boating with complete idiots, odds are you're still going to have a fun, relaxing time, because boating Maui's often-placid waters can't be beat. Since not all boating companies are created equal, our job is to steer you to the ones who seem to do the best job (and away from the idiots). We've anonymously ridden scads of boats off Maui, and the difference is striking. But re-member as you read these critiques: Even bad boat trips are usually fun.

We've noticed that there seem to be two types of crews. One is composed of cocky guys and gals who spend all their time and energy showing their crewmates and you how impossibly cool they are. (The old *don't you wish you were as cool as me?* syndrome.) Then there are crews who channel more of their effort to help ensure that *you* have a good time. We obviously lean toward the latter.

The prices we show may be different from what they advertise. Boating companies tend to tack on a number of garbage extras, such as harbor fees and fuel surcharges (particularly galling during times when fuel prices are lower), so we have calculated your out-the-door price.

MOLOKINI SNORKEL TOURS

Molokini is a small, crescent-shaped island 3 miles off the coast of South Maui. It's actually a submerged volcano crater; the sliver you see sticking up above the waves is what remains of the crater rim. The whole area is now a bird and marine sanctuary, and one of the best snorkel and SCUBA spots in the entire state.

It's illegal to feed the fish here, but you'll quickly realize that these little beggars *are* hand fed. (We've even seen boat personnel feeding them after telling passengers not to do it.) There's no need for you to do it; the fish *assume* you will. The fish count isn't as great as some other places on Maui (when it comes to sea life, Molokini's reputation is a bit overhyped), but it's still high. The bottom topography isn't overly interesting either, just a gently sloping floor. But it's covered with colorful coral, and there's no runoff, so underwater visibility is an *unbelievable* 100–180 feet.

We've repeatedly snorkeled the entire crater, and the best snorkeling is usually on the inside left (from the outside looking in—the side closest to Maui.) Boats that

Molokini is where you'll find the best water visibility in all Maui. Dive boats use the submerged corner and snorkel boats explore the inside.

park elsewhere will likely tell you *they* park in the best spot, but they're wrong. (SCUBA diving is a different matter.) The inside right is a close second, with the center the least interesting. (That's relative; the center still has lots of coral and fish.) Don't stay in one place; swim over near the shore to see more coral, then to deeper water for more fish. During normal trade winds, floating debris tends to accumulate in the center-left, and the water gets more churned up, so it's best to avoid that part. But it's usually reasonably calm. A big, clear pool for you to play in. A giant fishbowl in the middle of the open ocean.

The biggest problem with Molokini is its popularity. On a given day more than 1,000 snorkelers may visit the crater—twice that many during peak times. Each boat moors in a certain spot, and you are told to stay close to your boat. (Boat crews will tell you it's a Coast Guard regulation so you won't get mad, but we checked with the Coast Guard, and it's not.) If you're in the less interesting center part of the crater, you may need to violate *the tour boat's* rules and swim left or right through a sea of snorkelers to get to a better part. But stay inside the crater and away from the far edges, especially the far-right side (as you're looking inside)

where the crater wall is submerged. Powerful currents there can be bad.

Most boats that go to Molokini in the morning go to a second location after, such as **Turtle Town**. *Where is Turtle Town?* Wherever they say it is. It's a marketing gimmick. (After all, doesn't the name *sound* intriguing?) The term refers to several reefs along the South Maui coast. Different companies go to different turtle towns, and despite the picture they put in your head, the odds of actually seeing honu (the Hawaiian word for turtle) are probably 50-50 or less. Don't go with the expectation that you'll swim with sea turtles. If you do, great. Otherwise, just enjoy the water, coral and fish. Visibility will seem merely fair, but that's because you just got spoiled at Molokini on the first stop. People who would have been *thrilled* with 80-foot visibility before, suddenly sniff indignantly because it's not 180 feet like Molokini on a good day. By the way, many companies are now using the name *Turtle Arches*, which sounds even better, doesn't it?

Similar to Turtle Town, **Coral Gardens** refers to multiple locations off the West Maui coast. Boat tours drop you farther out, meaning you'll have better visibility than shore-bound snorkelers, but these reefs are mainly a fallback spot when the surf is too rough at better locations, or they can be a primary destination on afternoon tours.

The double-decker **Four Winds II** used to be our favorite of the big boats for Molokini tours, until they got dethroned by the mighty triple-deck **Calypso**. Read the individual reviews to see the differences and what to expect. Trips aboard power catamarans like these tend to be a relaxed experience, especially great for families. **Pacific Whale Foundation Eco-Adventures**, the **Pride of Maui** and **Lani Kai** are your other options in this category.

Aqua Adventures is a smaller, single-hull power vessel.

If you want to feel more at one with the sea, consider taking a sailing catamaran with **Sail Maui**, **Trilogy**, **Kai Kanani II** or **Alii Nui**.

Then you've got the rigid-hull inflatables (RIBs). It's a bouncier experience where you forgo comfort in exchange for more adventure, and some of them explore less-visited areas, such as Molokini's back side

Boat	Phone (808)	Max. Passengers	Type of Boat	Departs	Alcohol	Snorkel Stops	Rest Rooms	Food
Alii Nui	875-0333	60	65' Sailing Cat	Ma'alaea	Yes	2	Yes	Buffet
Aqua Adventures	472-2782	40	50' Single Hull	Ma'alaea	Yes	2	Yes	Deli
Blue Water Rafting	879-7238	24	27' & 30' RIB	Kihei	No	3	No	Deli
Calypso	856-4260	149	70' Power Cat	Ma'alaea	Yes	2	Yes	Buffet
Cinderella	344-3906	6	51' Sailing Sloop	Ma'alaea	Yes	1	No	Buffet
Four Winds II	879-8188	122	55' Sailing Cat	Ma'alaea	Yes	1	Yes	BBQ
Gemini	669-1700	49	64' Sailing Cat	Ka'anapali	Yes	1	Yes	Buffet
Hawaii Ocean Proj.	667-6165	80	65' Single Hull	Lahaina	No	2	Yes	Deli
Hula Girl	667-5980	49	65' Sailing Cat	Ka'anapali	Yes	1	Yes	Menu $
Insane	633-3138	20	30' Jet Boat	Ka'anapali	No	0	No	None
Ka'anapali Ocean	633-3138	32	46' Single Hull	Ka'anapali	BYOB	3	Yes	Deli
Kai Kanani II	879-7218	80	65' Sailing Cat	Maluaka Bch	Yes	2	Yes	Deli
Kainani Sails	495-1001	6	43' Sailing Yacht	Ka'anapali	BYOB	1	Yes	Deli
Lani Kai	244-1979	59	53' Power Cat	Ma'alaea	Yes	2	Yes	Deli
Leilani	242-0955	40	50' Motor Yacht	Ma'alaea	Yes	2	Yes	BBQ
Malolo	856-4260	66	55' Power Cat	Ma'alaea	Yes	2	Yes	Deli
Maui Adventure	661-5550	36	49' RIB	Lahaina	BYOB	1	Yes	Deli
Maui Magic	879-8188	45	54' Power Cat	Ma'alaea	Yes	2	Yes	BBQ
Maui Ocean Riders	661-3586	18	30' RIB	Mala Wharf	No	3	No	Deli
Maui Sailing Canoe	281-9301	6	Sailing Canoe	Polo Beach	No	1	No	None
Maui Snorkel	270-8776	18	40' RIB	Kihei	BYOB	2	Yes	Deli
Pacific Whale	249-8811	34–149	Sailing/Power Cats	Ma' & Lah	Yes	2	Yes	BBQ
Pride of Maui	242-0955	136	65' Power Cat	Ma'alaea	Yes	2	Yes	BBQ
Quicksilver	856-4260	125	55' Power Cat	Ma'alaea	Yes	2	Yes	BBQ
Redline Rafting	201-7450	24	35' RIB	Kihei	No	4	Sort of	Deli
Sail Maui	427-3281	38/30	47' Sailing Cat	Ma' & Lah	No	1	Yes	Deli
Scotch Mist II	661-0386	22	50' Sailing Sloop	Lahaina	Yes	1	No	Deli
Seafire	879-2201	22	40' RIB	Kihei	BYOB	2	No	Barely
Teralani	661-7245	49	65' Sailing Cat	Ka'anapali	Yes	2	Yes	BBQ
Trilogy I–VI	874-5649	49–96	Sailing Cats	Ma', Lah, Ka'	Yes	2	Yes	Deli/BBQ
Ultimate Whale	667-5678	22	30' & 47' RIB	Lahaina	BYOB	2	Yes	Deli

or the rugged lava rock formations of the **Kanaio Coast** (far south end of Maui, where it's too rough for most tour boats to go). Check the entries for **Seafire**, **Redline Rafting**, **Blue Water Rafting** and **Maui Snorkel Charters**.

All boats listed above depart from **Ma'alaea Harbor** (10 miles from Molokini) or the **Kihei Boat Ramp** (6 miles away) in South Maui.

In addition to morning tours, many of these boats also offer shorter, cheaper afternoon tours that go to Molokini when conditions allow. But the wind usually picks up in the afternoons, so more often than not they'll just go to a location somewhere along the coast.

If Molokini is the destination for you (and if it's your first time on Maui, it probably should be), feel free to skip ahead to the individual boat reviews now. Otherwise, read on.

LANA'I SNORKEL TOURS

The island of Lana'i is another popular snorkel destination. There are tours that go there and land so you can snorkel from the beach, tours that take you to snorkel off the coast but don't land (that's the *Michael Collins on Apollo 11* experience), and there are some boats that go all the way around the island, providing scenic views while hitting multiple snorkel stops along the way.

Most boats that go to Lana'i (but not all the way around) snorkel at **Manele Bay**, which is a marine reserve filled with sea life. Those that land give you the option of heading over to nearby **Hulopo'e Beach** in front of the Four Seasons, where you can snorkel a different part of the reserve from shore. (Be sure to read the Hulopo'e Beach entry to get the snorkeling details.)

Other tours go to the more remote **Shark Fin Cove**. This is a convenient place to park big boats but comparatively dull. The exception is if you're on a small boat

that moors near the shark-fin-shaped rock for which the cove is named, where the snorkeling is much better. It drops off quickly, but a staggering variety of colorful butterfly fish gathers near the spot where the triangular rock breaks the surface.

Water quality is not always the best. Runoff from heavy rainstorms can muck up visibility all around the island, and the effect can last for months. So while snorkeling Lana'i *can* be good, it's not guaranteed like Molokini. But you've got the best odds of seeing dolphins on trips to Lana'i since they usually hangout near the island.

Trilogy was the original Lana'i tour company and still the only one with permission to take people by shuttle from Manele Harbor to Hulopo'e Beach to snorkel. (All others require passengers to hoof it a half mile each way). **Sail Maui** snorkels off the boat in Manele Bay, then lands. Both of those catamarans usually sail on this trip. **Maui Adventure Cruises** uses a RIB to snorkel off the coast, then lands.

Pacific Whale, **Quicksilver**, and **Hawaii Ocean Project** all use double-decker power catamarans—more comfortable and better for families with young kids, but less adventurous. Pacific Whale and Hawaii Ocean Project tend to default to Manele Bay, Quicksilver to Shark Fin. None of them lands.

There are only two boats that we know of that consistently circumnavigate the island. Of those, **Ka'anapali Ocean Adventures** is the most comfortable. The other option, **Maui Ocean Riders**, uses a rigid-hull inflatable, and 70 miles is a looooong way to go by RIB.

With these all-day tours, you'll get to see more of the island than anyone else, including a huge, ghostly shipwreck that most guides incorrectly refer to as a WWII Liberty Ship. Actually, it's **YOGN-42**, a barge that was used to haul fuel. In 1943 in the South Pacific near Vanuatu, the

This WWII fuel hauler was purposefully run aground off Lana'i in the late 40s.

tug towing it was sunk by a Japanese torpedo. The barge was returned to Pearl Harbor, and the Navy eventually abandoned it here after the war. The reason it still looks relatively intact after more than 70 years exposed to saltwater and pounding surf is because it was constructed out of reinforced *concrete*, since steel was in short supply.

Another interesting sight you'll see on the back side of Lana'i is an otherworldly place called "Pinnacles" or "The Four Sisters." You might get told that the giant pillars of rock sticking out of the ocean are where lava sprayed up like a geyser and solidified in place. Neat! But not even remotely true. They are common sea stacks—harder areas of land left standing after the surrounding cliffs eroded away.

Tours around the island are best for intermediate to advanced snorkelers since you're often in deeper water that is more exposed and farther from shore.

Boat tours to Lana'i leave from **Lahaina Harbor**, **Mala Boat Ramp**, or **Ka'anapali Beach**, all in West Maui.

Finally, if you're looking for a much cheaper, no-frills way to get to Lana'i just to go snorkeling from shore, you can take the **Expeditions Maui–Lana'i Ferry**.

WEST MAUI COAST SNORKEL TOURS

For tours along the West Maui coast, boats slide right up onto the sand at Ka'anapali Beach to pick up their passengers. *Super* convenient if you're staying at one of the nearby resorts, but less appealing if not, since you'll likely have to shell out an extra $30–$40 to park at Whalers Village. (Most boats don't validate.)

The goal of these snorkel tours is to head north, wrapping along the coast to **Honolua Bay** or one of the others in the area like **Slaughterhouse** or the "Cliff House" cove at **Kapalua Beach**. Honolua is a protected reserve, with lots of fish and tons of coral—more than Molokini. If the surf isn't cooperating, which is more likely to happen in the winter, boats may divert south to another location where conditions will be more favorable, such as **Coral Gardens**.

Before you read any further, you should know that you can just as easily *drive* to these locations and snorkel from shore *for free*. (See *Beaches*.) So only book one of these tours if you're excited about the experience of riding on a boat.

That said, boat tours along the West Maui coast are effortless and great fun: Just walk to the beach and hop on. You stand a decent chance of encountering dolphins along the way, you'll snorkel, enjoy lunch at a beautiful place, and usually sail (or whale watch) on the way back.

Gemini, **Hula Girl**, **Teralani**, and **Trilogy** are all similar-sized sailing catamarans, and the experience will be largely the same no matter which you pick, but read the individual reviews to see the differences in price, tour length, and nuances like which ones have the better food, which have an open bar, etc. **Pacific Whale** also has a catamaran that leaves from Lahaina Harbor.

In addition to snorkel tours, most of these boats offer dedicated whale watching tours in season as well as sunset cruises. But don't dress too fancy for a sunset champagne cruise—wear shorts or a dress you can pull up over your knees, since you *will* get wet getting onto the boat.

A FEW TIPS

Some companies can be real stingy with the food. After your first snorkel you're apt to be pretty hungry and may not be offered any food. Consider bringing your own stash of snacks with you. You may be able to sell them to other hungry customers at prices confiscatory enough to pay for your trip. *I have a bid of $8 for a chocolate chip cookie. Do I hear $9?*

Another consideration is warmth. Though the water temps range from 75 °F to 80 °F, you may want to consider renting a thin wetsuit from a dive shop to keep you snug. The second snorkel site tends to chill people, especially in the winter. (February has the coldest water.) Of course, boats that rent wetsuits tend to *under*-report the temperature about 5–10 °F to convince you to rent.

Catamarans are twin-hulled and slice through the water much more cleanly than single-hull boats and, if wide enough, are more stable (less rocking) on the water. At the other end of the spectrum

are rafts and RIBs (rigid-hull inflatables), which are much bumpier and not recommended for pregnant women or people with bad backs.

If you're uncomfortable using the boat's snorkel gear (either for sanitary or fitting reasons), consider renting it elsewhere and bringing it along. Most boats have only one size mask. Also, when you defog your mask (using either dedicated goo or your own spit), rub it hard into the inside glass then rinse quickly.

If you want a towel, you'll probably have to bring your own.

Small, white tip reef sharks, which are essentially harmless, are sometimes seen at Molokini. *Don't worry* about them. Worry about getting sunburned.

Below deck is a bad place to be if you're worried about getting seasick. Without a reference point, you're much more likely to let 'er rip down there. If you *tied one on* the night before, do yourself a favor and take Dramamine, Bonine or apply Scopolamine patches *before* you go. Ginger is also a very good preventative and treatment for seasickness. If none of that works, head to the rear and shoot for distance.

People come off these trips *toasted*, especially in the summer. Make *sure* you slather on the sunscreen, or you'll be sorry for the rest of your trip. However, the coral at Molokini is showing signs of stress, and sunscreen from snorkelers is one theory. If possible, wear a shirt or rent a rash guard while snorkeling, then use the sunscreen when you get out of the water. Most boats won't allow you to use spray-on sunscreen.

Morning snorkel trips nearly always offer better snorkeling and calmer seas. If you're one of the first boats at Molokini, you'll have a much better shot at seeing bigger life, such as eagle rays, eels or an octopus. The only upside for **afternoon snorkel trips** is price. The only time we recommend windier afternoon trips is when you only want to sail.

SNUBA (see page 247) is often available. Inside Molokini Crater it's harder to justify the extra $60–$70 as you really won't see much more than the snorkelers see a few feet above, but it's kind of fun. (Other locations make more sense for SNUBA.)

PURE SAILING TRIPS

You're not really heading anywhere, and you aren't really interested in doing anything—you just want to sail. Most boats are sloops (a single hull with little or no shade other than what the sail provides). If you're up front, sloops require you to move more often than the twin-hulled catamarans (cats).

When it's too windy to go on a snorkel trip, it's probably great for sailing on the **Scotch Mist II**, **Cinderella**, **Sail Maui** or **Kainani Sails**. If you're looking for a cul-tural experience, **Maui Sailing Canoe** is real Hawaiian outrigger sailing canoe. In addition to sailboats listed in this sections, pretty much every catamaran that has a snorkel tour also offers two-hour sailing cruises at sunset.

THE BOATS

Alii Nui (808-875-0333) is a first-rate, 65-foot sailing catamaran with a good crew. Their six-hour snorkel tour goes to Molokini Crater and Turtle Arches. They feed you very well—full breakfast and lunch, plus beer, wine and champagne. SNUBA is available for an extra $65, SCUBA for $75 per tank. Even when fully loaded with 60 passengers, the boat doesn't feel as crowded as some of the others. Unfortunately, they moor near the center of the crater, which is not a great spot. A couple notable perks: They'll pick you up from anywhere in South or West Maui

Hey, a double rainbow! Grab the camera.

for no additional charge, and they provide complimentary towels and wetsuit tops. But at $199 (kids 4–12 are $149), you pay a hefty premium for all this, which perhaps explains the reason for the boat's name, which means *big royalty*. Ma'alaea Harbor, slip 56.

Aqua Adventures (866-472-2782) uses a 50-foot boat with two 350-horse diesel engines to get you to Molokini more quickly than most. The boat can feel crowded, especially when full with 40 people, and particularly when negotiating the ladder to the upper deck. However, other aspects of their tours are much better. Most boat crews start the day with a lot of energy, but their enthusiasm fades by lunchtime. Not these guys. They will probably remember your name, treat you like a long-lost cousin and give honest, accurate information about the area. The deli lunch is ample, and they practically guilt you into taking seconds and thirds. And the boat moors toward the interesting right side of the crater. Complimentary beer and mai tais follow their second snorkel stop at Turtle Arches. $110 for a five-hour tour, add $55 for SNUBA. Kids 3–13 are $70. Ma'alaea Harbor slip 51.

Blue Water Rafting (808-879-7238) uses rigid-hull inflatables (a V-shaped hull surrounded by a rubber pontoon). They do things differently and are more likely to go out in rougher seas than other companies.

From Kihei Boat Ramp you head down the coast, past La Pérouse Bay to an old lava flow at Kanaio (which literally means *the bastard sandalwood tree*). After exploring the unusual lava formations, you head back, usually to La Pérouse Bay to a rather dull snorkeling area, then stop at another, better site for snorkeling and a deli lunch.

The boat does a scorching 40 knots, and the ride is a blast (though less comfortable than a cushier boat and certainly wetter). Little shade. Consider a light, waterproof jacket for the morning trip out and for wet riding later. $115 for four hours. (Kids 4–12 are $94, no kids under 4). They also have a 5.5-hour trip for $140 that includes Molokini, but we recommend the shorter trip. Best seats are on the back, left side. Winds past La Pérouse can be fierce, hence their early start. No alcohol allowed.

P.S. Despite ads you may see, they no longer go into the sea caves.

Calypso by Quicksilver Charters (808-856-4260) is the biggest, most tricked-out tour boat on Maui. The 70-foot power cat has 4,000 square feet of space spread over three decks, two slides (the one off the front has an 8-foot drop into the water), a 15-foot-high jumping platform from the second level, and a glass bottom. It's basically a floating playhouse that takes you on a 5.5-hour tour to Molokini and Turtle Town for $130. (It's $90 for kids under 13; one kid 6 and under for free per paying adult.)

The boat was built in 2017 in Honolulu, and the designers clearly put a lot of thought into how to comfortably carry a lot of people without the boat feeling crowded. They've got *11* ladders off the back, so even with a full load of 149 people, you never have a long wait to get into or out of the water. Every seat has a table so you don't have to awkwardly try to balance your food in your lap while eating, and you'll get a real breakfast (as opposed to standard continental) with scrambled eggs and ham. Lunch is hearty, but it's prepared in advance and isn't as good as the food you'll get on the boats that grill at sea. Here, it's rather dry chicken and pulled pork. $2 drinks from the bar.

Seating is first-come, first-serve, so you'll want to be sure to get in line early if you want to get a prime front-row seat on the bow, or somewhere up top on the third deck. (Keep in mind, though, that if you tend to suffer from motion sickness, the higher up you go, the more you'll feel it rolling.)

Their mooring location within the crater is OK, but it's as close to the undesirable middle as we like to go. Head straight back to the crater wall, then slowly work your way to the right for better snorkeling. SNUBA for an extra $62.

A couple of minor complaints: The dark blue deck can get scorching hot, so bring your flip-flops to wear on the boat. And don't rely on their estimates of water temperature when they ask if you want to rent a wetsuit. (*Is the water really only in the high 60s in summer? This ain't Lake Michigan!*) Stick your toe in before paying. Bottom line: Unless you want to go sailing (and if you're not scared off by the price), this is the Molokini trip you should pick. Find the boat on the far side of Ma'alaea Harbor, all the way at the end. Can't miss it. Wheelchair accessible.

Their sister ship, **Malolo**, is a single-story power cat that also hits two snorkel spots. Virtually no storage means that the crowded deck always feels cluttered, and you're often bumping into people and stuff. $100 for adults and $50 for kids is the retail rate, but you'd be foolish to pay that since this is their discount boat. Odds are you'll probably get $20 off. Price includes food, but beer and mai tais are extra. Hard to get excited about this one, unless price is paramount.

Cinderella (808-344-3906) is a nice-looking 51-foot sailing yacht. Comfortable in back, less so up front; it holds six. Pricey at $808 for a private two-hour sunset sail. (Or you can rent it by the hour). Five-hour snorkel trip available for $1,670. (Ouch.) They have a deli meal, but you can shave off some of the price if you want to bring your own food. BYOB. Ma'alaea Harbor, slip 41.

The **Expeditions Maui–Lana'i Ferry** (808-661-3756) runs daily between West Maui and the island of Lana'i. Tickets costs $60 round trip ($40 kids 2-11), making it a cheaper and more popular option than flying over to go sightseeing or stay on the island. It's also a cheap alternative to taking a boat tour if all you want to do is go snorkeling from desirable Hulopo'e Beach (without a vehicle you won't be going to explore anywhere else

Calypso's design works very well for Molokini tours.

on island.) You'll have to pack your own food and drink, and they certainly aren't going to divert from schedule to check out any dolphins you may encounter on the way. Think of it as a bus route. Depart from Lahaina Harbor in the morning, land at the harbor at Manele Bay, and walk to the beach.

The trip takes about 45 minutes each way, and all adults must show ID. Sit on the right/ starboard side going over. The first ferry trip departs Lahaina at 6:45 a.m., and the last trip of the day leaves Lana'i at 6:45 p.m. Miss it, and you'll be stranded and sleeping on the beach.

Among the best of the boats is the **Four Winds II** (808-879-8188). This 55-foot, double-deck power catamaran makes morning treks to Molokini. Though they take up to 122 people, the boat is nicely designed to accommodate many people without feeling as crowded as some of the others. There's a good mix of sun and shade, and the upper deck perimeter bench seats allow you to spin around and face the water while resting on the railing—a nice touch. Their usual mooring spot toward the most interesting left side of the crater normally has clear water, though fish counts might be better elsewhere. Their food setup is also the best of the lot. All the pulled-pork sandwiches, chicken, hot dogs and veggie burgers you want are waiting for you when you get out of the water. Open bar (beer and wine only) stays open longer than any of the others.

One somewhat negative aspect—that they don't go to a second site—can be a positive in that they spend more time at the crater, making it feel more leisurely. (Their second "turtle town stop" is where they stop just outside the harbor on the way back and point out turtles. In fairness, it *is* a good place to spot them—you just won't swim with them.) Our only real gripe (in both readers and our experience) is that their website can be unresponsive at times. Calling them direct to book a tour seems to be the best bet. All in all, the Four Winds is a winner.

The five-hour morning Molokini trip is $105 ($75 for kids 3–12), and the shorter afternoon trip to Coral Gardens or occasionally Molokini (conditions permitting) is $57 ($43 for kids). They have wetsuits and underwater cameras available for rent, and you can add on SNUBA for an extra $59. Their hefty see-through sea-boards are *very* nice for timid kids and adults. The "glass bottom" on the boat itself works well for kids (staff are really good with children), but adults might not be too impressed. There's a freshwater hose shower on board and a slide into the water. You'll find it docked at Ma'alaea Harbor, slip 80, on the far side.

Their other boat, **Maui Magic** is a very different product, and we're not as fond of it as we are the Four Winds II. The boat's older, less comfortable and feels more crowded. The five-hour tour heads down the interesting Kanaio Coast (but stays so far from shore that you won't appreciate much detail) on the way to Molokini in hopes of spotting dolphins. SNUBA also available. BBQ and an open bar (after the snorkel), but other outfits can do it for less than the $120 they charge. In short, stick with the Four Winds II.

Gemini (808-669-1700) is a 64-foot sailing cat that leaves from Ka'anapali Beach and usually heads to Honolua Bay to snorkel. Hot buffet lunch and a pretty good crew on the four-hour tour of the West Maui coast for for $127 (includes an open bar). Teens $109, kids ages 2–12 for $75.

Hawaii Ocean Project (808-667-6165) has three boats in their fleet. The **Kaulana** (a 65-foot double decker catamaran with a slide from the upper deck) goes to Lana'i to snorkel at Manele Bay. This tour includes a BBQ lunch and one complimentary drink from the bar. $100 for adults, $60 for kids 7–12 (6 and under are free with a paying adult). Their 120-foot **Maui Princess** is used for dinner cruises (see *Lunch & Dinner Cruises* on page 314) with pricing identical to their Lana'i snorkel tour. The **Lahaina Princess** is mainly used for seasonal whale watching. Though the price is good at $25 for adults, $20 for kids 7–12, we don't recommend it as much. This 65-foot, single-hull yacht, is narrow and tall, meaning it's less stable than a twin-hulled catamaran. Even in calm seas, you'll notice it rocking. The downstairs is totally enclosed except for a few seats on the bow; the upper deck doesn't have any shade. Up top they've got plastic lawn chairs bolted down in front of tables instead of benches, which makes it difficult to get into and out of your seat. They sometimes use this boat if one of the others is in for maintenance—confirm which boat you'll be on when booking a tour, and try to avoid Lahaina Princess.

One of the best tours of the West Maui coast is **Hula Girl** (808-667-5980). The crew (including hands-on owners) is particularly laid back and friendly, and boat is well-designed with a luxurious, spacious feel, even when full. They leave from **Ka'anapali Beach** and go to **Honolua Bay** for snorkeling. (They usually *sail* back rather than *motor*.) The 65-foot catamaran cuts nicely through the water, even in big seas. When they sail downwind, the trampolines up front are fantastic places to be. SCUBA is available for $70 ($81 for an intro). One thing that is unusual is the food. It costs extra (so does the bar). So instead of a free but limited menu, you get a larger selection, and the quality is very good. But expect to spend an extra $10–$30 in addition to the $99 price for the five-hour tour. It's $85 for kids 2–12.

Ka'anapali Ocean Adventures (808-633-3138) is our preferred choice for circumnavigating Lana'i. Their single-hull boat **Sanity** is 46 feet long with padded seats, room enough to get up and stretch your legs, and plenty of shade. The $130, 4-hour scenic tour includes two snorkel stops, plus they visit one of the shipwrecks.

Friendly crew, but they're not great at directing you to the coolest underwater features. And they sometimes underestimate how much food to bring along for lunch, so if you're the last one back on the boat after snorkeling, you might find that all the deli meat is gone and end up filling up on chips. So there are a few things that could stand improvement. But overall, we're fans.

Now, for something totally different, they also have a 30-foot, flat-bottom *jet boat* called **Insane** that they use for one-hour thrill rides. Prepare for gut-wrenching 360-degree spins, slides, fast acceleration and dead stops where you'll feel the G's. Getting wet is a certainty. They'll go tearing off south toward Lahaina doing all sorts of tricks along the way, then, if conditions allow, they'll speed north to Kapalua Bay so you can climb up and jump off the cliff. $99 for adrenaline junkies only. Both boats leave from Ka'anapali Beach (they'll load you up using a skiff), and neither allows kids under 5.

The **Kai Kanani II** (808-879-7218) is a beautiful boat, but crowded when full. Rated to hold 80 passengers, even with just 55 (the most they'll take) it feels packed. Luckily the staff is helpful, the food is good, and the open bar has beer and mai tais. Their sleek boat takes much less time to get to Molokini than boats leaving from Ma'alaea, and it powers through big waves as if it were the calmest of days. No wetsuits for rent, but they'll happily *sell* you a top for $60, and in the winter time you might just be desperate enough to buy it. Super quick to Molokini because its launching point is from Maluaka Beach, though if seas are rough, it might be a

Ka'anapali tours start the right way—with your feet wet and sand between your toes.

challenge climbing aboard (you have to wade to the boat so you'll get wet either way). And don't expect the sails to be raised going out, *maybe* coming back. $199 for a 3.5-hour Molokini and Turtle Town trip. (Kids 3–12 are $162.) They'll pick you up from any Wailea resort for $5.

Kainani Sails (808-495-1001) is a *private-tour* outfit that runs $325 per hour, with a three-hour minimum. Their sailboat is a 43-foot Beneteau Oceanis that is set up nicely. Six-person max, and BYOB. Call for their customizable tours out of Ka'anapali. They've also got a liveaboard cruise option if you want to sail to Lana'i or Molokai, but it's $1,500 *per night*, so you aren't exactly going to save money by not having to get a hotel room.

Lani Kai (808-244-1979) is a crowded, 53-foot power cat that takes 59 people to Molokini and Turtle Town on a five-hour tour for $108. It takes them close to an hour to get out to the crater (and they often depart late), but they have a dedicated spot on the interesting right side, so at least no one who gets there before you is going to steal your place. SNUBA available for an extra $60, and there's a slide off the front. (Use the bucket to wet it down for the most fun.) Stairs make it easy to get back out of the water. Small upper deck. Friendly crew, but the boat just feels cramped and inadequate compared to the competition. Open bar (beer and mai tais), but they can be skimpy with the food. You can do better. Ma'alaea Harbor, slip 76.

Maui Adventure Cruises (808-661-5550) has two RIB tours to Lana'i. You can go to the island and snorkel at two spots (but not land) on a five-hour tour for $109, or, go on a seven-hour tour for $150 that includes a stop on the island. You'll walk about 15 minutes over the hill to **Hulopo'e Beach**, where you'll have three hours to snorkel from the shore. You aren't exactly welcome at the nearby Four Seasons unless you're spending money there. But the trip, beach stop and crew make this one a winner. Deli lunch, minimal shade. Summer brings more chances of a south swell that can disrupt the snorkeling. Head to slip 11 at Lahaina Harbor.

Maui Ocean Riders (808-661-3586) launches a 30-foot rigid-hull inflatable from Mala Boat Ramp in Lahaina and then circumnavigates Lana'i for $149.

(Children aren't much cheaper at $129.) RIBs are rougher and wetter than more traditional craft, and shade is not too ample. But they snorkel three spots, and it's nice to see Lana'i's more interesting windward side. They even visit Lana'i's shipwrecks and come ashore nearby. With 18 passengers plus crew, you won't be able to wander around for this 7.5-hour trip. Some food, no alcohol. You're gonna be tired at the end of this grueling trip. More taxing than relaxing.

If you want something a little different, **Maui Sailing Canoe** (808-281-9301) takes up to six people on a genuine Hawaiian sailing canoe. It's not the fastest boat on the water, but it's a thrill to glide just above the surface on the boat's trampoline. You'll launch from Polo Beach (in front of the Fairmont) and sail up and down the coast, snorkeling at one spot off the Grand Wailea. The captain has been sailing and racing since he was 16 and fills the trip with history and legends.

Here's our issue: Although the captain usually has someone with him, we've done this trip when he was by himself and were alarmed when he got in the water *with us* and left the boat tied up offshore, empty, while he went off spearfishing. Good thing he tied it up well... $179 ($129 for kids 5–12). The three-hour tour takes off at 9 a.m.

Maui Snorkel Charters (808-270-8776) takes their 40-foot, rigid-hull inflatable, the No Ka Oi, from Kihei Boat Ramp to Molokini (only 6 miles), then to "Turtle Town" for a 4.5-hour tour. Up to 18 people (which can feel crowded) are served continental breakfast, deli wraps for lunch, and juices and sodas. They do provide wetsuits, but for $156 ($145 for kids 5–12) you might want a little more. At least the crew is enthusiastic and good with kids.

Pacific Whale Foundation Eco-Adventures (808-249-8811) has been offering whale watching tours since the 1980s, os-

tensibly as a way of raising money for their nonprofit foundation's education and research efforts. Today, they're a juggernaut that takes more people on the water than any other tour operator on Maui. If all their many boats run at full capacity, they can carry more than 1,000 people per day.

It's easy from their promotional materials to get the impression that you're helping save the whales when you take one of their boats. But make no mistake: Your host is a *for-profit corporation* owned by the non-profit Pacific Whale Foundation. And sure, according to their own website, they've raised "hundreds of thousands of dollars to support marine research" since 1980. That's not nothing, but considering they've carried *5 million* passengers during the same time, that's... *close* to nothing: an average of less than 20 cents per ticket. The point is, make your decision based on whether their tours offer what you want (which they might), and *not* because you want a significant part of your fee to help the whales.

In addition to seasonal whale watching, they've got year-round snorkeling tours. Their most popular excursion is a five-hour tour that goes to two snorkel spots, Molokini and Turtle Arches, for $125. ($75 for kids under 13.) You'll go out on one of the PWF's nearly identical sister ships, likely **Ocean Odyssey**, **Ocean Voyager, Ocean Guardian** or **Ocean Discovery**. These are big, 65-foot, double-decker power cats that take up to 130 people each. They offer easy water entry, a slide, hot showers, continental breakfast, and a BBQ lunch, plus one complimentary drink from the bar. Our biggest complaint with this trip is that their snorkel location at Molokini is not very good. They moor toward the center of the crescent, where the coral is sparser and floating debris tends to accumulate. Tours depart from Ma'alaea Harbor.

They've got a similar six-hour snorkel tour aboard the very utilitarian-looking **Ocean Explorer**, which *might* include snorkeling Molokini's backside. The boat is 54-feet long with a really narrow design that doesn't encourage walking around, and no shade. Avoid it.

They've got two tours out of Lahaina Harbor in west Maui.

Ocean Spirit is a top-of-the-line, 65-foot sailing cat (it even features A/C in the bathrooms) outfitted with lots of eco- and whale-friendly technology, which they will *definitely* tell you about. When the humpbacks aren't in town, the five-hour tour cruises up to Honolua Bay and one additional snorkel spot for $130 ($80 for kids under 13.) BBQ and an open bar await after the second snorkel.

Ocean Quest is a 65-foot, double-deck power catamaran (similar to the ones used for the Molokini tours) that takes up to 110 people to snorkel at one spot off Lana'i for $105 ($65 kids under 13). Pretty good odds of seeing dolphins during this five-hour tour, but sometimes their eco-approach can get heavy-handed to the point of being silly. On one of our trips a pod of dolphins cruised through a sea of snorkelers, went beyond them a hundred yards, then came back to be with the swimmers again. Chance of a lifetime, right? But Pacific Whale yanked everyone out of the water! When we asked why, they piously responded, "We don't swim with dolphins; it's illegal." (Which is untrue. It *might* be illegal to jump in *after* you encounter them because it might alter their behavior, but it's perfectly legal to *stay* in the water when the *dolphins* are clearly initiating the encounter.) We haven't seen any evidence that they've changed this policy.

Don't get us wrong: Pacific Whale does a good job for the most part. Their snorkel tours are competitively priced, and they're *great* with kids. And for whale watching, they remain our top choice because of their knowledgeable crews. But they also spend *a lot* of energy soliciting donations and memberships to their foundation. Expect long, slow-moving lines when you check in. And don't lose your drinking cup onboard, or you'll be shamed when you try to get another.

Pride of Maui (808-242-0955) is a 65-foot catamaran that offers a five-hour tour to Molokini. (They also have a 50-foot, single-hull, rather spartan and uninspiring sister boat called **Leilani**.) Pride feels *very* crowded with 136 people packed on board: the quintessential cattle boat. Even with smaller crowds it feels packed like the last lifeboat on a sinking ship. Uncomfortable backless benches on top with no shade.

On the plus side, they moor in a good spot at Molokini. They have a slide and SCUBA and SNUBA available, and a small number of wetsuit rentals for snorkeling and camera rentals that you will hear plenty about. For their BBQ lunch they start cooking as soon as you take off from Molokini, serving up burgers, chicken, hot dogs and veggie burgers en route to the second snorkel site. Get in line early as it can take *forever*. Open bar after second stop, usually lasting about 20 minutes.

At $124, the trip is not a good deal. (Kids 3–12 cost $94.) Oh, and about that waterslide. It seems fiendishly designed with the horizontal bend at the end to *maximize* your chances of doing a nasty back flop onto the water. (Voice of experience...)

Quicksilver (808-661-3333) is a 55-foot, two-story power cat that carries up to 110 people. It's crowded when full, and the single stairway between decks is congested almost all the time. Most of the seats are in the shade, and they have a slide into the ocean. They go from Lahaina to Lana'i on a five-hour trip, with about 1.5 hours of snorkeling at Shark

Fin Cove, for $129. (Kids 7–12 are $55, 6 and under free with a paying adult.) Drinks aren't free, but they're cheap ($2). Breakfast includes scrambled eggs with ham, and lunch is chicken and pulled pork. Lahaina Harbor slip 1.

Redline Rafting (808-201-7450) is a RIB that goes to Molokini Crater and then down the wild Kanaio Coast. Five hours, four snorkel stops. On their Molokini portion they snorkel inside *and the back side* of the crater—very cool. Good crew. Good trip for $145. (No kids under 8). Deli lunch.

Sail Maui (808-244-2087) uses 47-foot sailing catamarans, **Paragon I** and **II**, for tours to Molokini and Lana'i. These guys *really* like sailing and are much quicker to raise and maintain their sails than most companies, often sailing both ways, not part of one way. (Their piddly 90 horsepower outboard motor is probably also a good reason to keep the sails up.) The boat takes 38 max on their Molokini trip, and there's shade for one-third of the passengers, plus what the sails provide. Riding the net (lying on the front trampolines) is a hoot on the way back. Soothing and dry if it's calm, thrilling and wet if seas are up. The outsides of the trampolines are the wettest.

At Molokini they moor at a pretty good spot toward the interesting right side, and they let you roam the crater—no short leashes. Their deli lunch isn't anything to write home about, but beer and wine is included, and the smaller group size means much more personalized interaction with the crew.

The five-hour trips are $140; it's $70 for kids 3–12, no second snorkel spot. Depart from Ma'alaea Harbor, slip 72. For their 7.5-hour Lana'i trip (which leaves from Lahaina Harbor), they snorkel at Manele Bay, then land and give you a picnic lunch, then do a blue water snorkel farther off Maui on the way back. They're

Sailing at sunset—yeah, we're happy.

only on-island for 1.5 hours, though, so you'll have to rush through lunch if you want to snorkel from the beach. (It's a 1-mile round trip walk from the harbor.) $200 ($100 for kids) for the Lana'i trip, which only takes 30.

The **Scotch Mist II** (808-661-0386) is a 50-foot sailboat that accommodates up to 22 (which is too crowded for comfort since it's not a wider catamaran), but they usually take about a dozen, and they'll go out with as few as six passengers. Their two-hour afternoon sail for $60 ($35 for kids 5–12) is just right to whet your nautical appetite. No shade except for the sail. Below deck is a bit dreary, but on top it's a nice, clean boat, and the experience is fun. Sodas, beer and wine provided. (What, no Scotch?) The $69 sunset trip, their most popular tour, adds champagne. (No kids under 13 on this one.) These guys don't just go out and bob around in the water; they really sail and can clear as much as 20 miles in two hours if there's a good wind. Out of Lahaina Harbor (slip 2). They also have a four-hour morning snorkel sail along the coast for $110 ($59 for kids).

Seafire (808-879-2201) is a badass-looking, 40-foot rigid-hull inflatable with minimal shade that goes to Molokini and Turtle Town for $79. (Cash only, paid at the Kihei Boat Ramp launch site.) Conditions and time permitting, they may stop at the backside of Molokini or St. Anthony's wreck. Cheap, no frills, three hours, two (sometimes three) stops.

Teralani (808-661-7245) has a five-hour West Maui coast tour from Ka'anapali Beach for $152. ($91 for kids 3–12.) Competitively priced, considering they hit two snorkel stops instead of just one like most of the others that head to Honolua Bay, but they take the unusual step of charging $79 for infants, which really rankles. SNUBA available for an additional $73. BBQ lunch and open bar included. They also have a shorter four-hour, one-stop snorkel trip available for less, but with sandwiches instead of a BBQ lunch. Both of their 65-foot catamarans will usually raise the sails, but you may get passed by a faster boat.

The longest running operator on the island is **Trilogy** (808-874-5649). Their six big sailing catamarans (cleverly named **Trilogy I, II, III**, etc.) run with some of the friendliest crews we've encountered. You can snorkel Molokini or cruise the West Maui coast, but their all-day trip

Sometimes swimming in a crowd isn't so bad.

to Lanaʻi is their signature tour. At $220 (kids are $120), it's super pricey, but worth it.

Once there, they'll take you by shuttle to relax and snorkel at **Hulopoʻe Beach**. They also offer a free scenic ride into **Lanaʻi City**. (You're on-island for four hours, so you have more than enough time to do both.) Dolphins sometimes mingle with swimmers at Hulopoʻe. But the fact that they require you to wear a floatation device—even if you're a Navy Seal—is annoying. This is the policy on all their tours and our biggest gripe with them.

Before leaving you'll have a BBQ lunch under their private pavilion. (The place is starting to look like Camp Trilogy.) Then they try to sail on the way home, depending on the wind. Usually they serve ice cream, and you can get two free beers or mai tais as you cruise back to the harbor.

Their service is top-notch and makes others look pedestrian. (You have to walk to the beach from the harbor if you go with anyone else who lands.) Their 5.5-hour Maʻalaea to Molokini trips are $140 ($85 for kids 3–12). Kaʻanapali to Honolua Bay area is $135 ($80 kids), and unlike most boats offering West Maui coast tours, they actually have reserved parking. SNU-BA available on all tours for $65. Our only gripe is the boats can feel crowded. They have a range of other tours, including whale watching trips.

Ultimate Whale Watch & Snorkel (808-667-5678) is the name, but "Bare Bones" Whale Watch & Snorkel is just as descriptive (plus it matches the price). Whale watches are the main tours during the winter months, but they also do snorkel trips to Lanaʻi throughout the year. Their boats are the popular RIB-style—fast, maneuverable and make for pretty good viewing no matter where you're seated. (You might get wet during the ride, though.) Seating is shaded, with eight padded bench seats in the back, plus two in the front and along the sides for those who want to be close to the action. There's a maximum of 26 passengers on most tours (fewer for snorkel trips), which can feel crowded, but there's no place to move around anyway.

Tours range from a no-frills to some-frills affair. Whale watches have no refreshments except an ice water cooler (you'll have to ask for it—they aren't good about offering) while snorkel trips include banana bread, wraps and coconut water (BYOB but no glass). The crew is friendly and to the point—they're geared to maximizing time spotting whales or getting to snorkel spots. Our main gripe has to do with their hydrophone—the underwater microphone to hear the crooning whales. It's an advertised part of their tours, but they don't always have one available. It's not a deal breaker, but if it's important to you to get the "ultimate" experience, ask about it before booking. Whale Watches are 1.5, 2 or 3 hours, $33–$89 (kids 4 and over $25–$89). Lana'i snorkel tours (gear provided, wetsuit tops for rent) are 4 or 6 hours, from $99–$140 (kids 5 and over $75–$119). Tours depart from Lahaina and are a good option for the price.

DEPARTURE POINTS

With a few exceptions noted in the individual reviews, boat tours depart from these common locations in South and West Maui.

Ma'alaea Harbor is centrally located between West Maui and South Maui (near Kihei). Most tours to Molokini Crater (10 miles away) depart from here. Early mornings are bustling with activity, so be sure to allow yourself plenty of time to find a parking spot. And don't forget to pay—after the boats depart, the parking attendants swoop in. (If you can't find space at the harbor, you may need to park at the aquarium and walk.)

The **Kihei Boat Ramp** is in South Maui, south of Kihei. It's 6 miles to Molokini from here. Free parking.

Lahaina Harbor is on the ocean side of the giant banyan tree on Front Street. Street parking in this area is only good for three hours (same goes for the free lot on Prison Street), so you'll need to find one of the nearby pay lots. (The big one on Dickenson Street requires more walking but is less expensive than ones closer to the harbor.)

The **Mala Boat Ramp** is on the north end of Lahaina. Parking is free (but finding a spot may tax your patience.) If you're not tired of snorkeling after your tour, there's good shore snorkeling straight out from the breakwater (aim for the leftmost post sticking out of the water, the one with the attached navigation sign) and around the old Mala Wharf to the left of the boat ramp.

For tours departing from **Ka'anapali Beach**, the boats will pick you up **right off the sand**. If you aren't staying at one of the nearby hotels, you'll probably have to try to find one of the few free spots, or pay to park at **Whalers Village**. Lots of Lana'i and West Maui coast tours depart from here.

WHALE WATCHING

See page 251.

LUNCH & DINNER CRUISES

See page 314.

Boogie Boarding (riders are derisively referred to as *spongers* by surfers) is where you ride a wave on what is essentially a sawed-off surfboard. It can be a real blast. You need short, stubby fins to catch bigger waves (which break in deeper water), but you can snare small waves by simply standing in shallow water and lurching forward as the wave is breaking. If you've never done it before, stay away from big waves; they can drill you. Smooth-bottom boards work best. If you're not going to boogie board with shorty fins (which some consider difficult to learn), then you should boogie board with water shoes or some other kind of water footwear. It allows you to scramble around in the water without fear of tearing your feet up on a rock or urchin. Shirts are very important, especially for men. (Women already have this problem covered.) Sand and the board itself can rub you so raw your *da kines* will glow in the dark.

In **South Maui**, if the surf is low (as is often the case), your best chance to catch waves is at **Kama'ole Beach III**. You also stand a good chance at the far south end of Wailea Beach. If there are moderate

Sponger shreddin' 'em. (Surfer lingo translation: Boogie boarder riding waves.)

waves, Kamaʻole III is probably too strong. Consider the middle of the beach at Kamaʻole I, midway along Wailea Beach, Mokapu Beach, Keawakapu Beach (especially in the middle just south of the two-story house with the blue tile roof) and Big Beach. A great spot when the swells are right is at Chang's Beach next to Poʻolenalena Beach (see page 171).

In **West Maui**, consider Hanakaʻoʻo/Canoe Beach, Kaʻanapali Beach, left side of Oneloa Beach, and Slaughterhouse Beach in the summer. Some shoreline stretches south of Lahaina can be great. Just drive along and look for good conditions.

Boards are easy to rent anywhere. They should cost about $5–$10 per day, $15–$20 per week.

CAMPING

Ah, camping in the tropics. The ultimate in low-cost housing. Although Maui isn't loaded with camping opportunities, there are several places worth noting.

Haleakala National Park has some of the best camping on the island. Drive-up campgrounds are at the seashore at Kipahulu (near the pools at ʻOheʻo), and at Hosmer Grove near the crater. Three-night maximum. *Inside* the crater, overnight tent camping at Holua and Paliku requires free permits. Apply in person at the park the day of your trip; no advance reservations. If they're booked up, tough toe-nails. Same three-night max (two nights at a site).

There are three *highly* coveted cabins inside Haleakala Crater, with free wood (limited) for the wood-burning stove, and *everybody* wants them. We know people who schedule a trip to Maui simply because they were able to get reservations at a cabin in the crater. The cabins hold up to 12, but it's only one party per cabin, and you'll have to reserve six months *or more* in advance. You can try calling (877) 444-6777. It's the federal government's main camping and permit line and they may be painfully unfamiliar with the options in Hawaiʻi. Or go online. Your whole party is required to watch a leave-no-trace video (the purpose of which is to discourage you from pooping on the trail) before descending into the crater. Cabins cost $75 per night.

They also have **car camping** available at the Kipahulu portion of the park at the

Seven Sacred Pools. Your $30 per car fee takes care of your camping fees.

State campgrounds are near Wai'anapanapa Black Sand Beach and at Polipoli Spring (high in the mountain). Call **State Parks** at (808) 984-8109 for permit information or camping.ehawaii.gov on the web. $18 per night per party. Five-night max. Wai'anapanapa has 12 overpriced cabins available for $90 per night (they're *really* basic—don't expect linens or even toilet paper!), and there's one cabin at Polipoli also for $90. Cabins have a two-night minimum (unless only available one night).

There is only one **county campground**: Papalaua Wayside Park (near Lahaina). Call (808) 270-7389 for $10–$20 per person permits.

The **YMCA** in Ke'anae is one of the best deals on the island. For $35 you can share a cabin (tent camping is $30 per adult and $15 per child 12 and under). They also have two, more modern oceanview cottages for $575 (for two nights). BBQ grill available (bring food, charcoal and linens). They're busy year round with large groups—book in advance by calling (808) 248-8355.

Camp Olowalu (808-661-4303), on the way to Lahaina in Olowalu, has tent camping for $24 per person per night and two adult (plus two children) tentalows (a tent on a platform) $140–$195 per night, which is too much considering how densely packed they are. (Two twin beds, cots are extra.) The grounds feel crowded if just half of the sites are taken. Basic amenities with hot water showers.

Camp stove gas can usually be found at **Ace Hardware** (808-877-3931) and **Walmart** (808-871-7820) in Kahului.

If you're planning on camping in east Maui and don't want to worry about collecting your gear in Kahului and hauling it with you, **Hana Camp Gear** (800-332-4022) has you covered. From tents and sleeping pads to cookware and stoves, they can rent you anything you need to spend the night in the great outdoors. Packages available. In west part of Hana, across the street from Hana Fresh.

FISHING BASICS

Deep sea fishing is synonymous with Hawai'i. Reeling in a massive marlin, tuna or tough-fighting ono is a dream of many fishermen. When there's a strike, the adrenaline level of everyone on board shoots through the roof. Most talked about are the marlin (very strong fighters known for multiple runs). These goliaths can tip the scales at over 1,000 pounds. Also in abundance are ono, also called wahoo (one of the fastest fish in the ocean and indescribably delicious), mahimahi (vigorous fighters—excellent on light tackle), 'ahi (delicious yellowfin tuna) and billfish.

Most big fish like to cruise through deeper waters than those found off the leeward side of Maui. (The Big Island is blessed with deep water right off the Kona shore.) The shallow water here that the whales love tends to be shunned by large pelagics. On Maui you'll have to take a 30- to 60-minute boat trip to areas where the undersea topography drops off steeply. But fear not. Once there, large game fish await.

Most boats troll nonstop since the lure darting out of the water simulates a panicky bait fish—the favored meal for large game fish. On some boats, each person is assigned a certain reel. Experienced anglers usually vie for the corner poles with the assumption that strikes coming from the sides are more likely to hit corners first.

You should know in advance that in Hawai'i, the fish belongs to the boat. What happens to the fish is entirely up to the captain, and he usually keeps it. You could catch a 1,000-pound marlin and be told that you can't have as much as a steak from it. If this bothers you, you're out of luck. If the ono or other small fish are striking a lot, and there is a glut of them, you might be allowed to keep it—or half of it. You *may* be able to make arrangements in advance to the contrary.

Charters leave from Lahaina and Ma'alaea. Though there are 4-, 6- and 8-hour charters, many won't do 4 hours since half the time is eaten traveling to and from the fishing grounds. We recommend the 6-hour trips. Mornings offer best conditions. Prices are $180 and up per person for a 4-hour shared charter. You can do a private 6-hour charter for $1,050–$1,400. 8-hour private charters go for $1,250–$1,600 or more for the big boats. Usually, the bigger the boat, the higher the price since nearly all are licensed to take only six passengers. Individual boat rates can change often depending on the season, fishing conditions and whims of the owners. Consequently, we'll forgo listing individual boat rates since this information is so perishable and instead list a few companies that we recommend. Call directly to get current rates. If you have four or more people, make it a private charter so you can exercise more control. If you book a shared tour and the (usual) minimum of four spaces isn't filled, you could be bumped in favor of another customer booking a private charter.

If you're easy-queasy, take an anti-seasickness medication before you get on board. There are people who never get sick, regardless of conditions, and those who turn green just watching *A Perfect Storm* on DVD. Nothing can ruin an ocean outing quicker than being hunched over the stern feeding the fish. Scopolamine patches prescribed by doctors can have side effects, including (occasionally) blurred vision that can last a week. Dramamine or Bonine taken the night before and the morning of a trip also seems to work well for many, though some drowsiness may occur. Ginger is a mild preventative. Try powdered ginger, ginger pills or even *real* ginger ale—can't hurt, right?

Tipping: 10–15 percent split between the captain and deckhand is customary, if you are pleased with their performance. If the captain is a jerk and the deck hand throws up on you, you're not obligated to give 'em diddly.

West Maui Fishing

In West Maui, there are several boats that depart from Lahaina Harbor to consider. **Luckey Strike** (808-661-4606) has two boats: the Reel Luckey (slip 51) and Luckey Strike II (slip 50). They take up to 20 anglers and are popular for bachelor parties and other large groups. **Finest Kind** (877-688-0999) lets you keep what you catch. Slip 7. **Start Me Up** (808-667-2774) trolls for fish. Slip 12.

South Maui Fishing

In Ma'alaea there's **Piper Sportfishing** (808-283-2628) at Slip 61. They are almost exclusively private charters—call to see if you can get a shared one. **Rascal** (808-874-8633) in Slip 13 is a typical 6-pack. Their fighting chair looks more like an electric chair, but at least they let you keep some of the fish. $268 per person or $1,554 for the boat for 8 hours. They'll also tag and release marlin.

FLY FISHING & SHORELINE

All types of fishing require skill, knowledge and luck. Fly fishing brings these requirements to another level (as any fly fisherman will tell you—*endlessly*). Though Hawai'i isn't known as a fly fishing destination, it still has the right ingredients to make for a great experience. **Local Fishing Knowledge** (808-385-1337) is the only outfit on Maui that can give you that experience. Either wading out to the reef or paddling in kayaks, Captain Jon Jon will take you to his favorite spots for bonefish (the favored fish of saltwater fly fishermen). A 4-hour tour will run you $500, which includes gear, water and your guide. Expensive, but you are basically paying for a lifetime's worth of experience from your guide, and without that knowledge, all you'll have is luck. He also offers rentals for fishing gear of all types and has great shoreline fishing spots that families will enjoy.

In West Maui, **All About Fish Maui** (808-669-1710) offers shoreline fishing gear rentals and can also point you in the right direction for good fishing spots.

OK, OK, let's be honest. A place that's known as the *windsurfing* capital of the world surely can't have world-class golf, right? So you'd think. But the truth is the golfing on Maui can be outrageous. Granted, it's probably not *quite* as good as some

on the Big Island, but some courses are pretty close and will blow away most of the courses you've ever played on the mainland. The trick here is to play *early.* Wind can be the instrument of your doom here, and the later you play, the greater the doom.

At both South and West Maui courses, *greens break toward the ocean*, no matter what your eye tells you. They may even break uphill if it's toward the sea. Also, dress codes (collared shirts) are enforced more here. **Carts** are included and mandatory, unless otherwise noted.

MAUI GOLF COURSES

If you only get a chance to golf once on Maui, we recommend golfing at the Wailea in South Maui. The exceptional morning weather, views of Kaho'olawe and Moloki-ni, and two of the best courses on Maui make the golfing incredible. **Wailea's Gold** or **Emerald** courses never disappoint. Emerald is the wider of the two. The nearby **Old Blue Course**, set among luxury homes off Kaukahi, is (as the name implies) older and noticeably duller.

Course	Phone	Par	Yards	Rating	Fees
Dunes at Maui Lani	(808) 873-0422	72	6,841	64.4	$112*
Ka'anapali Kai	(866) 454-4653	70	6,388	71.6	$205
Kahili	(808) 242-4653	72	6,554	72.2	$109*
Kapalua Bay Course	(808) 669-8044	72	6,600	72.4	$229
Kapalua Plantation	(808) 669-8044	73	7,284	75.2	$359
Maui Nui Golf Club	(808) 874-0777	71	6,404	71.1	$100*
Pukalani Country Club	(808) 572-1314	72	6,882	73.4	$89*
Royal Ka'anapali	(866) 454-4653	71	6,700	73.7	$255
Waiehu Municipal	(808) 270-7400	72	6,330	70.5	$63
Wailea Golf Club Emerald	(808) 879-2530	72	6,407	70.8	$250*
Wailea Golf Club Gold	(808) 879-2530	72	6,653	72.1	$250*
Wailea Golf Club Old Blue	(808) 879-2530	71	6,545	70.5	$200*

Carts are included and mandatory at all courses except Waiehu.
Yards and ratings are from the blue tees.
* Lower fees may be available in summer months at these courses.

In West Maui, you're gonna pay more bucks. **Kapalua Plantation** is hard, windy and stupid expensive. This is a serious course for serious golfers who seem to universally wear serious expressions. None of the dreamy glow of other courses; this is golfing to the death. Super early tee times usually bring less wind and lower scores. **Kapalua Bay Course** is closer to the beach, but ironically there's not an overabundance of sand. The fairways meander among several golf course communities. The **Ka'anapali Golf Courses** are flatter, have fewer hazards and usually are less windy than Kapalua. The **Royal (North) Course** is the harder of the two and the most popular. Cars and homes are always close by. The **Kai Course** is easier. The hardest thing here is crossing Ka'anapali Parkway in your cart. Fewer people make more leisurely play, especially in the afternoon (though that may bring winds).

Central and Upcountry courses are cheaper. **Dunes at Maui Lani** in Kahului may be the most underrated course on the island. Though not close to the ocean (and winds can be fierce), this course has smashing views of the West Maui Mountains, and the designer made splendid use of the rolling terrain of this natural sand dune area. At **Kahili**, in Central Maui, the layout, views and price make this a compelling course. The fairways are often undulating, and they make good use of sand traps and a few water hazards. Winds can really pick up in the afternoons. **Waiehu Municipal** in Kahului is cheap and right on the shoreline in Wailuku. No credit cards. **Pukalani Country Club** in Upcountry is cheap—and straight—and that's about it.

At Kihei's **Maui Nui Golf Club**, they've had the same problems for years. The fairways aren't in the same league as the Wailea, and the views are marginal at best. Rates can be pretty good (ask about any specials) but maybe not a compelling enough reason to miss out on Wailea.

Space doesn't allow us to go into more detail here, but our smartphone app, *Hawaii Revealed* has more thorough reviews.

If this section seems shorter than you would expect, it's because we put *lots* of shorter hikes in the *Hana Highway Sights*

Wailea Emerald has some of the best kept fairways of any Maui course.

chapter and elsewhere. There are many 10- to 30-minute hikes sprinkled in those sections since we felt that you were more likely to hike them on a driving tour than head out there for that purpose alone. Also, one of the tastiest trails on the island, at **'Ohe'o Gulch (aka Seven Sacred Pools)** is in *Southeast Maui Sights* on page 110. See more in *Hikes Described Elsewhere* on page 222.

If you're going to do much stream hiking or wet rock hopping, pick up tabis (fuzzy mittens for your feet), which cling well. You'll find them at the various **Longs Drugs** or at **Walmart** in Kahului.

WEST MAUI HIKES

Kapalua Coastal Trail
(3.5 Miles Round Trip)

Let's start this section off with an easy hike that has surprises even the trail builders didn't realize. Although it's less than 2 miles from end to end, you can get 3-plus miles of hiking out of it (plus the return), if you take other opportunities.

The trailhead starts at D.T. Fleming Beach Park near the Ritz-Carlton. (The other end is at Kapalua Beach, but it's tough to park there.) The first section is not along the coast and is fairly boring, so we suggest you park near the corner of Office and Lower Honoapi'ilani roads. You can start with a diversion to Dragon's Teeth (mentioned on page 59) before walking down the road to the beach access at Oneloa Beach. Head to the beach from there, turn left, and you're walking along the shoreline.

Cruise the boardwalk here with beautiful Oneloa on one side and insanely expensive condos on the other. As the trail ascends slightly, keep an eye out for a trail down to the point, though it's hard to spot. We suggest you stay on the main trail until the other half of the loop spur trail becomes obvious at an intersection where you either turn left (to stay on the main trail) or right, toward the ocean. Head right, heeding signs telling you to stay on the trail since birds nest in burrows in the ground here. Keep going toward the ocean and the point that extends into the sea.

This is Hawea Point, and it contains some absolutely *beautiful* tide-pools with clean, clear water. You'll have to boulder-scramble down to them if you want a closer look. One of the pools to the left makes a great place to take a dip on calm days because it's deep enough, and the large, rounded boulders don't have any fragile features that might be damaged by your feet. (Watch for the occasional sea urchin.) Next to that is a small pool shaped like a Japanese soaking tub that gets warmer thanks to the surrounding rock absorbing solar heat. Though partially protected by the ocean, stay away from the pools if the ocean is raging or threatening, or you could get in trouble fast. Winter can bring particularly big waves and big dangers.

From here, you have the option to explore further. There are lots of cool things along the shoreline, and it's an old public access, so you're allowed to poke around. There's a cove littered with coral rubble, more t ide-pools and a trail that ends at Namalu Bay with protected waters. The bay is a popular place to cliff jump. Rocks and railings have been leapt from for years, but we'll leave it to you to look before you leap.

Ultimately, you work your way back to that intersection and continue on the Kapalua Coastal Trail, which cuts through some condos and ends at Kapalua Beach.

Two-Tiered Tide-Pools of Honolua
(0.6 Miles Round Trip)

Most of the island is composed of a porous lava shoreline, making deep tide-pools a rarity. The Olivine Pools (see page 64) are a classic example of such rare tide-pools, which we discovered for our first

The clean, clear waters of Namalu Bay along the Kapalua Coast Trail.

edition. More recently, we found the heretofore unknown two-tiered tide-pools of Honolua.

The shoreline along these stretches looks somewhat artistic and exotic. It's made from a fine-grain, light-colored rock and sandstone. At one area the ocean smashes against the shoreline, bathing an upper pool in a clean shower of seawater. As it fills, it overflows into the lower pool by way of a small but lovely waterfall, which is usually constant at high tide. This lower pool is attached to the ocean, and the cycle is repeated. The results make for a great place to take a dip and a wild, raw shoreline to explore.

These pools are best at high tide with the upper pool over 6 feet deep in places. This is not a good place to be when the ocean's raging. When 10-, 20- and even 30-foot waves tear up the shoreline, the pools become a dangerous washing machine, and you'd get turned into a limp rag if you got near them. Use your good judgment when assessing the safety here. When smaller but still active surf prevails, it's fun to be in the lower pool as waves come charging into the cove next to (but separated by lava from) the lower pool. Wear water shoes or, better yet, tabis so you can walk around the pools more easily. It's usually windy out here, but the lower pool is *partially* protected by some lava.

To get here, just before mile marker 34, pull over to the turnout on the ocean side. Underneath the ironwood pine trees you'll see a path leading down the hill that turns into an old washed-out road. Shortly, on the right side, you'll notice three thick posts along a side road. This leads you down a long hill with old broken glass to a point overlooking the sea. From this windy point you get great views of Punalau Beach to your right; the two-tiered pools are to your left.

Take the path behind you that leads up the hill to the dirt road. You'll pass through the remains of an old cattle gate, and another 300 feet ahead the road splits three ways. Take the road heading straight toward the tide-pools. When you're heading out, you can bypass the hike down to the windy lookout by just following the dirt road back to your car. Though previously private, the land here is now owned by the state and is open to the public.

Acid War Zone to the Blowhole
(0.5 to 0.75 Miles One Way)

There's a quicker way to reach the Nakalele Blowhole (shown on page 61), but hiking to it along this route is definitely more fascinating. There is a small parking lot near mile marker 38 past Kapalua near the northernmost point on the island on Hwy 30. You are allowed to hike on the old jeep road and past the light beacon that leads to the blowhole. This is not a long hike—at most 30 minutes each way without side trips—but the terrain is excellent.

See map on page 62. From the parking lot, go down the old abandoned road slightly right toward the ocean. You will encounter the shoreline just passed a stone labyrinth. Go right along the shoreline. If you want to avoid the shoreline, you can go to the right through the forest. There are several paths. In recent years people have been stacking stones at the grassy field, creating a quirky atmosphere. Please don't stack any in the acid war zone. The trail is vague and spotty, but you shouldn't have trouble making your way as you first walk through a gulch toward your right before reaching the cliff. (Other paths are more inland but less interesting.) Keep going right. The cliffs are pockmarked with crags and caves, and the bouldery landscape around you is awesome.

About 10–15 minutes into the walk, just before a light beacon, you'll notice some small pools below the cliffs. From down there you can see how big the sea arch you saw from the cliffs really is.

Down at the pools there's decent swimming and a crack in the rock toward the sea that snorts air during high surf. The scenery is pretty down there, but access is tricky. You need to hop along boulders, then scale a questionable ladder with a questionable rope tied to a questionable rock. During our last visit, fishing pole holders in the rock indicated that it is popular with shoreline fishermen, which might also explain why there was no ladder. It was BYOL, which you probably forgot to bring, didn't you?

Back on the trail, you descend past the lighthouse, and here the trail snags the uninformed. A small blowhole shooting from the notch of a lava shelf and wall fools most hikers. Probably 90 percent turn around here. But wait: This *ain't* the blowhole! Continue along the shoreline, and soon you come to an alien landscape. It looks like a war zone fought with acid. Billions of tons of sea spray blown by the wind have carved up the soft rock here. The land is literally being eaten in front of you. Take your time to examine some of the lava formations up close. This part

The land is literally being dissolved along the acid war zone hike.

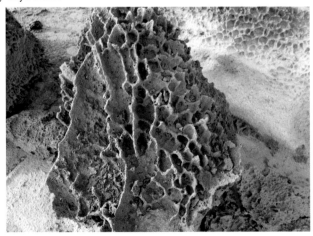

of the island is like no other. The surroundings are so surreal that we're amazed no one has used this area in a movie yet.

About 20–30 minutes into the hike you come to the **Nakalele Blowhole**. There's a nice vantage point above and slightly upwind of the hole. (But you can still get wet when the ocean behind you occasionally explodes sea spray.) You can make your way around the lava to the bottom. Stay upwind to remain dry. See page 62 for more on the blowhole itself. Return the way you came.

Though not overly strenuous, this hike can be a windy affair, sometimes too windy. (Nakalele means *the leaning* because the wind is sometimes strong enough, especially during the summer, to lean into it.) If the wind is blowing you away and you still want to see the blowhole, see page 62 for a more direct (though less interesting) route. Wear good shoes; flip-flops are a bit too casual for this terrain.

Ohai Trail (1.2 Miles Round Trip)

In a previous edition we called this trail remarkably dull. That's because when presented with a 50–50 choice, we did it the wrong way. We rehiked it again and discovered that this 1.2 mile loop trail is infinitely better if you go *to the right* at the sign, counterclockwise.

Just past mile marker 40.5 on Hwy 30, pull into the parking lot, and you'll see the trailhead. You'll be walking through native plants ranging from 2 feet to head high. You're inland at first and there's very little to see... just be patient. Halfway into the path you'll turn to the ocean and see a small side trail on your right side heading out on a point. Walk out here and look to the east. This is your first view of the coastline leading up to the pointed Kahakuloa Head.

Now as you continue the trail, you'll find yourself walking along a windswept area with small rocky hills dotting the view. There is even a bench for you to sit and contemplate the ocean. The last quarter of the hike rewards you with great views of the coastline and the Nakalele Blowhole in the distance. The highest hill you pass has a side trail to the top that affords the best views.

An easy hike, yes. But you get plenty of bang for your buck on the last half.

Mushroom Rock Shore Hike
(0.25 Miles Round Trip)

This is one of those *you're-on-your-own* hikes. Explore a wild, gorgeous shoreline, go as long as your desire takes you, then take the easy way back. The hiking is makeshift much of the way. Not much trail, just make your way, and be careful of the wind and crumbly soil and rock. It's not strenuous unless you want it to be. Like the blowhole hike, wind can sometimes be a problem here.

In West Maui after mile marker 41 on Hwy 30 (and just after the *End Of State Hwy* sign) there's a turnout on the ocean side. (See map on page 66.) From here, walk toward the ocean, then toward your left to a bluff overlooking the shoreline. The cliffs in front of you are striking, even for Maui. After overlooking a small islet, you'll see several discontiguous cow paths (and sometimes no paths) to your right. If you amble the right way, you'll quickly come to a cove with a shallow reef and a rusty old fishing pole holder driven into the rock. The little rock sticking out is an enviable place to ponder the shoreline if you're not too afraid of heights. All this is presided over by a mushroom-shaped rock to your right. By the way, the snorkeling on the downwind side of the reef below is exciting, but only when calm (which is not too often). Experts only. From here, either make your way back the way you came or trudge up a gully-looking feature in the crumbly soil. Then make your way back to the shoreline to your right. Perhaps you'll stop at the mushroom-shaped rock before making your way around and then along the shoreline.

From here there's no real trail most of the time. You're exploring. Sometimes you're along the shore, sometimes you'll have to make your way inland around the large lava hills. The scenery is wild, raw, striking and, quite often, it's all yours. You can't really get lost since you're following the ocean, and the highway is not too far inland. You can spend from 30 minutes to several hours, depending on how far along the shore you want to go and how fast you go. But you won't soon forget this piece of shoreline. This is a delicious, secluded Maui ocean hike. The wind and spray have carved and chewed the landscape with unequaled artistry, and, with no crowds or trails, sometimes you feel like you're the only person in the world.

If you hike a mile along the shoreline (less as the crow flies), you'll come to the **Olivine Pools** (see page 64). Keep an eye out for yellow/orange stripes in the lava. These are deposits of ash from when the island was young and restless. Gigantic volcanic explosions caused the ash layers that were covered with later lava flows. Erosion now reveals what a violent volcano this was in its youth. Not far past here you'll have to ascend from the ocean and walk along the sea cliffs. There are areas southeast of here where residents of **Kahakuloa** have dumped some of their garbage, the only mood spoiler. Continue as long as you want, then make your way inland to the highway and walk back to your car.

Waihe'e Ridge Trail (5 Miles Round Trip)

A very pretty trail with smashing valley views and a vigorous forest to gawk at. You'll gain about 1,500 feet over the 2.5 miles to the end (then return).

You'll want to do this hike early since clouds moving in later in the morning diminish the view. Start hiking by 8 a.m. (7 is better) to maximize your chances.

From Kahului, get on Hwy 340 heading north. (See map on page 218.) At 0.9 miles past mile marker 6, you'll see the road

Waihe'e Ridge Trail climbs to some fantastic views.

Waihe'e Ridge Trail

Makamaka'ole

Waihe'e Ridge Trail

Swinging Bridges

Waihe'e Valley Trail (Closed)

'Ali'ele Falls

Abandoned Ditch

Waihe'e Valley Rd

340

0   1/2 MILE

© 2020 Wizard Publications, Inc.

on the other. If you've got your head in the clouds, enjoy the aural and visual silence.

Lahaina Pali
(5.5 Miles One Way)

This is a trail that slips up over part of the West Maui Mountain, peaking at almost 1,600 feet. Along the way you get excellent elevated views. Unfortunately, this is a shuttle hike, with trailheads 6 miles apart (by car), a bit less by foot. Either hike to the top and return, or go one way if you've arranged transportation at the other end.

The biggest tip is to start from the Ma'alaea side in the morning. (See map on page 49.) You're already 200 feet up, and the sun will be at your back. The bumpy dirt road (usually passable in a regular car) to the trailhead starts between mile markers 5 and 6 on Hwy 30 and goes toward the mountain. If the road is too junky for your car, you gotta add .4 miles to the trip. The incline starts out gently, which gives your body a chance to start revving up. Once at the slopes of the West Maui Mountains, the grade is steeper but unwavering. This was a road for people and horses built in the 1800s, and like all good road builders, they wanted the grade constant. (But it's steep enough that they probably had to keep their horses in first gear.)

There's virtually no shade, but the near-constant winds cool you enough to give you more stamina than you'd typically have. There's not much indication of how close you are to the top, and the ceaseless climbing can lull you into a thousand-yard, stare-type stupor. Don't forget to stop and turn around often.

to Maluhia Boy Scout Camp. Another 0.9 miles up that road (past the gate) is the trailhead.

The trail gets your heart pumping right away, as a cement road climbs 200 feet in short order. Then the dirt path to the left ascends through a forest of guava, kukui, swamp mahogany and Cook Island pines. In (a strenuous) 0.5 miles you've gained 400 feet. Shortly after, a switchback corner reveals a pretty gulch and a bench facing **Makamaka'ole Falls**. Ahead is a peak and the trail switchbacking up. Clouds often come up the gulch and down from the ridge, colliding right in front of you. (And sometimes *into* you.)

Soon you get your first incredible view of the green Waihe'e Valley. It's beautiful! Now the trail is along the ridge, and you're blessed with numerous commanding views (clouds permitting).

Several switchbacks and flat areas later, you'll eventually reach the end of the line—a hill called **Lani-lili** at 2,563 feet. There's a small deck with a picnic table. If the clouds haven't moved in yet, the views are grand. You can see Haleakala on one side, and all the way to Molokai

The grand views of central and south Maui are fantastic.

Without warning, the giant windmills from **Kaheawa Wind Farm** burst into view, signaling your proximity to the 1,600-foot level. The trail will ultimately cut between two of them, and the eerie sound of the whirring blades is something that'll stick with you. *Each of the 34 windmills generates 1.5 million watts.*

After climbing to the top, your vantage point changes as you descend to the other trailhead at Hwy 30's mile marker 11. The ocean and offshore island views create an exotic landscape. You'll overlap two roads on the way down. Bring lots of water 'cause you'll sweat it out.

UPCOUNTRY & HALEAKALA HIKES

Haleakala Crater Trails

There are more than 41 miles of trails inside Haleakala Crater (if you include the Kaupo Gap Trail), and the views from inside are incredible. The catch is that you need to descend 2,400 feet (and, of course, *ascend* on your return) down **Sliding Sands Trail** over a 3.8-mile span (each way) to get to the bottom. You can get to the bottom via **Halemauʻu Trail** (which is only 1,400 feet down and 4 miles each way), but that trail, though beautiful and less steep, is more vulnerable to bad weather. If you want to hike many of the trails at the bottom, you'll need to camp inside. Sliding Sands itself is incredibly scenic, even if you choose not to go all the way to the bottom. Consider just wandering down until just before you start to worry about the ascent. If you want a longer Haleakala hike, one of the best hikes on the island, see *Adventures* on page 265.

At the far end of the crater is the **Kaupo Trail**, which descends

all the way down the mountain. You'll only access it if you're camping. Though it's easy to look at a map and think that an all-downhill trail might be easy, don't be fooled. The footing in many places is slippery with soft dirt and fist-sized loose rocks, and it can be steep. The constant downhill can put enormous strain on knees and other things you didn't think of—like your toenails. If your shoes don't fit right, you may find that the unrelenting tapping will cause you to lose them. (Trust me. Been there. Done that.)

Polipoli Spring State Recreation Area Hiking

An example of the varied nature of the island, this is a hike through a redwood forest. Here? On Maui? Yup. Back in the 1920s and '30s the state and the Civilian Conservation Corps undertook a reforestation program in this area that had been destroyed by cattle. They planted redwood, sugi, cedar and many other types of trees (though these are not native to Hawaiʻi). The trees have since flourished.

Getting there is part of the fun—if you like narrow, winding roads. (See map on page 121.) From Kahului on Hwy 36, take 37 to the *second* 37/377 intersection (near mile marker 14 on 37), and take 377 north for 0.3 miles or so, then turn right on Waipoli Road. From here you'll have 6

Stop and listen to the windmills at the top of the Lahaina Pali Trail.

miles of a winding paved road that offers smashing views of all of West Maui and the valley between the two great volcanoes. Believe the signs that tell you to watch for mindless cattle on the road. You'll even pass through an open gate with a cattle guard. After 6 miles (it'll seem longer), the road becomes unpaved, *requiring 4WD*.

It hasn't always been this way. But when the dirt road *to this state park* started to become a hassle to maintain, the government had a choice: either keep the ruts out or keep non-4WD vehicles out. Score one for the ruts, and a big *tough luck* for the kinds of cars 95 percent of visitors rent. If you get there, you'll see lots of dead trees from a fire in 2007 that burned 1,700 acres and a tropical storm in 2014, but both spared the redwoods.

Once at the parking lot (you took the right fork near the end), you'll want to walk back up the road for 300 feet. Go through the yellow gate, head downhill along the road, and you'll find the start of the **Redwood Trail** (1.7 miles) to the right

of a cabin. Now you begin your descent into the forest. The area looks much more like Northern California than Hawai'i, and the coolness of the air at 6,000 feet is a refreshing change. The descent is fairly gentle and constant. Be aware of tree roots in the trail that may try to trip you.

About 25 minutes into the hike you come to the large redwoods. Some of the redwood trees are around 100 feet tall and dead-on straight with trunks up to 6 feet in diameter. Pretty impressive growth in so short a time. When the Redwood Trail ends, either retrace your steps, or take the **Plum Trail** and make it a 5-mile loop hike. (This is preferred.) You'll want to do this hike while there is plenty of light as deadfall sometimes obscures the trail. A trail map to Polipoli is on page 261.

Assuming you make it a loop, the Plum Trail somewhat gently regains most of the 1,000 feet you lost on the Redwood Trail. When the Plum Trail meets **Haleakala Ridge Trail**, (1.6 miles) take the left turn. Haleakala Ridge Trail ends at Waipoli Road. (You had to pass by the Polipoli

At the risk of shamelessly promoting our own products, some parts of Haleakala Crater, such as this remote area with vague trails, can only be accessed with our GPS-aware smartphone app, or you might very well get lost.

A forest of redwoods reaching for the clouds is the last thing you expect to find in the tropics, but Upcountry's Polipoli Spring State Rec. Area is one of Maui's surprises.

Trail.) Here you'll have a smashing and very expansive view all the way down the mountain to the shoreline. Weather permitting, you'll see three of the Big Island's volcanoes—Mauna Kea (nearly 14,000 feet high), Kohala in front of it and Mauna Loa to the right. Up till now you probably haven't had any wind on this hike, protected by the ridge from the normal trade winds. But here on the ridge the wind can be howling.

To get back to your car, you'll have to head back down Haleakala Ridge Trail and hang a right on Polipoli Trail.

These trails are very nice when the weather is good but dark when it gets really cloudy. Go early in the morning for the best conditions. It takes most people 3–4 hours to complete the loop, and it's moderately strenuous. Despite what you might hear, this trail is not open to mountain bikes.

Weather can be cold and rainy at this altitude. Other trails, such as the Boundary Trail, make nice, if long alternatives. Avoid the wretched Upper Waiakoa and Upper Waiohuli Trails unless you want to get lost and angry.

Waihou Springs Trail
(1.1 Miles Round Trip)

This short, loop trail isn't as exciting as many other hikes on Maui. Nor is it strenuous. Instead this trail takes you through an "experimental growth forest" started in the 1930s. The setting is quiet, peaceful and shows just what the idyllic climate of Maui can do for trees in a relatively short amount of time. There are towering Monterey cypress, Mexican pines and numerous other alien species whose presence transports you to someplace that doesn't feel Hawaiian, but more akin to the Pacific northwest.

A trail branches off from the loop and takes you down to the now-dry Waihou Springs. You lose about 300 feet in elevation, and the descent is fairly gradual. The trail leads to an overlook of the old irrigation tunnels drilled into the adjacent cliff face. (The tunnels are off limits—people regularly slip and injure themselves trying to reach them.) The trail ends here, and you will need to hoof it back uphill. (It *seems* steeper than when you descended.) Ultimately, it's an expendable hike, but the cool upcountry weather and lack of elevation gain (unless you hike down the springs trail) makes it great for families and those with mobility issues looking for a short excursion.

From Makawao, head uphill from Baldwin Avenue, which becomes Olinda Road past the 4-way stop in town. Drive slowly—the road is curvy with plenty of blind corners. Park next to the trailhead near the top end of Olinda Road, about .25 miles past the Olinda Endangered Species Propagation Facility. Don't leave any valuables in the car—lowlifes have been known to practice their smash-and-grab techniques here.

Kahakapao Loop Trail
(6.2 Miles Round Trip)

Kahakapao Loop Trail feels similar to Waihou Springs, except it is much bigger and actually has about 1,000 feet of elevation gain. The loop trail itself winds through a towering, non-native forest in the Makawao Forest Reserve. Despite the Upcountry location, the area doesn't have sweeping views of the island. Instead, you get a quiet hike through a cool, shaded forest where often the only sounds are birds chirping and the occasional mountain biker bombing down an adjacent trail.

The loop trail meanders along two ridges on either side of a shallow gulch, while a third trail, Fong Ridge, follows a dirt road along yet another ridge. Eucalyptus and tropical ash trees tower overhead through most of the loop trail hike while huge native koa trees offer some shade along Fong Ridge. Few things besides ferns can grow in the shade of these trees, offering a surprisingly open view of the forest around you.

From the parking lot, hike past the mountain bike courses and continue for about a quarter mile until you reach start of the Loop Trail. You have the choice of going left or right. We prefer going left to the East Loop. The forest is a little more open on the hike back down on the West Loop, and you really get to take in the incredible height of the trees. (It's easier to enjoy your surroundings when hiking *down*hill.) Alternatively, you could opt to take Fong Ridge to the top of the trail system, which is a little easier (but less shaded) than the loop.

Awaiting you at the top is an aromatherapist's dream of a eucalyptus forest with stands of ginger in the understory. The trail ends at a gate and fence line where you'll have to turn around and backtrack to a short, dogleg path to the loop trail. Consider bringing a lunch (and plenty of water) if you're planning to do the whole loop. There are plenty of logs to rest on as well as a picnic table near the start of the West Loop trail. Note that it's often muddy here, and you may want to stash a bag in your vehicle upon your return for your red, mud-caked shoes.

Find Kahakapao by taking Makawao Avenue toward Ha'iku. Turn right just out of town after St. Joseph's Church onto Piiholo Road. At 0.5 mile past the 1 mile marker, bear left onto Waiahiwi Road. After coming out of the narrow gulch, turn right onto Kahakapao Road and follow it to the top (another 1.3 miles). On the right, two parking lots are available, but use the upper—the lower lot is meant for horse trailers. Oh, and don't venture off the trail. Remember the woman who made national news in 2019 when she got lost in the forest for 17 days then was miraculously found alive? She was hiking in this area (but not the Loop Trail) when she lost her way.

HIKES DESCRIBED ELSEWHERE

Short and not-so-short trails are described in other parts of the book for several reasons, either because of their remoteness, adventurousness or shortness. They include **Punalau Falls** on page 86, the marvelous **Wailua Iki** on page 91 and

Upper Pua'a Ka'a Falls on page 91, the **Red Sand Beach** on page 101, **Venus Pool** on page 107, the **Pipiwai Trail** on page 112 with the waterfalls, and **Alelele Falls** on page 114. The *Adventures* chapter (starting on page 257) has the **The Four Falls of Na'ili'ili-haele**, **Mountain Bike Haleakala's Spine** (which you can also hike) and the **Haleakala Crater Grand Loop**. And West Maui has the **Olivine Pools** on page 64 and **'Iao Valley** on page 69. There's also the short trail around **Kealia Pond** on page 135 in *South Maui Sights*.

OTHER EAST MAUI HIKES

In addition to hikes mentioned above, there are a few other East Maui hikes worth mentioning.

Wai'anapanapa Coast Hike
(3 Mile-ish Round Trip)

One of the nicer coastal lava hikes you'll find. It displays the raw coastline, backed first by palm and hala trees, then showcases the most recent lava flow in the Hana area that created the black sand beach. Though there's no big climbing, the second portion of the trail is somewhat undulating, so you have lots of little climbs, and the footing is awkward. This hike can last anywhere from 30 minutes to 4 hours, depending on your thirst for scenery.

You start at Wai'anapanapa State Park near Hana. (See page 97 for directions.) Park to the right of the main beach, walk to the shoreline, and head right along the shore. Soon a low-hanging sea arch and a blowhole (that only blows during monster surf) indicate the kind of scenery you'll

Remember, there are lots of short hikes listed in Hana Highway Sights, like this one at Pua'a Ka'a, and a longer, delightful hike listed in the Southeast Maui Sights chapter.

see. (Don't get too close to the tapered blowhole; it's a one-way trip down.)

About 10 minutes into the hike, at an area marked by some offshore rocks and a couple of arches, stop and listen for a hissing sound. The ocean waves are undercutting the lava here in some places, and when the tide is right, waves will force air up through a tiny hole, and you can actually hear and feel the ocean breathing. (Get too close, and you'll feel it spitting, too.)

The colors are very vivid as you walk along. The raw black coastline smashed by white frothing water next to impossibly blue ocean all backed by lush, green palm trees makes a delicious meal for

Lava arches are common along the coast of the Wai'anapanapa hike.

be walking on young (500-year-old) lava that created the black sand beach as lava shattered on contact with the sea and the new sand drifted into the bay.

Watch for columnar lava. These (usually) six-sided lava columns are at the shoreline in several places. They form when unusually thick lava ponds, cools more slowly, shrinks and cracks. The cracks work their way deeper and deeper as the rock cools, so the lava literally pulls itself apart. When you pass an old fishing shack, it's 2 miles to **Hana Bay**. The prettiest part of the trail is behind you. Large red ants seem to be making a good living off the stark lava here. Keep walking until you're halfway to being tired, or you get to Hana Bay, whichever comes first, then turn around. It's about 7 miles (round trip) to Hana Bay, if you go that far. Make sure you bring water; lava fields make you thirsty.

your camera. Soon you'll pass an enormous grove of hala trees, noted for their cage-like roots. Some locals call them tourist pineapples, as their fruit does look similar. (Real pineapples grow on bushes, not trees.)

Angry seas can make this hike even more dramatic. The water is so clean and clear, and it's exhilarating to see large waves punish the shoreline here. At one point, the trail passes a natural split in the land. The lava bridge keeps you from falling in. A little farther along the trail there's a big step down; it's preferable to a vague trail going around.

In about 30 or so minutes you come to the meager remains of a small heiau (temple). Nobody knows what it was used for. The trail gets vague for a minute, but should become clearer shortly after. Ahu (small piles of rock) help mark the trail. The footing has been pretty good up till now, but from here it becomes harsher and clumsier. Hiking shoes or boots can be helpful, as can a walking stick. You'll

Waikamoi Nature Trail (0.8 Mile Loop)

Between mile markers 9 and 10 on the Hana Highway. Two nature loops, one about 10 minutes, the other about 30 minutes make a pleasant diversion on the Hana Highway drive if you need to stretch your legs a bit, but it's not worth driving out there just for this. This hike is good for families, and you gain, at most, 200 feet.

If you start from the left-most trail and work your way up the gradual incline, there are a few concrete benches scattered along the way. Sometimes there are nice views of the highway beneath you and the valley beyond. Patches of bamboo interrupt the hala, strawberry guava and huge, towering eucalyptus forest. At the intersection, either take a right (back to your car for the 10-minute hike) or left for the longer one. The latter eventually leads to a picnic area with BBQ. The sign there says end of trail, though, in fact, the path continues. When it forks, take a left, walk a few minutes, and the path leads down to a stream and dam. The view is nice there despite the lack of water flowing over the cliff.

If you're feeling adventurous, you could hike 0.3 miles up the stream itself from here. It's relatively flat, your feet will get wet, and it can get slick on the rocks. If you persevere, though, you'll come to a pretty 45-foot waterfall and pool in a natural amphitheater. Give yourself an extra hour or two for this side trip.

Back at the picnic area, on your way down to your car on a 4WD road, if you veer to the left, it leads to a small reservoir. Otherwise, continue back to your car.

SOUTH MAUI HIKES

Over the years we've watched as the State of Hawai'i has shut down most of the hiking in South Maui for one reason or another. These are your best options.

Eddie Pu Trail (1.15 Miles Round Trip)

It's slim pickings for hiking trails in South Maui. That being said, there's a short-and-sweet trail that often goes overlooked. The Eddie Pu Trail stretches from the south end of Kama'ole Beach (Kam III), skirts the coast past Kihei Surfside and Mana Kai Maui Resort, ending at Keawakapu Beach. At only a half-mile with next to no elevation gain or loss, it's more a leisurely, seaside stroll than a hike. There a few benches that dot the rocky shoreline that give serene vistas of the offshore islands Lana'i and Kaho'olawe. Kayakers, snorkelers and the occasional sea turtle may drift by. Wedge-tailed shearwaters nest in the area from April–December, and if you're lucky, you may even see a chick exploring its surroundings in

Some hikes require luscious treks through bamboo forests.

Keawanaku, a hidden oasis in a sea of harsh lava, is only available to those willing to hike to it.

late spring. The trail disappears as it crosses the Kihei boat ramp but is easy enough to spot if you keep close to the shore. It's also less defined by the Kihei Surfside since it becomes part of their well-manicured lawn—just stick to the oceanside to stay in the right-of-way. Reward yourself with a libation at Sarento's on the Beach when you get there.

The trail is named for the late Eddie Pu, also known as Mr. Aloha during his time as a park ranger at Haleakala National Park. For 25 years he made an annual journey around the entire island (211 miles) on the ancient King's Highway, or Alaloa. The road connected all the communities across Maui and was vital to trade, communication and access to sites sacred to Hawaiians (not to mention collecting taxes and warfare). These days, walking around the entire island isn't really feasible—private property and loss of the road to development being the main hindrances. Though this section of the Alaloa is hardly even a shadow of its former self, it still manages to capture some of the rugged beauty of an area now dominated by condos and restaurants. We have Eddie Pu's journey to reconnect with his roots and the land he loved to thank for the preservation of this slice of old Maui.

Hoapili Trail to Keawanaku Beach (5 Miles Round Trip)

A deserted beach in South Maui? Yup. This hike along a lava trail leads to a black and white sand beach that has been mostly forgotten. From the end of the road in south Maui, where most cars park at La Pérouse Bay, a lava trail (not the gated road mauka of the shoreline) begins your journey along a shoreline that is young and raw and where surf claws at the jagged lava. For the first half mile kiawe trees provide intermittent shade. Watch for wild goats that seem less skittish than other goat-filled areas we've hiked around the state. See map on page 141.

Once the trees are gone, the sun becomes unrelenting. Good thing you brought *lots* of water, because there's none along the way. You'll pass spur trails that lead to local fishing spots. After 2 miles you come to a light beacon. (Stay out of the calm-looking but dangerous tide-pools just north of the beacon.) A rough path along the shoreline goes down to an unexpectedly pretty point dominated by black and red lava, some green vegetation, cobalt blue ocean, bleached white coral litter and green pools. These are brackish anchialine ponds, caused by spring water seeping into lava depressions. They may look like inviting places to cool off, but they are way too fragile to accommodate recreational swimming. The area is hot and harsh, beautiful and lonely. But your destination is still a mile away. Take a vague trail (hopefully marked by some white coral) to the right of the most veg-etated pond *away* from the ocean till you come to a wide main lava trail where you'll turn right.

The trail (now called the **Hoapili Trail** or **Kings Highway**) cuts across Cape Hana-manioa. This 6-foot-wide path was made in the early 1800s and was probably used to transport cattle across the harsh lava. As you walk this part of the trail, keep this in mind: The ancient Hawaiians crossed trails worse than this *barefoot*. In fact, they often had to run through the sharp lava where there were no trails at all during battle. But for the rest of us tenderfoots, we recommend hiking boots to protect the ankles. The footing on the Hoapili Trail is made of mostly fist-sized chunks of lava and is obnoxious.

Just over 2 miles into the lava field trail you'll see lots of vegetation at the shoreline (700 feet away). A spur trail leading there starts at a small lava rock wall just to the right of the main trail. The main part of the spur trail leads to Keawanaku Beach. (Other vague trails leading off the spur trail are avoidable.) This area has several structures, including the remains of a Hawaiian heiau (religious site).

Normal trade winds build up along the southern flank of Haleakala and often howl along this part of the island. The beach itself is normally protected from these trade winds. We've hiked to this beach during unusually strong trade winds, when gusts exceeded 50 mph and the ocean was an ugly mess of whitecaps, only to find the bay at Keawanaku calm, wind-less and protected. (During less common Kona winds from the south, it would be a different story.) The snorkeling off to the left (east) of the bay is exceptional along the 10–20-foot lava wall, covered with coral and loaded with fish. The bay is usually (but not always) protected from much of the surf, and the water can be beautiful and clear. The natural protective wall extends farther than it looks from the shore, bending around to the left and extending farther. The right side has several caves that you can explore if there's no surge or surf. (Surge would bounce you around in there.)

This beach is a jewel set amid the un-forgiving lava, mostly black sand with white and a touch of green sand. (The latter comes from a semiprecious gem called olivine.) There are some beach boulders near the shoreline, but a gen-erous repository of sand offshore *usually* keeps the shoreline relatively sandy, ex-cept after severe storms, which can tem-porarily move the sand offshore, usually during the summer. The area (and a near-by point) was called Keawanaku, and some old-time Hawaiians used the name for the beach, but it is not listed in any of the old literature as having that name. (Perhaps because the flow is relatively recent and the beach so new, the Hawai-ians never named it.) Nonetheless, we have deferred to the old-timers and called it Keawanaku Beach. Sit on the beach under a kiawe tree and watch the waves striking the columnar lava. Piles of rocks attest to those hardy souls who have tried camping out here. (If only they'd known that, *at night*, the beach becomes *alive* with cockroaches.)

It was 3 miles getting to Keawanaku but only 2 going back since you'll stay on the Kings Highway all the way.

HORSEBACK RIDING

If you want to see the countryside but don't want to walk it yourself, you need your very own beast of burden. (I always loved that phrase.) Maui has lots of horseback rides, from forest to plains to lava fields. Some are awesome; some are a snore.

Choosing one trip over another depends on what you want to see and what kind of equine experience you seek for the price of admission. None of the companies will challenge the horsemanship skills of a truly advanced rider. It's generally recommended that you wear long pants, and closed-toed shoes are mandatory. For most trips, forgetting your sunscreen and/or bug spray could leave you fried or eaten.

If you've heard about the amazing horseback ride down into Haleakala Crater, you ain't gonna do it. See page 132 for an explanation.

THE BUCKAROOS

Mendes Ranch (808-871-5222) has a pretty nice ride on their beautiful ranch in West Maui. They ride up to a spectacular overlook of Waiheʻe Valley, then head to the ocean for more good views. Like most outfits, it's a nose-to-tail ride with only two *very* short runs allowed. (But hey, running is hard to come by on Maui rides.) Guides range from helpful and friendly to aloof. In all, a good 90-minute trip for $135. On Hwy 340 at mile marker 7. Minimum age 7, maximum weight 250 pounds.

One of the better outfits is **Maui Mountain Activities** (808-242-5558). It offers a similar product to their neighbors, Mendes Ranch, but with finer execution. The folks running the operation have been guiding for years and still have great enthusiasm. They might seem a little rough around the edges at first, but they're very friendly and knowledgeable once on the trail. You'll get history, culture and maybe eat a wild guava or two along the way. It's a nose-to-tail operation with two spots where the horses can run. The tour begins with a trek up to a nice overlook of Waiheʻe Valley and waterfalls. (It's a distant view, but they're upfront about it, which we appreciate.) After some photos, the ride heads downhill to another photo opportunity next to the ocean. It's not the beach (there is no beach in this area), but you'll still see a nice vista and have a relaxing experience. The horses are fairly well behaved, and beginners seem happy with the ride. Two guides go with the group to help keep everyone together and offer more narration (something that's lacking in many horseback tours). Water, juices and saddlebags are provided (a nice touch) so you can easily carry and access your beverage, camera, etc. 2–2.5-hour morning ride is $140; the 1.5–2-hour afternoon ride is $110. Minimum age 7, maximum weight 250 pounds.

Makena Stables (808-879-0244) is in South Maui on the expansive Ulupalakua Ranch. The small scale of this stable translates into very well cared-for horses, good equipment and personalized attention. They seem proud and protective of their horses, and they are particularly instructive with beginner riders. The opposite of lush, this ride goes through kiawe (mesquite) groves and lava fields (where you'll be grateful for your helmet) up to Kalua o Lapa Crater. Enjoy the really cool views of the island of Kahoʻolawe, La Pérouse Bay, ʻAhihi-Kinau and the lava flow from

If this doesn't satisfy your horseriding needs, then we don't know what will.

this intensely windy 500-foot elevation. Ride back down through shaded stretches of the King's Highway, often spotting feral goats among the rocks. The 1.5-hour rides are $170 in the mornings and $195 for sunset trips. As far as sunset rides go, this one has great views. Sincere, dedicated guides, but we've seen them run short on snacks and long on local politics. Minimum age 13, maximum weight 200 pounds.

Lahaina Stables (808-667-2222) in West Maui is our *least* favorite. The views over Lahaina of the offshore islands are this outfit's best asset. Most of the ride is spent on poor trails. With no shade. In a subdivision. Instead of a hands-on safety/how-to demonstration, you'll watch a video in the office. Though your guide will likely be friendly and helpful, those needing extra instruction might find the experience lacking. The destination is a little anticlimactic—a man-made reservoir at the mouth of a beautiful valley. (You'll take photos of the valley but won't go in.) Snacks, water and juices are provided, but

might look a little beaten up from riding along with previous tours. It feels like there's a lot of corners cut in the whole product that could be easily fixed. The 2-hour morning ride is $135 and the sunset ride (including champagne and chocolate) is $189. Minimum age 7, maximum weight 250 pounds.

Also in West Maui, **Ironwood Ranch** (808-669-4991) is a tidy stable and, although the greeter may be short on social graces, they are long on safety and use the info you give in a survey about your skills to match you up with one of their celebrity-named horses. The trail goes through some boring fields but is punctuated by ironwood groves and the Maile Pai Valley where you'll find ferns, dry creek beds and some nice rock outcroppings. Those in the back will not likely hear any of the narration. You emerge from the valley onto the upper reaches of the plantation, providing grand views of offshore islands and the West Maui Mountains to your back. This ride is all about the views. The contrasts are particularly nice at sunset. 1.5-hour morning ride is $110; 2-hour morning or sunset rides are $170. Minimum age is 7, maximum weight 220 pounds.

Upcountry there's **Pi'iholo Ranch** (808-740-0727) in Makawao. This is a good place to experience a bit more free rein (literally) on a very nice operating cattle ranch. You drive up and away from the coastal plains into a cool eucalyptus forest, then arrive at their posh ranch center. Although this spread has a showy rodeo air, trail rides don't hold second-class status here. Their work shows in nicely laid trails and eager horses.

On the trail you'll meander through forested valleys and wind-swept pasture

Flyboarding is like wearing a Jet ski.

lands. Axis deer are common here and are known to spook the horses when they pop out of the bush. And some of the guides might be pretty generous with salty cowboy language. The climax of the ride (hold your hat) is the ascent to windy Pi'iholo Hill with 360-degree views. The elevation allows you to escape the extreme weather conditions that can accompany rides at lower and higher elevations, making it a particularly good choice for a midday ride. *Private rides only* with the 2-hour ride at $458 per couple and 3-hour ride at $698 per couple, including lunch. Minimum age 8, maximum weight 225 pounds.

Jet Skiing

Call them Jet Skis or Wave Runners (both are brand names) or personal watercraft—whatever your name for them, these motorcycles of the sea can be rented near Lahaina from **Maui Watersports** aka **Pacific Jet Sports** aka **Jet Ski Maui** (808-667-2001) from mid-May to mid-December. (They have to close during whale season.) They use fairly powerful 1100s and pretty much give you free rein in their circular course. That's good because it gives you more freedom... but it also leaves you free to hurt yourself. If you've never ridden before, these animals are a scream (literally, for many riders).

Early morning is usually very smooth, late afternoon choppy. Late morning seems a good balance, giving the water some texture. They offer a half hour for $79, full hour $124. The half hour will tucker out most people, especially if you're like me, and you drive it like it's stolen. Spend the extra few bucks for the goggles, and experiment with different ways to hold your feet while you sit.

Despite their brochure's claims, you're actually given little instruction, so be careful. If you go fast enough during bumpy seas, turns will feel like a controlled crash, so don't turn too quickly unless you know what you're doing. Extra riders (or just observers who hang out on their floating "island") are allowed for $20, but we recommend one person per craft. Doubling up seems to increase the risk of the passenger falling off, from what we observed. They meet on Ka'anapali Beach in front of the Hyatt and in front of Whaler's Village. They use a tiny boat to get out to the area, and you (and your electronic stuff) might get wet.

Another thing they have is a **Flyboard**. This is where they take the output of the jet ski and send it through a huge hose that is attached to jets and a board strapped to your feet. It's absolutely epic! We first did this on O'ahu (where it's much more expensive) and found it easier to learn than we expected. It feels similar to a snowboard. Turning takes some practice, and if you are proficient enough, they might let you dive like a dolphin. Keep a constant eye on the jet ski. You are pulling it (and the instructor who controls your throttle) around, and if you get too close, they'll kill your jets to keep you from smacking into it. It's $159 for 30 minutes.

It's not a Jet Ski, but **Ka'anapali Ocean Adventures** offers one-hour thrill rides on a *jet boat*. See *Boat Tours* on page 200.

Kayaks are a fun way to see the coastline. Not one of Maui's rivers is fit for kayaking, but the shoreline offers lots to explore.

Areas to kayak are south of Olowalu in West Maui starting at Papalaua Wayside Park between mile markers 11 and 12. Paddle southeast along the pretty shoreline below the highway, staying close to land to keep winds from making your life more difficult. Most put in near Mile Marker 14, but it's much less interesting there.

If you can arrange it, in the afternoon it's nice to put in at Kihei and let the wind help you go down the coast, then come out at Makena Landing. Kihei winds tend to blow from north to south along the coast; West Maui winds tend to go from nothing to blowing offshore, which is more dangerous.

The coastline south of Big Beach at 'Ahihi Cove heading south to La Pérouse Bay is unfortunately off-limits. The area is a protected reserve and commercial activities are banned in the area (which includes the use of *rented* kayaks). You can, however, snorkel in the area as long as you don't go ashore in the protected area.

Some companies put in at Makena Landing because it's so easy to launch. The kayaking from there is fairly good, though not great.

Winds will be your biggest factor. Don't let a breeze help you down a shoreline if you have to paddle back against it. Unless you've arranged for pickup, better to paddle in less breezy areas. The ocean can go from calm and light winds to wavy with strong winds over a span of about 100 feet. Whitecaps on the water are caused by wind, and it's easy to drift from a protected area to an exposed area. Stay alert. Google the name Nahid Davoodabadi for an eyebrow-raising story about a Maui kayak trip gone terribly wrong.

Many of the big resorts rent kayaks by the hour for confiscatory amounts.

WEST MAUI KAYAKING

Maui Kayaks (808-874-4000) has single kayaks for the day for $49 and doubles for $65. On the south end of Front Street, **Maui Ocean Sports** (808-667-6611) lets you rent for 2-hours, just long enough to paddle around the protected waters of Lahaina. Singles are $35, $49 for the day, Doubles $49, $65 for the day.

SOUTH MAUI KAYAKING

In South Maui **South Pacific Kayaks** (808-875-4848) has singles for $45 and doubles for $65 at Makena Landing. **Big Kahuna Adventures** (808-875-6395) in Kihei has singles for $50, doubles for $60. **Clear Kayaks Maui** (808-664-3000) in Kihei has pricy see through-bottomed kayaks, all of which are doubles. It's moderately cool for those not wanting to get in the water, but unless the water is shallow, your view won't change much. $75 for 2 hours launching from Makena Landing, where you stand a chance of spotting turtles.

HANA KAYAKING

In Hana, **Hana-Maui Kayak & Snorkel Reef Watch** (808-248-7711) has 3-hour kayak/snorkel trips around Hana Bay for $109. Cash only.

GUIDED KAYAK TOURS

For *guided* tours, most companies explore the Makena areas, Olowalu and Honolua. Cost typically runs between $60 and $115, and includes snacks and water. Consider **Maui Eco Tours** (808-270-5015), **Maui Kayaks** (808-874-4000), **South Pacific Kayaks** (808-875-4848) and **Aloha Kayaks Maui** (808-270-3318). **Hawaiian Paddle Sports** (808-442-6436) only takes private groups, which can make for a great experience if cost isn't a factor. (It's $139–$159 each, even if you bring four people along.) They, along with **Maui Kayak Adventures** (808-442-6465), also offer a tour *to Molokini* for $199–$249. That's not an easy paddle, so don't underestimate it.

OUTRIGGER CANOE PADDLING

If you're looking for an authentic cultural experience, how about trying the official state sport? No not surfing—the original state sport is *paddling*. Kids here grow up paddling outrigger canoes, and the recreational clubs are an important part of social life. (Depending on the club, competition can be fierce.) On Tuesdays and Thursdays, casual visitors are welcome to join the **Kihei Canoe Club** (808-879-5505) for an invigorating morning paddle.

Just an everyday scene from life on Maui. And you're invited to join in.

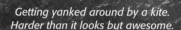

*Getting yanked around by a kite.
Harder than it looks but awesome.*

It's not at all touristy—just something you could do as part of your regular exercise routine if you lived here and were a member of the club. The program is volunteer run, and they'll put an experienced steersman in your canoe. This also isn't a thrill ride like on O'ahu were guides take you out to catch a wave to ride back to Waikiki Beach, just a nice paddle in an outrigger canoe where *you* provide the power. Sign-in starts at 7 a.m. and is first-come, first-serve, no reservations. They'll take you out for a short paddle and then do a little swimming or snorkeling from the boat before paddling back. Our only complaint is that we wish they did a better job of grouping more athletic people together in the same boat, so that those who want to spend the whole hour paddling, can. (You're just getting into the rhythm when they stop to rest.) Even with that caveat, you may unexpectedly find it is the most enjoyable part of your vacation. The suggested donation is $40 per adult—*ouch.* But hey, you *said* you wanted an authentic experience, and overpaying for things is *definitely* an authentic Maui experience. (Kids are free, though.) On the north end of South Kihei Road; look for the distinctive red and yellow canoes by the Uwapo Road T-junction. Wear your bathing suit and bring a towel and water; they'll hold keys and anything you don't want to get wet.

Also called kitesurfing. Imagine a modified surfboard, shorter and boxier than a typical board, with fins at both ends and straps for your feet. Then let a special, controllable, four-line kite drag you along. As in windsurfing, you don't have to go the direction the wind takes you—you have control. Despite what some instructors tell you when they want to sign you up, it's harder to get up on the board than windsurfing. But *oh,* what fun it is! More fun than windsurfing once you're comfortable on the board. One way you can prepare before you get here is to buy a two-line kite and master it so that you can instinctively maneuver the kite. It's not that hard, but it helps if you can steer the kite without thinking.

Lessons are *expensive*––multi-day courses can easily go into the thousands of dollars. The best places to learn are **Action Sports** (808-283-7913), **Kiteboarding School of Maui** (808-873-0015), and **Aqua Sports** (808-242-8015) all in Kahului. Most companies don't have a brick and mortar store—just meet on the beach. **Action Sports** has a 3-hour lesson for $165. This is a group lesson but only for 2 to 3 students. **Kiteboarding School of Maui** has 1.5-hour group lessons for $95,

3-hour private lessons for $350 and 9-hour lessons (over three days) for $950. **Aqua Sports** (808-242-8015) has 3-hour intro lessons starting at $240. We love how they use radio helmets to give you tips once you're soloing.

Teaching methods differ. First you need to learn how to operate the kite (which is a hoot). Next comes body dragging. Though it sounds like something they do to you if your credit card is declined, it's actually when you let the kite drag you through the ocean while you manipulate it. Then comes the good part—*riding the board.*

Some companies claim you'll be riding the board after the first lesson, but don't be disappointed if that doesn't happen. It ain't easy, brah, and instructors privately concede that few are able to get on the board the first day.

If you want to *watch* kiteboarding, head over to Kanaha in Kahului. Kiteboarders use the west (left) end.

Maui's landscape is vast and varied. We try to give you the best information for exploring the Valley Isle on your own, but there are plenty of offerings where you'll need explicit permission or expertise that we can't provide. Farm tours, garden tours and excursions that highlight Maui's natural attractions are our main focus here. Some of the items are mentioned in the Sights chapters but deserved a little more detail.

FARM TOURS

If it's food you want, we grow lots of our own here on the Valley Island. Many farms offer guided tours of their operations and they're pretty popular—tours regularly sell out and require some advance planning to ensure a spot.

Upcountry Maui has some of the best farm tours. One of our favorites is **Maui Pineapple Tours** (808-665-5491). You'll tour both the fields and packing facility, eat the ripest pineapple you've ever tasted straight from the field, and even get a pineapple to take home. $65 for the standard, two-hour tour. Add on a tour of the neighboring **Haili'imaile Distilling Company** (808-633-3609) for an extra $10 to see (and taste) how pineapple can be made into vodka.

Speaking of vodka, there's also the **Hawaii Sea Spirits Organic Farm and Distillery** (808-877-0009) tour where the locally popular Ocean Vodka is made. $15 for the half-hour tour. Their neighbor, **Surfing Goat Dairy** (808-878-2870) has a more kid-friendly tour where you can sample cheeses and help with farm work. $12 for the casual tour and up to $50 for the grand tour. **Kula Country Farms** (808-878-8381) is a local favorite thanks to their seasonal offerings like pick-your-own strawberries in February and pumpkin patch in October. $3 entrance for seasonal events.

A unique option in West Maui is **Punakea Palms** (808-269-4455), an organic coconut farm that offers tasting tours. For $50, the two-hour tour will take you through the life cycle and many uses of coconut, as well as a few hands-on activities.

GARDEN TOURS

Though this ain't the Garden Isle (that would be Kaua'i), Maui isn't lacking when it comes to places to appreciate the variety of plants that grow in a tropical climate. Some of these are mentioned in the *Sights* chapters.

Central Maui has a couple of convenient and inexpensive options. **Maui Nui Botanical Gardens** (808-249-2798) in Kahului is a small garden that features only native and Polynesian-introduced plants. It might

Ali'i Kula Lavender garden is where you can learn and eat all things lavender.

not be the prettiest garden, but their efforts are more in education and preservation. Open Monday–Saturdays, entrance is $5, free on Saturdays. Across the street from the War Memorial Stadium on Kanaloa Avenue. Nearby on Honoapi'ilani Highway (30) in Wailuku, **Maui Tropical Plantation** (808-244-7643) is what most people think of when thinking botanical garden. Though something of a tourist trap, it's free and has plenty of tropical scenery for the photo album.

Upcountry has a number of good options. Most notable are **Ali'i Kula Lavender** (808-878-3004) and the nearby **Kula Botanical Garden** (808-878-1715). Both are iconic for the area and just the drive up to them can feel like a garden tour, especially in the spring months when the roadside trees are flowering. Entrance is $3 and $10, respectively. A more unique garden option can be found between Ha'iku and Makawao. **The Sacred Garden** (808-573-7700) features an extensive garden/nursery and two labyrinths. Entrance is free and it's a definite hit with anyone looking for a quiet, relaxing atmosphere. On Kalanui Road off Baldwin Avenue.

The Hana Highway has two notable gardens that can be visited in one day. The **Garden of Eden** (808-572-9899) has an extensive collection of plants that any gardener will appreciate for $15. Just outside of Hana is **Kahanu Garden** (808-248-8912), part of the National Tropical Botanical Garden family. Rich local history is a big part of this garden—this is the site of the state's largest heiau, Pi'ilanihale. Planted all around the site are native and Polynesian-introduced plants vital to ancient Hawaiian life. It's an impressive spot that should be experienced at least once. $10 for the self-guided tour, guided tours $25 (by reservation only).

OTHER LAND TOURS

If you've visited the summit of Haleakala while the stars are out, you've seen that the night sky is so vast that constellations you'd usually recognize nearly get lost in the cosmic soup. While the cheap and easy method for making sense of things would be a smartphone app of the stars, context and a high-powered telescope can take the experience to another level. That's where **Maui Stargazing** (808-298-8254) comes in. If you have five hours to spare, this is the best stargazing tour on Maui (the other is by boat). You don't get to visit the big observatories of Science

City (they're off limits to everyone but officials), but you do get a wealth of information, incredible views through a 12-inch aperture Dobsonian telescope, winter gear, hot cocoa and snacks. This is a decidedly more technical and science-based tour than others available, but you don't need to be a space fanatic to enjoy the experience. The owner, Jan, is usually the guide and brings over a decade of experience finding deep-sky objects. (Her sometimes curt manner might trigger flashbacks of science class and pop quizzes.) There's always something interesting to see (the moon is a crowd pleaser), so time of year doesn't matter—weather is the biggest limiting factor. They do a good job of keeping up on conditions and will cancel (and refund) tours if it's not looking good. (If the tour isn't cancelled, but visibility is still extremely limited, you get a partial refund.)

Tours are limited to 11 people—make sure to be friendly with everyone on the shuttle ride since lining up to take turns at the telescope can get a little disorganized. You'll meet at Kula Lodge 2.5 hours before sunset (bring a to-go dinner along), then pile into the shuttle van and head to the summit to enjoy sunset while they get the telescope ready. Actual star gazing location is weather-dependent. $170 per person ($158 for 15 and under, but kids under 10 probably won't enjoy it as much).

For those vacationing with their in-laws, may we suggest a lively game of paintball? For those unfamiliar, paintball is a simulated combat experience using air-powered paint ball launchers, called *markers* to shoot opponents. Generally, the goal is for either individuals or teams to eliminate opponents by tagging them with paint. It can be a real hoot, too.

Maui Paintball (808-866-7034) has a 10-acre property (though they only use half of it or less), which—if you're into the sport—is more of a recreational course rather than a speed course, though they can get more of a speed setup going for private groups. We've seen family reunion groups come off the field grinning ear to ear. You're required to wear safety gear that protects your face, and they have optional chest protection plates as well. Just so you know, getting shot with a paintball can hurt like a *buggah*. You'll almost certainly get a welt from it, and if you're prone to bruising, you'll end up looking like a dropped banana. Luckily their course has plenty of cover.

The excitement of running and dodging around a paintball course is probably the most fun part. They have tree forts and a number of features they are always moving and changing. On open play days (Fri–Sun), you're assigned a team when you show up. Private groups Mon–Thur. They include all the gear you need in the $30 rental/entrance fee. Paintballs are an extra fee, as well as upgrades for even better equipment. Kids 10–12 must be accompanied by an adult. Run by guys who love the sport and enjoy making it work.

In west Maui, on the north side of Olowalu. Take the first road north of mile marker 16 (look for the green Recycling and Refuse Center sign), then take the immediate right onto the access road. The paintball course is at the end.

Parasailing is where you become a human kite, attached to a parachute and pulled by a boat via a long rope. It's an 8- to 10-minute ride, though that includes reeling in and reeling out. It's been our experience that parasailing *looks* more fun and thrilling than it really is and doesn't seem worth the money. Think of it as a $85-plus amusement ride. (People afraid of heights, however, will no doubt be properly terrified.)

Off Lahaina and Ka'anapali, at least views of the town or mountains are grand. All companies depart from West Maui from mid-May to mid-December. (They have to close during whale season.)

One tip (*especially* for guys): Don't wear any slippery shorts, or you may cinch forward in your harness resulting in... the *longest* 10 minutes of your life.

West Maui Parasail (808-661-4060) has 800- and 1,200-foot lines for $84 and $94. Tandem and triple rides available. **UFO Parasailing** (808-661-7836) has a 10-minute 800-foot ride for $89 and a 1,200-foot ride for $99.

OK, here's where Maui's often placid waters pays off. The diving here can be incredible. The usually calm morning waters off South and West Maui make boat rides short and sweet. In addition to its nearshore dives, Maui has two great offshore dives. West Maui has the awesome **Cathedrals II** on Lana'i, and South Maui has the humbling **back wall of Molokini**.

We've noticed that, overall, the dive operations on Maui seem to be of a slightly higher caliber than the other islands, perhaps because there's so much competition. Prices can be lower, too. (It's good to see that some things are actually cheaper on Maui!) They're usually more professional here with less of the dive shop attitude. You know the attitude—when you go into a shop, and the guy behind the counter never gets off his stool or takes off his sunglasses, doing everything he can to convey the impression: I'm so cool—don't you wish you were just like me?

However, many of the dive companies have provocative brochures showing divers cavorting with all sorts of critters, including the holy grail of scuba encounters, the whale shark. We're not saying it doesn't happen; just don't expect it. People have been known to experience spontaneous human combustion, but we've never seen that happen either. We only know one friend who claims to have swum with a whale shark here. (And he lies a lot.)

So you'll know our perspective when we review companies, we should tell you what we do and don't like when we go on a dive. On a bad dive, the dive master takes the group on a nonstop excursion that keeps you kicking the whole time. No time to stop and explore the nooks and crannies. Good outfits will give you a briefing, tell you about some of the endemic species here, what to look for, and will point out various things on the dives, keeping it moving but not too fast. Bad outfits kick a lot. Good outfits explain the unique qualities of Hawai'i's environment. Bad dive masters may tell you what they saw (but you missed). Good companies work around your needs, wishes and desires. Bad companies keep everyone on a short leash. Good dive masters know their stuff and share it with you. Bad dive masters don't know squat but imply they know it all in order to impress you. As divers, we like companies that wander toward the boat for the latter part of the dive and allow you to go up when you are near the end of your tank, as opposed to requiring everyone to go up when the heaviest breather has burned up his/her bottle.

During times when we feel the diving conditions are bad (poor vis or big swells), we like to call around and ask about conditions. We appreciate the companies who admit it's bad, and we hold it against those who tell us how wonderful conditions are.

What's not to love about a healthy coral reef?

THE TOPS ON MAUI

The best companies we've found have been in South Maui. Regardless of the profession, it seems that the cream sooner or later rises to the top. So it is with the dive industry on Maui. Without question, the best dive outfits on the island are **Prodiver Maui** and **Mike Severns**.

South Maui Dive Companies

Prodiver (808-875-4004) takes only six to 11 people on their ample boat, so you never feel crowded. They have a good boat, good crew, good pace and a good attitude. They treat you well and handle the dives just right. After lamenting their lack of snacks, we are pleased to see that the current owners are now feeding their divers more. You can tell that the joy of diving hasn't left them—an easy outfit to recommend. It's $146 per two-tank; gear is $22.

Mike Severns (808-879-6596) is also a quality outfit top to bottom. Everyone gets a computer, good gear and plenty of snacks. Their knowledge is so accurate it borders on wisdom, and their briefings are the most precise we've found. With perfectly led dives, a good 12-passenger boat (two groups, which can get a bit cramped and clumsy) and the right attitude, this is a great company to go with. With so many years of experience, they are very adept at finding critters and showing them to you, and their knowledge is phenomenal. Since they know the sites so well, they key in on what to brief you on before the dives. Many companies do this, but nobody does it as well. $139 for a two-tank, $20 extra for gear. Book both in advance.

Ed Robinson (808-879-3584) is also a very well-run company and is a very acceptable alternative. Good ascent policy, good briefing—they go nice and slowly during the dives, and their divemasters seem pretty knowledgeable, if a bit cocky. But most do a good job and have a good attitude. They have a 12-passenger boat (groups of 6). As opposed to Mike Severns' bent toward education, these guys tend to stress the fun of diving and lean toward finding rare stuff to round out your dive sightings résumé. They also perform the best in the food department. An easy company to recommend. It's $146 for two-tank, plus $22 for gear, but they usually won't do the Molokini back wall except on the $191 3-tank, which is a very good excursion. (They only want experienced divers on that 3-tank dive.)

Maui Dreams (808-874-5332) does good shore dives along South Maui. Their enthusiasm is evident and welcome. It's as if you're diving with friends. They'll go out with only one person, if necessary, even for a night dive. That's unusual for a dive company. (They could use a better briefing and maybe some food.) $89 for one tank, $119 for two, gear included. Boat dives are $149, plus $20 for gear. The shop is on the small side but prices are reasonable. The boat is at Ma'alaea Harbor, slip 23.

Maui Dive Shop has several locations on the island, including a large shop in Kihei (808-879-3388). Their shop personnel seem to be either super friendly or snotty and short with customers, with not much in between, and you certainly won't find many steals. As for diving, they do a pretty decent job, though it's a bit of a processing machine. Not bad, but not in the same league as the others mentioned above. They have boat, shore and night dives. Ma'alaea Harbor, slip 66.

West Maui Dive Companies

West Maui companies don't fare as well. The best boat dive company is probably **Extended Horizons** (808-667-0611), though it's not their services that shine. Light snacks for food, and their shorties are, frankly, insufficient for many people. What sets them apart, however, is their lust to go to more than the standard dive sites. 12 divers max, which is crowded. They often go to Lana'i. $189 for two-tank plus $36 for gear. Shore dives are $109 for one-tank.

Lahaina Divers (808-667-7496) is a big company with fairly big boats that hold up to 24 people. If full, it's pretty crowded, but when there are fewer divers, it's a good trip. They have a loose policy on keeping divers together underwater. That's good unless you're a novice or want

things pointed out. Friendly crews. We liked their Carthaginian (a sunken ship) dive. $149 for the shipwreck, $169 for their Lana'i trip. It's $27 for gear and another $14 if you want a regulator with dive computer. They also have the training to handle divers with disabilities.

OTHER DIVE COMPANIES

There are tons of them out there. There's absolutely nothing about **Boss Frog** that we like—pushy, rude and abrupt. **Makena Coast** (808-874-1273) is adequate. **5-Star Scuba** (808-662-8207) has painless shore dives at Black Rock for $89. **B&B Scuba** (808-875-2861) has a pretty nice shop in Kihei. They *sometimes* offer a unique dive to a well-preserved WWII bomber wreck in Ma'alaea Harbor. And **SCUBA Shack** (808-879-3483) has a 700-plus horsepower rocket that gets you out to Molokini in 10–15 minutes—faster, depending on who's driving. It's one cool ride.

WHERE TO DIVE

Though most boat captains will poll their customers, asking where they want to go, the captains will try to steer you to places they think are good that day. Three offshore places stand out as some of the best diving in Hawai'i.

One of the coolest is **Cathedrals II** off Lana'i. Most boats leave from Lahaina. Not only is the large lava room with several entrances here dramatic, but also the sea life can be great. On a two-tank dive here we saw, among other things, four reef sharks, two *huge* octopuses, a frogfish (*very cool*), harlequin shrimp, ghost shrimp, pipefish, a titan scorpionfish, lots of black coral, slipper lobster and— oh, yes—*a pod of dolphins!* (This was one of the single greatest day dives we've ever done.) Obviously, Cathedrals won't always deliver dives like that, but it *can* be awesome. Not necessarily an advanced dive. You need to specifically book this

Hawaiian Reefs—*Why is it that…?*

What is that crackling sound, like bacon frying, I always hear while snorkeling or diving?
For years this baffled people. In the early days of submarines, the sound interfered with sonar operations. Finally we know the answer. It's hidden snapping shrimp defining their territory. One variety is even responsible for all the dark cracks and channels you see in smooth lobe coral. A pair creates the channels, then "farms" the algae inside.

Why are there so few shellfish in Hawai'i? It's too warm for some of the more familiar shellfish (which tend to be filter-feeders, and Hawaiian waters don't have as much stuff to filter). But Hawai'i has more shellfish than most people are aware of. They hide well under rocks and in sand. Also, people tend to collect shells (which is illegal), and that depletes the numbers.

Why do coral cuts take so long to heal? Coral contains a live animal. When you scrape coral, it leaves proteinaceous matter in your body, which takes much longer for your body to dispatch.

How did the early fish get here over the vast open ocean? Often in the form of larvae, which could travel in the ocean's current for long periods of time without the need to feed in the inhospitable open ocean.

What do turtles eat? Dolphins. (Just teasing.) They primarily eat plants growing on rocks, as well as jellyfish when they are lucky enough to encounter them. Unfortunately for turtles and lucky for us, jellyfish aren't numerous here.

Is it harmful when people play with an octopus? Yes, if the octopus gets harmed while trying to get it out of its hole. Best to leave them alone.

Why does the ocean rarely smell fishy here in Hawai'i? Two reasons. We have relatively small tide changes, so the ocean doesn't strand large amounts of smelly seaweed at low tide. Also, the water is fairly sterile compared to mainland water, which owes much of its smell to algae and seaweed that thrives in the bacteria-rich runoff from industrial sources. We don't have an upwelling of cold, nutrient-rich waters common on the mainland, which causes plankton there to thrive.

Why is the water so clear here? Because relatively little junk is poured into our water compared to the mainland. Also, natural currents tend to flush the water with a continuous supply of fresh, clean ocean water.

Why do my ears hurt when I dive deep, and how are scuba divers able to get over it? Because the increasing weight of the ocean is pressing on your ears the farther down you go. Divers alleviate this by equalizing their ears. Sounds high tech, but that simply means holding your nose while trying to blow out of it. This forces air into the eustachian tubes, creating equal pressures with the outside ocean. (It doesn't work if your sinuses are clogged.) Anything with air between it gets compressed. So if you know someone who gets a headache whenever they go under water…well, they must be an airhead.

trip. Boats leaving from Lahaina offer shorter treks. Dive lights are helpful. **Cathedrals I** is also great, but not as good as Cathedrals II.

Another standout location is the **Back Wall of Molokini**. This is *outside* the crater. It's not necessarily the fish life that makes this a good dive, though the fish are numerous. Rather, it's the dramatic way that the wall plunges into the abyss. Its presence is never far from your mind. And as you round the corner from Molokini's shadow to the sunlight (penetrating to an incredible depth), the wall forms an awesome spectacle. Later, you may look down and see a black tip reef shark cruising the neighborhood 90 feet below you—and another one 90 feet above you. This is an easy dive on which to go deep, and most companies will screen to make sure you're up to the task. Since there's nothing much to stop you from going all the way down, it's important that you're comfortable regulating your buoyancy. We don't want you setting any new depth records in your state of rapture of the deep. Bring a light for the shadow side.

The *inside* of Molokini isn't nearly as dramatic to dive as the outside, but it's easier. Either way, trips to Molokini are very short. It's only 6 miles from the Kihei Boat Ramp.

The closest we come to a shipwreck is the **Carthaginian**. Scuttled here in 2005, it rests in 95 feet of water. The boat was painted and rigged to resemble an old whaling boat, and under water the wreck appears older. The easily accessed interior is fairly wide open, and in time the fish count should increase.

Good Shore Dive Locations

From South Maui to West, all are described in greater details in *Beaches*.

Black Sand Beach (Pu'u Ola'i) has good coral, turtle and fish life, but you'll have to swim along the hill's shoreline over 800 feet to get to the areas deep enough to justify SCUBA. Around the point, before Little Beach, there are some excellent caves. Ocean entry is over a lava shelf; try only during calm seas. Visibility is poor until you leave the shoreline area. Just follow the hill around as far as your will takes you. Dive boat captains call this site *Red Hill*.

Ulua is where intros usually take place in South Maui. There's lots of good reef, though visibility tends to be poor.

Makena Landing is usually calm with easy entry, making it a popular place for intro or night dives. The visibility is best on the north side, which also has good coral.

Five Graves/Five Caves (see page 171) can be excellent.

Scenic Lookout (see page 166) can be exciting, though the gear-hauling and entry is a bit annoying.

Black Rock is fun, and there are dive companies at nearby resorts.

Kahekili Beach Park is a popular intro spot because of the easy entry. Kick straight out for best conditions.

Honolua Bay *can* be incredible. (See photo on page 2.) Though depths rarely exceed 40 feet, the right side of the bay has an extensive reef area and lots of fish. Eels are common. Head out 100–200 feet before dropping.

Mala Wharf is a twisted pile of rubble from a badly constructed wharf that makes a great artificial reef. Night dives are best. At no deeper than 30 feet we've seen conger eels, octopuses and even oval squid. From Mala Ramp, you can see the old broken wharf and how to get there.

IF YOU'VE NEVER DIVED BEFORE

Intro dives are how nearly all of us certified divers started. You'll get instruction, and a dive instructor will be nearby during the dive. Most do these as shore dives.

Though certified, we still do intros with companies to see how they perform. Most intros take place at Ulua Beach in South Maui or Kahekili Beach in West Maui.

Of the companies we've listed above, **Maui Dreams** (808-874-5332) in South Maui does the best job for intro dives, and they are very reasonably priced at $99 for a one-tank, $129 for a two-tank.

Many of the big resorts also offer intro dives. You need to be age 12 to be certified through NAUI, or age 10 to be certified through PADI to SCUBA.

The two things that annoy us with companies doing intros are patronizing attitudes and the use of 63-cubic foot (or smaller) tanks. Most new divers suck a lot of air, and 80s, though heavier, are the way to go, not the smaller 63s. (Perhaps this is cynical, but maybe some use 63s so that they can get you in and out faster since your air won't last as long.)

If you have asthma, heart disease, high blood pressure, ear problems or are on medication, call the dive company before you arrive. They may need a signoff from your doctor for some things.

NIGHT & SCOOTER DIVES

Most (though not all) companies do night dives. Examples are **Maui Dreams**, which does one-tank shore dives for $99. **Ed Robinson** has two-tank shore night dives for $100–$150. **Maui Dive Shop** does one-tank night dives in South Maui for $129.

Scooter Dives aren't your usual cerebral exploration. These dives are an unabashed thrill ride, like an underwater roller coaster. Forget finding exotic fish or colorful reefs. Here, the object is to cruise like you belong here. It wasn't until my first scooter dive that I realized that humans can be incredibly graceful in the water. Usually we look clumsy and awkward. But scooters allow you to maneuver like a sea lion. They are amazingly precise and easy to learn—just not super

fast. After just a few minutes' practice, it's easy to skim the bottom, do loops and corkscrews, and soar like an underwater eagle. In short, they're a blast! Just don't forget that scooters don't change biology, so don't bounce your depths too much.

Maui Dreams also does one-tank scooter dives for $139 and two-tanks for $169. **5-Star Scuba** (808-662-8207) has several locations, such as the one at the Sheraton, and charges $119. They like to stop often and explore the reef by fin, which isn't as much fun as a nonstop ride. Tell them if you don't want to stop. They also have a shore dive package that includes a day, a night and a scooter dive for $297.

A FEW SCUBA TIPS

Despite assurances that the gear has been checked out, if you rent gear to dive on your own, it's a good idea to hook the regulator to the tank before you drive away from the shop. Though we have our own gear, we often rent from shops and boats to evaluate the gear, and we've had problems with leaking regulators and tanks not filled completely with some shops. Anyone can have it happen once, but if it happens twice at a shop, we'll dump on them.

Dives, like snorkeling, are usually best in the morning. Afternoon winds can lower visibility and raise surf.

Some companies try to put you in 63-cubic foot tanks. If you don't want to be rushed, tell them you want 80s. Many will comply.

I'd like to pass on a tip that has helped my diving more than any other. I used to be a less-than-stellar breather, never the last one out. I tried skip breathing—holding your breath while not ascending, which, of course, you're *not* supposed to do—but only got marginally better results at the cost of headaches caused by a buildup of CO_2. Then I learned the secret to make a tank last a long time. Breathe *continuously*,

*Hey—what are **you** looking at?*

never stop, but do it slowly. A long, slow, deep inhalation followed immediately by a drawn out exhalation keeps CO_2 from building up and keeps your body from thinking it's low on air. (I use my tongue at the top of my mouth to spray the air out slowly.) You never feel deprived, and the tank lasts *oh, so long*. The only downside is less silence during your dive. Now, I'm almost always the last one out, and only the tables tell me when to come up, not my gauge. See your dive instructor. (That's the diving disclaimer equivalent of *see your doctor*.)

Shopping

There are zillions of places to shop on the island, and it's not practical to list and evaluate them all. So here's some general guidance on *where* you'll want to shop. If you're looking for gifts to bring back home for family and friends (or maybe something for yourself), Lahaina in **West Maui** is where you'll find the most extensive shopping on the island. Front Street is lined with art galleries and clothing shops; for marathon shopping, start near Banyan

Tree Park on the south end, and then work your way up one side of the street and then back down the other. The Old Courthouse Building (near the harbor) has a good selection of Hawai'i souvenirs. Whalers Village in Ka'anapali is a beachside mall filled with high-end stores.

In **Central Maui**, the town of Pa'ia has a large art community, making it one of the most eclectic places on the island to shop. Here too, you'll find lots of boutique clothing shops, including popular local swimsuit designers Maui Girl and San Lorenzo. Nearby Makawao in Upcountry is an often-overlooked shopping destination, and in some ways it's even better than Pa'ia.

South Maui is spread out, so you won't find a dense concentration of shops where it's easy to walk from one to another just to browse. But there are a few at the Ma'alaea Harbor Village where you can find stereotypical Hawai'i knickknacks. The gift shop at the Maui Ocean Center is the biggest and best souvenir store on the island, and you don't have to pay admission to check it out. Kihei Kalama Village (across from Kalama Park—the one with the big sculpture of a humpback whale) is where you'll find cheap souvenirs like carved wooden tikis and coconuts to mail home, that kind of thing. There's parking in back. The Shops at Wailea is south Maui's upscale shopping venue.

If you're running short on time and still have a long list of people to buy gifts for, the Walmart close to the airport sells boxes of chocolate covered macadamia nuts and Hawaiian coffee as cheap as any place you'll find on the island.

Skydiving in Hawai'i is a special experience, but doing it in the remote paradise of Hana is *incredible*. The drive along the Hana Highway, through the rainforest and gulches, is a journey you won't soon forget. But to see that gorgeous scenery from the air, then go hurtling back toward that landscape while experiencing a huge adrenaline rush is the stuff you'll remember for a lifetime.

There's only one company offering skydiving on this island—**Maui Skydiving** (808-379-7455). They're relatively new to the scene on Maui, but the crew has years of experience in the industry. They do a good job of catering to each customer's needs—if you're a first-timer and feeling nervous, they'll walk you through the whole process; if you're excited and ready to have fun, they are, too. The whole process takes around an hour, though weather and group size are big factors. All jumps are done tandem (where you're attached to the instructor). Their zebra-striped plane, a Cessna 182, is on the small side, and only two jumpers (plus their instructors and the pilot) can fit—so if you have more than two in your party, you'll have to draw straws for who gets the first jump. They cruise to an altitude of 8,000–10,000 feet, giving you about half a minute of free fall time (which can feel *way* longer). The jump is made just offshore, allowing the trade winds to help push you toward the landing zone. (When the winds blow from the other direction, the jump is done more inland.)

Weather conditions play a big role in making the jump, and they err on the side of caution when making the call to jump or not. They've had no serious accidents to date. Our only ding is that they weren't as upfront as we would have liked when we asked about any previous incidents. *We already knew*, for example, that winds didn't cooperate one day in early 2019, and tandem skydivers landed

The biggest and best souvineer shop on the island is at the Maui Ocean Center. This guy, however, ain't for sale.

Skydiving in Hana—
how's that for crossing something off your bucket list?

in the ocean. They're always equipped with proper safety gear for such incidents, and there were no injuries, but it's best to get in front of these stories rather than avoid them.

Morning jumps usually provide the best conditions—winds are lighter and rain is less likely. Try to avoid booking a jump toward the end of the day. Any weather delays in the day that push earlier appointments later means the last jumps could be bumped to the next day. Plan at least 2 hours of travel time to get to the Hana Airport from Kahului. If you've never driven the Hana Highway before, know that you won't have time to stop and see sights along the way. Note that you must be 18 years old.

Prices are steeper than you find on O'ahu and Kaua'i, but considering the location, it's justifiable. A solo tandem jump runs $299; two jumpers for $498. If you're the only one jumping from your group and another single jumper is booked, you can get a standby rate of $250. Photo and video add-ons start at $95 and range up to the $520 Big Kahuna package where you get GoPro photos and video from your instructor's hand cameras, plus footage shot videographer-style by another instructor who jumps alongside you. All in all, it's a good product that will have you grinning for days to come. At the Hana Airport, park and bear right of the terminal. You'll find them at the small, cloth hangar on the grass.

Here we go again, frothing at the mouth about the water. But give us the benefit of the doubt here. The truth is that snorkeling on Maui can be outrageous—clean, clear water in many locations, calm surf much of the time, and gobs of fish and coral. The trick is knowing where to go. We've literally snorkeled miles and miles of coastline, from the top of West Maui to the bottom of South Maui, looking for good spots. In general, the best snorkeling is in South Maui, though West Maui does have a few gems.

We'll admit that we're snorkeling junkies and never tire of experiencing the water here. If you snorkel often, you can go right to our list below of recommended areas. But if you're completely or relatively inexperienced, you should read on.

For identifying ocean critters, the best books we've seen are *Shore Fishes of Hawai'i* by John Randall and *Hawaiian Reef Fish* by Casey Mahaney. They're what we use. You should see plenty of butterflyfish, wrasse, convict tang, Achilles tang, parrotfish, angelfish, damselfish, Moorish idol, pufferfish, trumpetfish, moray eel, and humuhumunukunukuapua'a or Picasso triggerfish—a beautiful but very skittish fish. (It's as if they somehow *know* how good they look in aquariums.)

We know people who have a fear of putting on a mask and snorkel. Gives 'em the willies. For them, we recommend boogie boards with clear windows to observe the life below.

SNORKELING TIPS

- Feeding the fish is generally not recommended because it introduces unnatural behavior to the reef.
- Rub spit on the inside of your mask (or spread a *thin* layer of anti-fog drops) and then do a quick rinse to prevent fogging. If it's leaking, tightening it more might not help. That might make it leak more while giving you a facial condition called *mask squeeze*, which makes you look weird.
- Most damage to coral comes when people grab it or stand on it. If your mask starts to leak or you get water in your snorkel, be careful not to stand on the coral to clear them. Find a spot where you won't damage coral or drift into it. Fish and future snorkelers (not to mention the coral) will thank you.
- Don't use your arms much, or you will spook the fish. Just gentle fin motion. Any rapid motion can cause the little critters to scatter.
- The trick to swimming with sea turtles is to act indifferent, repeatedly moving

your hands from the rocks to your mouth, as if you're eating. *You're here to graze on limu (seaweed), I'm here to graze on limu, no one's a predator, we're just a couple of sea creatures, each doing our own thing. We cool? Yeah, we cool.* They'll often get comfortable and ignore you, sometimes coming quite close as long as you don't spook them. Don't harass the sea turtles. Definitely don't touch them. And please, for the love of Neptune— don't try to ride them.
- Water temps range from 75 °F in February to 80 °F in September. The lower end may seem chilly; consider renting a short, thin wetsuit.
- We prefer using divers' fins (the kind that slip over water shoes), so that we can walk easily into and out of the water without tearing up our feet. (If you wear socks or nylons under the shoes, it'll keep you from rubbing the tops of your toes raw.)
- If you have a mustache and have trouble with a leaking mask, try a little Vaseline. Don't get any on the glass—it can get *really* ugly.

THE BEST AREAS TO SNORKEL

See the write-ups in the *Beaches* chapter for info on each area. Some snorkeling sites have specifics you'll need to know.

South Maui Snorkeling

The entire point separating **Po'olenalena Beach** from **Palauea Beach** is great, especially from the Po'olenalena side. Also, the south end of Po'olenalena is good. Between **Maluaka Beach** and Black Sand Beach there's some good snorkeling. The point separating **Kama'ole I and II** is pretty decent. North of **Keawakapu** works pretty well, as does south of **Wailea Beach**, though you'll have to go out farther there. **'Ahihi Cove** can be great, though it's often crowded with fishermen. Just past there is **Dumps**, which is acceptable.

West Maui Snorkeling

The scenic lookout between mile markers 8 and 9 is good if you can deal with the dicey entry and exit. Experts only. **Honolua Bay** offers excellent snorkeling about two-thirds of the time. *When it's calm*, the right side of **Slaughterhouse Beach** is excellent. (Say hi to the many turtles there.) Also when calm, it's nice to snorkel all the way to Honolua Bay. **Black Rock** at Ka'anapali Beach can be superb. The south end of **Oneloa** in Kapalua is good much of the time. In Lahaina, **Pu'unoa Beach** is a good, shallow option for first timers, and nearby **Mala Wharf** can be interesting for those with more experience. The **Mile Marker 14** on Hwy 30 is ridiculously overrated, but the area below the cliffs **southeast of mile marker 11** is good if you're up for a long swim.

ODDS & ENDS

Renting snorkeling gear is easy. Maui is littered with rental places, and you won't have any trouble finding them. For South Maui, we probably lean toward **Maui Dive Shop** (808-879-3388). They also have wetsuits and divers' fins available for extra that will fit over your water shoes. In West Maui, **Snorkel Bob's** (808-661-4421) many locations are convenient and the gear is higher quality than others in the area. Most places charge about $2–$8 per day, $10–$30 per week for gear. Many shops have low prices in hopes of luring you in and then selling you other activities or timeshares. Also keep in mind that at some shops, the employee gets a commission for selling you more expensive gear. Get what *you* want, not what *they* want you to get. Make sure the mask fits without having to suck in too hard through your nose. Snorkels with drain valves and dry snorkels work better than ordinary tubes.

The most common way that visitors get bad **sunburns** is while snorkeling. You don't feel it coming because of the cool water. Do yourself a favor and consider a rashguard (which you can buy or rent from a surf shop).

Don't judge a snorkeling site by the first 20 feet. Shorelines are often cloudy. You'll usually have to venture farther out for good quality.

It's a good idea to check on the **snorkeling conditions** the day before you plan to snorkel. Call 808-944-3756 for a weather forecast. For a surf forecast, call 808-572-7873, or check out the **Weather and Surf Links** page on our website.

SNUBA is a lot like SCUBA, except that you breathe through a hose connected to a raft on the surface instead of wearing an air tank on your back. The maximum depth is 20 feet, and you'll be guided by an instructor the whole time, so you don't need any special training—just a brief lesson immediately beforehand. Anyone 8 and older can do it.

For private tours just off the beach, **Shoreline SNUBA** (808-281-3483) offers tours from Mile Marker 14 and Airport Beach in West Maui, or around Makena Landing in South Maui. Rates start at $311 per person and includes all the gear, wetsuit rental and pictures. Expect about 30 minutes underwater. They dive different areas depending on conditions. Up to six people per tour. Mornings are usually better.

Many of the boats listed in the *Boat Tours* section also have SNUBA available as an add-on for around $60–$70. Remember, that's *in addition* to the cost of the snorkel tour, and for that you'll give up part of your snorkeling time in exchange for spending 20–30 minutes underwater. Specifically, read the entries for **Alii Nui**, **Aqua Adventures**, **Calypso**, **Four Winds II**, **Lani Kai**, **Pride of Maui**, **Teralani** and **Trilogy**.

SNUBA is sort of like scuba-lite. Good for those nervous about taking the plunge. This is at Molokini.

Breathing underwater is totally unnatural for mammals (even dolphins and whales have to surface for air), so the first time doing it feels strange and exciting. If you're hesitant about trying SCUBA but want to immerse yourself in the underwater world, consider giving SNUBA a shot.

If you're looking to be pampered, there are lots of spas on the island. Some are definitely better than others.

The grandest by far is appropriately named **Spa Grande** at Grand Wailea (808-875-1234, ext. 4949). It's the largest (50,000 sq. ft.), most elaborately decorated, rich-feeling spa on the island. You name it, they've got it. They also have a unique series of specialty baths, in addition to your treatment. Like most spas, you might feel a bit processed at the beginning (there are 40 treatment rooms), and the service isn't as grand as the surroundings. Also, try not to look too closely, or you'll notice that the infrastructure could use a bit of a facelift. But once you start, they'll transform you from a raving lunatic to a smiling idiot. And make sure you take advantage of the awesome facilities before or after your treatment. (Mornings are slowest.)

The **Four Seasons Spa** (808-874-2925), also in Wailea, is smaller but has something called a cocoon floating bodywork treatment—part of the Wellness Your Way body treatment—which is the closest you'll ever get to having your bones liquefied. (50 minutes for $195, 110 minutes for $399.) They also offer oceanside massages and in-ocean or pool water therapy. The locker rooms are beautiful and furnished with pretty much everything you'll need and then some. Nice treatment rooms.

In West Maui, the Hyatt Ka'anapali spa is part of a nationwide chain. Their **Kamaha'o: A Marilyn Monroe Spa** (808-667-4500) has ocean views from the hair and pedicure salon as well as some treatment rooms. (Though from the latter you'll probably have your eyes closed.)

The **Spa Montage** (808-665-8282) in Kapalua is an amazing experience, but it ain't cheap. Full body massages start at $215 and can go up to $810 for couples. Fitness and spa facility are available for the day with the purchase of $100 treatment. To justify the prices, be prepared to stay the day and just relax in their beautiful facility. They also offer family experiences as long as a guardian is present. The infinity pool and hot tub area is for men and women. Separate areas for soaking with cascading waterfall.

The **Westin Maui's Heavenly Spa** (808-661-2525) rooms are dark, moody, quiet and relaxing. Services are good, including the Hapai Prenatal Massage for moms-to-be ($150), traditional Hawaiian lomi-lomi massage ($155–$215), and the Pamper Me in Paradise body treatment, which will work you over from head to toe ($225). Includes use of the fitness room.

submarine

You won't *Run Silent, Run Deep*. You won't hear the sound of sonar pinging away in the background. And it's rare that anyone shoots torpedoes at you. But if you want to see the undersea world and *refuse* to get wet, *dis is da buggah*. **Atlantis Submarine** (808-667-2494) uses a 48-passenger sub out of Lahaina that ambles along over a reef, which is, to be honest, a bit plainer than the type you'd choose to snorkel or SCUBA, but it's still cool. They also visit a sunken wreck called the Carthaginian. This is the opposite of an aquarium—this world belongs to the fish, and *you* are the oddity.

This $124, 40-minute ride is a kick. Most kids (36-inches or more in height) like it if they are old enough to appreciate the sights. (Plus, one kid gets in free with a paying adult.) We took friends on this trip once, and a huge manta ray cruised by the window. Of course, their 2-and-a-half-year-old son was *far* more impressed with the plastic fish card tied to the inside hull than the 14-foot ray just outside the window. But adults like it, and even certified divers like us get a kick out of it. Claustrophobics will probably be too busy staring through the windows to be nervous.

Photographers will want to use a fast shutter speed and turn off the flash.

Mornings are usually best. Wear a bright red shirt, and watch what happens to its color on the way down. Also, if you book the last trip of the day during whale season, you might get to spend extra time on the transport boat whale watching. Lastly, remember that you *and everyone else in line* has to ascend and descend a ladder to get into and out of the sub. Skirt-owning women will want to contemplate that tidbit when choosing the day's outfit.

An inferior but cheaper substitute to a submarine is the **Reefdancer** (808-667-2133). It's a semi-submersible—a boat with large windows below. After a 20-minute (each way) ride to the site, they glide over a shallow reef for 20 minutes as divers scavenge for critters to bring to the window. Kids under 8 will probably love it, as will those too skittish to try snorkeling. It's also roomier than the sub. Adults $45, kids $20, and under 3 are free. The 1.5 hour ride is too long; stick with the hour.

SURFING

Ho, da shreddin's da kine, brah. (Just trying to get you in the mood.) Surfing is synonymous with Hawai'i. And why not? Hawaiians invented da buggah. Lessons aren't as difficult as you may think. They put you on a large, soft board the size of a garage door (well... almost), so it's fairly easy to master, at least at this level. Surf is usually very small in South Maui, often too small even for beginners, and the wind that arrives late morning and in the afternoon complicates the learning process. Lahaina is a *much* better place to learn. Plus, the South Maui area where they teach—Cove Park because of its fairly reliable surf—often has cloudy water. (See page 166 for more on that.)

WEST MAUI SURF SCHOOLS

In Lahaina, try **Goofy Foot Surf School** (808-244-9283). They're very good teachers and guarantee that you'll ride a wave or it's free. Two-hour lessons are $70 per person for groups of 5, $170 for a private lesson, $280 for a couple. By the way, a goofy footer is a person (in this case the owner) who surfs with his *right* foot forward instead of the usual left. Pretty goofy, huh? We also liked **Maui Surfer Girls** (808-670-3886), they have *mostly* female instructors. $89 per person. They seem to do really well with kids, taking keiki as young as 5 (gotta book a private lesson for the extra supervision, though). **Outrageous Surf** (808-669-1400) offers well priced group lessons for $50 and private lessons for couples at $150.

SOUTH MAUI SURF SCHOOLS

If you're in Kihei and don't want to drive to Lahaina, try **Big Kahuna Adventures** (808-875-6395) or **Maui Wave Riders** (808-875-4761). $65 for two hours with Big Kahuna, $5 more with Wave Riders.

SURF SPOTS

If you're experienced, West Maui has easily accessible water, so you may want to simply drive along and look for the kind of waves that work best for you since it's very swell-direction dependent. **Ukumehame** can have good conditions for beginners. **Launiupoko Beach Park** (down Kai Hele Ku St. north of mile marker 1 on Hwy 3000) often has a good break, though it's kind of far out there. The area south of mile marker 19 on Hanoapiilani Hwy can also be good.

Lahaina Harbor and the area just to the south, called **Shark Pit** (a reference to the mostly harmless, reef sharks that frequent the area), has a very dependable break, even in fairly low surf.

Honolua Bay is one of the best sites—if you know what you're doing.

One site that's received national attention is **Jaws**. An unusual formation below the surface kicks in when the surf gets bigger than 15 feet (which happens about a dozen times a year in the winter). Then the waves become magnified and form a curved shape. They have been known to reach 70 feet here. Only a handful of experts can surf Jaws (using Jet Skis to tow them out and save their bacon when needed). Less than 15-foot surf means zippo is happening, and there is no reason to visit here. (We're assuming you only want to *watch* Jaws in action.) If the surf is pounding, the most direct route from Hwy 36 is Hahana Road (between mile markers 13 and 14). Go to the left on Hahana after the fork, and take the public access dirt road at the end of Hahana. It's along a gulch (there will be trees and such along your right). Regular cars are likely to get stuck, only 4WDs should try. If wet, consider one of the other roads among the fields. (See map on page 121.)

SURF SHOPS

The best surf shops are in **Kahului**. They include **Second Wind** (808-877-7467) and **Hi-Tech** (808-877-2111). **Pa'ia** also has a **Hi-Tech** (808-579-9297) and **Sailboards Maui** (808-579-8432)...which only carries surfboards, despite the name. In **Lahaina**, try **Honolua Surf Co.** (808-661-8848) or their **Kihei** shop (808-874-0999).

SURFING TERMS

By the way, a collection of surfboards is known in surfing lingo here as a *quiver*. A little kid surfer who doesn't have a job or car yet is called a *grommet*. Double *overhead* is when the waves are huge, and if you get good enough, you might get a chance to visit the *green room*. If someone says your girlfriend is *filthy*, it's a compliment. And a *landshark* is someone who says he surfs... but doesn't.

Advice to boogie boarders—duck!

Lest you think of yourself as da best island surfer, consider this: Hawaiian legend states that Chief Kihapiilani once surfed a wave from Maui to Moloka'i. He was said to have been adorned with leis, and that no surf spray was found on the flowers. *Hey, we don't make up the legends, we just report them.*

STAND UP PADDLING

Stand Up Paddling, or **SUP**, is extremely popular with residents and visitors on Maui. The hardest part about learning to surf is standing up on the board while it's moving. This sport has made things easier by giving you a board big enough to dance on. SUP boards are wider, thicker and longer than the biggest longboards people commonly learn to surf on. SUP instruction focuses on keeping your balance while using a tall paddle to move you into the waves. (This provides an excellent central core workout, with your feet—of all things—hurting the most.)

The sight of people standing and dipping long paddles in the water has earned SUP surfers the derogatory titles of "janitors" or "moppers" from traditional surfers.

The size of the board, as well as the fact that you are already standing up, gives you an advantage in catching waves early. You don't have to drop in exactly where the wave is breaking. Moppers can catch waves behind the lineup, but all surfing rules apply once you've caught the wave. Traditional surfers will be more inclined to drop in on your wave since they'll feel that you didn't work as hard to get it as they did.

For rentals and lessons call the surfing guys above.

Maui is the undisputed whale watching capital of Hawai'i. The shallow water between islands here is the whales' preferred birthing area.

Few industries in Hawai'i bring as much shameless phony advertising as whale watching. Photoshop allows companies to create fake scenes with relative ease. (For the record, we don't doctor our photos.) Some show whales leaping so close to boats you think they're going to get swamped. Just so you know, boats are forbidden by federal law from getting closer than 100 yards. The fine for violating a whale's personal space is obscene. Whales are allowed to initiate closer contact (and they're rarely fined), but in general, count on staying a football field away. That's OK, because these oversized buggahs are so big that even at that distance they're still incredibly impressive.

Though they're not the only whales here, **humpbacks** are the stars. They work in Alaska during the summer, building up fat, then vacation here from mid-December to early April where the females bear their young, and the males sing the blues. More than *ten thousand* whales come to the islands each year, and the mothers and calves stay close to shore. Only the males sing, and they all sing the same song, usually with their heads pointed down. (Try sticking your head about five feet under while swimming, and you'll likely hear them.) No air bubbles come out while singing, and scientists aren't sure how the big guys do it. Humpbacks can grow up to 60 feet long and weigh 45 *tons*, but they don't eat while they're here and may lose up to one-third of their body weight during their stay. (It's doubtful that many *human* visitors to Hawai'i can make that claim.)

There's no question that whale activity levels vary from year to year. Some years the humpbacks are boisterous and raising hell, constantly breaching, slapping their fins on the surface, and generally having a good time. Other years they seem strangely subdued, as if hung over from their Alaska trip. What's really going on is that some years Maui's whales visit other Hawaiian islands. Water temperature seems to have a lot to do with it. Or perhaps whales, too, want to avoid getting into a rut.

The most knowledgeable company for whale watching, not surprisingly, is **Pacific**

Hard-core windsurfers, you have arrived. You've reached the promised land at Ho'okipa.

Whale Foundation Eco-Adventures (808-249-8811). This is their passion after all. They even have hydro-phones to listen to the beasts. It's around $44 for a 2-hour trip. Of their many boats, you want one of their large double-decker catamarans. Avoid Ocean Explorer; it's narrow and tight.

Just about every vessel that floats offers whale-watching during whale season. But if you really want to observe the humpbacks, make sure you book a *dedicated whale-watching tour* that focuses on that and nothing else, since companies taking you on a snorkel trip will all claim to watch whales, but that essentially means they'll briefly pause to wave hello as you race past the behemoths on the way to your snorkel destination. See *Boat Tours* on page 189 for a description of the different companies and boats. Most outings are two hours. Bring binoculars if you have them.

From land, good places to spot whales are from the Scenic Lookout between mile markers 8 and 9, or the light station at McGregor Point between mile markers 7 and 8. Both are on Hwy 30 past Ma'alaea. During the peak season (January and February), you can often spot them anywhere along the coasts of South and West Maui. The **Humpback Whale Marine Sanctuary Visitors Center** (808-879-2818) on South Kihei Road in Kihei is good place to get tips and learn more. Whales are *much* easier to see when there are no whitecaps. Look for spouts (condensed water vapor that's really a big whale exhale).

WinDsurfing

Windsurfing is the result of taking a surfboard and attaching a sail to it. When properly instructed, you can zip along faster than the wind. It's a first-class adrenaline charge. The sport has diminished greatly around the rest of Hawai'i but remains strong here.

No matter where you go in the world, if you ask people where to find the best windsurfing on the planet, Maui is nearly always rated as the best. That's because of an accident of geography. Our amazingly consistent trade winds from the northeast are speeded up near Kahului by the venturi effect between the two mountains, so it's always windier there than the general trade speed. The shoreline orientation means the wind is usually along the shore to slightly onshore and parallel to the wave direction. Perfect!

By common agreement, no windsports are allowed before 11 a.m. (Surfers get to use the waves up till then.) This is strictly enforced by local residents. Also, if you're interested in advanced lessons or simply renting your gear (around $60 per day), local regs state that companies aren't allowed to deliver. You'll have to bring the gear yourself. (Beginners on longboards are exempt from the delivery rule and the 11 a.m. rule because winds after 11 are considered too difficult for learners.) Unless you're advanced, don't try to windsurf at Ho'okipa, the mecca of windsurf spots. Local users won't allow beginners at the sacred spot, and there is no shortage of young toughs there to enforce the ban on novices. Beginners, instead, will find **Kanaha Beach** near Kahului Airport the best place to learn.

A 2.5 hour lesson is about $100 per person with three people per class. During that time you'll actually windsurf, though tacking and jibing (changing directions by heading into or away from the wind) may elude you. In general, it's a hard sport to master at the beginning, and you should expect to fall in the water 70 or so times during your lesson. So don't be discouraged if you're not streaking over the water like the wind gods you see around the island.

(Falling's not so bad; in fact, you'll probably get really good at it.) Shorter and slimmer people seem to learn board balance more quickly. During your lesson, don't be shy about asking your instructor to show you *exactly* what you're doing wrong.

The companies we've had good luck with are **HST Windsurfing & Kitesurfing School** (808-871-5423) and **Action Sports** (808-283-7913). Both meet at Kanaha at 9 a.m., but you'll have to go to their nearby offices to pay. (No exchanging money at the beach.)

Wear a T-shirt to keep the mandatory life jacket from rubbing you, and wear water shoes while boarding. (Most companies will provide.)

Ever seen movies where military commandos don a harness, hook a pulley onto a steel cable and zip down into the action? This is similar—without the hostile fire at the end. Ziplining has become big business on Maui, and an arms race of sorts was created as companies sought longer and longer lines. Claims of longest, biggest and fastest are common. We zipped every single line on the island, and the differences are big. Some companies offer sunset or full moon zipping; contact them if this is a priority. Don't wear too-short shorts, or the harness will get under your skin (so to speak). Minimum age is generally 10, unless otherwise noted.

Flyin' Hawaiian Zipline (808-463-5786) is our favorite. They took an area that was a reserve and built *eight ziplines* stretching well over 2 miles, with the last one a wild 3,250 feet across a valley where my GPS showed a top speed of 56 mph. Instead of zipping back and forth across the same gulch, you make a continuous journey toward Ma'alaea Bay. The views are the best of the lot.

On the other hand, it'll take you five hours on the mountain to do this since you'll wait longer between zips (one person at a time) than with other companies. (The quality of your group will make a big difference since you'll get to know each other.) And the company has indicated that they won't take more than 40 people *per day* on this trip to minimize impact on the land, so you might want to book this far in advance.

There are short, steep hikes between zips, and winds are often *nukin'* in this area, especially in the afternoon. (It'll mostly be a quartering tailwind.) A *chicken skin* moment comes when your group actually plants an endangered flower somewhere along the course. (*Very* cool but not done all year round.) Wear sunscreen and sunglasses. You gotta weigh between 75 and 250 pounds to zip. Light snacks and juices served. $185. Meet at Maui Tropical Plantation in Central Maui on Hwy 30.

Our next choice is **Kapalua Ziplines** (808-756-9147). Their location is one of the biggest selling points for their tour, with sweeping views and cool features such as the 360-foot suspension bridge. Two people can zip beside each other on all seven lines of their course. (Though with all due respect to Isaac Newton, while zipping, all objects *don't* fall at the same rate. The bigger they are, the faster they fall.) You'll be given jackets in case it rains, and snacks and juices are provided. Like Flyin' Hawaiian and Pi'iholo, your harness keeps you facing straight ahead, and you don't have to stop yourself at the end—braking blocks do the deed. The staff is fun, and you even get some extra thrills when they drive you to the upper lines on the four-wheel drive Polaris ATVs. Book the full, seven-line course, not the five, since the zipping is duller and you won't get the 2,300-foot line. It's $210 for seven zips and takes around

3.5 hours. Minimal hiking. 60–250 pounds. No lunch provided.

Pi'iholo Ranch (808-572-1717) has a similar tour to Kapalua, but the scenery is different. Less tropical-feeling, more gulch-filled eucalyptus forest above Makawao at 2,800 feet elevation. It's pretty, but not *as pretty* as Kapalua. They have side-by-side zipping with one easily fixed flaw. At the end of the zip a dangling rope threatens to flog your face as you come crashing in. It's unnerving.

The tour is otherwise well run, and there's little hiking—just steep scrambles up wiggly ramps to the tops of the towers. Rain is not uncommon, and stinky jackets are available. The $140 four-line zip's farthest line is only 1,065 feet. Opt for the five-line zip for $165, if you can afford it. Then you'll have one ride that's 1,400 feet and a final one that's a magnificent 2,800 feet long. Zippers must weigh between 75 and 275 pounds and be age 8 or older.

North Shore Zipline (808-269-0671) in Ha'iku, also called Camp Maui (named after the WWII training camp there) takes a different approach than the other companies. It's cheaper, you're done more quickly, and once you start the first line, your feet won't touch the ground until you're get to the end of the last line. While not as scenic as other zip locations, with these guys you really get the chance to feel like a kid again. In fact, you feel like you've come to a summer camp outpost when you pull up to their headquarters— a yurt. The course feels very much like zipping from tree house to tree fort with a few suspension bridges and ladders thrown in for good measure. For $119, you zip along seven lines in all with the last the longest at 900 feet. They'll tell you you'll get up to 40 mph on that one, but most likely it will only be the heaviest of the zippers who attain that speed. We only got up to 28 mph, but it really did *feel* faster. If your group is small enough (four people), it can be all done in an hour. Zippers must weigh between 40–270 pounds and be age 5 or older.

Another option is **Jungle Zipline** (808-573-1529). These guys are the most con-

Ziplining across the West Maui Mountains—the ultimate leave-no-footprint experience.

venient if you're looking for a fun activity to incorporate into your drive to Hana or for exploring the Ha'iku area. On the grounds of an old plant nursery (with some remnants still in operation), this eight-line course is shaded, which is a nice change from many of the other companies. The lines are fairly short, though the sixth is 810 feet long and has the best scenery. It is also the fastest—we got up to 30 mph. This and line 3 have a magnetic breaking system, making for smoother landings. The guides could use a pep talk. Depending on your group size, the tour will take an hour or so. (The two hours advertised on their website must be for a full tour bus.) $135 for all eight lines. On Hana Highway in Huelo between mile markers 3 and 4, just past the Twin Falls turn out. Zipper must weigh between 50–250 pounds and must be age 6 or older.

Skyline Eco-Adventures (808-878-8400) started it all here with a tour upcountry in Haleakala and one above Lahaina (which they call Ka'anapali). In those days Skyline was pretty cool, and you had to book *way* in advance. Our review was pretty enthusiastic, and the product hasn't changed. But our job is to review companies *relative to each other*, and as early builders, they've lost the arms race in terms of length and speed, they seem quaint and underachieving by comparison, and you often zip back and forth on short hops across the same terrain. Their harness system means that landings are less structured—you have to stop yourself on a ramp (or one of the guides will help), though that may add to the adventure for some. You'll have more flexibility in your zipping position. No side-by-side zipping here. The longest zip at the Haleakala location is 710 feet. But it's cheaper at $110. The hiking is nearly all downhill. Zippers must weigh between 80–260 pounds and be at least 10 years old.

Skyline Eco-Adventures (808-662-1500) in West Maui is more exciting than the Haleakala location. Here, most zips are 500–700 feet, and the longest of the 11 zips is over 1,000 feet. (We got up to 33 mph on that one.) Ka'anapali is dusty and often hot when the breeze isn't blowing. But they feed you snacks and water, and the views are pleasing. Their marketing department deserves a medal because the photos are far more compelling than reality, and the zips are so short you often won't have time to look around. It's $170 for the 8-zip course, $190 for a 11-zip course. The 11-zip is worth the extra money—you get a side-by-side zip to race your partner, plus the second longest zip of the course. The tour is 3 to 4 hours, one of which is trucking up the mountain. The hiking is nearly all downhill. Zippers must weigh between 80–260 pounds and be at least 10 years old.

Last but... last in the zipline department is **Paradise Eco-Adventures** (808-264-6127), south of Lahaina. It's maybe an adventure if you're a small kid. They only have *one* line on their dragonfruit farm that you repeat four times. (And it's only 450 feet long.) What's good is that they let you hang upside down and generally do whatever kinds of tricks you want. $70 for kids 5–12, $90 for adults. More interesting is their **Aquaball**. This is where they roll you down a hill inside a giant hamster ball (actually a large, double-hulled, clear, inflated beach ball) with water inside splashing around. It's called *zorbing* in other parts of the world. It's actually really fun for kids and grownups, but not great for those with knee issues because you'll be jabbing your legs during the roll down. And the rolling is pretty slow. $70 for kids 5–12, $90 for adults. Price includes two rolls down the gently sloped, approximately 450-foot-long course. They have a $10 per-person walk-along fee—*really?*

Having adventurous fun and perhaps helping the environment—yeah, works for us.

Some of the activities described below are for the serious adventurer. They can be experiences of a lifetime. We are assuming that if you consider any of them that you are a person of sound judgment, capable of assessing risks. All adventures carry risks of one kind or another. Our descriptions below do not attempt to convey all risks associated with an activity. These *adventures* are not for everyone. Good preparation is essential. In the end, it comes down to your own good judgment. Also, please read our note about personal responsibility on page 45. It's particularly relevant to this chapter.

SPEAR AN INVASIVE FISH

This is one of those adventures that can also be good for the environment. In the 1950s some short-sighted government officials decided it would be a *great* idea to introduce a beautiful fish from French Polynesia to Hawaiian waters in an attempt to create new fisheries. So they brought in 2,000 peacock groupers (now known locally as roi.) It was a disaster. The fish thrived, consuming and pushing out native species. And to add insult to injury, the fish isn't even edible, because individual fish have an extremely high incidence of ciguatera (reef fish poisoning) in their flesh, which is toxic to humans. So now Hawai'i is stuck with a fish that doesn't belong here and is harmful to our environment. What to do? *Spear 'em, brah.*

Maui Spearfishing Academy (808-446-0352) does a great job. The owner and guides are passionate about free diving and are excellent teachers. The 5.5-hour tour is $189, with 2–3 hours in the water.

You'll spend the first two hours going over safety, fish ID and free-diving/breathing techniques. The latter is *really* important. The guides do a good job of evaluating customers' limitations and will have you holding your breath longer and diving

This hiker (pictured at the bottom of the falls) reached the fourth, and best, falls at Na'ili'ili-haele. It's not too far, but it does include overcoming a hurdle. (Literally.)

deeper than you ever thought you could. The longer you can stay down and the deeper you can go, the larger the fish get and the easier they are to spear.

Depending on conditions, you will most likely go out in West Maui around Ka'anapali or Olowalu. You swim over the reefs, taking turns with a spear gun in a leapfrog fashion, so as to maximize your hunting time. They have short wetsuits you can use included in the tour price, but we recommend renting a full-length wetsuit. You lose a lot of heat in the water, and being too cold will diminish your breath-holding ability.

Top Shot Spearfishing (808-205-8585), formerly Spearfish Maui, is less about the free diving training, more about the spearing fish. They do spear invasive fish, but they also teach what subsistence spear fishing is all about and will most likely send you home with some fish to eat.

Their intro dive is $189 and has you in the water at least two hours. We still really like their product, but if we're staying true to a *spearing invasive fish* adventure, Maui Spearfish Academy is your better bet. With Top Shot, you're likely to be more successful at spearing a *native* fish.

THE FOUR FALLS OF NA'ILI'ILI-HAELE

Quite a mouthful. But imagine *four* waterfalls, one right after another, in a beautiful setting, and all relatively near the highway. It's the kind of scene most people dream of.

First things first. The trail is on EMI land. (See page 80 for more on that.) Unlike most land EMI uses, they actually own this parcel. (Most of the rest is leased from the state.) Locals have simply used the trail for years without a problem, but we'll leave it up to you to secure permission from EMI. The trailhead is 0.1 miles past mile marker 6.5 on Hwy 360 across from some tall Cook Island pines. There's a turnout on the right. (There's usually *lots* of cars.)

At first the trail can be slippery, awkward and steep as it goes down through bamboo to a ditch, which you may have to hop over if there's no board there. (If you fall in, you'll have a very bad day.) Once across, don't take the narrow trail to the right; stay on one of the two main trails in front of you (they converge). This will take you to a stream. After you boulder-hop across—IMPORTANT!—follow the trail as it parallels the bank upstream to the left. Don't take one of the false trails heading up the hill. Soon after, you're likely to see an artificial waterfall coming from a reservoir across the stream, but it's not one of the four natural falls we're describing.

Several minutes later the trail peters out, and a spur trail to the left takes you to the first waterfall (which you'll hear). The 15-foot falls are nice but a bit too small. (Oh, my, we're getting spoiled.)

Cross the stream (boulder-hop again), and the trail continues on the other (east) side (with a slippery and dicey incline at the beginning). Up through the bamboo (with a few awkward spots), and you'll soon come to waterfall No. 2. This is as far as many will go. Falls No. 2 has most of the ingredients people want. Very pretty with a nice swimming pool, rounded pebble shore with sun and shade. You

may find yourself falling asleep to the sound of the water.

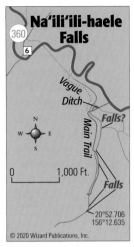

One of the things that separates a hike from an adventure is uncertainty of outcome. So it is here. On the left side of the falls, a trail leads up to...a dilemma. A fairly sheer 12-foot rock face is in your way. There are two more falls ahead. There may be a rope or a ladder or whatever (which we don't vouch for) to assist your climb, but it's not easy. And coming back down isn't much fun either. Most will probably settle for the first two falls. If you don't, here's what to expect.

It has probably taken you 30 minutes to get to falls No. 2. After overcoming the rockface, head upstream for 10–15 minutes, and you'll come to a long pool. A trail on the right side through the wild ginger helps, but eventually you'll have to get in the water and swim 100 or so feet up the pool. (Have I lost you yet?)

Don't try to go up and over; you *gotta* get in the water. Then you'll scale a man-high waterfall (No. 3), walk around the bend, and claim your prize: a gorgeous waterfall, at least 35 feet high (maybe more) in a drop-dead gorgeous scene. It's official. You have now arrived at paradise.

Now, that's a lot to go through to get to a waterfall, even a beautiful one. Why do it? Because it's a lot to go through, and it rewards you with a beautiful waterfall. That's it. Nothing deeper than that. Just an adventure you never would have had back home.

In case you're wondering, *yes*, there are more waterfalls past No. 4. And *no*, you'll never see them. It would be crazy to scale falls No. 4. Don't even think about it.

Water shoes or tabis are a big help for the last part of the journey. If you want to take a photo of falls No. 4, either get a waterproof bag, waterproof camera, or hold your camera high while swimming the length of the natural pool. (Hard to do.)

The spine of Haleakala with its chain of craters makes a glorious mountain bike ride. All downhill without the crowds.

MOUNTAIN BIKE HALEAKALA'S SPINE

OK, so everyone's heard of the Haleakala Downhill bike ride mentioned in *Biking* on page 187. But few are aware of this—there's a road called Skyline that meanders down the *other* side of the volcano, and it makes an incredible downhill *mountain bike* ride. After Skyline's downhill trek, you have 2 miles of relatively flat dirt road, then almost 6 miles of paved, downhill, *yee-haw* riding. Best of all, there are no commercial operators clogging the roads. (Some might tell you that you're not allowed to mountain bike it, but the truth is *they're* not allowed to do it *commercially*.)

Here's the deal: To do this you'll probably need two cars—one to leave at the end of paved part of Waipoli Road (which has to be a 4WD vehicle—see page 219 for more on that), the other to take you and your bikes to the summit of Haleakala. You'll probably find that renting a cheap-o car for a day is less expensive than renting a mountain bike (which is kind of odd when you think about it). Leave the car and a bike rack (which you get when you rent the mountain bikes) at Waipoli and Hwy 377 (the upper highway—see map on page 121), then head to the summit (not the upper visitor center).

Once at the top, ride your bikes down the short road, hang a right (mile marker 21 is there), and at the next intersection stay to the left to get to Skyline Road. (If the nasty government sign or gate bothers you, see page 131 to calm your nerves.) Skyline is just over a mile downhill from the summit.

Once on Skyline (marked by a gate), you'll hate what you see in the road. The first mile is an intimidating surface of loose lava rocks, and you'll be forgiven if you want to walk your bike on parts of it. It's an easy walk, and the views are awesome. The road gets progressively smoother, though it's always on a loose surface, so don't get too crazy. Avoid locking your front tire, or it will wash out. The road continues to improve the lower you get, and the riding gets more fun since you're a bit less worried about your traction. A gate at 3.5 miles into the trail is easy to walk around and is only there to prevent motorized vehicles from getting through. it is legal for you to cross it with a bike.

Watch for the Mamane Trailhead at almost 5.5 miles into Skyline; it's on the right and easy to miss. This is perhaps the best part of the ride. It's just over a mile on a smooth but narrow trail with killer views, and it seems tailor-made for mountain biking.

The intersection of Mamane and Waiohuli is marked by a large lava pit crater. This was an eruption vent, where the lava gurgled down the mountain. Stop and poke around for a minute. Also, it makes an ideal shelter if it starts raining.

The short trail segment from the Mamane/Waiohuli intersection to Waipoli Road is the steepest, and you may want to walk the bike over part of it.

Once on Waipoli Road, the free ride is over. It's 2 miles, mostly flat but with a little uphill, to the paved part of Waipoli Road. Raise the seat and take it slow. Once on the pavement, the 1.5-lane road is a delightful, extremely winding, downhill joyride. Keep the speed down, and watch for cars on this sparsely driven road. All told, you rode almost 16 miles and lost nearly 7,000 feet!

Some Tips

You'll probably want to lower your seat *a lot* for the downhill part, giving you more comfort, stability and a lower center

---

Map labels

21 Gate
Summit 10,023'
Science City
Gate
Gate

N E W S

Upper Waiakoa (2.6) — 7,800'
Skyline Trail (Closed 4WD Road)
Upper Waiohuli (3.8)
9,000'
8,000'
Waiakoa Loop
Waipoli Rd
4WD from here
Gate
8,000'
Kahua Rd
Boundary (.4)
6,800'
5,600'
Waiohuli (1.4)
Mamane (1.1)
7,200'
Gate
0   1 MILE
Redwood (1.7)
Tie
Parking (6,160')
5,300' Plum Trail (1.7)
5,900'

⌇ Foot Trails
⌇ Unpaved Roads
⌇ Contour Lines = 40 ft

Polipoli Trail (.6)–Lengths are in miles
Haleakala Ridge Trail (1.6)

© 2020 Wizard Publications, Inc.

of gravity. This also allows you to use the legs more to keep some weight off your 'okole on the bumpy parts. Rent a bike with front and rear shocks (for about $85) to keep your tush from getting tender.

It's good to cover your limbs and use a full face helmet (in case of a fall). Lava-induced road rash is a tad more severe than scrapes acquired from asphalt.

Some may not like the narrow Mamane section. (Readers have reported even carrying their bikes over their heads to navi-

Between the two of us, can you guess which one is excited to start the 1,700-foot climb back up the trail?

gate it.) They (and those who miss it) can continue on Skyline where it wraps around to Waipoli. Add 2 miles of pedaling if you do it this way.

This adventure will take most of the day, if you include the shuttling. A good time frame is to pick up the car in Kahului and pick up the bikes at around 9 a.m. (We like **Krank Cycles** (808-572-2299) in Makawao because they are a good shop and conveniently located for this.) Then head to Waipoli to leave the car.

This is not a maintained trail and several factors can make a big difference in the difficulty level (recent weather, ruts, experience, etc.). Experienced riders will probably think it's a great adventure, while novices may find it more harrowing. Sure, the riding surface is more challenging than the traditional downhill ride, but you go at your own pace, which is a big deal for safety. Oh, and bring a tire patch kit.

DAY TRIP TO MOLOKA'I'S KALAUPAPA

Moloka'i's formerly notorious Kalaupapa leprosy settlement (see page 151 for more) is an isolated peninsula on the island's spectacular north side. Backed by sea cliffs thousands of feet high, the views from here—not to mention the incredible history—are available as day trips from Maui.

The most popular way to reach this unique spot might not be available during your visit. Traversing the trail that spans the 1,700-foot cliff, via hiking or by mule, has been the only way to reach the settlement by land for over 100 years. A landslide in December 2018 destroyed a portion of the trail. This is not easily repaired and at press time, no time frame was available for its completion. Kalaupapa Guided Mule Tour aka Kekaula Tours (808-567-6088), is the company that will handle the adventure when the trail does reopen.

Until the repairs to the trail are completed, you can get to Kalaupapa in relative comfort via airplane. It may not be as thrilling as a mule ride or hike, but it is faster. There are a couple of options for this tour: Father Damien Tours (808-349-3006) and Kalaupapa Guided Mule Tour. The main difference being Father Damien use Mokulele Airlines, while the mule guys partnered with Makani Kai Air to stay in the game. Both offer a similar experience in shuttling and shuffling you from Maui to Moloka'i—you'll land topside and probably take the same plane down to the peninsula. Once on Kalaupapa, all groups combine for the tour. (You may have to wait for the different planes to land—we waited almost an hour on our last visit). The excursion takes you on a historic, four-hour bus tour of the settlement where Father Damien in the late 1800s ministered to those with leprosy (now known as Hansen's Disease). Lunch and a drink are included, but you won't be able to purchase any additional food or drink—consider bringing at least an extra bottle of water. (Supplies here are hard to come by. They only get barge service *once a year*.)

Tours are offered everyday of the week except Sunday (though tours of the rest of Moloka'i are available). Father Damien Tours is priced at $399. Kalaupapa Guided Mule Tour is the less expensive option at $349, though they can be difficult to get ahold of. Note that you must be at least 16 years old to visit Kalaupapa.

If you just want to have the bragging rights of landing at Kalaupapa (at the controls of the aircraft, no less), Maui Flight Academy (808-298-5188) will fly there during a flight lesson from Kahului Airport.

GROPE YOUR WAY TO A WATERFALL

We've shown you lots of waterfalls that you can hike to. Some have easy trails; some have difficult trails. Kanahuali'i Falls in Kipahulu is only a half mile from your car. How can that be an adventure? 'Cause this one has *no* trail. You're literally *in* the stream the whole time, walking on wet boulders.

You'll have to pick up some tabis for footwear. (Longs in the Maui Mall in Kahului is cheaper, but Hasegawa General Store in Hana is more convenient.) Then drive out to Hana, past mile marker 45 to the bridge over Wailua Stream. There might be a small fruit stand next to it. (The next stream *past* the Wailua Stream has Wailua Falls. You went too far. Go back to the Wailua Stream.) Once at Wailua Stream, park your car and make your way down to the stream for your trip upstream. All the land on the left side is public land. (The right side of the stream is private.)

Pick your way upstream. Keep a mental note of where you'd want to get to high ground should the stream start to flash flood. Remember that flooding occurs when heavy rain falls *uphill* from your location. Pay attention to weather conditions, and don't go if conditions seem unstable. As a rule of thumb, the stream depth shouldn't be over your knees.

At 0.5 miles into the stream you'll round a bend and be rewarded with your prize—a lovely waterfall, perhaps 20 feet tall, plunging into a waist-deep pool. Time to frolic and take pictures. Enjoy your private Eden. The setting is pristine and untouched

Rope don't fail me now.

(and I know you'll leave it that way when you're done).

CAPTAIN YOUR OWN BOAT TO MOLOKINI

There are lots of tour boats you can take to Molokini. But what if you want to do things your own way? One company, Aloha Outdoors (808-444-4044), rents power boats. They'll meet you at the Kihei Boat Ramp in South Maui and set you adrift. If you head to Molokini, you can arrange to be there after the tour boats leave and have it all to yourself.

The 24-foot Glacier Bay cats with twin 115 horsepower engines will do up to 30 mph, have shade and are easy to pilot. They include GPS so you can find the public mooring spots, but you'll have to have someone in your group dive down about 10 feet to grab the line. The catch? Price. They charge $695 for five hours (excluding taxes, fees and fuel). Now, that's a *big* chunk of money. But if you have four to six people, it's not quite as painful when you split it.

Seeing the area this way is a real hoot, but nobody ever said hoots were cheap. For liability reasons they prefer that you've at least driven a power boat before, and they don't want you to take the boat south

of Big Beach, where conditions are rougher. They have fishing poles, coolers, Porta-Potties, etc., available for extra. We've even taken SCUBA tanks and done drift dives off the back side of Molokini.

Whatever you do, make sure that when you're captain, you practice giving meaningless orders with an arrogant snarl. *Swab the decks, batten down the hatches, bring me a flagon of grog, matey, or ye'll walk the plank for sure. Arrrgh!*

RAPPEL OFF A WATERFALL

What if we told you that you could rappel off a rainforest waterfall on the Hana Highway? When we heard about Rappel Maui (808-445-6407), we were all in. The 6.5-hour tour includes three separate rappels, lunch (usually turkey and veggie wraps) and transportation—an hour each way—from central Maui. All you need to bring is a bathing suit, towel and a change of clothes (if you want to be dry for the ride back), though make sure the top you wear is something you don't mind getting wet. They provide all the gear, including tabis (neoprene booties with a mitten-like sole that grips wet surfaces). If you have a GoPro, bring it.

Rappel Maui brings you via their van to the Garden of Eden Botanical Garden, where they access the Puohokamoa drainage and falls. On the ride your guides will give you a rundown on rappelling and canyoneering. You'll start with a 60-foot rappel (the tallest) down a fern-covered cliff. It is a strange sensation, backing yourself up to such a steep drop and then walking down backward. You can go as quickly or as slowly as you want, since you're the one controlling the rope, but there is someone on belay at the bottom who can pull the rope and stop you from falling if necessary. You may be surprised at how much resistance there really is, and lighter people end up having to work harder, not having as much gravity on their side. Don't get so caught up you that forget to check out and enjoy your surroundings as you descend. Hey—*you're rappelling a waterfall.*

As extreme as rappelling may seem, we felt very safe and in control the whole time. The use of redundant anchoring systems and world-class instruction definitely helps put you at ease. Must be at least 10 years old and have $229 to burn. Their pace is slow—too slow—but you'll have a pretty cool memory.

HALEAKALA CRATER GRAND LOOP

One of most incredible hikes on the island, it takes you down into glorious Haleakala Crater, across the floor, then back up via another trail. The views are unspeakably good, and the colors are amazingly varied. All told, it's a 13-mile hike. Though you start at 9,800 feet and eventually drop to 6,600 feet, you'll only climb back up 1,400 feet to the 8,000-foot level. Granted, climbing 1,400 feet isn't a picnic, but it's much easier than recapturing the 3,200 feet of gravelly footing you lost coming down. See map on page 126.

Doing this hike necessitates leaving a vehicle at the Halemau'u Trailhead between mile markers 14 and 15 and starting at the Sliding Sands Trailhead past mile marker 20. You can either leave your car at Halemau'u and try to get a ride up, or rent an extra cheap-o car for the day. The latter is a sure thing, whereas getting a ride isn't.

Park at the Visitor Center and start at the Sliding Sands Trailhead around the corner. It's downhill virtually the entire way—and hard on the knees—then you'll pay the piper during the last 2.5 miles. More on that later. On the way down, you may want to take the side trip to Ka Ku'u o ka 'O'o. The crater reveals its character only as you continue changing elevations and angles.

After the trail levels, descends, then levels out again, you'll take the spur trail (there's a horse hitch at the intersection) to the left, heading north. Looking at the map, you'll want to veer right, then left at the next intersections to visit Kawilinau, formerly the Bottomless Pit. See page 130 for more on this pit. Turn left and about 100 yards past the pit is an area called Pele's Paint Pot. Minerals in the rock created this colorful rock canvas.

If you have a few extra calories you need to burn, you can take a side (unmaintained) trail up a ridge near here that overlooks the Dinosaur spine and the grandness of the crater itself. This is one of the most expansive views on the island and a real treat. Only go up as far as time permits; you *don't* want to be hiking out of here in the dark.

After the Silversword Loop, our old friend green will start to return as the vegetation increases, and you get closer to the mountain and the Ko'olau Gap. Stop and rest at Holua Cabin if you wish, envying the forward-thinking bug-

Parts of Haleakala Crater are peppered with life...

gahs who planned *way* in advance to stay there.

In another mile, it will be time to pay your dues. In terms of elevation, you've had it pretty easy for these last 10 miles. Now it's time to sweat. Fortunately, the trail switchbacks are only moderately steep. One of the seemingly endless switchbacks wanders over to the other side of the mountain, giving you a magnificent view (clouds permitting) of the Koʻolau Gap. Make sure to stop many times on the way up to enjoy the incredible views.

A Few Basics

Bring *gobs* of water with you. You lose water at a ferocious clip at this altitude. Since the only real climbing is at the end, it's no big a deal to drag more water than you *think* you'll need, *suck 'em up* all day, and pour out the excess before starting the climb. Also, bring a hat and sunscreen. You fry fast up here. Rain is possible, especially at the end as you're climbing back up. A light rain jacket is a good idea, especially in the winter. Dress warm for the top and cool for the bottom.

You never know what kind of weather you'll encounter on this hike. I was once up on Dinosaur Spine GPS-ing the trail for our smartphone app and exploring past the point where the trail was obvious, looking (unsuccessfully, it turned out) for more trail. Thick clouds moved in so fast that, if I hadn't had my GPS breadcrumb trail to follow back, I would have been lost and stranded in the clouds.

Speaking of the app, since you might purchase it, there is a vague but rewarding alternative route from Dinosaur Spine back to the base of your climb back out. Cool, but harder, and without the app it's easy to lose the trail, which is why I didn't put that trail on the map in this book.

HUNT A WILD PIG

Imagine creeping through Hawaiian forests with just the beginnings of sunrise streaming through the dense foliage, hunting dogs panting ahead of you with their noses to the ground. It's nearly silent except for the pounding of your heart. Suddenly the dogs begin to bay, and you're dashing through ferns and ducking tree branches, trying to catch up to the pack before your prey has a chance to escape. The hunt is on.

A wild pig hunt is exhilarating and invokes something truly primal, but this is not an adventure for everyone. You need to prepare for the experience before you even arrive on Maui. A hunting license for nonresidents is $105 and can be obtained online through the Hawai'i Division of Forestry and Wildlife website. But getting a hunting license here requires that you have a hunter safety card. (You can't be grandfathered in. As in most states, you must pass a hunter's education course—on the mainland is fine—to get a hunting license in Hawai'i.)

For those curious about this unique offering, some background information is in order. Pigs were brought to the Hawaiian islands by the Polynesians as a source of food and, over time, established themselves in the environment. When westerners came to the islands, they brought additional species of pigs. Though wild pig hunting provides an important source of food for local families and is part of a deeply rooted tradition, it is also integral to protecting the native ecosystems. Pigs cause incredible damage to the native forests of Hawai'i, especially the wetlands in the upper elevations. Decades of work have gone into fencing them out of sensitive areas. But pigs are very intelligent, are prolific breeders, and even the best efforts to keep them out of protected areas are often thwarted by these wily buggahs. So hunting is considered an important tool in managing the protected forest systems, and it helps maintain a connection to the land for local families that is increasingly difficult to find.

The experience is about more than harvesting game. The camaraderie between you, your party and your guide is one of the best perks. Personally, I've never been a hunter, just because it wasn't a part of my life growing up. But taking part in something that stretches back over a thousand years of Hawaiian culture and helps protect the threatened forests for future generations seems like a laudable goal. If you're successful, you can even take some of the meat back to where you're staying.

Lopaka's Aloha Adventures (808-298-3145) is your best bet. The traditional method of pig hunting in Hawai'i is called "dog and knife," and that's how Lopaka does it. On your own you'd never even see a pig. The vegetation is too dense, the pigs too alert. Dogs are necessary to track 'em. Just watching how the dogs work together and take cues from the lead dog is something to be appreciated.

Once you book your trip, you'll meet the day before your hunt at the Pu'u Kukui

...Others seem more like a moonscape.

It's hard to believe that swimming with sharks can be so relaxing. But on this dive, it is.

Watershed Headquarters in Kapalua to sign a waiver and learn about their conservation efforts in West Maui.

The next day you'll wake up stupid early and meet at a prearranged spot in West Maui at 5:30 a.m. The smaller your group, the better, since you need to be able to move quickly and somewhat quietly, making this popular with father-son teams. Though the dogs really do the hard part, you need to be able to hike a few miles over rough terrain. Lopaka is good at determining his clients' abilities/limitations and won't push you more than is needed. You'll probably spend a lot of time waiting for a dog or two to come back to the group, and there is the chance you won't find any pigs (though the game is prevalent and Lopaka has a few alternative spots to try if you have the time).

The hunt costs $500 and will take 6–8 hours with lunch included.

SWIMMING WITH SHARKS

Have you ever visited a large aquarium and wished you could observe the fish and sharks from the *other* side of the glass? Here's your chance, and the experience is ridiculously cool.

Three times a week the Maui Ocean Center (808-270-7000) in Ma'alaea allows two pairs of divers to spend around 40 minutes swimming with sharks, stingrays, puffer fish and all the other species in their three-quarter million gallon exhibit. And while the draw might be the 20 or so sharks in the tank, it's surprising that after a short amount of time many people start to forget that they're supposed to be afraid of sharks and find themselves oddly at home. Actually, we found it one of the most relaxing dives we've ever done, and during our dive the spotted eagle ray was the star. She loved to be touched and fed clams in their shells. We never realized how incredibly *loud* rays are when they crunch clam shells. In fact, you might not realize just how noisy the open ocean is until you've dived in this quiet tank. And with no current, surge or long swimming, you may be amazed at how little air you draw from your 50-cubic foot tank.

There's nothing about this dive we didn't like—except the price. It's $260 per person which includes all SCUBA gear. (They say the price is steep because their insurance rates are so high.)

Don't think of this as a death-defying shark encounter. The sharks don't seem very interested in feeding on divers. Think of this as the best chance you'll ever have to spend quality bonding time with sea creatures. In the open ocean these animals avoid you. But in this tank, you're one of the gang. The adventure here is to discover just how wondrous these animals really are when you're given the chance to observe them close up for so long.

You need to be a certified SCUBA diver and at least 12 years old. Since they take so few people, call them well in advance.

MARATHON SNORKELING TO PRISTINE COVES

In South Maui, if you drive your car south as far as the road takes you, you'll come to La Pérouse Bay. There's no sand beach here, except for some small pockets at the south end of the bay, but the fish life is rich—if you know where to go.

La Pérouse Bay is a great example of incomplete information. When you're standing next to your car at the end of the road, intimidating signs go on and on about all the things you *can't* do here. But what you *can* do is snorkel. Unfortunately, the snorkeling where you enter the water isn't very good. Visibility is usually poor and fish life minimal. All the good stuff is on the far side of the bay, and since it's illegal to hike over there (this being a protected reserve), the only way you're gonna see the beautiful coves is to make a long distance swim.

Before we go on, we need to make something clear. You need to be a reasonably strong swimmer. You could be looking at half of a mile of swimming (round trip), and there's the potential of having a head wind on the way back. You need fins and the legs to kick 'em. Early mornings are *usually* best and less windy. Wear a shirt as opposed to sunblock to keep the water pristine, and don't feed the fish. (They've got plenty to munch on without our help.)

When you first get in the water, you'll notice the cloudiness from the cove to your right where an estate resides. But if you go past their little cove, staying along the shoreline on the right, each successive cove usually gets clearer (though never crystal clear), and the fish life gets better and better. The cove 1,100 feet from where you enter usually has amazing fish life. Since this is a natural area reserve, it's illegal to come ashore in those coves, so just stay in the water and observe without touching. Don't go past the point on the left side of the photo. Yes, there's more snorkeling, but you're more exposed to the whims of the open ocean, and the return gets more burdensome.

Gonna have to earn those coves on the far side.

Yes, this table will do just fine, thank you.

By their very nature, restaurant reviews are the most subjective part of any guide. Nothing strains the credibility of a reviewer more. No matter what we say, if you eat at enough restaurants here, you will eventually have a dining experience directly in conflict with what this book leads you to believe. All it takes is one person to wreck what is usually a good meal. Many of us have had the experience when a friend referred us to a restaurant using reverent terms indicating that they were about to experience dining ecstasy. And, of course, when you go there, the food is awful and the waiter is a jerk. There are many variables involved in getting a good or bad meal. Is the chef new? Was the place sold last month? Was the waitress just released from prison for mauling a customer? We truly hope that our reviews match your experience. If they don't, *please* let us know. (It alerts us to both problems *and* jewels to check.)

This Island Dining chapter was pretty overwhelming for us. A huge number of choices made it difficult to select which ones to include. (And hey, we can only *eat* so much!) We have over 150 restaurant reviews in this edition and we've reviewed *even more*. Books have limited space, apps do not. So if you get our *Hawaii Revealed* app you'll find *many* more restaurant reviews there. Restaurants come and go, but if there's a place that you *really* loved, but we missed (and don't forget the ones you *really* hated), please drop us an email.

Unlike some travel writers who announce themselves to restaurants (to cop a free meal, if the truth be told), we always review *anonymously* and only expose ourselves after a meal (not literally, of course) *by phone* if we need additional information. By their reviews, many guidebooks lead you to believe that every meal you eat in Hawai'i will be a feast, the best food in the free world. Frankly, that's not our style. Like anywhere else, there's ample opportunity to have lousy food served with a rotten ambiance by uncaring waiters. In the interest of space, we've left out *some* of the dives. We did, however, leave in enough of these turkeys just to demonstrate that we know we live in the real world. Restaurants that stand out from the others in some way are highlighted with **ono** our *ono* symbol.

For each restaurant, we list the price *per person* you can expect to pay. It ranges from the least expensive entrées alone to the most expensive plus a beverage and usually appetizers. You can spend more if you try, but this is a good guideline. *The price excludes alcoholic beverages since this component of a meal can be so variable.* Obviously, everyone's ordering pattern is different, but we thought that it would be easier to compare various restaurants using dollar amounts than if we used different numbers of dollar signs or drawings of forks or whatever to differentiate prices between various restaurants. All restaurants take credit cards unless otherwise noted. When we mention that prices are reasonable, please take it in context. We mean reasonable *for Maui*. (We *know* you pay less back home.) Food in Hawai'i is expensive, even if it's grown here. (You probably pay less for our fruit on the mainland than *we* do here.)

When we give directions to a restaurant, *mauka side* of highway means "toward the mountain" (or away from the ocean).

The definition of **local food** is tricky. Basically, local food combines Hawaiian, American, Japanese, Chinese, Filipino and several other types and is (not surprisingly) eaten mainly by locals.

Pacific Rim is sort of a fusion of American and various countries' cuisines around the Pacific, including Asian and Hawaiian. It's a fine (and subjective) line between American and Pacific Rim, so we chickened out and included them under the American section. We don't have a separate **Seafood** section because nearly every restaurant on Maui serves fish.

Lu'au, those giant outdoor Hawaiian parties, are described at the end.

When a restaurant requires **resort wear**, that means collared shirts for men (though nice shorts are *usually* OK) and dressy sportswear or dresses for women.

Some restaurants have the annoying and presumptuous habit of including the tip in the bill automatically. Be on the alert for it or you may double-tip. And what if you get horrible service and don't *want* to tip? Then you're left in the awkward position of making them remove it.

Dining at the resorts is expensive, but you probably aren't being gouged as much as you think because their costs are exorbitant. One resort GM we know confided that they had over $7 million in revenue for their food and beverage department one year, but only made $100,000 in profit. (And this was the first year they had ever made *any* profit on food.)

Below are descriptions of various island foods. Not all are Hawaiian, but this might be of assistance if you encounter unfamiliar dishes.

ISLAND FISH & SEAFOOD

'Ahi—Tuna; raw in sashimi or poke, also seared, blackened, baked or grilled; good in fish sandwiches. Try painting 'ahi steaks with mayonnaise, which *completely* burns off when BBQ'd but seals in the moisture. You end up tasting only the moist ocean steak. Most plentiful April through September.

Lobster–Hawaiian spiny lobster is quite good; also called "bugs" by lobster hunters. Keahole Lobster is simply Maine lobster flown to the Big Island where it's revived in cold water.

Mahimahi–Deep ocean fish also known as a dolphinfish; served at a lu'au; very common in restaurants. Sometimes tastes fishy (especially if frozen), which can be offset in the preparation.

Marlin–Tasty when smoked, otherwise can be tough; the Pacific Blue Marlin is available almost year round.

Monchong–Excellent tasting deepwater fish, available year round. Usually served marinated and grilled.

Onaga–Also known as a ruby snapper; excellent eating in many preparations.

Ono–(Wahoo) *Awesome* eating fish and can be prepared many ways; most plentiful May through October. Ono is also the Hawaiian word for delicious.

Opah–(Moonfish) Excellent eating in many different preparations; generally available April through August.

'Opakapaka–(Crimson snapper) Great tasting fish generally cooked several ways. Common October through February.

'Opihi–Limpets found on ocean rocks. Eaten raw mixed with salt. Texture is similar to clams or mussels.

Poke–Fresh raw fish or octopus (tako) mixed with seaweed (limu), sesame seed and other seasonings and oil.

Shutome–Swordfish; dense meat that can be cooked several ways. Most plentiful March through July.

Walu–Also goes by other names such as butterfish and escolar. Be careful not to eat more than 6 ounces. The Hawaiian nickname for this oily fish is maku'u, which means—*ahem*, this is awkward—"uncontrollable bowel discharge." Eat too much, and you may pay more dearly than you intend.

LU'AU FOODS

Chicken lu'au–Chicken cooked in coconut milk and taro leaves.

Haupia–Coconut custard.

Kalua pig–Pig cooked in an underground oven called an imu (hot rocks go *inside* the beast), shredded and mixed with Hawaiian sea salt. Outstanding!

Laulau–Pork, beef or fish wrapped in taro and ti leaves and steamed. (You don't eat the ti leaf wrapping.)

Lomi salmon–Chilled salad consisting of raw salted salmon, tomatoes and two kinds of onions.

Poi–Steamed taro root pounded into a paste. It's a starch that will take on the taste of other foods mixed with it. Best eaten with kalua pig or fish. Visitors are encouraged to try it so they can badmouth it with authority.

OTHER ISLAND FOODS

Apple bananas–A smaller, denser, smoother texture than regular (Cavendish) bananas. Most people mistakenly eat them unripe. You need to wait until the skin turns predominantly brown.

Barbecue sticks–Teriyaki-marinated pork, chicken or beef pieces barbecued and served on bamboo sticks.

Bento–Japanese box lunch.

Breadfruit–Melon-sized starchy fruit; served baked, deep fried, steamed, or boiled. Definitely an acquired taste.

Crackseed–Chinese-style, spicy preserved fruits and seeds. Li Hing Mui is one of the most popular flavors.

Dim Sum–Think tapas, Chinese-style. Small portion items served off a cart. It's intended to give you a huge variety of food during one meal.

Guava–Tart fruit whose inside is full of seeds, so it is rarely eaten raw. Usually prepared with lots of sugar, so it's used primarily for juice, jelly or jam.

Hawaiian supersweet corn–The finest corn you ever had, even raw. We'll lie, cheat, steal or maim to get it fresh.

Huli huli chicken–Hawaiian BBQ style.

Ka'u oranges–Grown on the Big Island. Usually, the uglier the orange, the better it tastes.

Kim chee–A Korean relish consisting of pickled cabbage, onions, radishes, garlic and chilies.

Kulolo–Steamed taro pudding.

Liliko'i–Passion fruit.

Loco moco–Rice, meat patty, egg and gravy. *Never* served as health food.

Lychee–A reddish, woody peel that is discarded for the sweet, white fruit inside. Be careful of the pit. Small seed (or chicken-tongue) lychees are so good, they should be illegal.

Macadamia nut–A large, round nut grown primarily on the Big Island.

Malasada–Portuguese donut that is dipped in sugar.

Manapua–Steamed or baked bun filled with meat.

Mango–Bright orange fruit with yellow pink skin. Distinct, tasty flavor.

Manju–Cookie filled with a sweet center.

Maui onions–Grown in Kula; sweet. Some people eat them like apples.

Musubi–Cold steamed rice, often with sliced Spam rolled in black seaweed.

Papaya–Melon-like, pear-shaped fruit with yellow skin best eaten chilled. Good at breakfast.

Pipi Kaula–Hawaiian-style beef jerky. Excellent when dipped in poi. (Even if you don't like poi, this combo works.)

Plate lunch–An island favorite as an inexpensive, filling lunch. Consists of "two-scoop rice," a scoop of macaroni salad and some type of meat, either beef, chicken or fish. Also called a Box Lunch. Great for take-out.

Portuguese sausage–Pork sausage, highly seasoned with red pepper.

Pupu–Appetizer, finger foods or snack.

Saimin–Thin Chinese noodles cooked in a Japanese-style chicken, pork or fish broth. Word is peculiar to Hawai'i. Local Japanese say the dish comes from China. Local Chinese say it comes from Japan.

Shave ice–A block of ice is "shaved" into a ball with flavored syrup poured over the top. Best served with ice cream on the bottom. Very delicious.

Smoothie–Usually papaya, mango, frozen passion fruit and frozen banana, but almost any fruit can be used to make this milkshake-like drink. Add milk for creaminess.

Taro chips–Sliced and deep-fried taro; resembles potato chips.

WEST MAUI AMERICAN

808 Grindz Café
843 Wainee St, Lahaina • (808) 868-4147

ono Apparently the owners of this small breakfast diner haven't heard that food is supposed to cost more here in Hawai'i. (And don't *you* tell 'em.) For $8.08 (a nice homage to the state's area code) you get three eggs, toast, hash browns, bacon, Spam and Vienna sausage. Not filling enough? The $15 *Breakfast for Champions* includes an 8-ounce steak with four choices of meat, three eggs, choice of starch and a waffle. An *outstanding* value and delicious as well. They also have yogurt, pancakes and plenty of menu items done in the loco moco-style. A little off the beaten path (look for it in the Foodland Shopping Center), but easy enough to get to from either Front Street or Hwy 30 by taking Lahainaluna Road to Waine'e. It's $7–$15 for breakfast until 2 p.m. Closed Mondays.

Bad Ass Coffee Company
3636 Lwr Honoapiilani Rd, Honokowai
(800) 738-8223

Words cannot convey how much we agree

with their name, but probably not the way they intended. Wretched Kona coffee. (Their name is supposed to refer to donkeys used in days gone by to haul bags of coffee on the Big Island.) They also have lots of merchandise featuring their logo for sale as well as mac nuts and some packaged chocolate treats. Go for the latter, not the coffee. Two locations (one on Front Street in Lahaina), both skippable. This one is across from Honokowai Beach Park. **$3–$6.**

Betty's Beach Café
505 Front St, Lahaina • (808) 662-0300

onó This hidden gem escaped us for years until savvy readers tipped us off. If you like a tacky, tiki bar atmosphere, look no further. The food is good, but the view takes things to another level. Large windows run the length of the restaurant, giving a nearly unobstructed view of the ocean and the island of Lana'i. The menu is American café-style. Breakfast features the usual lineup of omelets, Benedicts (love the blackened mahimahi), plus pancakes and a couple of Mexican-style dishes. Lunch/dinner brings burgers, sandwiches, more Mexican dishes, seafood and salads. On lobster nights—Wednesdays and Saturdays—you can get a whole Maine lobster (from the Big Island) for only $20. Prime rib on Friday (prime rib night) goes for the same price. No live music, but the grounds are basically right in front of the **Feast at Lele** lu'au, which runs nightly from 5:30–8:30 p.m. It makes for loud dining, but you basically get a free lu'au show (though whether that's a pro or con, you'll need to decide for yourself). **$10–$20** for breakfast, **$11–$25** for lunch and dinner. This is exactly the kind of place many visitors look for—close to the action (Front Street) but still somewhat hidden, with great views and friendly, attentive staff. While the food isn't fancy, it's simple and satisfying. In the back of the 505 building at the south end of Front Street.

Bubba Gump Shrimp Co.
889 Front St, Lahaina • (808) 661-3111

Remember the movie *Forrest Gump,* when Bubba describes all the ways you can fix shrimp? Well, the owners of this small chain apparently didn't see it because most of the recipes mentioned in the movie aren't on the menu. But that's OK because this is a fairly easy place to like. The whole restaurant is based on the movie, and the dishes are named after its characters. Very friendly service, fun, loud and over the water. Waves actually splash under the window tables, if you're lucky enough to get one. The food is mostly fairly sorta good (certainly not great) with lots of shrimp dishes (obviously!), fish, some steak, burgers and salads. The peel-and-eat shrimpers' net catch makes a good appetizer, and they have some very good fresh fish. Their Medal Margarita is smokin' good, and the portion is hefty (though sometimes watery). We only have two complaints: They don't take reservations (and long waits can occur—but if you call 30 minutes ahead, they'll put your name on the list), and they obviously want to turn tables over fast. When we eat here, *we* set the pace by finding a nice way to tell them we're not in a hurry. Overall, a fun atmosphere and acceptable food make a good but not great experience. Between Lahainaluna and Papalaua. **$14–$30** for lunch and dinner.

Captain Jack's Island Grill
672 Front St, Lahaina • (808) 667-0988

An open-air bar and grill with a pirate theme on the north end of the Wharf Cinema Center. The second floor location makes for a nice place to get away from the heat of Front Street, but there's no view. Standard bar fare with burgers, sandwiches, tacos, pasta, seafood and steaks. Fish and chips is a good option and they make a good mai tai. Though not quite an *ono,* they've improved since our last edition and are a solid choice for the price and area. Their good happy hour deals on both food and drinks from 2–5 p.m. are your best bet. Lunch is $15–$25, dinner is $15–$35.

Cheeseburger in Paradise
811 Front St, Lahaina • (808) 661-4855

ono A legendary place that is fun to try at least once. It shares a name with a song by Jimmy Buffet, who promptly sued them when he discovered the restaurant, so they settled and changed the name of future locations. Buffet then launched his own national chain of the same name, but it's unrelated to the Cheeseburger restaurants here in Hawai'i. There are two on Maui and three on O'ahu, and the menu is the same at both Maui locations.

We've been negative on this place in the past (and so have readers), but the food has gotten better. Lots of varieties of big cheeseburgers to choose from. The BBQ burger is piled so high you'll have structural integrity issues trying to hold it together while eating. They also have a veggie burger available. Their ultra-prominent, two-story location on the ocean side of Front Street (at the intersection of Lahainaluna) is open-air on both sides, creating a nice cross breeze. The decor is stereotypical "old Hawaii" with plenty of eye-candy to keep your eyes busy. The Polynesian coconut shrimp are tasty but come with only six shrimp—that's more than $2 per shrimp! Their cocktails tend to be fruity and tasty.

The food alone isn't enough to earn the coveted *ono* rating, but combined with setting, we're comfortable awarding the designation for the *Lahaina* location. (But if you're looking for a *really* good burger in Lahaina and don't care as much about the setting, try **Teddy's Bigger Burgers**.)

They are often packed, but things usually seem to run pretty well (they claim to be able to serve up to 1,200 customers a day during peak times). $9–$16 for breakfast (be cautious—they skimp on portions in the morning); It's $15–$20 for lunch and dinner. Live music starting late afternoon.

They also have a location at the Shops at Wailea in south Maui called **Cheeseburger Grille & Tap Room**, but it lacks the energy of the Lahaina location, there's no view, and the kitchen doesn't seem to do quite as good a job.

Cool Cat Café
658 Front St, Lahaina • (808) 667-0908
Lots of good hand-formed burger combinations (but fries are extra), sandwiches, fish tacos, ribs and steak. Their onion rings are a good choice for a side. Desserts include malts, shakes (made the old-fashioned way, thick and tasty), root beer floats and brownie sundaes. Service, however, is simply joyless, so no *ono*. $17–$27 for lunch and dinner. (More if you move to pricier items such as the steak or ribs.) On the top floor of the Wharf Cinema overlooking Banyan Tree Park. Bartending is weak—stick with beer.

Duke's Beach House
130 Kai Malina Pkwy, Kaanapali • (808) 662-2900

ono Is there a killer view here? *Check.* Great fresh food? *Check.* Ka'anapali prices? *Check.* Part of a local chain that runs a tight ship, Duke's is no different. Breakfast has some great choices, such as the giant kahuna pancakes and seared 'ahi Benedict. Lunch brings salads, burgers and some fresh fish choices (which they tend to do very well). With dinner comes great seats for sunset, more seafood and steak. Dinner can get pricey—arrive for the end of happy hour (3–5 p.m.) to get better deals on starters and drinks. We really like that they strive to use locally sourced ingredients, even macadamia nuts from Moloka'i. The portion sizes can be lacking for seafood entrées—add a side such as salad or soup if you're on the hungry side. Biggest complaint is that the kitchen gets backed up at dinner, and entrées can take too long to make it to your table. $12–$20 for breakfast, $15–$20 for lunch, $18–$50 for dinner. Reservations recommended. At the Honua Kai Resort, near Keka'a (North) Beach. Free valet parking, though you'll have to walk a ways through the big resort.

Fleetwood's on Front Street
744 Front St, Lahaina • (808) 669-6425

ono Legendary Fleetwood Mac drummer, Mick Fleetwood, has a restaurant in Lahaina, and though a bit shaky in the past, they mostly get it right these days. The location (especially the rooftop dining area) is amazing, the food quality is great, there's a nice wine selection, and the events and entertainment can be a blast. The nightly sunset ceremony has become a favorite in Lahaina (complete with bagpiper), and the view is basically open from the mountains to the ocean. The menu embraces seafood more these days and a variety of fish are usually available, as well as steak and various grilled meats. Lunch is $16–$25, dinner is $26–$50. Pricey, but they do have some great happy hour deals as well. Between Dickenson and Lahainaluna streets.

Gazebo
5315 Lwr Honoapiilani Rd, Napili • (808) 669-5621

ono Gazebo benefits a lot from its location. Eating near the shore with wicked ocean, Napili Bay and Moloka'i views for... *relatively* little money (for this area, at least) makes the food and service seem better. They've got a good selection of omelets, and their signature mac nut pancakes are pretty good. Lunch is burgers, sandwiches and salads. Both are served simultaneously from 7:30 a.m. to 2 p.m., though breakfast items are better than lunch. Birds can be a problem. They only have 14 tables and fill up quickly (they don't take reservations), so either

arrive well before they open, or you'll have to wait, perhaps a *long* time. $9–$15 for breakfast, $11–$17 for lunch. South of Kapalua. Park at Napili Shores toward the back and walk through the resort. Our review never changes because this place never changes.

Honu Seafood & Pizza
1295 Front St, Lahaina • (808) 667-9390

ono At the shoreline literally within spitting distance to the water (but don't embarrass us by testing that description), this seafood-oriented restaurant also has pizzas (big enough for two, especially with an appetizer), 'ahi bolognese ('ahi tuna sausage in a cool preparation), seafood, sandwiches and a burger. Dinner menu is similar, but they have more fish entrées, raising the price to $50. Salads are their weak point, and some items might be under salted. Flavors are more subtle than bold here—to the point that it almost cost them the *ono*.

It's at the north end of Lahaina away from the high-energy vibe. We like the outdoor tables, especially when the surf is smacking the shoreline. Indoor tables mostly have ocean views. Good place to watch the sunset. Their cocktails are well-executed and varied—even non-alcoholic ones like the No-jito. Overall, this is a good place to dine while staying cozy with the ocean, looking at boats moored offshore and Moloka'i looming in the distance. $15–$30 for lunch (unless you get the $39 mac and cheese, which is certainly overpriced but deadly), $15–$50 for dinner. Reservations recommended for dinner.

Hula Grill
2435 Kaanapali Pkwy, Kaanapali • (808) 667-6636

ono They've been consistent the last couple of editions. Good food. Good cocktails. Their desserts are outrageous, and they make some great fish. The ambiance is *very* nice—next to Ka'anapali Beach with great water views and killer sunsets. Sandwiches, burgers and lots of salads for lunch; steak, seafood and pasta for dinner. Consider the lobster and scallop potstickers at dinner, but avoid the chicken. In Whalers Village. **$16–$25** for lunch, **$25–$50** for dinner.

Kimo's

845 Front St, Lahaina • (808) 661-4811

ono Dreamy location along the water's edge for lunch. Dinner is upstairs and slightly away from the water. (Some of the otherwise excellent dinner views are cut off by the roofline.) Lunch items are hit or miss, but mostly pretty good. Good burgers (need better fries, though). Their Hula Pie for dessert is worth the accolades. At dinner you can eat downstairs (which at night is designated as the bar) where some cheaper items are available. Otherwise, dinner is steak and seafood, usually with good results. Kimo's has a good atmosphere and usually good food. **$14–$22** for lunch. **$25–$50** for dinner (except the cheaper burgers). Good place for a sunset cocktail. Between Lahainaluna and Papalaua. Reservations recommended for dinner.

Lahaina Coolers

180 Dickenson St, Lahaina • (808) 661-7082

An acceptable place for a meal and a cocktail. (They have some nicely concocted tropical drinks.) Food's not bad. There's enough outdoor seating for 30, but not a single level table to be had. (Don't have 'em fill your coffee cup too high, or it'll spill.) Indoor seating is nice. Burgers, sandwiches, fish tacos, pasta and salad for lunch. Mostly steak with some chicken and fish and pizza for dinner. None of the entrées has us fantasizing about coming back, and the ingredients taste a bit cheap. But we won't steer you away either. **$10–$17** for breakfast (love the homemade corned beef hash), **$13–$20** for lunch, **$18–$35** for dinner. On Dickenson near Wainee Street.

Lahaina Fish Co.

831 Front St, Lahaina • (808) 661-3472

A fixture along Front Street for some time. They tend to feature several varieties of fish, which can be good if you've mostly been finding only mahimahi other places. Opah, also known as moonfish, is very good, and they usually cook the entrées nicely. (We've had 'em overcooked, though.) A section of the menu embraces local, sustainable ingredients that taste better than they sound, such as the taro and lentil steak. (A good vegetarian choice, but we like to stick with the fish.) Besides seafood, they have a decent variety of salads, burgers and chicken dishes. At dinner they add pastas and prime rib. The view is great at sunset, but the service can be slow even when it is not that packed. No *ono*, but we won't steer you away either. Lunch is **$15–$23**, dinner is **$22–$42**. Reservations recommended for dinner. Between Lahainaluna and Papalaua streets.

Lahaina Grill

127 Lahainaluna Rd, Lahaina • (808) 667-5117

ono One of the nicest restaurants in West Maui. Food, service and setting are all rock solid. There's no view here, but the tasteful decor is complemented by outstanding food. This chef *really* knows flavors, such as the tequila shrimp and firecracker rice. Unbelievable flavor combinations. Duck, steak, lamb, fresh fish. We haven't had a bad meal here yet. Prices are *very* high, but if you're looking to splurge, you'll be pleased with the results. It's the kind of place that doesn't seem to change over the years. **$45–$65** for dinner. Reservations recommended. Near Front Street.

Leilani's on the Beach

2435 Kaanapali Pkwy, Kaanapali • (808) 661-4495

ono Two totally different menus and two totally different experiences. Downstairs, the **Beachside Grill** menu is a bargain, considering the location and setting vs. the price. The bar is popular and gets *loud*. The sriracha-guava chicken wings are a tasty, if overpriced, appetizer at the beachside setting. (Killer Hula Pie dessert.) You can order this menu at lunch or dinner. $16–$27. For the regular dinner menu upstairs at Leilani's, it's mostly steak, seafood and ribs for $23–$55. *Usually* good service and fairly good food, but with a *tasty* view, hence the *ono*. At Whalers Village. Often busy, reservations recommended, though they *do* reserve some space for walk-ins.

Leoda's Kitchen & Pie Shop
820 Olowalu Village Rd, Olowalu • (808) 662-3600

ono This is the kind of place a lot of people look for when traveling. A restaurant in the middle of nowhere but *on your way* to somewhere, which uses fresh local ingredients and combines them into wonderful dishes. Olowalu's finest— and only—eatery bakes their own bread (a loaf is $7 or spend $3 for day-old), makes their own deadly pies, creates their own pot pies, and whips up burgers, great sandwiches (try the seared 'ahi) and salads. Love the chicken and gravy on a waffle— it's better than it sounds. Also consider the roast pork sandwich with garlic bok choy. Prices on some items seem a tad high, but the quality of the ingredients and preparation mitigates that. At mile marker 15 between Ma'alaea and Lahaina. $5–$20 for breakfast, $8–$22 for lunch and dinner, which assumes you'll snag one of their hand-held pies. Sometimes lines are pretty long.

Maui Brewing Co.
4405 Honoapiilani Hwy, Kahana • (808) 669-3474
Much improved since our last edition. This is the original location for Maui Brewing, and the restaurant here is independent of the others found around the state. The food tends to be better here than at other locations, but it's still not quite an *ono*. The

menu is what you hope to find at a bar, and they incorporate the beer into many dishes. Burgers, sandwiches (the Black Rock Dip is a standout), flatbreads, mac and cheese, plus a few local-style dishes such as loco moco. The beers can be hit or miss, though the coconut porter is one of the best options—consider getting a flight to find your favorite. $12–$20 for lunch and dinner. In the Kahana Gateway Center. Note that they only allow one check per table. Reservations are recommended for dinner, especially on weekends.

Merriman's Kapalua
1 Bay Club Pl, Kapalua • (808) 669-6400

ono Master Hawaiian chef Peter Merriman has restaurants across the state. Mostly hits, some misses. This one is a major hit. The oceanfront location overlooking Kapalua Beach goes a long way, but the quality of the food delivers as well. Billed as the "Home of Hawaii Regional Cuisine," you can be assured that all the ingredients are fresh and local whenever possible. Fresh fish, lobster, steaks and a veritable farm stand of vegetables fill the menus. And it ain't cheap. Dinner will run you $42–$80. The bar menu features only pupus, but they are all well-presented, delicious and (somewhat) easier on the wallet at $13–$60. Brunch is available on Sundays—if you can choose just one dish, brunch will run you $14–$30. Off Lower Honoapiilani Road, just past Sea House Restaurant. Complimentary valet parking, or park at the Kapalua Golf and Tennis Club across the street for $10. Look for the large Cook Island pines.

Monkeypod Kitchen
2435 Kaanapali Pky, Kaanapali • (808) 878-6763

ono Monkeypod is one of Peter Merriman's better restaurants, and both Maui locations are top notch. While the original Wailea restaurant relies on quality food (known as Hawai'i Regional Cuisine), the Ka'anapali restaurant gets a boost from its awesome location. Though not right next to the beach like Leilani's or Hula Grill, the large, open dining space embraces the ocean (and cooling breezes) in a way that makes for a casual and inviting atmosphere. Even when packed (which is often), it doesn't feel crowded. Plus, service tends to be swift, even during the hustle and bustle of happy hour (3–5:30 p.m. daily). The menu is no different than at the other location—wood-fired pizzas, burgers, sandwiches, some good salads and tempura fish and chips for lunch; add fresh fish (for which they are renowned) and steak (from Big Island) for dinner. Cocktails and desserts are also a hit—we haven't had a bad meal here, although price shock is another story. $16–$30 for lunch, upper range goes to $50 for dinner. At Whaler's Village on Ka'anapali Parkway. Reservations recommended, especially for dinner. One last tip—you have to *touch* the spigot at the bathroom sinks for water to come out.

Pacific 'O
505 Front St, Lahaina • (808) 667-4341

ono Thanks to the awesome outdoor location next to the beach, sunsets are fantastic from here. This farm-to-table restaurant offers a relatively small but varied lunch menu of sandwiches, burgers, fresh fish and fish tacos. Dinner has a large fish selection, plus chicken, lamb and steak, as well as a vegetarian offering. (Love the shrimp wontons.) The tasting menu is a pricey $99 (plus $30 with wine pairing) and shifts to seasonal dishes. Their bartending is decidedly high end with clever concoctions such as the watermelon royal—gin poured over watermelon ice cubes with mint, syrup and sparkling wine. It's great *if* you're patient and let it melt a bit. Sundays bring brunch and even more creative flavor pairings, such as kimchee sausage sliders. Service is good, but the pace is slow. $13–$22 for lunch and brunch, $35–$50 for dinner.

Reservations recommended for dinner. South Lahaina at the 505 Front St. Shopping Center. You'll pay to park across the street.

Pioneer Inn Grill & Bar
658 Wharf St, Lahaina • (808) 661-3636

ono A good place to go for breakfast, especially if you're taking a boat trip from adjacent Lahaina Harbor, because they open at 7 a.m. Service is fast and efficient. The big kahuna pancakes are giant, plate-covering items that are pretty impossible to finish off. (And hard to syrup without making a mess.) Lunch and dinner (same menu) are steak, salads, fish, burgers and sandwiches. $7–$20 for breakfast, $11–$30 for lunch and dinner. Their resident parrots can be a little noisy, but one does a great impression of R2-D2. (It never gets old.) At the Pioneer Inn.

Roy's Ka'anapali
2290 Kaanapali Pkwy, Kaanapali • (808) 669-6999

ono Roy's is a local chain, and they serve wonderful and often smartly conceived food. Consider the tonkatsu sandwich at lunch with avocado. The dinner menu changes nightly and runs from fish to pastas to steak, all served with an Asian/island twist. Their fish is always a winner. We've never had a bad meal here, though service can be hit or miss—sometimes slow, sometimes rushed. Their baked chocolate soufflé is deadly but takes a while, so order it while you're still eating dinner. $14–$20 for breakfast, $15–$30 for lunch, $30–$50 for dinner. On the corner of Hwy 30 and Ka'anapali Parkway with a golf course view. Resort wear is recommended, as well as reservations for dinner.

Sea House
5900 Lwr Honoapiilani Rd, Napili
(808) 669-1500

ono Spectacular location right next to the beach at Napili Bay. Try to reserve a window table. They thoughtfully leave sun screens down during the brightest part of the late afternoon, then raise them for sunsets, which are awesome from here. *Yeah, but what about the food?* Well, it's good, too. Dinner is fresh fish (which they *occasionally* overcook—it's easy to do), lobster, filet mignon or chicken. Quality is usually very good and service is fair. Lunch is sandwiches, some seafood and salads. Their happy hour deals (2–4:30 p.m.) are a great way to test what you want for dinner. $10–$20 for breakfast, $12–$20 for lunch, $21–$40 for dinner. They do a great job with presentation. On Lower Honoapiilani Road at Napili Kai Beach Resort. The south parking lot is small and fills up, so consider the northern lot. Both require you to grope your way (especially after dark) through the resort to the restaurant.

Slappy Cakes
3350 Lwr Honoapiilani Rd, Honokowai
(808) 419-6600

ono Make-your-own pancakes? OK, you have our attention. The tables have their own griddle in the middle where you cook your pancakes, but I'm getting ahead of myself. The fare is basically breakfast all day with a few lunch plates, such as burgers and sandwiches. For the pancakes, it's $8 to start with your choice of batter (buttermilk, chocolate, gluten-free/vegan or seasonal). Fixins to go in the batter range from sweet to savory at $2 to $5 apiece. Then you choose toppings and sauces for $3. And just so it's not all breakfast talk, the cocktails are original and pretty amazing. (Love the Mauimosa—strawberries and coconut with citrusy additions). Good family place. $15–$25 for breakfast. Next to Times Supermarket on Lower Honoapiilani Road north of Ka'anapali.

Soup Nutz & Java Jazz
3350 Lwr Honoapiilani Rd, Honokowai
(808) 667-0787

ono The ambiance is really hard to describe. Call it assorted kookiness. Nearly all the artwork was created by the owner, who occasionally plays guitar during dinner. The food is usually good, though they've slipped to the point that the *ono* is marginal. Small menus for all meals, but the taste works. Breakfast is probably their weakest showing, but the breakfast burrito is a crowd pleaser. Sandwiches, salads, wraps and burgers for lunch. Steak, pasta, fish and lobster for dinner. Sounds like a bigger menu than it is. But Hawaiian lobster (when available) for $38 is a good deal. $7–$20 for breakfast and lunch, $13–$40 for dinner. In Honokowai Marketplace, south part of Lower Honoapiilani Road. They open at 6 a.m. and have lots of coffee drinks, though refills are extra.

Sunrise Café
693 Front St, Lahaina • (808) 661-8558
This tiny hole in the wall with just a few tables in front (more in back) opens early (though opening hours are squirrelly), but it maintains the *we are the only restaurant open* attitude all day long. Lousy coffee but the breakfast croissant sandwich (spring for the bacon) is not a bad way to start the morning. Good loco mocos if you need something more hearty. Breakfast and lunch served all day, nothing over $14. Limited typical breakfast choices, local-style sandwiches for lunch. Food's not real flavorful, but it's not real bad. (Well...the pancakes are real bad.) At Market and Front streets. Cash only. $8–$15.

Teddy's Bigger Burgers
335 Keawe St, Lahaina • (808) 661-9111
ono A retro burger joint with the look and feel of a fast food place, but the food is much higher quality, and you'll have to wait while they make it.

Build your own (choose from one-third pound, half-pound, or absolutely kill it by ordering the one-pound monster double), then add toppings, or pick one of the many specialty burgers. Burgers are their signature item (they use ground chuck instead of the typical ground beef), but they also have a really good crispy chicken sandwiches, fish sandwiches, as well as a few chicken or fish baskets. The shakes are made with Roselani Ice Cream (made on Maui) and are just barely liquid enough to drink with a straw. You can skip the upgrade to the butter garlic fries. Veggie burger available as well as a cheaper kids' menu. Across the highway from the Cannery Mall, in the Lahaina Gateway shopping center. Part of a local chain (there are several on O'ahu), but this is their only fixed location on Maui. **$8–$18.** BYOB. They also have a food truck roving around, and the food is reasonably close in quality.

WEST MAUI CHINESE

China Boat
4474 Lwr Honoapiilani Rd, Kahana
(808) 669-5089

ono Quality food that is good enough to merit an *ono*. Tell them to spice up your food, and they will *fully* comply. **$8–$17** for lunch, **$12–$30** for dinner (over $50 if you go for the whole Peking roast duck). Full bar. Service can be rushed and a bit overbearing. Ask 'em to slow it down if you need to. From Honoapiilani Hwy (30), turn onto the road at Kahana Gateway Shopping Center, then turn right on Lower Honoapiilani Road. Across from Kahana Reef. Sunday is dinner-only.

Fu Lin
1312 Front St, Lahaina • (808) 661-7071

ono Popular with the local Chinese community (usually a good sign), Fu Lin also has great views at sunset. You'll find lots of familiar dishes as well

as some you'll have to look up on your smartphone. Their sizzling platters make for a dramatic presentation (think fajitas, but priced better). One of the best surprises is the tasty herbal tea. The colorful presentation is exotic, and there is a natural sweetness to it with no sugar added. Couple the food with the amazing ocean view at sunset, and you have an easy *ono*. Service can be a little slow at sunset, plus they're pricier than other Chinese places in the area. Lunch and dinner are **$10–$30.** At the corner of Kapunakea and Front Street, at the north end of town before Front Street ends.

WEST MAUI FRENCH

Gerard's
174 Lahainaluna Rd, Lahaina • (808) 661-8939
Some people are shocked and angry that we didn't give Gerard's an *ono*. We admit, the food's good. But it's just too overpriced. This chapter has lots of expensive restaurants, many providing an atmosphere you can't get back home. Gerard's, on the other hand, doesn't have anything you probably can't find in a reasonably sized city on the mainland, and it's *very* expensive. Lamb, pork, beef, veal, lots of fresh fish and seafood. There is no view, and the atmosphere at the courtyard and lanai tables is accompanied by traffic noise. Service is attentive, but we're appalled by the prices—even dessert. I mean, a *tiny* crème brûlée is $12. If you're overlooking a gorgeous beach, *maybe*. But here? We feel it's about a third overpriced, but maybe we're just savages. **$40–$60** for dinner. Reservations are a must and leave the beach attire at the condo. At the Plantation Inn.

WEST MAUI ITALIAN

Lahaina Pizza Company
730 Front St, Lahaina • (808) 661-0700

ono One of the best pizza places on Maui. They serve Chicago-style deep-dish pizzas (hard to find in Hawai'i) with a super-thick crust that is surprisingly light. They also have some pastas and sandwiches. Pizzas take a while, and if you're not paying close attention to the menu when you order, your first comment to the waiter is going to be, "I didn't order it with tomatoes." They know. All pizzas come with very light sauce and stewed tomatoes. (They're quick to point out you'll find tomatoes in the sauce). They'll serve it without the tomatoes if you request it. Beers, wine, and mixed drinks. Whole pies, sandwiches and pasta dishes for $12–$32. A 10-inch is filling enough for two. Good views overlooking the harbor and a popular surf spot. Upstairs on Front Street.

Penne Pasta Café
180 Dickenson St, Lahaina • (808) 661-6633

Ah, so you *can* eat in Lahaina without paying a fortune. The food quality/price ratio is fairly good here. Pasta, sandwiches and salads with a little flatbread pizza. (The latter has an ultra-thin crust and makes a good appetizer for two.) You can also get brown rice pasta as well as gluten- and flour-free pizza crust for an extra $3. Daily specials bring different proteins to the menu, such as fresh fish or lamb osso buco. Portions are more than fair, and the flavors work. It's not great. But you're not paying for great. Order at the counter, and they'll bring it to you. On Dickenson near Wainee. $12–$20 for lunch and dinner.

Pi Artisan Pizzeria
900 Front St, Lahaina • (808) 667-0791

onō Right up front you are first presented with two bars—one for drinks, one for pizza. Choose wisely, my friend. As the name suggests, pizza is their main game here, but they also have some good sandwiches, pasta and sides. (The meatballs are great in any of them.) Pizzas are personal-sized with their suggested styles staying under $18. You can also build your own with their gourmet ingredients and easily spend over $20. We suggest fewer toppings per pie and ordering a few different styles. We haven't had a bad meal here, but we especially liked the prosciutto pie. They have a knack for pairing craft beers to their pizzas here. Lunch and dinner are $11–$25, more if you do things family-style. On Front street at the north end of Lahaina.

Pizza Paradiso
3350 Lwr Honoapiilani Rd, Honokowai
(808) 667-2929

If the name didn't give it away, pizza is the mainstay here. While the pizza can be good (we've been historically lukewarm on the quality), it's really the Greek and Mediterranean items that bring us back. Gyros are probably the best bet, though the kabobs are also a good, hearty choice. The pizza is small for the price ($22 for a "large" 14-inch cheese) and definitely tastes better the fresher it is. Service tends to be surly but quick. (You pay up front, and there's a definite tip-to-surliness ratio.) Dessert consists of ice cream, gelato, baklava and halva (a sesame butter and chocolate, nougat-like dish). In all, not a *ono*, but we won't turn you away either. $12–$30 for lunch and dinner, $4–$5 for pizza by the slice. At Honokowai Marketplace.

Surfside Woodfire Pizza Kitchen
505 Front St, Lahaina • (808) 793-2650

A fairly simple menu of wood fire pizzas, salads, calzones and a few sandwiches. Ingredients are fresh and creative. (Can't say we've seen bacon jam as sauce before—but hey, it works.) Despite being on Front Street, they're not very visible, and their quest for a competitive edge means great deals for us. At lunch you can get a three-topping calzone or personal pizza for $8. Add a salad (which is good) and drink for $4 more. The food's nothing to write home about, but it's a great deal, and those ain't easy to come by on Front Street. All in all, a solid and filling choice. $8–$19 for lunch, a few bucks more for dinner. On the ground floor of the 505 Front St. building.

WEST MAUI JAPANESE

Sansei Seafood & Sushi
600 Office Rd, Kapalua • (808) 669-6286

ono Sushi, as well as non-Japanese food, such as seafood pasta, lobster, beef and duck served in a soothing atmosphere. Consider starting with the fresh Hawaiian ʻahi tataki (great, tangy flavors). Check out their nightly specials for the freshest, locally sourced selections. They take the art side of crafting sushi seriously, and their presentation is impressive. Rolls are pretty darned pricey, but you'll like the taste. $25–$50 or more for dinner. Thursday and friday they have karaoke and half-priced sushi after 10 p.m. On Office Road near the intersection of Village Road in Kapalua. They have another location in Kihei, but we find Kapalua to be the better of the two. Reservations recommended.

Star Noodle
286 Kupuohi St, Lahaina • (808) 667-5400

ono A little off the beaten path, these guys are worth the trek. Our best attempt at classifying them is modern-Asian fusion, and the vibe is reflected in their menu, music and decor. Best known for their noodle dishes, they have a little bit of everything to keep you trying new things. Many dishes are inexpensive but small. One strategy here is to order a few things at first, share, and then see where your taste buds take you. Their use of sauces and fresh ingredients take seemingly simple dishes to new heights. The regular menu is great, and you can trust 'em on their specials, too. $15–$30 for lunch and dinner. This place is popular, and you may have to wait if you arrive at peak times—reservations recommended. On north side of Lahaina near the Cannery Mall. Turn mauka onto Keawe Street, right on Kupouhi Street, and follow it to the end.

WEST MAUI LOCAL

Aloha Mixed Plate
1285 Front St, Lahaina • (808) 661-3322

ono This is a particularly great place for lunch. Decent and varied local style food, meaning it may be a bit fattier than mainland tastes, but most visitors seem to like items such as kalua pig sandwich, furikake garlic fries and chow fun noodles. If these sound a little too alien, don't worry. There's something for pretty much everyone. Prices are reasonable for what you get, and portions are large for most (though not all) items. Service is usually friendly but understaffed. They have an outdoor deck and beachside tables, all with lots of shade. The great setting and prices go a long way in giving them an *ono* as the food quality has been hit-or-miss in recent years. $10–$25 for breakfast, lunch and dinner. North of downtown Lahaina near the Mala Ramp.

Honokowai Food Trucks
130 Kai Malina Pkwy, Honokowai

A convenient dining option for the Honokowai area. Here's the deal: 8 to 10 food trucks converge circle-the-wagons style around a bunch of picnic tables, giving lots of options in one spot. The actual food trucks may come and go, not all the trucks may be open at the same time, and if the weather's bad, there's not really any place to shelter. That being said, you'll often find a range of cuisine types, such as Thai, Chinese, Japanese, Mexican and American, many with a local-style/Island twist. Hours can vary, but most trucks follow a general 11 a.m.–8 p.m. schedule. Expect to pay anywhere from $8–$25, with most items around $12. On the ocean side of Lower Honoapi'ilani Road, across the street from Times Supermarket. The best parking is off Kai Malina Parkway— bear right onto Honoapiilani Park Access Road. The public lot is on the right.

Honokowai Okazuya Deli
3600 Lwr Honoapiilani Rd, Honokowai
(808) 665-0512

ono How refreshing! A place in northern West Maui that serves good food but doesn't feel the need to soak you. Ambiance is... well, none, actually. Best to get it to go. The original owner was a former executive chef at Mama's Fish House and the Fairmont Kea Lani, so they knew how to cook here. But instead of opening another highbrow (and high-cost) restaurant, they channeled their energies toward the lower-end market. The menu is diverse enough to eat here repeatedly. Teriyaki steak, spaghetti and sausage, fresh fish, kung pao chicken, steamed tofu—the menu is all over the place, and we weren't sure how to classify them. We like to take the food over to nearby Honokowai Beach Park if it's not too windy. (There are a few stools inside, but it's hot.) This place doesn't change much from year to year, and we're glad. $10–$20 for lunch and dinner. North of Ka'anapali on Lower Honoapiilani Road just north of Honokowai Beach in the AAAAA Rent-A-Space Mall. No credit cards. Closed Sundays.

WEST MAUI MEXICAN

Frida's Beach House
1287 Front St, Lahaina • (808) 661-1287

ono A great view and contemporary, gourmet Mexican food. Many of their dishes go for the fresh rather than the usually heavy style of Mexican food. There are lots of choices to pique most everyone's interest, such as the pomegranate guacamole and grilled Span-

ish octopus. The tacos are very good and the cocktails will make you want to come back to try more. (The complimentary, fruity chasers for tequila shots are nice touch.) A bit overpriced, but when you consider the oceanfront view and the non-traditional menu, you'll probably like it. They have a veritable army of staff here. Lunch and dinner entrées are $16–$42. North Lahaina, behind the Cannery Mall.

Nachos Grande
3350 Lwr Honoapiilani Rd, Honokowai
(808) 662-0890

ono There's a sign that warns you must be 18 to order the XXX salsa. It's just a joke of course, but it's no joke. That stuff will *hurt* you (but in a good way that primes your taste buds for the main course). Let the owner talk you into getting the carne asada burrito—it's marinated overnight and a strong contender for the title best Mexican dish in all Hawai'i. *So delicious.* Simple menu of tacos (and taco salads), enchiladas, burritos, chimichangas, quesadillas, nachos, and fajitas. Generous portions for a very reasonable (by West Maui standards) $11–$14. Off Highway 30 between mile markers 25 and 26, a short distance from the Ka'anapali area resorts. Real friendly place, but a dumpy little building. The kitchen is open late—good to know on an island where most everyone goes to bed early— and there's an attached dive bar cantina.

WEST MAUI THAI

Thai Chef
878 Front St, Lahaina • (808) 667-2814

ono A friendly, family-owned Thai restaurant that has eluded us in the past. Tucked away in the Old Lahaina Center near Front Street, the menu is similar to **Maui Thai Bistro** in Kihei, only cheaper. The service is warm and the curries warmer, just as we like them. Seating is limited, and large tables are often shared, making it a social occasion. Drinking is BYOB with no corkage fee. **$12–$27** for dinner (most dishes are around $15), and they close when they feel like it. Closed Sunday.

WEST MAUI TREATS

Island Cream Co.
305 Keawe St, Lahaina • (808) 298-0916

ono This feels like a cross between gelato and ice cream with lots of traditional and creative flavors, plus a flavor-your-own shave ice station, making this one of our favorite places for an icy treat. They make the ice cream, the waffle cones and bowls, as well as the fudge and other toppings and syrups. They're always experimenting with flavors, and we haven't found one we didn't like (even the coconut poi flavor). You can sample as much as you like, or go all in and get the six-scoop sampler. They're a bit pricey, but worth it—easy recommendation for cooling off in the Lahaina sun. **$6–$12**. In the Lahaina Gateway Mall.

Local Boys West
624 Front St, Lahaina • (808) 344-9779

ono Shave ice is so abundant on Maui, it's sometimes hard to call out which ones shine the most. This place has nailed it pretty well. Snow-like consistency, great flavors and huge sizes. And they chill the syrups to avoid the dreaded icing on the bottom. Every time we're near Lahaina, we re-review them, just to be sure. **$4–$8**. Across from Banyan Tree Park.

Ono Gelato & Espresso
815 Front St, Lahaina • (808) 495-0203

Delicious ice cream. That's the literal translation of this restaurant's name (gelato is Italian-style ice cream), but it's pretty descriptive of the product, too. Traditional as well as local flavors (they do coconut well) make this a great way to cool down on a hot day. All the gelato is made in house. Small, simple and good. Plus, there's a selection of dairy-free and gluten-free options. Depending on size, expect to spend **$6–$8**. They can also satisfy that coffee craving with anything from an iced coffee to an espresso. With your treat in hand, head to the back of the building for the best part—a private, shaded lanai overlooking Lahaina Harbor. On Front Street near the intersection of Lahainaluna.

WEST MAUI VEGETARIAN

Moku Roots
335 Keawe St, Lahaina • (808) 214-5106

ono Gone are the days of comparing vegan cuisine to rabbit food. Moku Roots deftly combines flavors and different cuisines to make some darned good stuff that even meat lovers can appreciate (individual results may vary). The menu changes a lot due to availability of local produce, which keeps the choices interesting.

Popular (and usually available) options are items like taro burgers, mushroom meatloaf and spicy buffalo cauliflower (think hot wings minus the wings). Breakfast options are more limited (Sunday brunch has more variety) but offer one of the few non-vegan items—eggs. As an aside, they take the farm-to-table concept a step further with table-to-farm practices where they donate food waste back to farms for compost and feed for chickens. (The eggs in your breakfast burrito maybe came from a chicken that ate yesterday's special.)

Their beverages are creative and feature lots of local ingredients such as lavender from Kula and Maui-grown coffee. The setting is casual with a variety of seating options both inside and out, plus it stays surprisingly cool inside. An easy recommendation for those already into healthy cuisine. **$12–$17** for breakfast, a few bucks more for lunch and dinner. In the Lahaina Gateway Mall at the corner of Keawe and Honoapiilani Highway.

WEST MAUI VIETNAMESE

Pho Saigon 808
658 Front St, Lahaina • (808) 661-6628

ono A quiet place in the Wharf Cinema Center. Their specialty is—drum roll, please—phở. This beef and noodle soup is the national dish of Vietnam. And this place has the absolute best on the island (spicy beef noodle phở is amazing). Also try the summer rolls, which are cool and light. Service is friendly but can get slow. $10–$17 for lunch and dinner.

SOUTH MAUI AMERICAN

808 Deli
2511 S Kihei Rd, Kihei • (808) 879-1111

ono Prices are super reasonable for the quality of the food. *Love* the chicken pesto panini, and Red Rooster hits the spot when you need something spicy. Gotta try the turkey and cranberry sandwich. Between the hot and cold sandwiches, panini and the salads, odds are they have something you'll want. They also have a few egg sandwiches and bagels at breakfast. Grab your food and head across the street to Kam II Beach since seating at the deli is limited, and it gets hot. $6–$8 for breakfast, $6–$11 for lunch. Great prices on keiki menu, too.

Beach Bums BBQ
300 Maalaea Rd, Maalaea • (808) 243-2286

Comfortable menu of BBQ items such as pulled pork, ribs and brisket, half-pound burgers, fish tacos (we prefer the blackened rather than the grilled) and sandwiches (love the smoked TBA). Consider having them bring you an empty bowl if you want to mix your sandwich meat with BBQ sauce instead of simply drizzling it on top. Lots of tropical drinks, most of which are tasty (but we are still diligently working our way through the complete list—just for you), but the appetizers are too pricey. They are not needed, really, because portions are ample. Across a small street with views of the boat harbor, though obscured by vegetation, which is a shame. They get points for convenience if you've got a boat tour planned, but the quality has gone down to merely adequate, no longer earning them an *ono*. $8–$12 for breakfast (the $3 bloody mary and screwdrivers are a good deal), but they don't open till 8 a.m. because they're busy catering for many of the boats at the harbor. $11–$30 for lunch and dinner. All meats are smoked in-house. In the Ma'alaea Harbor Village. Live music most nights. Tuesdays are crowded since their special that night is prime rib and lobster for $35. Biggest ding is that midges sometimes pester you while you dine.

Café O'Lei
2439 S Kihei Rd, Kihei • (808) 891-1368

ono Enthusiastic readers first tipped us off to this place and continue to send glowing reports. Not impressive from the outside, it's much bigger and more elegant than you'd think inside. A reliably easy place to like with good food and reasonable prices at lunch, and pricier but dependable food at dinner. (Still less than you'd pay at the fancy resort restaurants, though). Lunch is a random selection of fish, chicken, pasta and sandwiches. Most items are great. Love the mac nut-crusted chicken sandwich, and you gotta try the Manoa lettuce wraps as an appetizer or the onion soup. Dinner features mostly steak, seafood, some pastas and sushi. Some vegetarian and vegan dishes, too. They'll serve you some lunch items at dinner if you ask. Our only complaint is the noise—it's often super loud inside. $8–$16 for lunch, $18–$27 for dinner entrées. In the Rainbow Mall. They have a second location in central Maui at The Dunes Golf Course, off Highway 380 (Kuihelani Highway) that is popular with the local business crowd, but that one is less interesting for a visitor.

Carl's Jr.
15 Kapoli St, Maalaea • (808) 249-0787
Look, we don't normally review fast food restaurants, but we wanted to tell you that you can avoid this one without fear. A must-miss.

Cinnamon Roll Place
2463 S Kihei Rd, Kihei • (808) 879-5177
Just like the name says. Cinnamon rolls, bread pudding, banana bread, scones and muffins are the usual pastry lineup, and all under $5. They also have breakfast sandwiches and coffee drinks, as well as deli sandwiches after 10 a.m. The cinnamon rolls are very popular and go quickly—you'll hear the baker shouting a countdown for the next batch throughout the morning. Only gripe is the limited seating (about five outside tables), but it's just as easy to grab and go across the street for a beachside breakfast. $3–$10 for breakfast and lunch. At Kama'ole Shopping Center, downstairs. Open at 5:30 a.m.

Coconut's Fish Café
1279 S Kihei Rd, Kihei • (808) 875-9979
ono You're in Hawai'i, and you want fish without paying a fortune. These are the cats to hit. (The place is named after the owner's kitty, Coconut.) Simply great seafood tacos, fishburgers, fish and chips (which are not at all greasy), etc., as well as pasta, salads and soups. Presentation is better than you'd expect for these prices, and if you order a sandwich, your sides will come stacked on top. They make everything on the spot, and they have nice buns, if we do say so ourselves. The place has a funky, surfer/rec hall feel (and impressive surfboard tables) and is popular with locals. The downside is that their popularity often brings long waits. Expect to share your table with others. $13–$22 for lunch and dinner. In

Azeka Mauka Shopping Center. Easy to recommend, though they *occasionally* disappoint. They also have a location at Kama'ole Shopping Center.

Eskimo Candy Seafood Market & Café
2665 Wai Wai Pl, Kihei • (808) 891-8898
ono Hard to find but worth the effort, this place is popular with local repeats. Eskimo Candy's main business is actually selling fish wholesale to other island restaurants, but you can get it direct for less here. They have a great selection of seafood items like fish and chips (go for the ono over the marlin), shrimp tacos, seafood pasta, and local items like the excellent wasabi poke, burgers and ribs. (For a seafood place, the burger is quite good.) Keep looking around at the signs, and you'll see something you like. Nearly every item is very reasonably priced, and service seems genuinely friendly. Limited seating; consider taking it out (although the pirate- and shark-themed interior is fun for kids). From South Kihei Road turn mauka onto Hale Kuai Street. Across from Napa Auto. $11–$20 for lunch and dinner. Open until 7 p.m. Closed weekends. Note that locally caught fresh fish prices have skyrocketed in Hawai'i, so you will pay higher market prices for the never-frozen, fresh-catch options.

Fat Daddy's
1913 S Kihei Rd, Kihei • (808) 879-8711
ono A BBQ joint with pulled pork, brisket, ribs, chili and brats. The atmosphere is a cross between a Maui lounge and a southern BBQ. Though the brisket is sliced in thickish slabs, we much prefer the pulled pork, which goes well with their excellent and savory BBQ beans. Service can be a bit scant, but it is still a good place to fill your BBQ craving. $10–$30 for dinner, more if you go for the full rack. As a reader says, "It's a nice change after a week of fish." In the Kihei Kalama Village.

Five Palms

2960 S Kihei Rd, Kihei • (808) 879-2607

They have one of the tastiest views of any restaurant. We liked it so much, we used a photo of it for the *Island Dining* chapter opener for past editions. It's right on the water and looks down Keawakapu Beach. They also have outdoor tables. There are few bad tables in this place. The food is steak, seafood and sushi for dinner. In all the years we've been reviewing them, they *still* have the same problem far too often: food being served warm rather than hot. And spending $45 for fish and scant vegetables, then receiving it at nearly room temperature is hard to swallow, especially with the slow service here. But the food *can* be good. Consider the Hama Kama pupu. One of their better dinner entrées (if it isn't cold), the Upcountry Pasta, is also the most affordable. Despite the great setting, they need to get more cylinders running to get an *ono*. $12–$25 for breakfast (which features $15 pancakes), $18–$30 for lunch, $25–$55 for dinner (reservations recommended). In the Mana Kai Resort.

Haui's Life's a Beach

1913 S Kihei Rd, Kihei • (808) 891-8010

Burgers, Mexican items, some fried seafood and salads. A local watering hole. The atmosphere is funky, trashy, sticky, mangy and loud. (This is *not* a family place.) They take cheap-tasting ingredients and combine them fairly well, and overall, it's priced about right. Good 3–7 p.m. happy hour with cheap mai tais and beer. $8–$20 for lunch and dinner, plus $5 specials at lunch. Across from Kalama Park.

Humuhumunukunukuapua'a

3850 Wailea Alanui Dr, Wailea • (808) 875-1234

Often called simply Humu (for reasons that should be obvious to anyone who sprains their tongue trying to pronounce it the other way), this is a truly memorable place to eat and *is sometimes* one of our favorites on the island. We say *sometimes* because they get good, then they lose their steam in a cycle almost as regular as sunspot activity. (They're back on their game lately and readers have reported good experiences.) You're surrounded by and actually *over* a huge fishpond. Some of the fish and lobster swimming around are the main course (but don't tell them). Waterfalls and thatched roofs along with killer sunset views add to the exotic, Polynesian feel. It's very expensive steak, lobster and seafood. The service is not commensurate with the prices. If you catch them in the right phase (during their circular journey between awesome and complacent), you'll love the results. In the Grand Wailea Resort; allow an extra 10 minutes to walk through the fabulous grounds, or save time (and valet fees) by parking at the Wailea Beach access lot. $35–$65 for dinner. Reservations and resort wear are recommended.

Ka'ana Kitchen

3550 Wailea Alanui Dr, Wailea • (808) 573-1234

ono Restaurants are almost always expensive at fancy resorts. Accept that going in. This place has great food, but you pay dearly, especially for alcohol. More seafood than steak here, with excellent quality and presentation. Whether you choose the Wagyu beef, local fish or Berkshire pork belly, they don't skimp on the basic ingredients. The kitchen is wide open, and you are encouraged to visit, if you like.

Sunsets can be good from the outdoor tables (not so much from the indoor ones). Be careful ordering from the bar if you're near your credit limit, because the high prices and small pours can kill ya. (The mai tai does not taste like a mai tai, but the Ka'ana old fashioned hits the mark. Too bad its volume is so dominated by the giant ice cube.)

Consider the coconut sundae for dessert—you'll like what's on the bottom.

Free valet parking at the Andaz Resort in Wailea. **$21–$35** (or $49 for the buffet) at breakfast, **$25–$60** for dinner, plus what you imbibe. The *ono* is for the dinner. Breakfast is just too outrageously expensive.

Kihei Caffe
1945 S Kihei Rd, Kihei • (808) 879-2230

ono Breakfast is best (they open at 5 a.m.) with good omelettes, hearty breakfast burritos, huge loco mocos, biscuits and gravy (though they're a little salty), some truly kickin' raspberry twisties and the best turnovers in South Maui, plus coffee drinks. Some of the outdoor tables are almost penned in, making it popular with parents trying to corral their keiki. (Kids seem to like the teddy bear or whale pancakes.) Lunch is mostly sandwiches, burgers and salads. Kihei Caffe makes mostly good food, and the breakfast selection is fantastic. The *ono* is mainly for families with kids. The price certainly is reasonable. Long waits are not uncommon, and you order from the counter. Across from Kalama Park on the corner of Alahele. **$8–$16** for breakfast and lunch. Cash only.

Ko
4100 Wailea Alanui Dr, Wailea • (808) 875-2210

ono Here's the concept: Serve food inspired by the various immigrant groups brought in to work the sugar plantations in days past. Chinese, Filipino, Japanese, etc. I promise you—this *ain't* how they ate. And certainly this ain't what they *spent* on food. But Ko does a good job of taking the flavors of those countries and spinning them into tasty—and breathtakingly expensive—dishes. Flavors are clean and fresh, and ingredients are top quality. We like the modern, open-air atmosphere by the swimming pool. Their bar serves some really tasty cocktails. Straight rum sippers will *really* appreciate the complex banana bread old fashioned with nice finishes. **$25–$50** for lunch,

$30–$70 for dinner. Reservations recommended. At the Fairmont Kea Lani.

Lava Rock Bar & Grill
1945 S Kihei Rd, Kihei • (808) 727-2521
An open, ocean-view seating, high off the ground can go a long way on hot days in Kihei. Though the view isn't great, the open-air patio here captures the breeze and makes for a pleasant experience. The owners are Argentine, and the menu showcases a few dishes inspired by that meat-loving country. The empanadas are easy to recommend, and all the meat dishes, from burgers to steaks, are done well (and made with local beef). Their house-made chimichurri sauce is served with many of the dishes and pushes decent food into deliciousness. Service can be aloof but friendly. Breakfast has a lot of familiar options like omelettes, eggs Benedicts, and pancakes—many with a local or island twist. They stay open late and cater to the bar and club crowd. In all, a decent choice for the area, especially if you take advantage of their happy hour deals. **$10–$17** for breakfast, **$13–$30** for lunch and dinner. In the big building across from Kalama Park in Kihei.

MBC Kihei
605 Lipoa Pkwy, Kihei • (808) 201-2337
Mixed feelings about this one. This large, warehouse-like location works. It looks and *feels* like a brewery with lots of open space and simple yet bold designs. There's both a tasting room and a restaurant. The menu features familiar bar appetizers with a local twist, salads, pizza, burgers and a few seafood dishes. In general, the food is overpriced for what you get. The fish and chips is tempting and their tartar sauce is good, but the portions can be too small and greasy. Luckily they have some decent happy hour deals that make the the prices easier to swallow (a few extra pints helps, too). Go for the pizza, but avoid the pricey (and meatless) nachos.

If it's not happy hour, go elsewhere. The beer is not good enough to make this a destination. $14–$32 for lunch and dinner with pints around $7 and up. At the end of Lipoa Parkway in North Kihei.

Moose McGillycuddy's

2511 S Kihei Rd, Kihei • (808) 891-8600

This is a hopping place at night. Dinner is mostly steak (cow, not moose) and some seafood. It's popular with singles looking for... well, what singles are *always* looking for. Entertainment and dancing at night. Lunch consists mostly of burgers. However, avoid having breakfast here. We used to gripe about the wait times but they improved (mostly by having you seat yourself). The food...has not. The fried rice is decent but just about anything else will leave you disappointed. Be warned they tend to play the same music at breakfast as at night– not a popular choice among those in need of morning coffee. $7–$12 for breakfast, $12–$24 for lunch, $15–$35 for dinner. In South Kihei.

Nick's Fishmarket

4100 Wailea Alanui Dr, Wailea • (808) 879-7224

ono One of the finest restaurants in South Maui. Exceptional seafood in an elegant setting. The menu changes often, but we've never had a bad meal here. Their Hawaiian lobster is fantastic. So is everything else. Consider the chocolate "decadence" for dessert. World-class wine list. The service is unbelievable. Order a drink and see if it takes more than a minute. It's like a contest to see how excellent they can make the service, but the tag team approach seems to confuse some diners. Though attentive, they *don't* come around every five minutes, when your mouth is full, asking, "How is everything?" They just keep a watchful eye on you. We've never seen a water glass go empty. So what's the catch? *Exactly what you think.* Nick's isn't cheap. But if you want steak and seafood and need a good

pampering, Nick's is the place to go. $35–$60 or more for dinner. In the Fairmont Kea Lani. Reservations recommended. Resort wear required.

Peggy Sue's

1279 S Kihei Rd, Kihei • (808) 214-6786

ono Small but effective 1950's-style diner serving generous-sized burgers (a second 6-ounce patty is $4 extra), ribs, salads, hot dogs and some sandwiches, such as steak, chicken and fish. Their burgers are fairly good. Portions are fairly generous for the price, and they have a good keiki (kid) selection with PB&J and grilled cheese sandwiches. Service can be slow because they are often busy, especially at lunch, and the servers seem overworked. (This has been going on for years.) Getting a table can be hard at peak eating times. Real milkshakes are tasty (love the peanut butter), and the jukebox (with quarter-fed players at each table) playing old 45s adds to the flavor. The food by itself wouldn't get them an *ono*, but when added to the atmosphere, the place works. In Azeka Mauka Shopping Center. $8–$12 for breakfast (Sunday through Tuesday only), $8–$16 for lunch and dinner.

Sarento's on the Beach

2980 S Kihei Rd, Kihei • (808) 875-7555

ono Over the years we've gotten spurts of bad e-mails about the service at Sarento's. The restaurant employs a tag team approach that can be irritating to some diners. You get lots of attention from various staff, so if you want to be left alone, you might not like it here. Personally, though, we like the extra fawning. The relaxed, open-air setting is right on Keawakapu Beach, one of the most intimate beach locations on the island. (The view is terrific, and the binoculars on the table during whale season are a nice touch.) Fresh fish, steak, osso bucco (veal shank) and pasta. It's hard to classify the style, sort of a Pacific Rim/Italian plus American/local brunch (they do a great loco moco). $14–$25 for brunch, $28–$56 for dinner. In our experience the food is usually great, but some readers have complained that the quality doesn't match the price. The wine list is vast with a number of bottles costing more than $1,000. (Sorry, but that's just insane to spend $25 *per sip* of wine.) At the Maui Oceanfront Inn. Reservations recommended. Valet-only parking. The sister restaurant to **Nick's Fishmarket**.

Seascape
192 Maalaea Rd, Maalaea • (808) 270-7068

ono I know what you're thinking: a seafood restaurant at an aquarium—do I *really* want to hear the special? Not to fear, they have a lot more than seafood, and, of course, the catch comes from offshore waters. Lunch menu is sandwiches, fish and chips, daily catch, fish tacos and half-pound wagyu beef burgers (which are great). Dinner entrées bring even more fish and protein options, such as coconut crusted Polynesian chicken and mac nut-crusted mahimahi. The view overlooking the harbor and boats is very relaxing. Flavors are fresh, and ingredients are high quality. Portions can be small though, and service inattentive. If you don't get a table along the edge overlooking the harbor, shoot for one against the glass of an aquarium tank. Very cool. $15–$30 for lunch, $23–$50 for dinner. Happy hour is 3 p.m.–5 p.m. daily with a smaller menu with better prices. Dinner is only Friday–Sunday and reservations are recommended.

South Shore Tiki Lounge
1913 S Kihei Rd, Kihei • (808) 874-6444

They know how to decorate and how to set a scene. They just don't know how to serve food or drinks. Sandwiches, burgers and pizza. The atmosphere is their best offering. The outdoor tables have a bamboo tiki decor with water sport videos playing against a backdrop of eclectic music. Pizza is average. Everything is average. All served on paper plates. And despite their tiki bar feel, drinks sound far tastier than they really are. Service can be indifferent. Yeah, that about covers it. Open till 2 a.m. $10–$20 for lunch and dinner, more for specialty pizzas. In Kihei Kalama Village.

Spago
3900 Wailea Alanui Dr, Wailea • (808) 879-2999

ono Lots of hype about this place, but guess what? They live up to it. This is Wolfgang Puck's Maui restaurant. (On those few occasions that old Wolfgang himself shows up, the staff tries to shoo him out of the kitchen.) The dishes are simply unbelievable. The spicy 'ahi tuna poke in sesame-miso cones is unlike any appetizer we've ever had. The various preparation of fish and their accompanying sauces are *ohhh,* so good. Actually, everything we've had is good. Portions are pretty small, and you can drop a lot of money quick here. Appetizer prices are crazy high and can destroy your wallet. But their fantastic ocean view and world-class cooking make it a treat. Dinner is $42–$90 and up. (The menu changes slightly each night and sometimes has items for $100.) In the Four Seasons Resort. Reservations and resort wear recommended.

Stewz Maui Burgers
1819 S Kihei Rd, Kihei • (808) 879-0497

ono With its convenient location next to Starbucks in the Kukui Mall, the burgers are better than most you can find in the area. Hamburgers, fries and milkshakes are the specialty, with burgers named after different towns on Maui that feature some varied (and tasty) local ingredients. We really like the Kula burger with the roasted poblano chili pepper on it. The sweet potato fries are consistently good (not too greasy). If you build your own burger, the price depends on how many patties you get—$9 for a single, $13 for a double and a big ol' triple for $17. If you get a specialty burger, a single patty starts at $9.50. They also have an indoor space called **Little Bar at Stewz**. It's kid friendly and a good place to beat the heat while enjoying an adult beverage. The menu changes a bit in the bar—here burgers come with fries or onion rings (it's à la carte at the window outside), and prices start at $14.

Three's Bar & Grill
1945 S Kihei Rd, Kihei • (808) 879-3133

ono The name refers to the chefs. One local, one Texan and one Coloradan, and the food is a fusion of all three. The ambiance is about as varied as the menu with outdoor seating, a quiet but small dining room, and also a bar/lounge environment with large leather couches and low bar tables. The food is great, presentation is professional, and it's priced reasonably. At night the bar turns into a nightclub with live music and some darned good drinks. Breakfast is their weakest showing, and the *ono* only applies to lunch and dinner. $9–$18 for breakfast, $14–$20 for lunch, $20–$40 for dinner. In the Triangle across from Kalama Beach Park. Consider reservations for dinner.

Tommy Bahama
3750 Wailea Alanui Dr, Wailea • (808) 875-9983

ono If you've ever shopped at a Tommy Bahama clothing store, this is the same concept. It ain't cheap, but it's good quality in an islandy, tropical, tasteful atmosphere. This is where you'll find a $19 burger (but it's a *really* good burger), $37 ribs (same observation), some seafood and unexpected items such as scallop sliders, as well as lots of pricey, well-conceived salads. The cheapest appetizer is the chips with guacamole and cheese spread for $15. It's $24 for a plate of roasted vegetables. Tropical drinks are *exactly* what you'd ex-

pect from Tommy Bahama. And the desserts are scrumptious. Dinner adds steak, fish and chicken. It's $17–$45 for lunch, $24–$45 for dinner. In the Shops at Wailea. Some outdoor seating (but no view), and live (but unobtrusive) music at night. Great tasting food that's easy to recommend unless you want cheap eats. Be sure to ask them to validate your parking. Reservations recommended.

Volcano Bar
3850 Wailea Alanui Dr, Wailea • (808) 875-1234
Poolside at the Grand Wailea resort. Lunch is outrageously priced ($18 for a hot dog, $24 for nachos) but you can grab something to drink ($17 for a mai tai) and head to the beach for a relaxing afternoon. The most interesting part is that there's a swim-up bar in a cave off the lazy river. We once asked the bartender how often people actually leave to go to the bathroom. He just shrugged and said, "Always nice when they do." Eww.

SOUTH MAUI INDIAN

Monsoon India
760 S Kihei Rd, Kihei • (808) 875-6666
Indian food with great ocean proximity. They have a good selection of curries, tandoori kabobs, naan and vegetarian dishes, and the results are usually acceptable. (Some readers disagree.) Try the monsoon kabob for an appetizer. Dishes can be hit-or-miss, but this is a really good location. Service is deferential but sometimes a bit thin. Full bar. $11–$20 for lunch, $17–$30 for dinner. Dinner only on Mondays and Tuesdays. At the Menehune Shores in North Kihei.

SOUTH MAUI IRISH

Mulligan's on the Blue
100 Kaukahi St, Wailea • (808) 874-1131

ono Irish food such as shepherd's pie, fish and chips, corned beef, and

Irish stew (lamb braised in Guinness beef stock—awesome) all served in a campy, Irish pub atmosphere sometimes accompanied by Irish or other local live music most nights. Sunday is Celtic night. When he's in town, Hawaiian singer/songwriter and blues man Willie K. knocks 'em dead on Wednesdays, but you'll pay $75 for a three-course dinner that night. Make sure you get an indoor table when Willie is there—reserve in advance. Most of the food items are pretty good. (Awesome apple pie.) Indoor and outdoor tables. Service can be slow. **$13–$20** for lunch, **$16–$30** for dinner. At the Wailea Blue Golf Course.

SOUTH MAUI ITALIAN

Fabiani's
95 E Lipoa St, Kihei • (808) 874-0888

ono The former pastry chef from Longhi's opened this bakery/pizzeria, and the results are outstanding. Everything is homemade, even the bagels. Quiches, croissants, cinnamon rolls, and an amazing Italian-style loco moco for breakfast (only at Kihei location), plus pizzas, pasta and panini for dinner. Lunch is the same, but add hamburgers and sandwiches. The 12-inch thin crust pizzas are tasty. Or add the bolognese sauce to the cheese ravioli for a delicious dish. Even their bartending skills are top notch.

For a place that takes obvious pride in their product and service, they missed one big thing that possibly should cost them their *ono*: It's loud inside. What? *I said it's so bloody loud inside, you should only come here with someone you don't want to talk to.* Our voices were raw after just trying to talk to the server. **$5–$15** for breakfast, **$10–$20** for lunch, **$16–$30** for dinner. In the South Maui Center between S. Kihei Road and Piilani Highway. The Wailea Gateway location is smaller with no bakery but is less noisy, with great happy hour specials at the bar and a larger dinner selection.

Ferraro's at the Four Seasons
3900 Wailea Alanui Dr, Wailea • (808) 874-8000

Not a bad place to overpay if you're looking for a good view, and service and price are less of a consideration. While it's true that $12 gelato can *never* be justified (unless you're eating it in Venice), the dreamy location overlooking Wailea Beach at lunch is simply wonderful. Food consists of pretty good *$21* burgers (though a bit greasy), stone oven-baked pizzas, sandwiches, sashimi, salads and panini. Dinner is upscale Italian-style steak, seafood and pasta. Tables are outdoors, and those closest to the beach are most recommended. Their homemade lemonade is especially good on hot days. **$18–$30** at lunch, **$40–$60** for dinner. Reservations required.

Longhi's
3750 Wailea Alanui Dr, Wailea • (808) 891-8883

ono Longhi's does food well. The upscale Italian/seafood menu has historically been excellent and can be a favorite with many locals and visitors. They do wonderful things with lobster, shrimp and fresh fish. One tip to save money is to inquire about the portion size, they are often generous enough to split an order. A good place for a breakfast (killer fish and eggs, or try the French toast with Grand Marnier), and late risers can reserve by phone some quiches and their renowned pastries for late breakfasts. Extensive wine list. Dinner is expensive (and everything is à la carte) at **$28–$140** per person (the latter price if you order their Lobster Longhi), **$13–$30** for lunch, **$11–$30** for breakfast. In The Shops at Wailea. Reservations and resort wear recommended. We could have put them in either the American or Italian category (they call it Mediterranean).

Maui Brick Oven
1215 S Kihei Rd, Kihei • (808) 875-7896

ono Maui Brick Oven is *all gluten-free, all the time*. Their surprisingly varied menu tends more toward Italian/ Mediterranean. The pizza itself is pretty good (considering it's gluten-free) with a thin, crisp crust, but it's a little pricey. Their onion rings are about as fresh as they get—they don't even slice 'em until you order. The fish and chips is a good choice, but can be heavy on the grease. (No malt vinegar here, but the balsamic is wheat-free). The stuffed chicken is a real treat. The service is friendly, and though the space is small and narrow, it is much cooler toward the back of the restaurant. $16–$35 for dinner. In the Longs Center, corner of Kihei and Piikea. Closed Sundays.

Shaka Pizza
1770 S Kihei Rd, Kihei • (808) 874-0331

A popular local pizza joint with a no-frills atmosphere. The hot sandwiches are actually *better* when you take 'em out. (Being wrapped up improves the bread.) Pizza, on the other hand, is best ordered by the slice. (The reheating helps the crust.) Their regular pizza has extremely thin and fairly tasty crust, but unremarkable sauce and toppings. It's so thin that you'll be surprised at how much pizza surface area you can dispose of. They also have gourmet pizzas, such as spinach, chicken pesto and white pies that are fine, but cheesesteaks and other sandwiches are also available. Overall, the sandwiches and fresh-cut fries are their best asset, though pricey: A 14-inch sandwich starts at $18. $4–$20 for lunch and dinner. By-the-slice pizza reasonably priced. South of Welakahao Street.

SOUTH MAUI JAPANESE

Koiso Sushi Bar
2395 S Kihei Rd, Kihei • (808) 875-8258

ono This small-time operation has earned no small claim: Best Sushi on Maui, in our opinion. Make reser-vations (in *advance*) to occupy one of the 12 seats at the sushi bar where the smiling owner/ chef will serve up amazing traditional sushi. No fancy rolls or tricks here, just a small menu (written on the wall) and a single four-person table away from the bar. The fish is always melt-in-your-mouth fresh with clean flavors. This is the kind of place where your best bet is to order the chef's choice, sit back and watch the master do his thing. You won't be disappointed. Don't take anyone here who is looking for a way to move wasabi to their mouth; it would be a waste of good fish. There are two sittings—at 6 p.m. and around 8:30 p.m., closing at 10 p.m. Plan on spending $30 plus per person, which is worth every penny. In Dolphin Plaza. Closed Sundays and Mondays.

Miso Phat Sushi
1279 S Kihei Rd, Kihei • (808) 891-6476

ono The second location of an awesome restaurant with a good sense of humor—if the name didn't give it away. Kihei has some amazing sushi joints that are decidedly more authentic, but they tend to be intimidating if you're not already a sushi pro. That's not the case here—the food is excellent, and the staff does a good job of making you feel comfortable. If you like to spice things up with more than wasabi, ask to substitute any tobiko (those tiny, orange fish eggs on so many rolls) with their habanero-style tobiko—it's got a nice kick. The space is on the small side, but it doesn't detract from the experience. It can be hard to calculate a price range at sushi joints since everyone has their own style of ordering, but you can expect to pay at least $20–$40 for lunch and dinner, more if you're really hungry. In the Azeka Shopping Center. Their original restaurant location is in Kahana near Hoohui Road.

SOUTH MAUI LOCAL

Nalu's South Shore Grill
1280 S Kihei Rd, Kihei • (808) 891-8650

ono ᐟ A wide open, tropical sports bar feel, but it's not really a sports bar. Local food with other foods, such as a Cuban sandwich, apple brie burgers, and ribs served with kimchee. Nothing is typical here, and they combine flavors well. (Great chicken salads.) Service is quick and friendly. Tables are a mix of four-tops, community benches, kids' tables and a bar. It's a quirky place that works for us, and there's live music most nights. Order at the counter, and they will bring it to your table. $10–$15 for breakfast, $10–$20 for lunch and dinner. In Azeka Makai Shopping Center. Reservations recommended for dinner shows on Wednesdays and Saturdays.

South Maui Fish Company
22 Alahele Pl, Kihei • (808) 419-8980

ono ᐟ A great spot for to get your local fish fix. This food truck found behind the 76 station across from Kalama Park has fresh fish and lots of aloha. Usually just grilled plus a couple of styles of poke, the simple menu uses all local ingredients from farmers' markets in the area. They even sell fresh fish to take home and grill—perfect for folks staying in condos. Ask for their spice blend, and they'll walk you through the best way to prepare the fish. Easy to recommend. $9–$15 for lunch. Open till 3 p.m. but often sell out earlier. Closed Sundays.

SOUTH MAUI MEDITERRANEAN

Pita Paradise
34 Wailea Gateway Pl, Wailea • (808) 879-7177

ono ᐟ We've never seen people who can do so much with pitas. Here they're freshly made and topped (not actually filled—it's more like a wrap) with all manner of ingredients. Chicken, veggies, fish, lamb and greens in clever combinations. Kebabs and lots of vegetarian options, too. Their ziziki bread and spinach tiropitas make good appetizers. Daily fresh fish specials come straight from the owner's fishing boat. (If you're there early enough, you might even see him bring the catch through the restaurant.) The cocktails are tasty, and presentation can be downright theatrical (try the Buddha Hand). Consider the baklava ice cream cake for dessert. $11–$25 for lunch, $20–$35 for dinner. Quality food, but a little pricey for the portion size. In Wailea Gateway Center. No view, so might as well wait until after sunset. Dinner reservations recommended.

SOUTH MAUI MEXICAN

Amigo's Authentic Mexican Food
1215 S Kihei Rd, Kihei • (808) 879-9952

A mixed bag. There's a large and diverse menu of mostly Mexican and a few non-Mexican items such as burgers, probably something for everyone. Portions are generous on some items like the burritos, standard on others such as the enchiladas. The chili verde is authentic, and they have a salsa bar to go with your chips. The food's acceptable—good, not great—but they have a nice selection of tequilas, including my favorite, Don Julio. But prices ain't cheap for what you get. Breakfast ($7–$12) available all day. It's $9–$18 for lunch and dinner. Slightly north of Piikea Avenue in the Longs Drugs Center. Two other locations (in Kahului and Lahaina), but this is the best of the three.

Fred's Mexican Café
2511 S Kihei Rd, Kihei • (808) 891-8600

I know. With a name like *Fred's,* you're expecting *scrupulous* authenticity. Actually Fred was a regular at Moose McGillycuddy's on the mainland and suggested they name a chain after him. Whaddyano, they did. Fred's has gone downhill lately.

Currently it feels more like a frathouse Cinco de Mayo party held over from Saturday night and exposed to the harsh light of Sunday morning. Décor is a mixture of crystal chandeliers and car hoods studded with light bulbs. Most items are under $13. Fajitas, tacos and massive burritos. The house margaritas aren't very good, but you'll like the top shelf. (Ask them not to load it up with too much ice.) The bar gets crazy on Taco Tuesdays, and the wait can be over 2 hours. All in all, Fred's just doesn't work for us. $8–$15 for breakfast (which should be avoided at all costs), $11–$20 for lunch and dinner. Across from Kama'ole Beach II.

Maui Tacos
2411 S Kihei Rd, Kihei • (808) 879-5005

ono This small, local chain is a good place to go for tacos and burritos. Nothing fancy, but it's not overly expensive. They have a good selection, and the portions are large. Their various locations are pretty different. The Kihei location in Kama'ole Beach Center is their best, followed by Kahului (Queen Ka'ahumanu Center), then Napili (Napili Plaza). Sometimes their food is warm instead of hot, and don't forget the condiments bar if you find you need more seasoning. $6–$11 for lunch and dinner. Some serve alcohol, some don't, and some are BYOB. Readers (and my own personal circle) are split on whether to give 'em an *ono*, so take that into consideration.

SOUTH MAUI THAI

Maui Thai Bistro
2439 S Kihei Rd, Kihei • (808) 874-5605

ono Maui has some great, traditional Thai food, but Thai Bistro brings you into modern Bangkok. Lots of classics dishes plus some with a contemporary spin rarely seen outside Southeast Asia. The menu gives good descriptions of dishes, so experiment here. (Be aware that the lunch versions are smaller and missing some great sides like noodles—it might be worth springing for the dinner version). Tom yum fried rice is a great treat. The fish here is usually frozen sea bass or mahimahi, but the sauces outshine the fact that the fish is not fresh. Many of their cocktails have some aspect of Thai cuisine in them, such as kaffir lime or even curry (hey, it works). Service is friendly and seems to improve the *busier* they get. Depending on what kind of protein you choose, expect $10–$25 for lunch, a few bucks more for dinner. In the back of the Rainbow Mall.

Nutcharee's Authentic Thai Food
1280 S Kihei Rd, Kihei • (808) 633-4840

ono Warning—this restaurant might prompt unfair comparisons with other Thai restaurants (*yeah, it's good, but is it Nutcharee's good?*). Nutcharee's has ruined us for a number of dishes. Most notable is the crispy fish with green mango salad. We don't usually rave about an item from the salad menu, but this is truly epic. They also do very well with curries, noodle dishes and starters (the E-San Sausage is great). You basically can't go wrong with anything labeled a "House Specialty." Desserts are the only things lacking, but if you eat like we do here, you won't have room anyway. $11–$20 for lunch and dinner. Tucked in the corner of the Azeka Shopping Center.

SOUTH MAUI TREATS

Maui Pie
1280 S Kihei Rd, Kihei • (808) 298-0473

ono What's not to love about a comforting slice of pie? That's what you get here. Many of the expected fruit and cream pies, whole for about $21, minis for $11, a slice for about $5. A la mode available. They also have a pot pie and quiche, but you came here for a treat. Turnovers are not as compelling—

stick with the pie. In Azeka Makai Shopping Center.

Peace Love Shave Ice
1280 S Kihei Rd, Kihei • (808) 264-9090

ono Sounds so much more enticing than *War and Anger Shave Ice*, doesn't it? This small shack in the Azeka Market parking lot does a good job. Though there's not a huge range of flavors, the ones offered are still extensive enough to satisfy most anyone. The syrups are all chilled and made with organic sugar, whether in natural or artificial flavors. The Thai tea shave ice is a good option (we're *pretty* sure those are tea leaves in the syrup). $6 for small, $8 for large. The owner is very nice and does a good job of helping you pick good flavor combos—she won't push toppings and additions if they don't mix well. Seating consists of bar stools around the shack as well as a tiny, keiki-sized picnic table. Easy to recommend. On South Kihei Road between Piikea and Lipoa.

SOUTH MAUI VIETNAMESE

Vietnamese Cuisine
1280 S Kihei Rd, Kihei • (808) 875-2088

ono We really like the food here. Flavors will appeal to most people. The build-your-own Vietnamese burritos are great. And you *have* to try the rice-in-a-clay-pot. Stir it up first and look for the slightly burned parts. They're the best! Noodle dishes, rice dishes, stir fry dishes, seafood, plus steak. Lots of vegetarian items, too. Flavors may not be authentic, but most items are tasty. $12–$30 for lunch and dinner. In the Azeka Makai Shopping Center.

CENTRAL MAUI AMERICAN

808 on Main
2051 Main St, Wailuku • (808) 242-1111

ono These guys can compete with any five-star restaurant on the island. Mostly gourmet paninis, sandwiches, salads, burgers. The Spicy Ranch panini is a personal favorite, with chicken, bacon, pepperoni, tomato, avocado, provolone and cheddar. They haven't missed yet with their daily soup specials. By the same people as **808 Deli** in south Maui, where you can find many of the same menu items for a few bucks less, but there's not much seating there. So, you are paying a little bit more for the sit-down atmosphere here. But the food is so good we don't even care. $11–$18 for lunch and dinner entrées. Upgrade to the loaded BBQ fries for $5 extra. Totally worth it. Kids menu also available. Full bar, with rotating monthly specials. The setting is about as nice as things get in old Wailuku (the visitor's bureau would probably rather we say historic... but it's old.) If they fix the bathroom situation (out back, in a building next door) we'd have nothing but praise for this place. Between Church and Market Street. Closed Sunday.

Café Des Amis
42 Baldwin Ave, Paia • (808) 579-6323

ono They call themselves French/Mediterranean/Indian. *Sooo*, we put it under American because we don't have a category like that, and you'd never look for it. This place nicely complements the Pa'ia vibe. The inside is a little cramped, but the outside seating in a converted alley makes the experience. Wood fencing, gravel floor and simple wood tables and chairs with umbrellas make it an authentic outdoor cafe where sipping wine and eating with your fingers is basically a requirement. The featured food is crepes, both sweet and savory, with some available only at breakfast. Wraps, salads and Indian-style curries round out the menu with Mediterranean platters (big enough for at least two) of cheeses, cured meats, hummus and pita bread as well as dips and chutneys. All ingredients are fresh, organic and local when possible. Happy hour from 4–6 p.m. daily brings half-priced beer, wine by the glass and cocktails. Lunch can get busy. $8–$20 for breakfast, lunch and dinner. On Baldwin Avenue kitty corner from Mana Foods.

Café Mambo
30 Baldwin Ave, Paia • (808) 579-8021

ONO A cool menu with unexpected items such as duck burgers (a good use of duck, we might add) and fajitas (we have to force ourselves not to get 'em every time), kalua pig salad, organic tofu burger, spinach nut falafel, etc., for lunch. Tasty sweet potato fries. The food is good, and they're friendly and quirky—exactly what you want in Pa'ia. Good drinks and beer selection, too, with pretty fair deals during their happy hour. Popular with locals; it can get loud inside. Hope you like onions, 'cause they sure do. $8–$15 for breakfast, $12–$18 for lunch, $13–$25 for dinner. On Baldwin Ave. about a block off Hana Hwy.

Charley's
142 Hana Hwy, Paia • (808) 579-8085

This is a great bar and music venue, but the restaurant has had its ups and downs. The menu has been all over the place, ranging from decent bar fare to mediocre gourmet cuisine. These days, the menu has been simplified and is back to burgers, sandwiches, pizza, steak and some seafood. (However, the sushi bar at dinner feels a little out of place.) Though it has improved, the food's still nothing to write home about and is a bit overpriced for what it is. Come for the atmosphere, music and booze. Their Sunday Bloody Mary bar is a fun tradition. Part-time Maui resident Willie Nelson is revered here at this occasional hangout for celebrities who have homes on the north shore of Haleakala. $13–$26 for breakfast, $15–$40 for lunch and dinner. So does Charley

himself do the cooking? Hope not. Charley was a dog who died in 1978. He lives on as the restaurant's logo. In Pa'ia near Luna Lane.

Da Shrimp Hale
70 E Kaahumanu Ave, Kahului • (808) 868-2361

Shrimp, clams, crawfish, catfish, etc. Pick your critter by the pound, pick your sauce, and choose your heat level. For example, try the shrimp with Cajun. (Note that it's served whole, head and all, making the bib and gloves useful.) They also serve your choice fried, if you like. Also consider the sausage tossed in a bag. Unfortunately, they bring the food out at different times, so you may not be eating at the same time as your dining partners. In the end the execution is not quite as likable as the menu and concept. It's good, but not great. $12–$25 for lunch and dinner. In the Maui Mall.

Fork & Salad
120 Hookele St, Kahului • (808) 793-3256

ONO A good place for healthy eats. The original location in Kihei got us onboard for their salads (which are easy to recommend). Once another location opened, we branched out a bit more. Turns out the whole menu is a hit. The founders are the same guys who started **Three's Bar & Grill**, which is known for creative dishes made with fresh, local ingredients—that tradition continues here. The sandwiches, such as the 'ahi melt or Asian-inspired kalua pork, are well conceived and look as good as they taste. The grain bowls (filled with things like quinoa and beets) are a heartier alternative to salad. Their Ni'ihau lamb chili is some of the best we've had anywhere (just don't tell my grandmother that). Even the lemonade and teas are above average. Service is fast, and you can order ahead online for an even speedier experience. Easy *ono*. $10–$20 for lunch and dinner. By Target and next to Starbucks on Hookele Street in Kahului.

Ku'au Store & Deli
701 Hana Hwy, Paia • (808) 579-8844

ono One of your better bets for picking up some grinds on your way out to Hana. Open at 6:30 a.m., they have a coffee bar, smoothies, cold case deli and some hot breakfast sandwiches. $7 for a burrito that is loaded, $6 for breakfast panini (meat or veggie). Poke, BBQ lunch plates and more panini and sandwiches. Lots of organic, local produce and natural foods for a decent price, considering it's a small store. (They even stick freshly cut lime in the half papayas in the cold case.) Lots of locally made baked goods, many loaded with superfoods and nuts. Easy to recommend. $10–$15 for breakfast and lunch. Makai side of Hana Highway, east of Pa'ia but before Ho'okipa. (Lotta Hawaiian words there, so you'll need to step up your game.)

Ma'alaea General Store
132 Maalaea Rd, Maalaea • (808) 242-8900

ono Right at Ma'alaea Harbor, your best bet for a morning coffee and a darned hearty breakfast English muffin sandwich or fruit-filled breakfast bowl before a boat ride. They also have deli sandwiches, burgers, smoothies, tacos and fresh fish. They also have a full bar. They get an *ono* for convenience alone. $8–$15 for breakfast, $10–$20 for lunch.

Mama's Fish House
799 Poho Pl, Kuau • (808) 579-8488

ono This is where we come when we want to treat ourselves, so let's cut to the chase: diabolically satisfying food and an extremely pleasing ambiance. They are right next to a beautiful beach and tide-pool; the only things between you and the sand are picturesque palm trees. Food, service, ambiance—all top notch. We like early dinners best. You know as soon as you walk up the gecko walkway and through the banyan tree root archway (which got that shape when it crushed a building) that this will be special. The mostly seafood recipes are very imaginative and change daily, so it doesn't make much sense to mention specific ones. But we've never had a bad meal here. They even give credit on the menu to the fishing boat or fisherman who caught each fish. Polish it off with a Polynesian Black Pearl dessert and a chocolate martini. This is a well-oiled machine that serves 1,000 meals a day and is often listed as one of the top 10 restaurants in the U.S. Other than the price, complaints are hard to think of. (OK, their drinks lean toward the sour side. There, now I'm not a slobbering bootlicker.) Same menu for lunch and dinner and it's $50–$80. Northeast of Pa'ia on Hwy 36 just past mile marker 8. Reservations required at least a month (or more) in advance.

Mana Foods
49 Baldwin Ave, Paia • (808) 579-8078

ono Why include a grocery store in dining? Well, the unassuming building hides one of the best grocery stores in the state, and once you walk in, the store seems to continuously expand in little nooks and corners. The reasonable prices (for Maui) also make us pause and wonder about the markup at Whole Foods. Head toward the back to find a food counter, which gets them their *ono*. Huge salad bar, hot dinner entrées, sandwiches and wraps all ready to go. Especially tasty and filling are the breakfast burritos that come out every morning. By the entrance is a small counter for local coffee and smoothies. Near the cashiers are some baked goods that surpass all expectations. $5–$15. About a block from Hana Hwy on Baldwin.

Maui Coffee Roasters
444 Hana Hwy, Kahului • (808) 877-2877

Ono ⌐⌐ An excellent place for coffee and a muffin in the morning. They also have breakfast sandwiches, eggs Benedict and various bagels. They get their baked goods elsewhere, and the results are flavorful. Lots of coffee flavors and coffee drinks, and it's the only place we can think of that sells coffee for around a buck. The coffees taste freshly roasted—not surprising since they do their own roasting next door. Lunch consists of tasty sandwiches and wraps at a good price. Near Dairy Road next to Marco's. $2–$10.

Mill House
1670 Honoapiilani Hwy, Waikapu
(808) 270-0333

Ono ⌐⌐ One of the cooler places to eat on Maui. Incredible ambiance backing up against the West Maui mountains in the central valley, they are ensconced in the Maui Tropical Plantation next to a serene pond. Indoor and outdoor tables are not too tightly spaced, and the interior includes the charm of *full-sized trains* as decoration. The food is fantastic with items that change often. It's hard to classify because the entrées and styles are all over the place. This is a farm-to-table establishment with much of the produce grown on the plantation. The only catch to all this is that the portions are fairly small, so order with this in mind. Prices are high, but the experience is worth it. From $14 burgers to $58 steak, lunch and dinner runs about $14–$60. Between Wailuku and Ma'alaea on Hwy 30. Reservations recommended for dinner.

Paia Bay Coffee & Bar
115 Hana Hwy, Paia • (808) 579-3111
Tucked away behind the shops at the (only) stoplight in Pa'ia. Paia Bay Coffee & Bar is presented as a hidden gem where amazing, local food is served and authentic musicians play. Well, the music is fine, but the rest of it is no gem. The space fits Pa'ia well—an open, courtyard-like setting. Breakfast has a handful of scrambled egg dishes, bagel sandwiches, yogurt and açai bowls. (Avoid the banana bread at all costs.) Lunch brings sandwiches and pricey salads. Dinner has appetizer-type dishes, poke, tacos, curry and a couple of sushi rolls (one of which is vegan). Pricing is all over the place with some of the same menu items costing more at lunch than at dinner, and some items inexplicably expensive ($10 for yogurt?). The cocktails tend to be on the weak side, which is disappointing when they're charging top-shelf prices. In all, stick with the coffee and the atmosphere—nearby **Café Des Amis** does food and cocktails much better. $10–$15 for breakfast and lunch, $7–$20 for dinner. On the alley-like Nalu Place, just before the stoplight.

Pa'ia Fish Market
100 Baldwin Ave, Paia • (808) 579-8030
Improved since our last edition, but the *ono* applies only to the Kihei restaurant. They have a very nice selection of fish, chicken, tacos, salads, sashimi, pasta, fajitas and burgers. Portions are large enough that many of the fish dishes are enough for two to share. Crowded seating, but no table service in Pa'ia—order and wait for them to call Beer and wine available. $10–$25 for lunch and dinner. On the corner of Baldwin Avenue in Pa'ia.

Rock & Brews
120 Hana Hwy, Paia • (808) 579-9011
Part-owned by KISS frontmen Gene Simmons and Paul Stanley, this chain restaurant tries to appeal to the rock fan by playing live recordings of various rock groups. But for a band often associated with wretched excesses, you'd expect a bit more competency behind the bar. If you spilled one of their mai tais, I doubt

even Gene Simmons would *Lick it Up*. (It's the name of a song, OK? Look it up on YouTube.) Otherwise, it has a sports bar-type feel with the usual fare that comes with it. Not necessarily the best place for entrées, but they do well with most appetizers, and service is friendly. One of the only places on Maui we've seen a giant baked pretzel, which is pretty tasty. Go for the mustard rather than paying extra for the cheese. $15–$25 for lunch and dinner. On highway in Pa'ia.

Wailuku Coffee Co.
26 N Market St, Wailuku • (808) 495-0259

A good spot for coffee and light food if you're exploring Wailuku. Their slogan is "where the hip come to sip," but they still served us—and we tend to swill coffee (to say nothing of our less-than-"hip" factor). The setting is simple, comfortable and decidedly not like a chain. Bagels, eggs, sandwiches, salads and smoothies round out the food options—nothing fancy, but it works. They have a good range of beverages, both coffee-based and not. $5–$15 for breakfast and lunch. Kitchen closes around an hour before the shop does. On Market Street between Main and Vineyard.

CENTRAL MAUI ITALIAN

Flatbread Company
89 Hana Hwy, Paia • (808) 579-8989

ono An easy place to love. Simple menu of flatbread pizzas (thin, slightly chewy crust) and salads, both with outrageously delicious results. You may find yourself clearing more pizza surface area than you anticipate. Ingredients are organic with chemical-free meats and produce from local suppliers. Their selection goes from fairly traditional to uniquely their own (the Mopsy is their most popular—it features kalua pork and Maui-grown pineapple), and the attention to quality is obvious. How they make it

healthy yet sinfully good is beyond us, but we wish all the islands had one. Great drink menu (a simple gin and tonic becomes so refreshing with mint and cucumber). Root beer fans will love the Hawaiian-made soda. (Free refills.) Friendly service and a casual, inviting, loud and festive atmosphere at dinner. If you ain't happy here, you must be having a bad day. Sorry to sound slobbering, but we're big fans. No reservations, but consider calling an hour ahead and asking to be put on the waiting list. Only ding: It gets really hot inside. $12–$24 for lunch and dinner.

Giannotto's Pizza
2050 Main St, Wailuku • (808) 244-8282

ono Your classic go-to pizza joint. The ultra-thin slices *look* a little sad, but you'll notice something about the pepperoni—it tastes better. More flavorful. That's because they cut the pepperoni fresh. By the slice for $2–$4 or full 16-inch pizzas for $17–$27. They also have homemade pasta, hot and cold sandwiches, salads and desserts. The zeppoli—a hot dough ball covered in powdered sugar—is *darned* good. Everything is from family recipes. The owner may seem like a gruff guy, but he greets his loyal regulars by name. Free delivery on orders over $20. On the corner of Main and Church.

Marco's Grill & Deli
444 Hana Hwy, Kahului • (808) 877-4446

An Italian restaurant set in a loud '50s-style diner. The pizza, pasta, sandwiches and salads are all heavily overpriced. (Sandwiches come with pasta salad, or you can substitute fries or salad for $4.50 more, but they take away the pasta salad—*hey, I paid for it; just give me both*.) Breakfast is more American–style (avoid the sad, doughy pancakes). The food tends to be bland. How bland? Italian hospitals probably serve more flavorful chicken parmigiano than Marco's. If you insist on eating here, avoid the acutely uncomfortable booths with their acute-angle seat backs. $6–$24 for breakfast, $10–$38 for lunch and dinner. On the corner of Dairy Road.

CENTRAL MAUI JAPANESE

Vana Paia
93 Hana Hwy, Paia • (808) 579-6002
Vana attempts to add a bit of elegance to a laid-back surf town, and the results are…mixed. Brunch is available every day and consists mainly of egg dishes, with Benedicts getting the most attention. The cardamom French toast is an interesting option, but the strong flavor might not be for everyone. The lunch side of brunch consists of a handful of sandwiches (BLT with avocado is probably the best bet) and salads. Dinner brings sushi and small-plate entrées. Presentation is great, and the outdoor café setting tucked away in the back of the inn can make for a romantic atmosphere. Portions and flavors, on the other hand, can be lacking (even with drinks). We won't turn you away, but you can spend less and get more at neighboring restaurants—go for the atmosphere. $11–$33 for brunch (weekends only), $15–$40 for dinner. Reservations for dinner recommended. At the Paia Inn, on Hana Highway in Pa'ia.

Wow Wee Maui Kava Bar & Grill
333 Dairy Rd, Kahului • (808) 871-1414
First of all, it's not really Japanese. It's really more American with burgers and sandwiches. But they *also* have a sushi bar which, frankly, is the only reason to stop here. The sushi's fresh and reasonably priced. Avoid the standard fare menu, which reads better than it tastes. At the Dairy Road Center near Alamaha. $9–$20 for lunch and dinner. It's $20 and more if you take our advice and get the sushi. They also have kava (called awa in Hawai'i), which is made from a root and tastes a little like woody water. It's a mild

relaxant/painkiller. Polynesians have been using it for generations, and it has cultural importance here. When you get a bowl, you're supposed to gulp it down fast; don't sip. It may make your mouth tingle. Consider trying it once for the novelty.

CENTRAL MAUI LOCAL

Da Kitchen Café
425 Koloa St, Kahului • (808) 871-7782
ono Island-style, gourmet comfort food. Nearly everyone who eats here ends up raving about it. Wide selection of local items, such as loco moco, teriyaki chicken, chicken katsu, lau lau, and kalua pork in a casually upscale setting. The saimin could use a little work—you're better off with the Kalbi fried noodles. The more adventurous will want to try the poke. If you're presently wanted by the cholesterol police, don't come here—they may raid the place. Portions are very generous. The Notorious B.I.G. loco moco is big enough to share and then some. Portuguese sausage: two giant beef patties, bacon, spam, Mexican chili with an egg all over rice. Don't order dessert; you won't have room for it. $11–$30 for lunch and dinner. BYOB. Consider making reservation for dinner—waits are usually 20 minutes or more. The *ono* rating only applies to the Kahului location off the Hana Highway, makai (ocean side) of Dairy Road. The Kihei location in the Rainbow Mall is the "Express" version with a smaller menu and less compelling atmosphere.

Tasty Crust
1770 Mill St, Wailuku • (808) 244-0845
Kind of dumpy, mostly windowless, and not as… kempt as one might like, but this longtime restaurant remains popular with the local community because it's cheap and hearty. (Probably also helps that it's one of the few restaurants open early for breakfast in this area.) Their pancakes are light, soft and large with a good texture;

they even serve peanut butter with them, if you want. (It's surprising how well the flavor combination works.) The banana pancakes taste like banana bread and are good... but they're missing banana slices on top, as you commonly find elsewhere in Hawai'i, so that's disappointing. They also have eggs, some omelettes, and loco moco (an egg over two beef patties on top of a bowl of rice, all smothered in gravy). In the traditional local way, Spam or Vienna sausage are available with breakfast. (Locals *love* Spam.) Lunch is saimin, pork chops, spare ribs and burgers. $6–$15 (add some pricier steaks at night). From Hwy 32 (coming from Kahului), go right on Central to the end. Turn right on Mill. Opens at 6 a.m. No dinner on Mondays.

Tin Roof
360 Papa Pl, Kahului • (808) 868-0753

ono Killer local grinds, brah. This is what happens when a local boy becomes an accomplished chef and uses his skills to make gourmet local food at food truck prices. Kau kau tins, dry mein, garlic shrimp, poke bowls. We haven't had a bad item. The selection is small, but they're all items most visitors are unfamiliar with, so no worries. $8–$15 for lunch. Only open 10 a.m. to 2 p.m. Lines can be long, and there are only a couple tables, so take it to go. Since the food might not be familiar to you, consider ordering on their website and picking it up. On Dairy Road near Hana Highway in the same center as the more visible Las Piñatas.

Zippy's
15 Hookele St, Kahului • (808) 856-7599

While the mainland has lots of regional, roadside diners, Hawai'i has Zippy's. (Think Hawaiian-style Denny's.) While the food is nothing to write home about, it's at least consistent. Some of the better options are chili, fried chicken (Korean-style is a favorite) and saimin. Their bakery also offers lots of dessert options. The atmos-

phere is very casual and family-friendly. (There's a good chance yours won't be the loudest table there, even if you have kids.) While the takeout counter is always open, the dining room is open from 6 a.m.–midnight weekdays and 24 hours Friday through Sunday. It's a decent option for anyone dealing with late flights or odd hours. $7–$16 for breakfast, $6–$22 for lunch and dinner. In Kahului on the corner of Hookele Street and Puunene/Maui Veterans Highway (near Target).

CENTRAL MAUI MEXICAN

Las Piñatas
395 Dairy Rd, Kahului • (808) 877-8707

ono This is the place to go for a quick bite, but you still want to sit down and eat reasonable quality, relatively inexpensive Mexican food in acceptable surroundings. (If that sounds less than glowing, it's because *you aren't paying* for a glow at this place.) The tasty Kitchen Sink burrito is a massive collection of ingredients. Chicken enchiladas are pretty tasty. Vegan and vegetarian options as well as a salsa bar. Mostly Mexican beers. Counter service only, and they are super nice here. We hear from Californians who say it's not as good as what they can get there. Well... *yeah*. But this ain't California. Large portions. And yes, they do have lots of piñatas hanging from the ceiling. $8–$12 for breakfast, $8–$17 for lunch and dinner. Between Hana Highway and the Maui Marketplace, next to FedEx.

Milagros
3 Baldwin Ave, Paia • (808) 579-8755

ono The food alone qualifies them for an *ono*, but what really impressed us was their reverence for tequila and margaritas. You won't find Jose Cuervo here. The metaphorical bar is raised a bit higher than that, and you will be more involved in how your 'rita is concocted. Do *not* ask for a top shelf tequila in your margarita, or they may throw you out. Such libations are only served in a snifter. And for the food, lunch is an accommodating menu of fresh fish, Mexican items and half-pound burgers. At dinner try the fajitas; they're sweet, smoky and delicious. Their seafood enchiladas (dinner only) and burritos are equally amazing. Most seating is outside, making it a perfect place to observe the diverse population of Pa'ia. At the stoplight on the highway. $12–$20 for lunch, $12–$25 for dinner. Look for their roving food truck. Smaller menu, but it's somehow tastier than the restaurant.

CENTRAL MAUI THAI

Thailand Cuisine II
70 E Kaahumanu Ave, Kahului • (808) 873-0225

ono If you want Thai atmosphere, this is the place. Though the place is small, the ambiance is thick enough that we notice something new each time we visit. The menu is large and, though the summer rolls are bit lackluster, the main dishes hold up well (the whole Cornish game hen is a favorite). They also have a good selection of vegetarian versions of their entrées with the curries as the standout. If you like it spicy, they won't believe you—be persuasive. Most dishes are under $17. It's $14–$25 for lunch and dinner; throw on a few more bucks for market-priced fish. Reservations on weekends recommended. Dinner-only on Sunday.

CENTRAL MAUI TREATS

Ululani's Shave Ice
115 Hana Hwy, Paia

ono A great assortment of flavors (made from natural, local juices whenever possible), toppings and the standard ice cream flavors for the bottom. The service is excellent with lots of aloha, and they have always poured the perfect amount of syrup for us. They have quickly become the local favorite and have expanded to many locations around the island (one in Kihei, Wailuku, Kahului, Pa'ia, Lahaina and Ka'anapali). Seriously, these guys make shave ice the way it should be. Depending on size and add-ons, expect to pay $5–$8. This is one of the best locations, mostly because they also carry Coconut Glen's Ice Cream. At the stoplight in Pa'ia.

CENTRAL MAUI VEGETARIAN

Choice Health Bar
11 Baldwin Ave, Paia • (808) 661-7711

ono In a town with a distinct hippie streak, this restaurant fills a niche that was strangely missing... and knocks it out of the park. The menu is fairly simple—açai and granola bowls, smoothies (*love* the cookie monster), fresh juices, salads, wraps, fresh soups, wraps and a couple of unusual items. The wildflower tacos really surprised us—they're filled with a taco-seasoned, walnut-pumpkin seed mix and wrapped in an edible nasturtium leaf. You can order on their website and grab to go. Only ding is how loud it can get inside (lots of hard surfaces and blenders whirring). $7–$12. On Baldwin Avenue next to Milagros. They also have locations in Lahaina and Whaler's Village in Ka'anapali.

CENTRAL MAUI VIETNAMESE

A Saigon Café (Jennifer's)
1792 Lower Main St, Wailuku • (808) 243-9560

ono One of the better restaurants in Central Maui (especially for vegetarians), their menu contains an eye-popping array of foods from several Asian countries. We've had outstanding meals here, but the quality has gone done since our last edition, and we nearly pulled the *ono*. Stick to the menu items with a star next to them, and you should still have a good experience. The shrimp pops (ground shrimp pasted on a stick of sugar cane, steamed and grilled) are a *great* way to start things. Consider the garden party shrimp, sizzling Naokee (16-ounce New York) steak, or any of the rice in a clay pot choices—just make sure you stir it as soon as it hits the table. Service is either rushed or playful. $13–$31 for lunch and dinner. It's tricky to find. If you take Hwy 32 from Kahului into Wailuku (as if you're heading toward 'Iao Needle), you'll see the rooftop sign barely sticking up above the road on the right, just past mile marker 0.5. (The highway is briefly elevated here, hence the difficulty). Turn right onto Central, take a quick right onto Nani, go right onto Kaniela, and it will be on your left side at Kaniela and Lower Main. Busy at lunch and weekends.

Ba-Le
270 Dairy Rd, Kahului • (808) 877-2400

ono You can forget classifying this place. They call themselves a French sandwich shop and bakery, but serve mostly Asian dishes, huge portions with flavorful results, very cheaply. Vietnamese plate lunches, French sandwiches, local entrées—and you'll probably spend about $12. Their phở (pronounced *fah*—do you know how *hard* that squiggly character is to type?) is pretty good, and the ginger chicken sandwich is our favorite thing on the menu. In the Kau Kau Food Court in Maui Marketplace and other places around the island. $7–$15 for lunch and dinner.

UPCOUNTRY DINING

Baked On Maui
375 W Kuiaha Rd, Pauwela • (808) 870-3042

ono American—The kind of café you hope for in a sleepy, surf town— laid back, tasty and killer, local coffee (almost worth the *ono* on its own). Breakfast features baked goods, waffles and French toast, as well as plenty of savory, egg-based

options. Lunch is a range of sandwiches and burgers. (House fries are available throughout the day and are a great addition.) The small, indoor space works fine, but the shaded seating outdoors is really the best place to settle in and people-watch. (If it's breezy, dust from the nearby parking lot can be an issue.) Service is friendly and fast, making for a good breakfast option when starting the drive to Hana. Breakfast runs $10–$20, $10–$15 for lunch. The only item we didn't love was the biscuits and gravy. (But finding good biscuits and gravy in Hawai'i is like finding good surfing in Iowa.) In the Pauwela Cannery Center on Kuiaha Road between mile markers 13 and 14 on the Hana Highway.

Casanova
1188 Makawao Ave, Makawao • (808) 572-0220

ono Italian—Dinners are their weak point here; the *ono* is for *lunch only*. Some portions are too small, but they have improved on some of their pasta dishes since our last edition. Their thin 12-inch pizzas make good appetizers if you can split them with others. (It's their best offering.) Breakfast and lunch are served in their deli and offer some of the best deals in Makawao. Tasty sliced pizza, sandwiches, and pasta of the day with a generous side salad for lunch. Attitudes in the dining room can be snotty, so remember—the *ono* is *narrowly focused*. $12–$30 for lunch, $14–$40 for dinner. Live music weekends and some week nights after 9 p.m. Wednesdays and Sundays are dinner only. In Makawao near Olinda Road.

Grandma's Coffee House
9232 Kula Hwy, Kula • (808) 878-2140

ono American—A good place to stop if you're coming 'round the mountain from Kaupo after the long Hana Highway drive, or if you're coming down from a Haleakala sunrise. Order at the counter and they'll bring the food out to you. They have a good variety of coffee drinks, and breakfast is their strongest showing. It's popular with residents as well as road bikers—weekend mornings are especially busy (though service can be surprisingly quick). Good coffee cake and other sweets. Consider the bulls-eye breakfast if you're in the mood for something hearty and colorful. On Hwy 37 between mile markers 16 and 17 south of Kula. Open 7 a.m. to 5 p.m. $8–$15 for breakfast and lunch. Lunch tastes exponentially better when you realize how few other places there are to get food around here.

Hali'imaile General Store
900 Haliimaile Rd, Haliimaile • (808) 572-2666

ono **Local**—The location for this somewhat upscale restaurant is unexpected. You have nowhere, then you have Hali'imaile, which is 3 miles south of nowhere. The food is pricey (given the remote location), but very good. Cuisine is mostly Pacific Rim with a smattering of American, Mexican and locally-inspired dishes. The menu is regularly updated but seafood and meat are always well-represented. Lunch (weekdays only) is slightly easier on the wallet—there's a few smaller versions of dinner entrées. Dinner brings items such as mac nut-crusted fish, ribeye steak and coconut seafood curry (very tasty). Desserts are rich enough to make you sweat. $14–$30 for lunch, $30–$45 for dinner. Between Baldwin Avenue and Haleakala Highway (37).

Komoda Store & Bakery
3674 Baldwin Ave, Makawao • (808) 572-7261

ono **Treats**—Who would expect that in this uninspiring, little, semi-dumpy building would reside some of the best bakers on Maui? Their cream puffs are legendary around the island (more like éclairs). Stick donuts, malasadas (Portuguese donuts) chocolate croissants—we've liked almost everything

we've tried here. (And we're quite diligent in reviewing them every time we're in the neighborhood.) They've been here since the island rose from the sea. (OK, OK, since 1916.) Service is either friendly or indifferent, and the price is very reasonable. As at most bakeries, coming in before noon is best. In Makawao just off Makawao Avenue. $2–$6. Closed Sunday and Wednesday.

Kula Bistro
4566 Lower Kula Rd, Kula • (808) 871-2960

ono **American**—Situated in historic Kula town, Kula Bistro is one of your best dining choices upcountry. Despite the good location, there's not much of a view—the windows face uphill. Luckily, they make up for that with quality food and overall charm. Breakfast has some killer eggs Benedict choices, frittatas and pancakes (which are huge). Lunch and dinner bring a number of pasta dishes, sandwiches and paninis, burgers and pizza, as well as steaks and seafood. They also have a bakery with rotating selection of desserts that are worth the stop alone. It's BYOB (with no corkage fees), and you can pick up your adult beverages across the street at Morihara Store. We have not had a bad meal here. $9–$18 for breakfast, $13–$30 for lunch and dinner. On Lower Kula Road, near the Holy Ghost Church.

Kula Lodge
15200 Haleakala Hwy, Kula • (808) 878-1535

American—Every time we sit down to review this place, we get sucked in by the setting and predict, *this* is when they'll get their *ono* back. Then the food comes, and we remember why they don't have it. With sweeping views down the mountain, you can see South Maui, the West Maui mountains and Kahului. An all-glass wall takes full advantage of the views with a somewhat lodge-like decor inside. They also have some cool outdoor tables and a pizza oven out there you just *gotta* see. (Lunch outside when weather permits.) Don't neglect their small but exotic garden to the right and below the restaurant. So that's the good stuff. Unfortunately, they are ill-served by the kitchen. Steak, ribs, fish and 12-inch pizzas are mediocre, and with prices like this it's a shame. Ingredients taste cheap, and this would be a kickin' restaurant if they put as much effort into the food as they do the garden. $15–$25 for breakfast, $20–$30 for lunch, $25–$45 for dinner. On Upper Highway (377) before 378 in Kula.

Nuka
780 Haiku Rd, Haiku • (808) 575-2939

ono **Japanese**—The key to good sushi is far more about the rice than most people realize, and these guys carry on the deep tradition of making the best rice possible. The pickling aspect of it produces delicious veggies that you can get as a side. (The eggplant has great tang and texture.) Atmosphere is a mix of traditional Japanese and a modern lounge—a very comfortable setting. Try the Nuka bowl, which has everything you could hope for in a Japanese rice bowl. Add avocado and meat to take it to the next level. These guys know their stuff, and we have yet to find something we didn't like here—at dinner. Lunch brings noodle bowls, hand rolls and burgers (no sushi). Their beef burgers are fine, but stick to the Asian fare for the best experience. Weekends are packed. Lunch (Monday through Fridays only) runs $6–$15, dinner is $15–$30 and up, no reservations. At the intersection of Haiku Road and Kokomo.

Polli's Mexican Restaurant
1202 Makawao Ave, Makawao • (808) 572-7808
Mexican—A solid option for Upcountry dining. They get very busy at pau hana (after work), so you may have a long wait if you're there just after 5 p.m. The flavors are good and portions are better than most Maui restaurants. Burritos are large and served enchilada-style. The chips and salsa are good, but $3 extra. (I don't know why I feel *entitled* to free chips in a Mexican restaurant...but I do.) Service is friendly and the ambiance is festive, but space can get cramped. BBQ and burgers also available. Check for specials, which can be a good deal. $12–$25 for lunch and dinner. On Makawao Avenue in Makawao. Their motto is, "Come in and eat, or we'll both starve."

Serpico's
7 Aewa Pl, Pukalani • (808) 572-8498
Italian—Historically, we've really liked this place. You can still get a decent meal with ample portions for a good price. Unfortunately, quality has declined enough to pull their *ono*. Breakfast is mainly American, while lunch and dinner turns Italian with thin crust pizza (which is probably their best offering), several parmigiana (including shrimp), pastas such as baked ravioli (avoid the fettuccine Alfredo), hot hoagies and salads. It ain't fancy, and you certainly won't drive all the way to Pukalani to eat here, but it's comforting food before or after a hard day exploring Haleakala. On Old Haleakala Highway and Aewa Place in Pukalani. $9–$15 for breakfast, $9–$30 for lunch and dinner, more if you for surf and turf. BYOB.

Stopwatch Bar & Grill
1127 Makawao Ave, Makawao • (808) 572-1380
American—In a town that prides itself on its cowboy heritage, it's surprisingly hard to get a decent burger in Makawao. The burgers here are pretty decent (though they may cook them more than the medium-well they claim—consider requesting medium or medium-rare). They also serve fish and chips, fresh fish, steak and sandwiches. Not much healthy stuff in this noisy sports bar; head down the road for that. $10–$20 for lunch and dinner. Good views. Service can be in-

different. Fridays bring live music and a cover charge after 9 p.m. In Makawao, southwest of Baldwin Avenue.

Ulupalakua Ranch Store

14800 Piilani Hwy, Kula • (808) 878-2561

ONO ʕ **American**—It's worth going in just to smell the burgers cooking on the grill—beef, venison, lamb and elk. Even taro burgers for vegetarians. They have some plate lunches, but it's all about the third-pound burger here, all raised on their ranch. The flavors and bun are good (though the patties could use a pinch of salt and pepper, in our humble opinion). Take your food outside to eat on the picnic tables. Flying bugs are an occasional problem, but it's relaxing out on the lawn. **$10–$18** for lunch. Way out on the way to (or coming from) Kaupo where Hwy 37 becomes Hwy 31.

ISLAND NIGHTLIFE

The sun has set and the scenery faded, but you don't want the day to end. If you're a night owl, you'll find that Maui probably has enough to keep you happy, but don't expect Las Vegas. This is still a relatively quiet island, especially in South Maui. Nightlife is something that's ever-changing. Many restaurants are constantly bringing in new musicians and trying new things. We hate to pass the buck, but by definition, nightlife is something that changes all the time. Different establishments do different things, sometimes every week. No one covers this week's action as well as an insert in Thursday's *Maui News* newspaper called *Maui Scene*. Grab a copy to see what's shakin' this week. It includes special events, concerts, movies, stage plays, resort entertainment, galleries, and it has coupons. Also look for *Maui Time* on free newsstands.

For **movies**, the best is in Kahului at the Maui Mall Megaplex 12 (808-249-2222). **Kihei's Regency Theater** (808-891-

1016) is small but quality. In Lahaina, the small **Wharf Cinema** has seen better days but is the only option (808-249-2222).

Note that the Maui authorities take DUI very seriously and make extensive use of sobriety checkpoints. We don't want you to arrive for vacation and leave on probation.

West Maui Nightlife

Lahaina is the center of West Maui nightlife. One of the most effective ways to feel out the nightlife in Lahaina is to walk along Front Street and see what strikes your fancy.

In Kaʻanapali, watching the cliff diver at sunset is a good way to start off an evening. Several of the beachside path restaurants there often have live music. Most of the resorts also have goings-on.

South Maui Nightlife

The hub is the **Kihei Kalama Village**, locally known as **The Triangle**. (a.k.a. **Bermuda Triangle**, and if you stay long enough, you'll get turned around and disoriented, too.) Bars like **Haui's Life's a Beach** (808-891-8010), **South Shore Tiki Lounge** (808-874-6444), **Lava Rock Bar & Grill** (808-727-2521), and **Three's** (808-879-3133) are hopping most nights of the week. **Kahale's** (808-215-9939) is a watering hole in the Triangle that might look a little rough around the edges because... well, it *is* rough around the edges. **Mulligan's on the Blue** (808-874-1131) at the Wailea Old Blue Golf Course, mauka of the Fairmont Kea Lani Resort, has live music every night and often sports one of the most festive atmospheres you'll find, especially when the Celtic band is playing on Sunday nights. **Willie K**, a master guitar player and vocalist, kills the place on most Wednesdays. It's $70 for dinner and show. Get early reservations if you want to eat inside. Outdoor tables may not have a view of the performer.) Service can be understaffed, and sometimes Willie likes to *talk story* about himself as much as he likes to play, but this guy has the chops for a master performance. **Fred's/Moose McGillycuddy's** (808-891-8600) at 2511 S. Kihei Road is a lively place for the younger crowd. Their Taco Tuesday has cheap tacos and boozy margaritas.

Nightlife Elsewhere

Every Friday night is a party somewhere on Maui. Appropriately named **Maui Friday Town Parties**, these small block parties showcase local musicians, craft vendors, food trucks, and kids activities. Best of all, entrance is free. **Wailuku** is home to the first Friday, second in **Lahaina**, third in **Makawao**, and fourth in **Kihei** at the Azeka Shopping Center. On those rare fifth Fridays of the month, the offshore island of **Lana'i** gets to host.

In **Hana**, find a bright light and watch the geckos eat night bugs—you crazy party animal, you. Actually, the **Travaasa Hana** (808-248-8211) often has some pretty good local musicians at their bar.

Upcountry isn't a nightlife mecca either. Might want to wander around Makawao and see what's shakin'. **Casanova** (808-572-0220) has a dance floor and lively music on weekends and some weeknights. Sometimes **Stopwatch** (808-572-1380) has live performers on Fridays with karaoke on Thursdays and Saturdays.

In **Pa'ia**, **Charley's** (808-579-8085) has music every night except Sundays with occasional drop-ins from local celebs like Willie Nelson.

In **Kahului**, the **Maui Arts & Cultural Center** is on Kahului Beach Road. Call (808) 242-7469 to see what's happening there. Their Castle Theatre is a great place for a movie or play. The two rows of balconies provide excellent vantages.

LU'AU

Hula dancers in grass skirts and coconut bras bending and swaying to the music. Smiling people in their finest aloha wear sitting together at a table with a mai tai in hand, and a plate of kalua pork in front of them. A performer on stage twirls a torch lit at both ends, to an urgent drumbeat. The idea of a lu'au that you probably already have in your head isn't that far off from reality. The pig is baked in an underground imu all day, creating succulent results when prepared right. Shows are usually exciting and fast-paced. Sure, it's one of the most touristy things you can do, but going to a lu'au can be a real blast, and if time allows, it's highly recommended.

Different lu'au are held on different nights, and schedules change based on the whims of the managers, so verify the days before making plans. The prices listed in this section are for a standard ticket and include tax. (You can upgrade to VIP packages that include perks like better seats.) *Most* places don't expect you to leave a tip. The buffets are all-you-can-eat, and your ticket price includes an open bar. Keep that in mind if the watered-down mai tai they hand you on your way in the door doesn't satisfy you; the bartender will make something more to your liking. Also remember the golden rule at the buffet line—the cheapest stuff comes first, so reserve enough plate real estate for the good stuff at the end. If you are a vegetarian or have food allergies, be sure to let them know when you book.

The best shows are in West Maui, but if you're staying in South Maui your calculus might be different since not having to drive an hour back afterward is a big advantage. You should also know that several of the lu'au here are put on by the same production company, **Tihati**. They put on a classic lu'au featuring dance styles from across Polynesia, not just Hawai'i. But they're a little bit formulaic; the shows are all similar, so they can interchange personnel, right down to the same emcee jokes.

West Maui Lu'au

Old Lahaina Lu'au
1251 Front St, Lahaina • (808) 667-1998

The Old Lahaina Lu'au is easily the best lu'au on Maui, and if it wasn't missing a couple of common elements found at more standard shows, it would be without question the best lu'au in the entire state. The professional crew is competent, friendly, and always up, and they make you feel welcome by giving everyone a fresh flower lei. The grounds, next to but not *on* the shore, have an assortment of thatched hale (buildings) giving things a distinctly Hawaiian feel. Drinks are served from their accommodating bar. The food is better than any other lu'au on Maui (except for their sister program **Feast at Lele**, but that's a different experience). The buffet offers all of the usual lu'au items plus many Hawaiian dishes you'll have a hard time finding elsewhere, such as laulau (pork wrapped in a taro leaf and cooked until tender) and poke (raw, cubed, and seasoned ahi). Unlike a typical lu'au that features dance styles from across Polynesia, this show strives for a more authentic Hawaiian and Tahitian feel. This means no lounge lizard emcee singing Hukilau, no shiny foil shirts. But it also means no fire knife dancers (because that's Samoan) and no heavily tattooed Maoris wagging their tongue at you. We really miss the fire knife show. They also don't give you an opportunity to get up on stage to learn to hula. If either of those things are important to you, look elsewhere. That said, the dancing here is captivating. It's so riveting that most people don't even get up to go get seconds during the show.

They've got shows seven nights a week but tickets sell out weeks, even months in advance, so book as soon as you know your dates. When you make your reservation you've got a choice of sitting at a regular table and chair, or what they call "traditional" seating in the first row, right next to the stage. Great view, but you'll have to sit cross-legged on the ground all night and dine from a low table (a configuration we suspect is set up to pack more people in without blocking the view of those behind.) Opt for the regular table unless you're limber. Another thing you should know is that unlike most lu'au, where gratuity is included, they have table service for drinks, and they'll lean on you to leave a tip. In Lahaina at the north end of Front Street, behind the Lahaina Cannery Mall. $120 adults, $75 kids 3–12.

Drums of the Pacific Luau
200 Nohea Kai Dr, Kaanapali • (808) 667-4727

If the elements that are missing from the Old Lahaina Lu'au are important to you, then you might prefer the Drums of the Pacific Lu'au at the Hyatt Regency in Ka'anapali. This is the best show if you're excited to get up on stage to learn to dance the hula (something that's always more popular with the women in the audience than the men, even though the hula was originally practiced exclusively by male warriors). Don't worry—they won't force you to get up on stage if you don't want to. They also have a dramatic three-man fire knife show at the end. Of the **Tihati** shows, this one has a bigger stage and better production values, but the setting is less appealing—very artificial. (The venue is next to the beach but you can't see the ocean from your seat.) The food is only okay, nothing special. And as with most lu'au, you might want to pass on the watered-down mai tais they hand you on the way in and consider the free open bar instead (though it's poorly stocked with exceptionally cheap well drinks). Nightly, it's $123, with one kid ages 6–12 included free per paying couple. (It's $76 for each additional. Under six are always free.) That makes it a pretty good value for families. $14 valet, or free self-parking with a long walk.

Maui Nui Lu'au

2605 Kaanapali Pkwy, Kaanapali • (877) 846-5554
The Maui Nui Lu'au at the Sheraton Maui is another **Tihati** production, meaning you can expect a Polynesian revue and a fire knife show. The usual setting is a lawn right behind Ka'anapali Beach with a scenic view of Black Rock, but if that one is occupied with another event you'll get shunted over to a secondary location away from the ocean closer to the hotel, where there are more distractions and the performers seem to have a harder time commanding the audience's attention. Try to confirm which they are using before booking, since it will affect your level of enjoyment. This is one of the better shows overall, but they commit the sin of forcing everyone to stand up to learn how to hula before the crowd has a chance to warm up and get into it. Good food, including more traditional items than you'll find at most other lu'au. Avoid the mai tais at the open bar—you could water your lawn with them and never give the worms a buzz. **$125** ($75 kids 6–12) on Monday, Wednesday and seasonal Fridays. It's $2 to self-park or $5 for valet. This part of the island can be terribly breezy at night so you might want a light jacket. Seating is first come, first serve, and they have a few preshow games and activities to keep you entertained. Everyone gets a flower lei.

Wailele Polynesian Lu'au

2365 Kaanapali Pkwy, Kaanapali • (808) 661-2992
The Wailele Polynesian Lu'au at The Westin Maui has some positive things going on: the food is good, the lit palm trees behind the stage provide an alluring backdrop long after the sun goes down, and they have a *great* fire knife finale, with the most fire knife dancers on the island. On the negative side, they don't offer an opportunity to learn the hula, the dancing is merely so-so, and they don't validate parking, so you'll have to pay an extra $20–$25 to park at Whalers Village on top of the **$120** ticket price ($65 for kids 6–12). That means you'll probably only want to consider this one if you are staying at the Westin or somewhere else in Ka'anapali that's in close enough proximity to walk. They keep an irregular schedule, so you'll have to call or check online to see which days they are performing. Prices rise during holidays.

Myths of Maui Luau

2780 Kekaa Dr, Kaanapali • (808) 425-9418
Our last choice in West Maui (heck, in all Hawai'i, for that matter) is the Myths of Maui Lu'au at the Royal Lahaina Resort. The small cast has some good dancers (including a fire knife dancer) and a good emcee, but you're packed into a table-filled gravel pit like sardines, and the food is simply bad. (*Promise* you won't eat the fish or the mac salad.) When the chicken nuggets are among the best things you can eat, you *know* you've arrived at a really poor lu'au. **$115** adults, $50 kids 6–12, plus $5 for parking. Expect to spend lots of time waiting.

Feast at Lele

505 Front St, Lahaina • (808) 667-5353
The Feast at Lele is not a typical lu'au (it's really more of a dinner show) so we put it at the end, but it's the classiest of the bunch. No unearthing the pig in an imu ceremony, no getting up to learn how to dance the hula, no buffet. Instead, they serve a five-course meal featuring dishes from Hawai'i, New Zealand, Tahiti, and Samoa (even including vegan options in the same cooking styles). The food at this aptly named feast is *incredible*. (Anyone who can serve squash

and have us clamoring for more gets our respect.) And each party gets their own private table, so no need to make polite small talk. Service is often stretched a bit thin though, so you may find yourself having to beg for another mai tai (which are exceptionally sneaky—you don't taste the rum... but it's there). And the accompanying hula show is only adequate. But they have an absolutely *killer* location next to a beach in Lahaina in West Maui.

Despite being owned by the same folks as the **Old Lahaina Lu'au**, they don't try to be authentically Hawaiian. Here, they allow more Polynesian and faux-Polynesian influences into the experience, including a fire knife dancer. It's pricey at **$136** (kids 2–12 are $99) plus $10 to park across the street, and since there is table service you'll probably feel compelled to leave a tip. But if you can stomach the wallet-choking cost, which includes a fresh flower lei, it's worth it. They seat 280 maximum, so book well in advance—your seats are determined at the time you make a reservation.

By the way: your table won't be right on beach, but you will be on sand, so take that into consideration when choosing your footwear.

South Maui Lu'au

Honua'ula Luau
3850 Wailea Alanui Dr, Wailea • (808) 874-2355
In South Maui it's between the Marriott and the Grand Wailea. We prefer the Honua'ula Lu'au at the Grand Wailea Resort, but it's a toss-up. The location, on a lawn right behind the beach, is wonderful. And this is one of the better options if you want to learn to hula (but they won't make you). The show itself is reasonably good, but at times it doesn't seem to know whether it wants to be a standard Polynesian revue, comedy, or tell a story. Several vignettes incorporate elements you won't see elsewhere, such as aerial silks.

They've got an *excellent* fire knife dancer. The food here is the better of the two South Maui options, and they've got good drinks. **$130** adults, $85 kids 6–12. Free valet parking. They ask you to be there early to reserve a table for your party, but once that's done you can wander the hotel grounds or walk on the beach while you wait. Shows Monday, Tuesday, Thursday, Friday and Saturday.

Te Au Moana
3700 Wailea Alanui Dr, Wailea • (877) 827-2740
Our second choice in South Maui is Te Au Moana on the grounds of the Marriott Wailea Beach Resort. *Beautiful* setting, and everyone gets a real flower lei. The stage is between you and the ocean, so you've got a prime view of the offshore island of Kaho'olawe until the sun goes down. (You'll probably want sunglasses until then.) What's weird is that there's a pathway running behind the stage, so you'll see disembodied heads bouncing along in the background during the show. The food is mostly good, although the pig is a little too salty and the steak is tough, and depending on when your table is called you may have to eat fast if you want seconds because they shut the buffet down fairly early. The mai tais might taste watered down... but they aren't. That's something you may appreciate when they start things off by forcing everyone to stand and learn to hula before giving the crowd a chance to loosen up. It's a standard **Tihati** show. The performers at this one are not the most technically proficient dancers, but they bring the energy even when the audience does not. Big smiles, loud whoops and hollers. Nice touch incorporating the sound of the conch shell throughout the show. Two fire knife dancers... one is a little clumsy. Seating is first come, first serve so make sure you get in line early. And you should know it's a long walk from the parking

area. **$124** adults, $79 kids 6–12. Free self-parking or valet parking available for $40. Shows Monday, Tuesday, Thursday, Friday and Saturday.

Feast at Mokapu
3550 Wailea Alanui Dr, Wailea • (808) 573-1234

The Feast at Mokapu at the Andaz Maui at Wailea Resort is a different kind of South Maui lu'au. For one thing, it's the most expensive lu'au on Maui at **$200** per person (kids 6–12 are $100, while 5 and under are free). Maybe because of the price, it tends to be a smaller affair with a maximum of 150 guests (though we've seen as few as 60). It also abandons the buffet-style feast for a family-style dinner, with each table getting platters to share across three courses. The food is better than the other lu'au in the area, though there's no imu ceremony—the whole pig is presented, but it was cooked above ground, not an underground oven. The mai tais are some of the better, and more potent, drinks at any luau we've been to, plus the bar is open throughout the show. The lu'au is on the Andaz lawn, with the stage a natural hill overlooking Mokapu Beach. (You can't see the beach, but the palm trees and sun setting behind offshore islands makes for a great backdrop.) The open setting and smaller size makes for a more casual start to the evening, where you're greeted with a nice shell and kukui nut lei, a mai tai and a greeter who escorts you to the table and seats (general seating is first-come, first-served, so you'll have better options if you get there right when they open). Since the tables are set directly on the lawn, and the lawn isn't level, you may find yourself sitting at an angle with your plate ready to spill into your lap. (The pricey, Premium seats seem to be more flush.) With the high price of admission comes a few perks—a professional photographer snaps your photo with the sunset, and at the end you get a quality print of the best shot plus free downloads of all the rest. There are a few cultural activities put on by the performers when you arrive, such as lei bracelet weaving and (temporary) Polynesian tattoos. These are a nice touches, though it's odd since these are the only kid-friendly aspects of this lu'au. The rest feels much more adult-oriented (it is billed as a *luxury* lu'au). The show is a Tihati production, with a tour of Polynesian dance styles, including a fire knife finalé. The performance feels more intimate than other Tihati shows thanks to the smaller crowd and setting. In all, the high quality of food, drink and setting make this our favorite of the South Maui lu'au, but only if you can stomach the price. Free valet-only parking. Sundays and Tuesdays from 5:30–8:30 p.m.

LUNCH & DINNER CRUISES

Not all the Hawaiian islands offer these, but Maui's often placid evening waters make dinner cruises a delight.

In West Maui the **Maui Princess** (808-667-6165) is a huge 120-foot yacht that feeds over 100 passengers at dinner. **$100** per person includes prime rib, chicken, fish or vegetarian, three drinks, live entertainment and dancing. While the brochure may show a cozy table for two, there are, in fact, four people seated at each table—just so you know. Tables are all on the open top deck: half along the railing, half in the middle.

If the anemic mai tais are too tame for you, don't hesitate to take them to the bar and have them *seasoned* for you; it's all included. The crew is good, and, while you may expect glorified airline food for such a large crowd, the food is better than we expected. Even the desserts are good. The slow cruise during the sun's golden hour creates pretty views of Lahaina and Ka'anapali. After dinner there's dancing below decks. You don't feel as crowded on this boat (except during boarding) as you may think. The boat is very smooth, and they stay out from 5:30–8 p.m., leaving from Lahaina Harbor. **Pacific Whale Foundation** (808-249-8811) has a $93 dinner cruise out of Lahaina for up to nearly 100 people. You may end up sharing your table with other guests, or you can pay $113 to ensure you'll get a private table.

There are also lots of sunset **cocktail cruises**. Most include the open bar in the price. Out of Lahaina the smallish **Scotch Mist** (808-661-0386) does a good job on their 50-foot sailboat for $70. No bar, just champagne, beer, wine and soft drinks. Out of Ka'anapali Beach the **Teralani** (808-661-7245) offers two different sunset cruises. Their original cruise consists of cocktails and appetizer/pupu style foods and lasts around 2 hours for $78. The full dinner cruise offering brings dinner and cocktails over 2.5 hours for $102.

From Ma'alaea **Pride of Maui** (808-242-0955) has a 2-hour trip. Heavy pupus and an open bar, but we've seen them run out of food in only 30 minutes. The crew's pretty unenthusiastic. $89.

Also out of Ma'alaea, **Pacific Whale** has a cocktail cruise with pupus for $65. On Fridays they offer the **Island Rhythms Sunset Cruise**, complete with live music, pupus, beer and wine for $85. On Saturdays, they also offer a unique tour dubbed the **Sunset & Celestial Cruise** that includes pupus, beverages and an entertaining star gazing and astronomy presentation for $69.

Calypso (808-856-4260) also has a 2-hour trip and is the nicest, most comfortable of the Ma'alaea bunch. It's full-on dinner with options such as prime rib and fresh fish (portions can be small—go for the ample pork ribs if you're really hungry), plus two free adult beverages. $100 though you might get a better deal booking directly. (Kids 6 and under are free with paying adult, but you'll be splitting a plate.)

The closest sunset cruise for those in Wailea, **Kai Kanani II** (808-879-7218) has a cocktail and appetizer sunset cruise for a pricey $156 (though it's closer to a dinner with things like seared 'ahi and rib-eye steaks).

From Ka'anapali, the **Hula Girl** (808-665-0344) is probably our favorite dinner cruise, though it ain't cheap. Rather than a buffet, it's handled more like a floating restaurant. $81 gets you onboard, then all your food from a menu and drinks are extra. Perhaps $23–$35 with drinks. But the quality, for a boat, is amazing. The vessel is in top shape, service is great, and the food would get them an *ono* on land. They'll sail if there's enough wind. Our only annoyance is that they tell you to check in at the beach in front of Leilani's at Whalers Village 30 minutes before departure, but there may not be anyone there until the boat actually comes ashore.

DINNER SHOWS

West Maui has a couple of night-time attractions that you should consider. One is a traditional dinner show. One is sort of a dinner show... with an optional dinner.

The best is **Warren & Annabelle's** (808-667-6244), probably the most amazing show in all Hawai'i. Put simply, our jaws never stop dropping through the whole show. After the first time we saw it, we were so impressed we told everyone we knew on Maui, "You gotta go see this." Most said, "Oh, I don't really like magic shows." Doesn't matter. It's not the kind of magic show you're thinking of. It might sound corny, but the whole evening's magic. Every person we've ever sent to this show has come back a raving fool. (Now the island is populated with raving fools. We're sorry to be the ones responsible.)

You enter the theater in a unique way. (We won't give it away.) Then you're in an incredibly beautiful parlor, elegant in every way. You spend some time inside having tasty (though pricey) pupus, desserts and cocktails while their resident ghost (Annabelle) plays at the piano. You call out a song, and she probably knows it. (Hey, wait a minute. If the ghost has been dead for 150 years, how come she knows the theme to *Cheers*?)

Then it's into the cozy 78-seat magic theater for—we promise you—the most amazing show you'll ever see. No smoke and mirrors, no elaborate props. Don't think David Copperfield or anything like that. Just a close-up view of a very engaging (and hilarious) man doing the absolute impossible. And we mean that literally. In fact, the first time we saw the show, we were so blown away that we were convinced that some of the audience members had to be plants. After the two-hour show, we told Warren our suspicions. I told him, "I've seen great magicians, but *nobody's* that good." He proceeded to do some of the same things for us. (We didn't tell him who we were that night—just viewers.) We don't want to give anything away, but we can tell you that Warren does things that have literally kept us awake at night. It's simply not possible, and we've come to the awkward conclusion that Warren is simply not of this world. We've seen lots of magicians and even taken one to see Warren. But none of us has ever seen anything like it, and we've since seen the show several times. When Warren is away he has four additional magicians, two of which take his place. They have been his replacements for years and have *nearly* equally astonishing magic and comedy skills.

If you only see one show on Maui, this is it for $74. Upgrade to the "Royal Flush Package" which includes gourmet appetizers (which can be a meal), dessert, two drinks from the full bar before the show and gratuity for additional $48. Book in advance. Though the act is "clean," it's for those age 21 and older.

The other show in West Maui is **George Kahumoku Jr's. Slack Key Show–Masters of Hawaiian Music** (808-669-3858). Held every Wednesday evening at the Napili Kai Beach Resort, the show features local slack key guitar and ukulele musicians from across the state. It's run by George Kahumoku Jr., a consummate entertainer who has some amazing stories of his life. He hosts nearly every show, mixing storytelling, humor and music. A handful of his students are regular performers, and most every week there is a special guest performance by a locally famous, Hawaiian slack key guitarist. It's really more of a show with an optional, separate dinner available from the neighboring Sea House restaurant. Dinner consists of three courses you choose from a set list—adequate but nothing to write home about.

The show is under a tent elsewhere on the property (you can still bring your beverage ordered from the restaurant bar). The venue is next to Napili Beach, but you won't have a sunset view. (The back wall is painted to look like the beach at sunset, which feels a little lame.) To warm up the crowd, 'ukulele are often handed out to anyone willing to give it a go, and an impromptu group lesson begins. The lesson is pretty gentle—you get to stay in your seat (you don't have to "perform" for everyone if you're dragged onstage at a lu'au), and some like it enough to buy the 'uke and book a class. The show itself is great if you're a music lover, enjoy storytelling and can comfortably sit for about two hours in a folding chair. Though kids are welcome, it's really only going to appeal to teenagers into live music—young kids will have a hard time sitting still. Bottom line, the dinner can be skipped in favor of nearby options, but the show is good for anyone who wants to see a true slack key guitar master. $95 for the dinner and show, $38 for just the show ($45 at the door).

About the Author

More than two decades ago, I bought a one-way ticket to the island of Kaua'i after another venture failed spectacularly. (That's a *really* good story… for another time.) I was devastated, broke, and working in the construction industry as an unskilled laborer just to survive, thinking that I had peaked at such a young age, and it was all downhill from there. But at least I was living in Hawai'i. I spent my free time exploring, but I got frustrated when weekend after weekend I couldn't find a particular beach I'd heard about that I wanted to go to. I looked at a couple of guidebooks, but they all referred to a road that hadn't existed in a long time. And I dreamed that maybe I could find a way to do it better.

Within days of of entertaining that dream, however, I had to return to the mainland due to the declining health of my mother, who passed away shortly thereafter.

It was while I was away that a plan emerged—I would return to Kaua'i and start writing guidebooks. There were just a few problems with this plan: I had no writing skills, I didn't know how a book was published, I wasn't good at photography, I didn't know how to use a computer, *and I had no money.*

So I spent a year on the mainland and applied for every credit card I could and tried to acquire the skills I would need to make my dream come true. Just when I was ready to return to the islands in 1992, I watched in horror as a category 4 hurricane smashed into Kaua'i, causing widespread devastation. I couldn't pick another island because Kaua'i was the one I knew, the island I had fallen in love with. Knowing that hurricanes clear out old growth, giving sunlight (and a chance) to encourage younger foliage, I figured that the same might be true in business. So with a huge stack of credit cards and two suitcases, I moved back to a ravaged island and got to work.

I completely covered one of the walls of my 290-square-foot rented room with highly detailed topographic maps of the island, so I could study them while drinking my morning coffee (gotta have coffee). This was before Google Earth, after all.

Over the next year, I spent my mornings exploring the island and checking out various visitor activities like helicopter rides and snorkel tours (which I did anonymously and paid for with my credit cards—*at 22 percent interest*). I'd review a restaurant at lunch, and then I'd spend my afternoons doing a hike or swimming a beach in multiple conditions to assess its safety, before returning to my room to have a simple dinner of canned chicken and rice (because it was so cheap), then worked into the evening making my own maps of the island. Before going to bed each night, I would read every book about Hawaiian history I could get my hands on.

The first edition of "the blue book" came out in March 1994. I paid to print the first 10,000 books (with cash advances from that stack of credit cards) and mailed free copies to newspapers for review. The first order was for only one case, but a year later a nationwide bookstore chain agreed to stock the book. It took off from there. Next came Big Island, then Maui and O'ahu. I packed up my equipment and lived for two years on each island researching, mapping, writing and photographing.

Today the *Revealed Series* is no longer a one-man show. I have an awesome team that has expanded over the years, but ultimately the books and the apps are an expression of what I think about Hawai'i and comes from the experience of actually *doing* all the things you'll read about. And our ability to keep current and find new things is greatly helped by feedback from our incredibly enthusiastic readers. Please keep it coming.

Once in a while, if you are *really* lucky in this life, you find the place and circumstance to which you belong. I hope you will fall in love with Hawai'i the way I did, and return often. But wherever you travel in life, take chances, embrace the uncertainty of outcome, go with an explorer's heart, and most importantly, share what you find with others.

—One lucky buggah, *Andrew Doughty*

INDEX

Island Dining Index on page 270

Island Dining Index on page 270

INDEX

Island Dining Index on page 270

Island Dining Index on page 270

INDEX

Island Dining Index on page 270

Island Dining Index on page 270

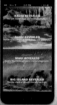